Securing AI–Generated Media With Blockchain Technologies

G. Revathy
SASTRA University, India

Arul Kumar Natarajan
Samarkand International University of Technology, Uzbekistan

Naresh Kshetri
Rochester Institute of Technology, USA

IGI Global
Scientific Publishing
Publishing Tomorrow's Research Today

Vice President of Editorial	Melissa Wagner
Director of Acquisitions	Mikaela Felty
Director of Book Development	Jocelynn Hessler
Production Manager	Mike Brehm
Cover Design	Jose Rosado

Published in the United States of America by
    IGI Global Scientific Publishing
    701 East Chocolate Avenue
    Hershey, PA, 17033, USA
    Tel: 717-533-8845
    Fax: 717-533-7115
    Website: https://www.igi-global.com E-mail: cust@igi-global.com

Library of Congress Cataloging-in-Publication Data

LCCN: 2025035574 (CIP Data Pending)
ISBN13: 9798337364810
Isbn13Softcover: 9798337364827
EISBN13: 9798337364834

British Cataloguing in Publication Data
A Cataloguing in Publication record for this book is available from the British Library.

Table of Contents

Detailed Table of Contents

Chapter 1
Ethical and Legal Considerations in AI-Generated Media 1

S. C. Vetrivel, Kongu Engineering College, India
P. Vidhyapriya, Kongu Engineering College, India
V. P. Arun, JKKN College of Engineering and Technology, India
V. Sabareeshwari, Amrita Vishwa Vidyapeetham, India

The rapid advancements in multimodal generative AI have revolutionized digital media production, enabling the creation of hyper-realistic content across text, image, video, and audio domains. However, this technological evolution raises significant ethical and legal concerns, including deepfake misinformation, copyright infringement, data privacy breaches, and algorithmic biases. This chapter explores the ethical dilemmas posed by AI-generated media, emphasizing the need for transparency, accountability, and responsible AI governance. It examines legal frameworks governing AI-generated content, including intellectual property rights, digital forensics, and emerging regulations such as the EU AI Act. The role of blockchain technology in ensuring content authenticity and traceability is also discussed as a potential solution to mitigate ethical and legal risks. By addressing these challenges, this chapter aims to provide a comprehensive understanding of the intersection between AI, blockchain, ethics, and law in digital media.

Chapter 2
Legal and Ethical Considerations of AI-Driven Adaptations in the Production
of Media 35

Suraj Patel Pinninti, Mahindra University, India
Raneeta Pal, Mahindra University, India

The rise in the integration of Artificial Intelligence (AI) into media productions for example remastering, dubbing and content adaptation has raised significant legal and ethical concerns. Central to these issues are the rights to adaptation under copyright law, which grant creators exclusive authority over derivative works and transformations of their original creations. These rights are often challenged by AI-driven processes like audiovisual quality enhancement, synthetic voice generation, cultural localization raising questions about ownership, fair use, and copyright compliance. This research proposal will therefore examine the legal effects of AI enhanced adaptations through a thorough evaluation of relevant case law, jurisdictional differences and market forces so as to strike a balance between innovation and maintaining respect for artists' rights.

Chapter 3

S. V. Divya, V.S.B. College of Engineering Technical Campus, Coimbatore, India

P. Venkadesh, V.S.B. College of Engineering Technical Campus, Coimbatore, India

S. Saravanaprabhu, Nandha College of Technology, Erode, India

Jelin Taric G., Noorul Islam Centre for Higher Education, Kumaracoil, India

S. Yazhini, V.S.B. College of Engineering Technical Campus, Coimbatore, India

M. Shify Antolin, V.S.B. College of Engineering Technical Campus, Coimbatore, India

Digital media has provided new frontiers where the challenge to authentication and copyright is unparalleled. The emergence of new solutions for safeguarding intellectual property rights and ensuring authenticity in content becomes necessary. This chapter introduces blockchain integration as a means of authenticating AI-generated content with secure attribution against risks of unlawful duplication or misappropriation and how blockchain-based systems allow verifiable ownership of digital assets through smart contracts that automate licensing, royalty collection, and the tracking of use. This chapter goes deeply into the technical architecture of blockchain applications in digital media, illuminating its capacity to create trust and accountability in this fast-evolving creative ecosystem. Ethical, legal, and scalability considerations discuss the role that blockchain is playing in building a fairer and more transparent digital economy.

Chapter 4

Bishwo Prakash Pokharel, Sault College of Applied Arts and Technology, Canada

Naresh Kshetri, Rochester Institute of Technology, USA

Suresh Raj Sharma, Tribhuvan University, Nepal

Soba Raj Paudel, Tribhuvan University, Nepal

Suresh Baral, Gupteshwor Mahadev Multiple Campus, Nepal

The rise of multimodal generative AI has revolutionized creative industries by enabling the production of high-quality text, images, audio, and video. However, this innovation has also introduced critical challenges, including content authenticity concerns, the proliferation of deepfakes, intellectual property disputes, and unethical manipulation of media. Addressing these issues requires a robust and scalable solution. This chapter introduces a blockchain-driven framework that integrates the strengths of blockchain's decentralized and immutable architecture with the creative potential of generative AI. It ensures verifiable content creation by embedding proof of originality into digital assets, facilitates transparent ownership through tokenization, and automates secure licensing and fair revenue sharing via smart contracts. By exploring the theoretical foundation, technical architecture, and practical applications of blockAuth, it presents a transformative solution to foster trust, transparency, and equity in the digital media ecosystem.

    Suresh Raj Sharma, Tribhuvan University, Nepal
    Naresh Kshetri, Rochester Institute of Technology, USA
    Sobaraj Poudel Paudel, Tribhuvan University, Nepal
    Bishwo Prakash Pokharel, Sault College of Applied Arts and
        Technology, Canada

AI-powered fact-checking systems, secured by blockchain technology, represent a transformative approach to combating misinformation in the digital age. Leveraging advanced artificial intelligence (AI) algorithms, particularly natural language processing (NLP), these systems efficiently analyze vast datasets to verify claims in real time. The integration of blockchain ensures data immutability, transparency, and security, enhancing trust in the fact-checking process. This convergence addresses the limitations of traditional fact-checking methods, which often fail to keep pace with the rapid spread of false information. By enabling real-time claim verification, monitoring live events, and predicting misinformation trends, AI-powered systems provide a critical tool for journalists and content creators to combat disinformation effectively. Blockchain further reinforces the integrity of the verification process by maintaining tamper-proof audit trails, fostering accountability, and ensuring the delivery of trustworthy information.

Chapter 6

GenBlock: A Secure Decentralized Model for Generative AI Integration With

Soba Raj Paudel, Tribhuvan University, Nepal
Suresh Raj Sharma, Tribhuvan University, Nepal
Bishwo Prakash Pokharel, Sault College of Applied Arts and
Technology, Canada

Generative AI, a branch of artificial intelligence, is revolutionizing the creation of original content, including text, images, music, and videos. When integrated with blockchain technology, it creates a powerful synergy that combines creativity with enhanced security. Blockchain's immutable and tamper-proof properties can authenticate generative AI outputs, ensuring trust and originality. For instance, artists can timestamp their works on the blockchain, providing undeniable proof of ownership and authenticity. This fusion also addresses critical challenges faced by businesses adopting generative AI chatbots like ChatGPT, including mitigating the risks of false outputs ("hallucinations") and safeguarding intellectual property used in AI training.

Chapter 7

Integrating Blockchain With Watermarking Systems for Tamper-Proof

K. Muthamil Sudar , Mepco Schlenk Engineering College, India
V. Vaissnave, SRM Institute of Science and Technology, Kattankulathur,
India
P. Nagaraj, SRM Institute of Science and Technology, Tiruchirappalli,
India

The emergence of digital content has created an instant need for ways of authenticity, ownership, and protection of intellectual property. This chapter elaborates the merging of blockchain with digital watermarking systems for credible attribution of tamper-proof images, videos, and documents. One can add watermark to a digital file. However, a copy of the ownership and copyright information, which is collected through uploading to blockchain's non-deletable and de-centralized ledger, is stored and comes with the entire assurance that the data is safely verifiable. The watermarking methods for use along with blockchain in this system include Discrete Cosine Transform (DCT) and Discrete Wavelet Transform (DWT). Watermark metadata, including cryptographic hash values, timestamps, and the details of the creator, are stored on the blockchain, making it possible to authenticate content easily and to derive its chain of evidence. Smart contracts will take complete charge of operations like licensing for content and royalties payments to ensure clear compliance with usage conversions.

Chapter 8

Anant Wairagade, Independent Researcher, USA
Sumit Ranjan, Independent Researcher, USA
Kunal Lanjewar, Independent Researcher, USA

Deepfake technology has emerged in recent years and has posed serious challenges to areas such as politics, cybersecurity, and media integrity. The advent of deepfake content using generative adversarial networks (GANs) has further aided in manipulating public opinion through dissemination of misinformation and security threats to nations across the world. This book chapter focuses on tracing the evolution of deepfake technology, its role in electoral interference, and security impacts, with consideration given to several case studies and comparative research on detection frameworks to assess the strengths and weaknesses of AI-based and forensic detection of deepfakes. A novel cybersecurity capacity-building model is presented that focuses on collaborative efforts among academia, industry, and governmental agencies in addressing the deepfake threat. Innovation in detection techniques, policy reform, and public education must work in tandem to ensure a capable digital ecosystem that withstands manipulation through synthetic media.

Chapter 9

Devendra Chapagain, Tribhuvan University, Nepal
Bindu Aryal, Tribhuvan University, Nepal
Bijay Bastakoti, The University of Texas at Arlington, USA
Dipendra Silwal, Oxford College of Engineering and Management,
    Nepal
Ayesha Arobee, Emporia State University, USA

Deepfakes and synthetic media, powered by AI technologies like Generative Adversarial Networks (GANs) and Diffusion Models, pose significant threats to digital trust and security. These tools enable the creation of highly realistic forgeries, which are increasingly exploited in social engineering attacks to spread misinformation, manipulate emotions, and impersonate trusted individuals. This chapter explores the role of deepfakes in enhancing social engineering tactics, such as phishing, CEO fraud, and disinformation campaigns. It reviews current detection methods, including machine learning techniques to identify inconsistencies in synthetic media, and discusses the ethical, societal, and policy challenges posed by this emerging threat. By examining the intersection of deepfakes and social engineering, this chapter highlights the need for robust detection technologies, public awareness, and regulatory measures to address the growing risks of AI-generated content in cybersecurity.

Chapter 10

M. Sridevi, Rajalakshmi Engineering College, India
P. Madhavasarma, SASTRA University, India
Jayaprakash J. Stanly, Mahendra Institute of Technology, India
Kumar M. Santhosh, Nandha Engineering College, India

Deepfakes, which are driven by generative AI, have revolutionized synthetic media, presenting both exciting opportunities and formidable obstacles. Deepfakes may be utilized for immersive experiences and imaginative storytelling, but they also present risks including false information, identity theft, and a decline in public confidence. The crucial role that blockchain technology plays in controlling AI-generated material and reducing the dangers of deepfakes is examined in this study. Digital media authenticity and provenance may be effectively verified thanks to blockchain's decentralized, unchangeable ledger. Blockchain and generative AI may be used to provide a strong foundation for content authentication, manipulation detection, and media production and distribution responsibility.

Chapter 11

C. P. Shabariram, PSG Institute of Technology and Applied Research,
*   India*
N. Shanthi, Kongu Engineering College, India
P. Ponnuswamy Priya, Vellore Institute of Technology, India

Due to the increased demand of intelligent edge applications, efficient computational offloading schemes and secure communication between edge and cloud server has become essential. This chapter presents an intelligent framework that integrates Blockchain technology and Generative AI to achieve intelligent computation offloading in an edge computing. The framework includes generative models to encode the sensitive data and blockchain based smart contract infrastructure. To ensure confidentiality, the generative adversarial network is used to encode the data into images or audio files. The smart contract is applied to log task metadata and verify the data integrity. The immutable execution logs are ensured by blockchain based infrastructure. The framework allows seamless computational offloading between edge and cloud server with end-to-end security. The experimental results depict the system overhead with respect to interception, latency and tampering. The fusion of AI-driven data masking provides a secure and intelligent computation offloading mechanism in the decentralized manner.

Chapter 12

This chapter delves into the transformative power of Non-Fungible Tokens (NFTs) as foundational components of the Web3 ecosystem. It examines the way tokenization is disrupting the digital asset ownership vector to bring decentralized exchange of assets and the redesign of industries like creative arts, real estate to finance. The chapter provides the whole picture of technical, legal and operational frameworks using which the NFT adoption takes place through a deep dive into token standards, smart contract architecture, decentralized storage, and cross chain interoperability. It also examines how security and authentication protocols, security mechanisms, and maintenance practices of decentralized systems work together to make sure of trust, provenance and usability in decentralized environments. Furthermore, the chapter investigates the integration of NFTs with metaverse platforms, the emergence of advanced token protocols, and the broader implications for identity, governance, and digital economies.

Preface

The rapid evolution of artificial intelligence (AI) has ushered in a new era of digital media production, where hyper-realistic content—spanning text, images, audio, and video—can be generated with unprecedented ease and sophistication. While these advancements in multimodal generative AI offer immense creative potential, they also introduce profound challenges, including ethical dilemmas, legal complexities, and cybersecurity risks. The proliferation of deepfakes, misinformation, intellectual property disputes, and data privacy concerns underscores the urgent need for innovative solutions to ensure trust, authenticity, and accountability in the digital ecosystem.

Securing AI-Generated Media With Blockchain Technologies addresses these challenges by exploring the transformative potential of blockchain technology as a cornerstone for securing AI-generated content. Blockchain's decentralized, immutable, and transparent architecture offers a robust framework for authenticating digital assets, protecting intellectual property, and fostering trust in media production and distribution. This book brings together a diverse group of researchers, academics, and industry experts to examine the intersection of AI, blockchain, ethics, law, and cybersecurity, providing a comprehensive resource for navigating the complexities of this rapidly evolving field.

The chapters in this book cover a wide range of topics, from ethical and legal considerations to technical frameworks and practical applications. They explore how blockchain can mitigate risks such as deepfake misinformation, copyright infringement, and unethical media manipulation while enabling secure content creation, distribution, and monetization. By integrating AI with blockchain, the contributors propose innovative solutions—such as smart contracts, tokenization, and watermarking systems—to create a fairer, more transparent, and trustworthy digital economy.

This book is intended for researchers, policymakers, technologists, and industry professionals seeking to understand the implications of AI-generated media and the role of blockchain in addressing its challenges. It aims to spark meaningful dialogue and inspire further innovation in building a secure and ethical digital future.

CHAPTER OVERVIEW

1. **Ethical and Legal Considerations in AI-Generated Media**

    Vetrivel SC, Vidhyapriya P, Arun VP, Sabareeshwari V
    This chapter explores the ethical and legal challenges posed by multimodal generative AI, including deepfake misinformation, copyright infringement, data privacy, and algorithmic biases. It emphasizes the need for transparency and accountability in AI governance, examines legal frameworks such as intellectual property rights and the EU AI Act, and discusses blockchain's role in ensuring content authenticity and traceability to mitigate risks.

2. **Legal and Ethical Considerations of AI-Driven Adaptations in Production of Media**

    Suraj Pinninti, Raneeta Pal
    This chapter examines the legal and ethical implications of AI-driven media adaptations, such as remastering, dubbing, and cultural localization. It analyzes copyright law challenges, including ownership and fair use, through case law and jurisdictional differences, aiming to balance innovation with respect for creators' rights.

3. **Blockchain for Content Authentication and Copyright Protection**

    S.V Divya, P Venkadesh, S Saravanaprabhu, Jelin Taric.G, S Yazhini, M Shify Antolin
    This chapter introduces blockchain as a solution for authenticating AI-generated content and protecting intellectual property. It explores how blockchain-based systems use smart contracts to automate licensing, royalty collection, and usage tracking, delving into technical architectures and addressing ethical, legal, and scalability considerations.

4. **blockAuth-A Blockchain-Driven Framework for Verifiable Content Creation and Secure Distribution in the Generative AI Era**

    Bishwo Pokharel, Naresh Kshetri, Suresh Sharma, Soba Paudel, Suresh Baral

This chapter presents blockAuth, a blockchain-driven framework integrating generative AI to ensure verifiable content creation, transparent ownership through tokenization, and secure licensing via smart contracts. It explores the framework's theoretical foundation, technical architecture, and practical applications to foster trust and equity in digital media.

5. **TrustChain AI-Powered Fact-Checking Systems Secured by Blockchain Technology**

Suresh Raj Sharma, Naresh Kshetri, Sobaraj Poudel Paudel, Bishwo Pokharel
This chapter discusses AI-powered fact-checking systems enhanced by blockchain to combat misinformation. Leveraging NLP and blockchain's immutable ledger, these systems enable real-time claim verification, live event monitoring, and tamper-proof audit trails, fostering trust and accountability in digital content.

6. **GenBlock A Secure Decentralized Model for Generative AI Integration with Blockchain**

Soba Paudel, Suresh Sharma, Bishwo Pokharel
This chapter explores the synergy between generative AI and blockchain, highlighting how blockchain's tamper-proof properties authenticate AI outputs, ensuring trust and originality. It addresses challenges like AI "hallucinations" and intellectual property protection, particularly for generative AI chatbots.

7. **Integrating Blockchain with Watermarking Systems for Tamper-Proof Attribution in Digital Media**

Muthamil Sudar K, Vaissnave V, Nagaraj P
This chapter examines the integration of blockchain with digital watermarking systems (e.g., DCT and DWT) to ensure tamper-proof attribution of digital content. It discusses how blockchain stores watermark metadata for authentication and uses smart contracts for licensing and royalty management.

8. **Deepfake Attacks Detection and Mitigation Techniques for Strengthening Cybersecurity in AI Era**

Anant Wairagade, Sumit Ranjan, Kunal Lanjewar
This chapter focuses on the cybersecurity challenges posed by deepfakes, tracing their evolution and impacts on politics and media integrity. It presents a novel cybersecurity model, combining AI-based and forensic detection techniques with

collaborative efforts among academia, industry, and government to counter deep-fake threats.

9. Deepfakes and Synthetic Media: Challenges and Solutions in Social Engineering Attacks

Devendra Chapagain, Bindu Aryal, Bijay Bastakoti, Dipendra Silwal, Ayesha Arobee

This chapter explores how deepfakes enhance social engineering attacks like phishing and CEO fraud. It reviews detection methods, ethical and societal challenges, and the need for robust technologies, public awareness, and regulatory measures to address AI-generated content risks.

10. Deepfakes Unleashed Exploring the Role of Blockchain in Managing AI-Generated Content

M Sridevi, P Madhavasarma, Stanly Jayaprakash J, Santhosh Kumar M

This chapter investigates blockchain's role in managing deepfake risks, leveraging its decentralized ledger for content authentication and manipulation detection. It highlights blockchain's potential to ensure authenticity, provenance, and accountability in AI-generated media.

11. Secure and Intelligent Computation Offloading between Edge and Cloud Servers using Generative AI and Blockchain

Shabariram C P, Shanthi N, Priya Ponnuswamy P

This chapter presents a framework integrating generative AI and blockchain for secure computation offloading in edge computing. Using generative models for data encoding and smart contracts for metadata logging, it ensures confidentiality, integrity, and seamless offloading with end-to-end security.

12. Mint, Tokenize, Authenticate - An NFT Perspective: An NFT Trilogy

Trisha Rami

This chapter explores Non-Fungible Tokens (NFTs) as transformative tools in the Web3 ecosystem, focusing on tokenization, smart contract architecture, and decentralized storage. It examines NFT integration with metaverse platforms and implications for digital identity, governance, and economies.

The integration of blockchain technology with AI-generated media offers a transformative approach to addressing the ethical, legal, and cybersecurity challenges of the digital age. By leveraging blockchain's decentralized, immutable, and transparent properties, the frameworks and solutions presented in this book—ranging from content authentication and copyright protection to fact-checking and secure computation offloading—provide robust mechanisms to ensure trust, authenticity, and accountability. As generative AI continues to reshape media production, the synergy with blockchain paves the way for a fairer, more secure, and equitable digital ecosystem. This book underscores the need for ongoing research, collaboration, and innovation to navigate the evolving landscape of AI-driven media and safeguard its integrity for future generations.

G Revathy
SASTRA Deemed University, India

Arul Kumar Natarajan
Samarkand International University of Technology, Uzbekistan

Naresh Kshetri
Rochester Institute of Technology, USA

Chapter 1
Ethical and Legal Considerations in AI–Generated Media

S. C. Vetrivel
iD https://orcid.org/0000-0003-3050-8211
Kongu Engineering College, India

P. Vidhyapriya
iD https://orcid.org/0000-0002-1421-8743
Kongu Engineering College, India

V. P. Arun
iD https://orcid.org/0009-0009-1211-2150
JKKN College of Engineering and Technology, India

V. Sabareeshwari
Amrita Vishwa Vidyapeetham, India

ABSTRACT

The rapid advancements in multimodal generative AI have revolutionized digital media production, enabling the creation of hyper-realistic content across text, image, video, and audio domains. However, this technological evolution raises significant ethical and legal concerns, including deepfake misinformation, copyright infringement, data privacy breaches, and algorithmic biases. This chapter explores the ethical dilemmas posed by AI-generated media, emphasizing the need for transparency, accountability, and responsible AI governance. It examines legal frameworks governing AI-generated content, including intellectual property rights, digital forensics, and emerging regulations such as the EU AI Act. The role of blockchain technology in ensuring content authenticity and traceability is also

DOI: 10.4018/979-8-3373-6481-0.ch001

discussed as a potential solution to mitigate ethical and legal risks. By addressing these challenges, this chapter aims to provide a comprehensive understanding of the intersection between AI, blockchain, ethics, and law in digital media.

1. INTRODUCTION

1.1 Overview of Generative AI in Digital Media

Generative Artificial Intelligence (AI) has emerged as a transformative force in digital media, capable of producing original content across text, image, video, and audio formats. At its core, generative AI utilizes deep learning architectures—especially Generative Adversarial Networks (GANs) and transformer-based models like GPT and DALL·E—to simulate human-like creativity (Kumar & Rana, 2023). These systems are trained on massive datasets and can generate outputs that are not only contextually relevant but also indistinguishable from human-created media. With the rise of platforms such as Midjourney, ChatGPT, and Synthesia, content creation has shifted from traditional tools to AI-powered environments that offer unprecedented speed, scale, and personalization (Ramesh et al., 2022). The proliferation of generative AI tools has disrupted conventional workflows in journalism, entertainment, advertising, and education. In India, media startups and regional film industries are increasingly using generative AI for voice dubbing, scriptwriting, and special effects—reducing both cost and production time (Chatterjee & Singh, 2023). This rapid adoption is further fueled by the widespread availability of open-source models and cloud-based APIs, democratizing access to sophisticated media-generation tools for individuals and small enterprises alike. According to a recent study, over 68% of surveyed Indian digital media professionals have experimented with generative AI tools in some form, marking a significant shift in content production dynamics (Verma & Iyer, 2023). Moreover, generative AI's multimodal capabilities—combining text, image, and sound—have enabled the development of immersive media experiences, from AI-generated podcasts to interactive storytelling platforms.

However, the rise of such technologies brings ethical dilemmas around authenticity, misinformation, and intellectual property. Concerns about the misuse of generative AI to produce deepfakes, synthetic news, and unauthorized reproductions of artistic works have been widely reported (Narayanan & Gupta, 2023). These challenges underscore the urgent need for robust ethical and legal frameworks to govern AI-generated media, especially as its influence continues to expand globally. The growing importance of generative AI in shaping media content highlights not just a technological shift, but also a cultural and regulatory one. As governments, educators, and content creators grapple with its implications, a nuanced understanding of this emerging field becomes essential for ensuring responsible innovation in digital media.

1.2 The Emergence of Multimodal Content and Its Implications

The rise of multimodal content—integrating text, audio, video, images, and interactive elements—marks a transformative moment in digital media production and consumption. Powered by advanced generative AI systems like GPT-4, DALL·E, and Runway, multimodal media allows users to create richly textured experiences that communicate across multiple sensory modalities. This shift from traditional linear narratives to immersive and interactive formats has vast implications for education, journalism, entertainment, and marketing (Benaich & Hogarth, 2023). For instance, models that simultaneously process and generate content across modalities—like OpenAI's GPT-4 with image and text capabilities—are already being used in newsrooms and educational platforms to streamline content creation and improve accessibility (Wu, Zhang, & Zhou, 2023).

From an ethical perspective, this convergence raises complex concerns. As multimodal content blurs the lines between reality and simulation, it challenges conventional notions of authenticity and truth. In India, the use of AI-generated synthetic content in regional language media outlets has spurred debate on the cultural and social risks of misinformation (Krishnamurthy & Ghosh, 2023). Furthermore, these systems can amplify biases encoded in training datasets—whether through the stereotyping of gender roles in generated images or unbalanced narrative framing in AI-written texts—highlighting the urgent need for inclusive dataset curation and algorithmic transparency (Muthukumar & Reddy, 2022).

The implications also extend to accessibility and engagement. In education, multimodal generative tools are revolutionizing pedagogy by catering to diverse learning styles. For example, AI-generated educational videos with sign language interpretation and multilingual voiceovers offer inclusive learning for students with hearing impairments or from non-dominant language backgrounds (Jain, Bhattacharya, & Menon, 2023). At the same time, concerns about the homogenization of global content and loss of local narrative autonomy remain pertinent, especially in the Global South where generative tools are often developed with Western-centric datasets.

1.3 Ethical and Legal Frameworks: An Urgent Need

The rapid deployment of generative AI technologies in digital media has far outpaced the development of corresponding ethical and legal safeguards, creating a pressing need for robust governance frameworks. As AI models increasingly produce hyper-realistic content—including text, images, audio, and video—traditional legal systems face challenges in attributing responsibility, protecting intellectual property, and ensuring ethical standards. Unlike conventional media production, AI-generated outputs are often created without direct human intervention, raising questions about authorship, consent, authenticity, and potential misuse (Tripathi & Joshi, 2023).

One major concern lies in the proliferation of deepfakes and synthetic media, which can be weaponized for misinformation, character assassination, and political manipulation. While some countries, including India, have started formulating data protection laws such as the Digital Personal Data Protection Act (DPDPA) 2023, these efforts remain fragmented and do not yet fully address the complexities introduced by multimodal AI systems (Kumar & Deshmukh, 2024). Moreover, global legal systems lack consensus on AI authorship and accountability. For instance, the U.S. Copyright Office recently reiterated that copyright does not extend to AI-generated content lacking human authorship, yet gray areas remain for co-created content (Levendowski, 2023).

Ethically, there is an urgent need to define boundaries for AI usage in media production—particularly regarding consent, cultural sensitivity, and algorithmic fairness. Generative AI tools can amplify biases embedded in training data, leading to discriminatory representations of race, gender, and ethnicity (Singh et al., 2022). The absence of internationally harmonized standards allows unethical practices to flourish, especially in jurisdictions with weaker regulatory environments. Blockchain, with its ability to record provenance and authenticate media, offers partial solutions but cannot substitute for comprehensive ethical frameworks (Mukherjee & Sanyal, 2023). Therefore, a multi-pronged approach combining technological design, legal reforms, and ethical codes is essential to mitigate harms and ensure responsible use of AI in media. Regulatory bodies, technologists, and media professionals must collaborate to design AI systems that are ethical-by-design, embedding transparency, explainability, and human oversight into their architecture (Sharma & Iyer, 2023). As AI continues to evolve, such frameworks will be indispensable in safeguarding both creators' rights and the public interest in digital media ecosystems.

2. UNDERSTANDING GENERATIVE AI AND BLOCKCHAIN IN MEDIA

2.1 Generative AI: From Text to Multimodal Media

Generative Artificial Intelligence (AI) has rapidly evolved from generating simple textual outputs to creating highly sophisticated multimodal content that includes images, audio, video, and interactive experiences. Initially recognized for its capacity to generate natural language using models like GPT, the scope of generative AI has expanded with the advent of diffusion models, transformers, and encoder-decoder architectures capable of interpreting and producing across multiple modalities (Goodfellow et al., 2022). Today's AI systems such as OpenAI's DALL·E, Google's Imagen, and Meta's Make-A-Video exemplify this evolution by seamlessly synthesizing content that merges linguistic, visual, and auditory elements in creative and context-aware ways (Gupta & Srivastava, 2023). These systems are increasingly used in journalism, advertising, design, and digital education, creating a paradigm shift in content creation and audience engagement.

In India, the use of generative AI in media has grown significantly, with platforms like Indic-GPT and BharatGPT designed to generate content in regional languages, helping bridge linguistic digital divides (Sundaram & Rao, 2023). This localization of generative AI has made the technology more inclusive and impactful in developing contexts, particularly for education, government outreach, and cultural storytelling. However, such widespread use also raises critical questions regarding cultural bias, semantic integrity, and the potential misuse of synthetically generated information (Mohan & Shetty, 2022). These challenges demand a closer examination of the ethical boundaries of creativity and representation in AI systems that are increasingly trained on unfiltered internet data, which often lacks adequate contextual filtering.

Multimodal AI systems not only perform generative tasks but also understand and interpret cross-modal relationships—for example, generating video summaries from audio-visual input or answering questions based on combined text and image prompts. These capabilities are now foundational in sectors like entertainment, edtech, and healthcare communications (Zhou et al., 2022). As AI-generated multimedia becomes indistinguishable from human-produced content, the authenticity, authorship, and accountability of such outputs must be critically addressed. Moreover, interdisciplinary collaborations are essential in ensuring that these powerful tools are deployed with safeguards that align with regional legal frameworks and socio-cultural norms, especially in media-sensitive democracies like India (Ramesh & Iyer, 2023).

2.2 Blockchain's Role in Verifiability and Traceability

Blockchain technology plays a vital role in strengthening the verifiability and traceability of AI-generated content, particularly in digital media where issues of authenticity and ownership are increasingly complex. By maintaining a decentralized and immutable ledger, blockchain enables transparent tracking of content origin, edits, and distribution pathways (Nguyen et al., 2022). Each instance of AI-generated content can be hashed and recorded with a timestamp and creator identification, ensuring that any future verification can be traced back to its original source.

In the context of generative media, especially deepfakes and synthetic text or imagery, blockchain addresses the growing concerns over misinformation and identity misrepresentation. For instance, by embedding cryptographic fingerprints into multimedia files, blockchain allows consumers and regulatory bodies to confirm the authenticity and unaltered nature of digital content (Das, 2023). This is particularly relevant in journalism, entertainment, and political communications, where fabricated content can have far-reaching implications.

India has also recognized the strategic importance of blockchain in digital governance and media authenticity. The Telangana Blockchain District initiative and the draft National Blockchain Strategy by NITI Aayog advocate blockchain's use for content certification, intellectual property protection, and enhancing trust in digital platforms (Sundararajan & Ramesh, 2021). Such frameworks aim to support Indian artists and content creators by offering a transparent system for asserting ownership and preventing unauthorized distribution. Blockchain's role is also significant in ensuring ethical use of data for training AI models. Since generative AI systems rely on vast datasets that may include copyrighted or sensitive content, blockchain can be used to log the provenance of datasets, ensuring ethical sourcing and usage rights. Researchers argue that combining blockchain with AI can also help track accountability by making it easier to audit how AI models were trained and how their outputs were derived (Chakraborty & Gupta, 2022). This traceability becomes essential not only for content authentication but also for ensuring compliance with regulatory frameworks and ethical standards.

2.3 Synergy between Generative AI and Blockchain for Ethical Media

The integration of generative AI and blockchain technologies holds immense potential for building a more ethical and transparent digital media ecosystem. While generative AI enables the creation of sophisticated content—ranging from hyper-realistic deepfakes to automatically generated articles and synthetic voiceovers—it also raises concerns about authorship, consent, manipulation, and accountability. Blockchain, with its capabilities in data immutability, decentralized verification, and provenance tracking, complements AI by providing the infrastructure to document and verify each stage of content generation and dissemination (Wang & Chen, 2023).

The synergy is particularly evident in combating misinformation and ensuring responsible use of AI-generated content. For example, when blockchain is integrated into AI workflows, it can record metadata about the dataset used for training, the version of the algorithm, and details of content generation. This ensures not only reproducibility but also accountability, especially in high-stakes media environments like journalism, election campaigns, or health communication (Bhardwaj et al., 2023). Blockchain-stored records can also include licenses, consent forms, or user agreements, allowing for ethical compliance even in automated generative pipelines.

In the Indian context, where both misinformation and copyright infringement are major concerns, the synergy of these technologies is being explored in sectors like digital art, entertainment, and vernacular journalism. Recent initiatives by Indian startups and digital platforms are experimenting with smart contracts to automate payments and licensing for AI-generated content, ensuring fair remuneration and transparency (Rajagopal & Mishra, 2022). These smart contracts are hosted on blockchain and executed without intermediaries, preventing content misuse and simplifying the attribution process. Additionally, the convergence of generative AI and blockchain provides a robust framework for defending user rights. For instance, individuals whose likeness or voice is used in synthetic content can have their consent validated through blockchain entries, creating an immutable legal and ethical trail. This traceability is vital as legal frameworks evolve to address questions of deepfake accountability, biometric data misuse, and synthetic defamation (Leung & Narayanan, 2023). The combined use of these technologies also supports inclusive and equitable AI development. Blockchain helps track and audit whether the data used by generative models is diverse and ethically sourced. This can help mitigate algorithmic bias, a known issue in many AI systems that disproportionately impact marginalized communities (Pillai & Thomas, 2022). Thus, the synergy of generative AI and blockchain not only enhances media innovation but also embeds ethical safeguards from data collection to content dissemination.

3. ETHICAL CHALLENGES OF AI-GENERATED MEDIA

3.1 Deepfakes, Misinformation, and Public Trust

The proliferation of deepfakes—hyper-realistic AI-generated videos, audios, and images—has emerged as a profound ethical challenge, particularly as generative AI becomes more accessible and sophisticated. These synthetic media artifacts are capable of distorting reality, manipulating public opinion, and eroding trust in digital content. The rise in misinformation campaigns, especially on social media platforms, has demonstrated how deepfakes can be used to impersonate political figures, spread disinformation during elections, or damage reputations through fabricated audio-visual materials (Kietzmann et al., 2020). A major concern associated with deepfakes is their potential to mislead audiences, creating a digital environment where viewers cannot distinguish between authentic and manipulated content. This phenomenon has been termed the "liar's dividend," wherein the existence of deepfake technology allows real events to be denied as fabrications, thus deepening public cynicism and weakening accountability (Fallis, 2021). In India, concerns around deepfakes have escalated, particularly in the political sphere. A notable case emerged during the Delhi Legislative Assembly elections in 2020, where AI-generated campaign videos of political leaders speaking in multiple languages were circulated—raising questions about transparency and consent (Mundkur & Pathak, 2021).

Furthermore, deepfake-driven misinformation poses a significant risk to journalism and free speech. News organizations may struggle to verify sources, and the proliferation of realistic fake content can blur the lines between real and fictional narratives. This undermines the role of media as a pillar of democracy and informed citizenship. Several scholars argue that the psychological effects of repeated exposure to deepfakes can also induce desensitization, where people begin to accept digital forgeries as a normative part of media consumption (Vaccari & Chadwick, 2020). Technological responses such as blockchain-based media authentication tools and AI-powered detection algorithms are being explored to mitigate the spread of misinformation. However, these measures must be integrated with legal frameworks and digital literacy campaigns to be effective. In India, the proposed Digital India Act 2023 is expected to address AI-generated misinformation, but the lack of specific legislation on deepfakes continues to create legal ambiguity and enforcement challenges (Singh & Bhatia, 2023).

3.2 Identity, Consent, and Privacy Issues in AI-Generated Media

The proliferation of generative artificial intelligence (AI) in media production has ushered in significant challenges concerning identity, consent, and privacy. AI systems capable of creating realistic images, videos, and audio can inadvertently infringe upon individual privacy rights by producing content that closely resembles real persons without their explicit consent. This raises critical ethical and legal questions about the unauthorized use of personal likenesses and the potential for identity misrepresentation. A paramount concern is the lack of informed consent in the creation and dissemination of AI-generated media. Individuals may find their images or voices replicated in synthetic media without prior knowledge or approval, leading to potential reputational harm and emotional distress. The European Union's General Data Protection Regulation (GDPR) emphasizes the necessity of obtaining explicit consent for processing personal data. However, the application of these regulations to AI-generated content remains complex and evolving. For instance, the creation of deepfake videos using publicly available data poses challenges in determining whether such content falls under the purview of existing data protection laws, especially when explicit consent has not been obtained (Bayer, 2024).

Moreover, the right to privacy is jeopardized when AI models memorize and reproduce sensitive information from their training data. Studies have demonstrated that generative models can inadvertently leak personal data, leading to potential privacy violations (Liu et al., 2024). This issue is exacerbated in scenarios where AI systems are trained on vast datasets scraped from the internet without adequate data minimization strategies, contravening principles that advocate for collecting only necessary data.

The right to be forgotten, as enshrined in data protection frameworks like the GDPR, presents additional challenges in the context of AI-generated media. Ensuring the erasure of personal data becomes complex when such data has been used to train AI models that generate synthetic media. Developing mechanisms to identify and remove personal data embedded within AI systems is imperative to uphold individuals' rights to data erasure (Bayer, 2024). Addressing these multifaceted issues necessitates a collaborative approach involving policymakers, technologists, and legal experts to establish comprehensive frameworks that safeguard individual rights in the era of AI-generated media.

3.3 Creative Ownership vs. Machine Authorship

One of the most contested ethical dilemmas in the realm of AI-generated media lies in determining who holds the ownership rights over creative outputs produced by generative models. Traditional intellectual property (IP) frameworks are founded on the assumption of human authorship, where the creator—be it a writer, artist, or composer—retains moral and economic rights over their work. However, when content is autonomously generated by AI systems, the attribution of authorship becomes murky (Samuelson, 2022). Generative AI models, such as DALL·E or GPT-4, can produce images, stories, music, and video that may closely resemble or even surpass human creativity. This blurs the legal and ethical distinction between tool and creator.

Indian copyright law, as governed by the Copyright Act of 1957, does not currently recognize non-human entities as authors. The Indian courts have so far taken a conservative stance, reinforcing that only natural persons or legally recognized entities like corporations can hold authorship rights (Sinha, 2023). This creates a legal vacuum where AI-generated outputs either fall into the public domain or require attribution to human programmers or the corporate body deploying the AI. Moreover, the question arises whether credit should go to the data curators, the AI developer, or the end-user who prompts the system (Gervais, 2021).

In contrast, jurisdictions like the United Kingdom have made limited attempts to attribute authorship of computer-generated works to the "person making the necessary arrangements," as per Section 9(3) of the UK Copyright, Designs and Patents Act 1988. However, this approach still centers on human agency, failing to fully account for unsupervised or autonomous creative processes executed by generative models (McCutcheon, 2022). Ethically, this raises concerns about distributive justice—if AI systems generate commercially valuable work, who deserves the economic benefit? And if the system is trained on pre-existing copyrighted materials, is the creative output a derivative work or an original one?

The global debate is also tied to questions of moral rights—should AI be acknowledged as a co-creator or simply a tool? Emerging perspectives suggest that while AI cannot have moral rights, humans guiding the prompts and curating the results might claim partial authorship (Sharma & Dey, 2023). However, the lack of international consensus complicates enforcement, particularly for AI-generated media circulated across digital platforms. Blockchain technologies are beginning to offer potential solutions, allowing for timestamped authorship and transparent licensing via smart contracts, but their legal standing remains uncertain in many countries (Hofmann & Kamps, 2021).

3.4 Algorithmic Bias and Fair Representation

One of the most pressing ethical concerns in AI-generated media is algorithmic bias, which refers to the tendency of AI systems to reproduce and even amplify societal prejudices embedded within training data. Since generative AI models are trained on massive datasets sourced from the internet, they are inevitably exposed to biased, stereotypical, or unbalanced content. These biases can manifest in ways that perpetuate racial, gender, cultural, and linguistic stereotypes, particularly in visual and textual media outputs (Mehrabi et al., 2021). For instance, AI-generated images often depict certain demographics—especially women and minorities—in stereotypical or hyper-sexualized roles due to the overrepresentation of such content in training datasets (Binns, 2018). Similarly, voice synthesis or text generation tools may preferentially use westernized English accents or idioms, marginalizing non-Western linguistic and cultural identities.

Bias becomes even more problematic in multimodal AI systems, where text, image, audio, and video are synthesized together, potentially compounding multiple forms of representation disparity. A study by Suresh and Guttag (2019) outlined how biases can enter through various sources in the AI pipeline, including problem framing, data collection, labeling practices, model design, and evaluation metrics. In the Indian context, Sharma and Dey (2022) found that natural language processing (NLP) models often misrepresent caste identities or fail to detect social nuances in vernacular languages due to underrepresentation in training data. This underlines the importance of diversifying datasets and applying fairness-aware learning methods to mitigate such issues.

Moreover, algorithmic bias isn't only a technical flaw—it poses significant ethical and legal implications for media creators and consumers alike. For instance, AI-generated news summaries or historical visualizations that erase marginalized groups' contributions can subtly reshape collective memory and public discourse (Crawford, 2021). As these systems are increasingly used in journalism, marketing, cinema, and even policymaking, the stakes are high. Without rigorous bias auditing protocols and ethical review processes, generative AI could exacerbate existing social divides, particularly in countries like India where digital media consumption is booming but literacy on AI fairness remains limited (Joshi & Arora, 2023). Therefore, achieving fair representation in AI-generated media requires a multi-stakeholder approach, combining technological innovations (e.g., explainable AI, inclusive training sets) with policy frameworks and cultural sensitivity training for developers. It also involves public participation, where impacted communities have a say in how they are represented in synthetic media spaces.

4. LEGAL AND REGULATORY CONSIDERATIONS

4.1 Intellectual Property Rights and Copyright Challenges

The rise of generative AI in digital media production has brought intellectual property (IP) rights into a realm of uncertainty. Traditionally, copyright protection has been extended to works created by human authors, provided they exhibit a degree of originality. However, with AI systems now capable of autonomously generating music, art, literature, and videos, questions arise as to who owns the rights to such creations—the programmer, the user, or the machine itself (Chesney & Citron, 2019). The issue becomes even more complicated when AI models are trained on copyrighted datasets without explicit permission, thereby raising concerns about derivative works and fair use exceptions (Elgammal et al., 2017).

Legal systems across the world are still grappling with how to classify AI-generated content. For instance, in India, the current Copyright Act of 1957 only protects works created by "authors," a term that does not explicitly include non-human agents. Consequently, when a generative AI model produces a piece of art or a film script, assigning legal authorship becomes ambiguous. Scholars argue for the introduction of "machine authorship" doctrines or shared ownership frameworks between developers and users (Ravichandar & Narayan, 2022). In contrast, jurisdictions such as the United Kingdom have provided more progressive stances; the

UK Copyright, Designs and Patents Act 1988 acknowledges computer-generated works and attributes authorship to the person "making the arrangements" necessary for the creation.

Another complexity arises with the remix culture proliferated by generative AI tools that draw from millions of online samples. The line between inspiration and infringement blurs, especially in the creation of deepfakes or AI-generated mash-ups, which may repurpose existing content with minimal transformation (Gervais, 2020). Blockchain technology has been proposed as a means to track provenance and manage licensing automatically, yet these solutions are still emerging and face scalability and legal recognition issues (Tripathi & Bansal, 2023).

In the context of India, the lack of AI-specific IP regulation has sparked judicial debates. A 2021 ruling by the Delhi High Court stressed that the law must evolve to accommodate AI-related disputes, particularly when such systems are used to generate commercial content. The legal vacuum not only hampers innovation but also discourages creators from leveraging generative AI tools due to concerns about ownership and liability (Sarkar & Menon, 2023).

4.2 Data Protection and Privacy Laws

Data protection and privacy laws play a pivotal role in regulating AI-generated content, particularly in the context of digital media where personal data can be scraped, synthesized, or manipulated without the consent of the data subjects. The General Data Protection Regulation (GDPR), implemented in the European Union, establishes stringent principles such as lawful data processing, purpose limitation, data minimization, and the right to be forgotten. These principles become critical when generative AI systems utilize large datasets scraped from social media, news portals, and video-sharing platforms for training purposes (Taddeo & Floridi, 2020). The GDPR mandates explicit consent from data subjects, posing a challenge for AI systems that operate on anonymized or publicly available data, yet may inadvertently generate identifiable content.

In the Indian context, the Information Technology (Intermediary Guidelines and Digital Media Ethics Code) Rules, 2021 and the recent Digital Personal Data Protection Act, 2023 introduce new compliance requirements for platforms using AI tools, particularly regarding notice and consent mechanisms, user rights, and data localization (Kumar & Ramesh, 2023). The Indian law also stresses the accountability of data fiduciaries and emphasizes "purpose limitation," which means that data collected for one reason (e.g., user interaction) should not be reused for AI training without informed consent. This aspect is particularly relevant for media platforms integrating generative AI, where content replication, deep personalization, and synthetic media production are common.

Furthermore, privacy concerns arise from the way generative models like GPT, Midjourney, and DALL·E may retain or regenerate sensitive or personally identifiable information (PII) from their training data. Studies have shown that such systems can "memorize" user-specific inputs or reveal private data under certain prompt conditions (Carlini et al., 2021). In jurisdictions where such disclosures fall under data breach, there are implications for civil liabilities and regulatory penalties.

Cross-border concerns further complicate privacy enforcement. AI-generated media platforms are often hosted across different jurisdictions, making it difficult to determine the applicable law or regulatory authority. This global disjunction necessitates harmonization of data protection frameworks and collaborative international governance (Saxena, 2023). While GDPR has set a global standard, emerging economies including India are evolving their legislation to balance innovation and rights protection.

4.3 Accountability and Liability of AI-Generated Content

As generative AI systems continue to proliferate in the digital media space, the issue of accountability and liability becomes a major ethical and legal concern. Traditional legal systems are designed to attribute responsibility to human actors or legal entities, such as corporations. However, the autonomous nature of generative AI—especially those systems capable of creating multimodal content like text, images, videos, and soundscapes—complicates the attribution of legal liability when harm or misinformation occurs. One of the key challenges is determining who is accountable when AI-generated content causes defamation, violates copyright, or spreads misinformation. The developers, deployers, and users of these systems may all share varying degrees of responsibility (Kaminski, 2019).

Some legal scholars argue for a model of "functional equivalence", where AI is treated analogously to human agents under the law in specific contexts, while others propose the creation of a new category of "electronic legal personhood" (Wischmeyer & Rademacher, 2020). However, these models remain largely theoretical and face considerable resistance due to ethical and regulatory implications. In countries like India, where digital literacy and content moderation mechanisms are still developing, these concerns are particularly pressing. The Information Technology (Intermediary Guidelines and Digital Media Ethics Code) Rules, 2021, assign due diligence obligations on intermediaries, but these laws are not well-equipped to handle liability arising from AI-generated content (Gurumurthy & Bharthur, 2022).

A key concern lies in the opacity of generative AI systems—often referred to as the "black box" problem. This lack of transparency in algorithmic decision-making makes it difficult to trace content creation and identify responsible agents (Pasquale, 2015). Blockchain integration has been proposed as a means to improve traceability and ensure that a digital record of AI content creation is maintained, but this is still in early implementation stages and cannot yet address all liability concerns.

International regulatory frameworks are also struggling to catch up. The European Union's draft AI Act includes provisions for high-risk AI systems that could help address accountability gaps, but its scope is limited to systems explicitly designated as high-risk (Veale & Borgesius, 2021). As such, many generative media systems may fall outside this classification despite their potential to cause serious harm. Overall, the legal landscape remains fragmented, and until there is a unified framework that clearly allocates responsibility, accountability in AI-generated media will continue to pose serious ethical and legal dilemmas.

4.4 Jurisdictional Complexities in Global Digital Media

One of the most challenging aspects of regulating AI-generated media lies in the jurisdictional complexities associated with the global nature of digital content creation and dissemination. As AI-generated content crosses borders instantly, determining the applicable legal framework becomes complicated. For example, an AI-generated video created in India, hosted on servers in the United States, and consumed by users in the European Union may potentially fall under the purview of at least three distinct legal systems, each with unique data protection, copyright, and liability regulations (Kesan & Hayes, 2022). This lack of uniformity often results in legal ambiguity, especially when it comes to enforcement and accountability.

Countries have adopted varied stances toward the regulation of AI and digital media. The European Union's AI Act proposes a risk-based classification system for AI applications, placing stricter obligations on systems deemed high-risk, such as those capable of generating deepfakes (European Commission, 2021). However, other jurisdictions like the United States emphasize sector-specific approaches, relying more heavily on private governance mechanisms. India, in contrast, is still evolving its regulatory framework with guidelines like the Information Technology (Intermediary Guidelines and Digital Media Ethics Code) Rules, 2021, which stress platform responsibility but lack specific directives for AI-generated content (Chander & Parmar, 2022).

Additionally, the issue of legal jurisdiction is complicated by the lack of consensus on whether the AI or the developer should be held accountable for harmful or infringing content. This is especially relevant when AI models are trained using global data sets that may incorporate culturally sensitive or legally protected materials across jurisdictions (Kumar & Tripathi, 2023). The transnational nature of blockchain, often used to verify and timestamp generative media, adds another layer of complexity as many countries have no specific legal infrastructure to manage smart contracts or decentralized records.

International cooperation, such as through multilateral forums like the OECD and UNESCO, is beginning to address these gaps by promoting interoperability and ethical standards, but a binding legal consensus remains distant. Without unified global frameworks, content creators and platforms often resort to geo-blocking or content moderation that aligns with the most restrictive jurisdictions, potentially stifling creative freedom and access (Brown & Marsden, 2023). Therefore, the urgent need is not just for robust national laws but also harmonized international legal instruments that can manage jurisdictional overlaps and facilitate fair regulation of AI-generated media.

5. BLOCKCHAIN AS A TOOL FOR ETHICAL COMPLIANCE

5.1 Content Authentication and Provenance Tracking

In an era dominated by generative AI, ensuring the authenticity of media content has become crucial. With AI models capable of producing hyper-realistic images, videos, and voices, there is a growing risk of digital forgeries and misinformation. This has created an urgent need for mechanisms that can verify the origin and authenticity of content. Blockchain technology is increasingly being seen as a powerful tool for this purpose, particularly through its capability to create immutable and time-stamped records of media creation and modification (Gupta et al., 2023). These records provide an auditable trail that can help users, platforms, and regulators verify the provenance of a digital asset, including its creator, licensing history, and any subsequent changes made to it.

One emerging solution is the use of blockchain-based content authenticity frameworks such as the Content Authenticity Initiative (CAI), which pairs metadata with digital assets. When integrated with AI-generated content, these systems can verify whether the media has been altered or synthetically generated (Sinnappan & Zutshi, 2022). This metadata, which includes source information, time of generation, and creator details, is hashed and stored on a blockchain ledger. If any alterations are made to the content, the hash no longer matches, signaling potential tampering. For example, the Adobe-led CAI has already begun testing such standards across creative and news platforms.

In the Indian context, researchers have advocated for blockchain-driven digital watermarking to protect cultural content, local journalism, and user-generated media (Mukherjee & Ghosh, 2022). With the increasing use of regional languages and AI tools in the Indian media space, tracking provenance is vital for maintaining trust, especially given the scale at which misinformation spreads on WhatsApp and similar platforms. Blockchain-based certificates embedded within images and videos could also support court admissibility of digital evidence in India, aligning with IT Act provisions and digital forensics guidelines (Kumar & Arora, 2021).

Furthermore, provenance tracking has immense implications in the art and entertainment industry. With Non-Fungible Tokens (NFTs) powered by blockchain, creators can assert authorship, protect against forgeries, and establish royalties using smart contracts (Siddiqui & Chang, 2023). This also helps in fighting unethical AI-generated replications by preserving a transparent ownership trail. Ultimately, blockchain-enabled provenance verification presents a scalable and decentralized response to ethical concerns in AI-generated media. As AI evolves to mimic human creativity, technologies like blockchain become essential not just for trust-building but also for reinforcing accountability in digital ecosystems (Hussain et al., 2023).

5.2 Smart Contracts for Licensing and Usage Rights

Smart contracts—self-executing contracts with terms directly written into code—are transforming the licensing and rights management of AI-generated media by introducing automation, transparency, and enforceability. In digital media ecosystems where content is being generated and distributed at unprecedented rates, smart contracts ensure that creators, distributors, and users engage in fair and pre-agreed terms without the need for intermediaries. This is particularly relevant for generative AI outputs, such as digital art, music, and video, where ownership and rights attribution are often blurred.

A key advantage of using smart contracts lies in their ability to automate licensing based on usage parameters embedded in the contract. For instance, when AI-generated content is used in a social media campaign or broadcast, smart contracts can instantly execute royalty payments or revoke usage rights upon expiry or violation of terms (Regner et al., 2019). This streamlines compliance and enforces accountability in a way that is currently difficult to achieve through conventional legal channels. Further, smart contracts can be encoded to reflect ethical considerations, such as ensuring attribution for human co-creators or limiting dissemination of content flagged as sensitive or biased (Schatsky et al., 2020).

In the Indian context, smart contracts have begun to gain traction in IP-intensive sectors like entertainment, music, and fashion. For example, media start-ups like Blocklogy Edutech and TDeFi-backed projects are integrating smart contract-based frameworks to protect digital creators and enable micro-licensing, especially in vernacular content platforms (Radhakrishnan & Shilpa, 2022). Despite the lack of a concrete legal definition of smart contracts under Indian law, the Information Technology Act, 2000 provides a general framework for digital signatures and electronic contracts, which can be extended to smart contracts (Malik & Joshi, 2021).

However, the use of smart contracts is not without challenges. One primary issue is the legal enforceability of these contracts across jurisdictions, especially since AI-generated content often circulates globally. Differences in copyright laws, contract recognition, and definitions of authorship can lead to conflicting interpretations of ownership and usage rights (De Filippi & Wright, 2018). Moreover, smart contracts are only as good as the code they are built upon—errors or security vulnerabilities in code could lead to unintended consequences, including unauthorized use or incorrect distribution of royalties. Nevertheless, smart contracts hold tremendous potential for democratizing access to content while simultaneously upholding ethical and legal norms in AI-generated media. They present a proactive, tech-enabled path for protecting creator rights and streamlining content governance in a rapidly evolving digital world.

5.3 Immutable Records for Dispute Resolution

One of the most significant contributions of blockchain technology to the ethical governance of AI-generated media is its ability to provide immutable records that can serve as credible evidence during disputes over content authenticity, usage, or ownership. The decentralized and time-stamped nature of blockchain ensures that once a record is created, it cannot be altered or deleted without consensus across the network, thus offering a transparent audit trail. This feature is particularly vital when AI-generated content, such as deepfakes or synthetic media, leads to misinformation, defamation, or copyright infringements (Kritikos, 2022). For example, when disputes arise regarding whether a generative AI has unlawfully copied style, voice, or content, a blockchain-based ledger that tracks the provenance and modification history can help resolve such conflicts with verifiable proof (Schoren et al., 2023).

Furthermore, these immutable records can be used to verify the originality and source of AI-generated media, especially in contexts such as journalism, advertising, and cinema where trust and attribution are critical (Pathak & Sundararajan, 2023). For instance, in the Indian legal and media landscape, where enforcement of digital rights remains fragmented, blockchain has the potential to serve as a neutral third-party record keeper that enhances evidentiary standards in judicial proceedings (Raman & Dubey, 2022). Smart contracts—self-executing agreements coded into the blockchain—can also facilitate automatic enforcement of usage terms and penalties, adding an additional layer of trust and legal robustness to AI-generated media distribution (Lee & Choi, 2023).

Notably, this capability extends beyond merely resolving ownership or licensing issues; it can also empower content creators to document their creative process in a secure, time-bound manner. Such documentation can later be used in cases of unauthorized reproduction or plagiarism allegations, even in cross-border contexts where jurisdictional overlap makes enforcement complex (Chugh & Srivastava, 2022). As disputes over AI content increase globally, the incorporation of blockchain-backed immutable records is emerging as a vital safeguard, contributing not only to ethical compliance but also to legal clarity in an evolving digital ecosystem.

5.4 Real-World Use Cases: NFTs and Media Attribution

The fusion of blockchain and generative AI has opened up novel opportunities in the realm of digital media, particularly in areas like non-fungible tokens (NFTs) and content attribution. NFTs, unique cryptographic tokens that represent ownership of digital assets, have revolutionized how creators assert rights over their AI-generated content. For instance, artists and developers are now minting AI-generated visuals, music, and even narratives as NFTs on decentralized platforms to establish indisputable ownership and provenance (Dowling, 2022). This mechanism not only authenticates originality but also embeds metadata such as time of creation, content lineage, and creator details directly on the blockchain, thereby ensuring traceability and attribution (Rosenblatt, 2022).

In the Indian context, AI-based artworks and music compositions have been increasingly tokenized on platforms like WazirX NFT Marketplace and Guardian-Link. These platforms allow Indian artists to monetize generative AI content while embedding licensing rights through smart contracts, automatically ensuring royalties are paid for every resale (Chopra & Singh, 2023). Moreover, platforms are adopting blockchain not only for transaction transparency but also for content moderation, ensuring that generative media is not plagiarized or misleading.

One of the significant advantages of blockchain in media attribution is the ability to maintain immutable records, which can be used in legal disputes involving ownership or misuse. For instance, in the case of AI-generated deepfake videos, embedding blockchain-based digital watermarks enables real-time verification of content authenticity and its origin (Krafft et al., 2023). This is particularly relevant for journalism and online media, where the credibility of sources and content is critical to public trust. Media organizations such as The New York Times have piloted blockchain-based content authentication through projects like "The News Provenance Project", which tags metadata and blockchain-stamped verification for each image published (Diakopoulos & Johnson, 2022). Additionally, NFTs can aid in combating unauthorized distribution. The metadata stored within the NFT smart contracts contains licensing details that can be automatically enforced, and these records can serve as legal evidence. In educational and research publishing, AI-generated textbooks and simulations are increasingly being protected through NFT-based registries, thereby facilitating transparent usage metrics and compliance with intellectual property rights (Menon & Suresh, 2023). In essence, these use cases demonstrate the growing relevance of blockchain-backed NFTs in legitimizing AI-generated media, by enhancing traceability, ownership, and legal enforceability. As these technologies mature, their integration is expected to create a more ethically governed digital media ecosystem.

6. POLICY FRAMEWORKS AND STANDARDS

6.1 Global Perspectives: UNESCO, OECD, EU AI Act

As the use of generative AI and blockchain technologies becomes mainstream in digital media, international organizations such as UNESCO, OECD, and the European Union (EU) have initiated critical frameworks aimed at ensuring ethical deployment of AI systems. UNESCO's *Recommendation on the Ethics of Artificial Intelligence*, adopted in 2021, is among the first global standard-setting instruments for AI ethics. It emphasizes human rights, transparency, accountability, and sustainability in AI design and application, and encourages member states to regulate AI-generated content through robust ethical governance (UNESCO, 2021).

The OECD AI Principles also serve as a foundational document promoting responsible AI. These principles, adopted by 46 countries including India and the USA, advocate for AI systems that are inclusive, safe, accountable, and transparent (OECD, 2019). Particularly relevant to digital media, these guidelines underscore the need for human-centred values and fairness in algorithmic design—an area often challenged by multimodal generative AI platforms. The European Union's AI Act, proposed in 2021, introduces a risk-based regulatory approach, classifying AI applications into unacceptable, high, limited, and minimal risk. Deepfakes and other AI-generated media used in misinformation campaigns are categorized under high-risk or even prohibited categories if used without disclosure or consent (Stix, 2021). The AI Act also calls for rigorous documentation, testing, and human oversight mechanisms, especially in cases of synthetic content generation and dissemination.

These international initiatives reveal growing recognition of the global implications of AI-generated media, yet they also highlight gaps in harmonization, particularly in enforcement across jurisdictions (Butcher & Beridze, 2022). In the context of blockchain, these frameworks are evolving to address how distributed ledger technologies could support provenance verification and intellectual property rights in AI-created content

6.2 National Approaches: India, USA, China, and Others

National-level strategies vary widely in scope and implementation. India, for instance, has adopted a relatively cautious but evolving approach. The *Information Technology (Intermediary Guidelines and Digital Media Ethics Code) Rules, 2021* address online content regulation, including AI-generated misinformation and deep-fakes. While India lacks a standalone AI law, the *National Strategy for Artificial Intelligence* by NITI Aayog proposes ethical frameworks based on transparency, accountability, and privacy (Mehta & Singh, 2022). However, there remains ambiguity in enforcement, particularly regarding generative content and copyright attribution.

In contrast, the United States relies on a sector-specific, decentralized approach. Agencies like the Federal Trade Commission (FTC) have issued warnings against the misuse of deepfake technology in advertising and political manipulation (Smith, 2023). Furthermore, multiple states including California and Texas have passed laws requiring disclosure when synthetic media is used in political contexts, particularly near elections.

China has adopted a stricter regime. The *Provisions on the Administration of Deep Synthesis Internet Information Services*, effective from 2023, require platforms to clearly label AI-generated content and prohibit the creation of false information through synthetic technologies (Li & Wang, 2023). These rules impose significant penalties for non-compliance and mandate identity verification, data security, and content traceability.

Other nations, such as Canada, Brazil, and South Korea, are developing national AI strategies with embedded ethics clauses, but few have enforced specific legal controls on AI-generated media. This patchwork of national policies emphasizes the need for international coordination to ensure that AI and blockchain technologies in media operate within an equitable and enforceable ethical-legal framework.

6.3 Industry-Led Ethical Guidelines and Self-Regulation

In the rapidly evolving domain of AI-generated media, industry-led ethical frameworks and self-regulatory practices have emerged as crucial mechanisms to address the limitations of slow-moving legislative processes. Companies and industry coalitions have recognized the urgency of establishing ethical boundaries, particularly to ensure transparency, accountability, and public trust. For instance, technology leaders such as OpenAI, Meta, and Adobe have introduced internal ethics boards and responsible AI frameworks to monitor and guide the development and deployment of generative tools (Jobin, Ienca, & Vayena, 2019). These initiatives typically focus on transparency in AI decision-making, data integrity, and the prevention of harms such as bias, misinformation, or deepfakes. One prominent example is the

Partnership on AI, a global coalition of over 100 organizations, including academia, civil society, and industry players. This initiative promotes best practices for AI and has published guidelines addressing the ethical design and deployment of generative systems (Whittlestone et al., 2019). Similarly, Adobe's Content Authenticity Initiative (CAI) is designed to ensure media attribution by embedding metadata about the origin and edits of visual content, thereby supporting media authentication and discouraging manipulation (McGregor et al., 2022).

In India, while government-led regulation is still nascent, major IT and media companies have taken proactive steps. The National Association of Software and Service Companies (NASSCOM) released the "Responsible AI Guidelines for India," highlighting the importance of fairness, transparency, and explainability in AI applications, including those related to content generation (NASSCOM, 2021). These industry guidelines emphasize community feedback loops and algorithm audits to minimize potential harms. Although not legally binding, they act as normative standards that influence practice and corporate governance.

However, the self-regulatory approach is not without criticism. Scholars argue that such frameworks often lack enforcement mechanisms and rely heavily on corporate goodwill, leading to uneven implementation (Rahwan et al., 2019). To improve the effectiveness of self-regulation, experts propose hybrid governance models where industry codes are complemented by public oversight and civil society involvement. This would ensure accountability while preserving innovation and adaptability in content creation technologies.

7. CASE STUDIES AND REAL-WORLD EXAMPLES

The advent of generative AI has introduced both innovative opportunities and significant challenges across various sectors. This section delves into three pertinent case studies that highlight the ethical, legal, and regulatory implications of AI-generated media.

7.1 Case Study: Deepfake Controversy and Legal Action in the U.S.

In October 2023, a distressing incident unfolded at Westfield High School in New Jersey, where 14-year-old Francesca Mani discovered AI-generated explicit images of herself and other female students circulating among peers. The school's initial response was inadequate, prompting the Mani family to advocate for legislative reforms. Their efforts contributed to the introduction of the Preventing Deepfakes of Intimate Images Act, aiming to criminalize the non-consensual creation and distribution of such content (The Guardian, 2024). Subsequently, in March 2024, New Jersey enacted legislation making the creation and dissemination of deceptive AI-generated media a criminal offense, punishable by up to five years in prison. This law also empowers victims to pursue civil lawsuits against perpetrators (Associated Press, 2024). These developments underscore the urgent need for comprehensive legal frameworks to address the misuse of AI in generating harmful content.

7.2 Case Study: Blockchain-Based Attribution in News Media

The proliferation of misinformation has compelled news organizations to seek innovative solutions to authenticate content. Italian news agency ANSA implemented a blockchain-based system to certify its news articles, ensuring each piece is timestamped and its origin verifiable. This initiative aims to bolster public trust by providing transparent and immutable records of news provenance (EY, n.d.). Similarly, Mediachain, a platform leveraging blockchain and machine learning, facilitates automatic attribution for digital content, addressing challenges related to copyright and content ownership (Forbes, 2016). These cases exemplify how blockchain technology can enhance content integrity and combat misinformation in the digital age.

7.3 Case Study: Use of Generative AI in Indian Cinema and Regulatory Gaps

The Indian film industry, known as Bollywood, has begun integrating AI technologies into various aspects of filmmaking, including scriptwriting, visual effects, and post-production. While AI offers creative possibilities, it also raises concerns regarding intellectual property rights and the authenticity of performances. For instance, the potential use of AI to recreate deceased actors or alter performances poses ethical and legal questions. Currently, India lacks specific regulations addressing the use of AI in cinema, leading to uncertainties about content ownership and the protection of artists' rights 3). This regulatory gap highlights the necessity for policymakers to establish clear guidelines that balance innovation with ethical considerations in the entertainment industry.

8. ROAD AHEAD: RECOMMENDATIONS AND FUTURE DIRECTIONS

As artificial intelligence (AI) becomes increasingly integrated into digital media, addressing the ethical and legal challenges associated with AI-generated content is paramount. The following recommendations and future directions aim to promote responsible development and deployment of AI in media.

8.1 Designing Ethical-by-Design AI Systems

Incorporating ethical considerations from the inception of AI system development ensures that these technologies align with societal values and human rights. An "ethics by design" approach emphasizes integrating principles such as transparency, fairness, privacy, and accountability throughout the AI lifecycle. This methodology not only fosters trust among users but also mitigates potential risks associated with AI deployment. For instance, the European Commission provides guidelines advocating for the inclusion of ethical principles in AI design to preserve respect for human agency and promote fairness (European Commission, 2020). Additionally, Trigyn Technologies highlights the importance of prioritizing transparency, fairness, privacy, accountability, human oversight, safety, and social impact in AI solutions (Trigyn Technologies, 2023).

8.2 Developing Cross-Border Legal Harmonization

The global nature of digital media necessitates harmonized legal frameworks to effectively address the challenges posed by AI-generated content. Disparities in national regulations can lead to legal uncertainties and hinder the enforcement of ethical standards across jurisdictions. Establishing international agreements and collaborative regulatory approaches can facilitate consistent standards for AI deployment worldwide. For example, discussions on creating unified global legal structures for AI emphasize the need for harmonization to navigate the complexities of cross-border data flows and AI applications (Mohamed, 2022). Furthermore, the proliferation of barriers to cross-border data flows underscores the importance of developing international rules to govern the digital economy effectively (White & Case LLP, 2022).

8.3 Public Awareness and Digital Literacy Campaigns

Enhancing public understanding of AI technologies and their implications is crucial in mitigating the spread of misinformation and fostering critical engagement with digital content. Digital literacy initiatives should focus on educating individuals about the capabilities and limitations of AI, enabling them to discern between authentic and AI-generated media. For instance, the Bertie County Center emphasizes that digital literacy now encompasses the ability to critically engage with content in an era of AI-generated media, highlighting the necessity of recognizing misinformation to preserve trust in media (Bertie County Center, 2025). Additionally, the European Broadcasting Union discusses how AI tools can enhance media literacy by enabling quick and efficient analysis of information, thereby helping users distinguish between credible and misleading content (European Broadcasting Union, 2023).

8.4 Future Role of Blockchain in Governing AI-Generated Media

Blockchain technology offers promising solutions for ensuring the authenticity and integrity of AI-generated media. By providing decentralized and immutable records, blockchain can be utilized to verify the provenance of digital content, thereby combating issues such as deepfakes and unauthorized alterations. Integrating blockchain with AI can enhance transparency and accountability in content creation and distribution. For example, KPMG highlights that blockchain's ability to decentralize identity and verification could be invaluable as AI assumes a more significant role in content generation (KPMG, 2023). Additionally, Columbia University's Data Science Institute discusses how blockchain can assist creators in gaining control over their work in the context of AI-generated art, emphasizing the importance of establishing provenance (Columbia Data Science Institute, 2023).

9. CONCLUSION

The evolving landscape of AI-generated media presents a complex intersection of innovation, ethics, and legal accountability. As technologies like generative AI and blockchain reshape content creation and dissemination, it becomes imperative to establish a robust framework that safeguards human rights, fosters transparency, and promotes global cooperation. Designing AI systems with ethical principles embedded from the outset, harmonizing legal standards across borders, educating the public through digital literacy, and leveraging blockchain for provenance and accountability are all essential steps toward building a responsible digital media ecosystem. By integrating these approaches, stakeholders can ensure that AI-generated media serves as a tool for creativity and progress—rather than a source of harm or misinformation—ultimately contributing to a more trustworthy and inclusive digital future.

REFERENCES

Bayer, J. (2024). Legal implications of using generative AI in the media. *Information & Communications Technology Law*, *33*(3), 310–329. DOI: 10.1080/13600834.2024.2352694

Benaich, I., & Hogarth, N. (2023). *State of AI Report 2023*. Air Street Capital. Retrieved from https://www.stateof.ai

Bhardwaj, A., Sharma, K., & Mehta, R. (2023). Integrating blockchain with generative AI for ethical media governance. *Journal of Digital Ethics and Technology*, *11*(1), 55–70. DOI: 10.1080/25741292.2023.1142785

Binns, R. (2018). Fairness in machine learning: Lessons from political philosophy. *Proceedings of the 2018 Conference on Fairness, Accountability and Transparency (FAT)**, 149–159. DOI: 10.1145/3287560.3287598

Brown, I., & Marsden, C. T. (2023). *Regulating Code: Good Governance and Better Regulation in the Information Age* (2nd ed.). MIT Press., DOI: 10.7551/mitpress/13764.001.0001

Butcher, J., & Beridze, I. (2022). Policy, legal and regulatory implications of AI: Understanding the challenges. *AI and Ethics*, *2*(3), 531–545. DOI: 10.1007/s43681-021-00082-2

Carlini, N., Tramer, F., Wallace, E., Jagielski, M., Herbert-Voss, A., Lee, K., & Song, D. (2021). Extracting training data from large language models. *Proceedings of the 30th USENIX Security Symposium*, 2633–2650. DOI: 10.48550/arXiv.2012.07805

Chakraborty, S., & Gupta, R. (2022). Blockchain for responsible AI: A framework for transparent and traceable content creation. *Journal of Ethics and Information Technology*, *24*(3), 389–405. DOI: 10.1007/s10676-022-09634-w

Chander, A., & Parmar, M. (2022). Digital sovereignty and AI regulation in India: A comparative study. *Indian Journal of Law and Technology*, *18*(2), 127–149. DOI: 10.2139/ssrn.4094321

Chatterjee, R., & Singh, M. (2023). Generative AI in Indian media: Opportunities and ethical considerations. *Journal of Emerging Media Technologies*, *12*(2), 155–169. DOI: 10.1016/j.jemt.2023.06.009

Chesney, R., & Citron, D. (2019). Deep Fakes: A Looming Challenge for Privacy, Democracy, and National Security. *California Law Review*, *107*(6), 1753–1820. DOI: 10.15779/Z38RV0D15J

Chopra, R., & Singh, V. (2023). Blockchain-powered NFTs and the Indian creative economy: Opportunities and regulatory challenges. *Journal of Digital Law and Policy, 4*(1), 34–48. DOI: 10.2139/ssrn.4348712

Chugh, R., & Srivastava, M. (2022). Blockchain in Creative Industries: Protecting Intellectual Property in the Age of AI. *Journal of Intellectual Property and Technology Law, 17*(2), 95–110. DOI: 10.2139/ssrn.4078143

Columbia Data Science Institute. (2023). AI art is here to stay: How blockchain can help creators gain control over their work. Columbia University. https://datascience .columbia.edu/news/2023/ai-art-is-here-to-stay-how-blockchain-can-help-creators -gain-control-over-their-work/

Crawford, K. (2021). *Atlas of AI: Power, Politics, and the Planetary Costs of Artificial Intelligence.* Yale University Press.

Das, P. (2023). Digital provenance and blockchain: Protecting originality in AI-generated media. *Indian Journal of Law and Technology, 19*(1), 33–51. DOI: 10.2139/ssrn.4532107

De Filippi, P., & Wright, A. (2018). *Blockchain and the law: The rule of code.* Harvard University Press.

Diakopoulos, N., & Johnson, S. (2022). Credibility and blockchain: The use of immutable records in news verification. *Digital Journalism (Abingdon, England), 10*(2), 233–251. DOI: 10.1080/21670811.2021.1925429

Dowling, M. (2022). Fertile LAND: Pricing non-fungible tokens. *Finance Research Letters, 44*, 102096. DOI: 10.1016/j.frl.2021.102096

Elgammal, A., Liu, B., Elhoseiny, M., & Mazzone, M. (2017). *CAN: Creative Adversarial Networks, Generating "Art" by Learning About Styles and Deviating from Style Norms.* In *Proceedings of the Eighth International Conference on Computational Creativity* (pp. 96–103). Association for Computational Creativity. DOI: 10.48550/arXiv.1706.07068

Bertie County Center. (2025). Digital literacy for the age of deepfakes: Recognizing misinformation in AI-generated media. North Carolina State University. https:// bertie.ces.ncsu.edu/2025/03/digital-literacy-for-the-age-of-deepfakes-recognizing -misinformation-in-ai-generated-media/

European Broadcasting Union. (2023). Navigating the digital frontier: The impact of AI on media literacy. https://www.ebu.ch/news/2023/10/navigating-the-digital -frontier--the-impact-of-ai-on-media-literacy

European Commission. (2021). Proposal for a Regulation of the European Parliament and of the Council Laying Down Harmonised Rules on Artificial Intelligence (Artificial Intelligence Act) and Amending Certain Union Legislative Acts. COM/2021/206 final. https://eur-lex.europa.eu/legal-content/EN/TXT/?uri=CELEX%3A52021PC0206

Gervais, D. (2020). AI and Copyright: Assessing the Challenge of Human-Machine Creativity. *Houston Law Review*, *57*(3), 803–843. DOI: 10.2139/ssrn.3359524

Gervais, D. (2021). The machine as author. *Iowa Law Review*, *105*(5), 2053–2102. DOI: 10.2139/ssrn.3359524

Goodfellow, I., Bengio, Y., & Courville, A. (2022). *Deep learning* (Vol. 1). MIT Press., DOI: 10.7551/mitpress/12094.001.0001

Gupta, R., Sharma, A., & Das, P. (2023). Blockchain and AI in media verification: An integrated framework. *Journal of Information Security Research*, *11*(2), 78–91. DOI: 10.1016/j.jisr.2023.04.005

Gupta, R., & Srivastava, M. (2023). Generative AI and multimodal content: Emerging trends in media communication. *Journal of Media Innovation*, *14*(2), 120–137. DOI: 10.1016/j.jmi.2023.03.005

Gurumurthy, A., & Bharthur, D. (2022). Platform governance and digital rights: Regulating the online public sphere in India. *International Journal of Communication*, *16*, 1506–1525. https://ijoc.org/index.php/ijoc/article/view/18630

Hofmann, J., & Kamps, J. (2021). Smart copyrights: Blockchain technology and copyright management. *Journal of Intellectual Property Law & Practice*, *16*(6), 561–569. DOI: 10.1093/jiplp/jpab055

Hussain, S., Luo, J., & Kim, S. (2023). Decentralized provenance tracking for AI-generated content using blockchain and smart contracts. *Journal of Digital Ethics and Technology*, *6*(1), 33–47. DOI: 10.1016/j.jdet.2023.01.004

Jain, A., Bhattacharya, R., & Menon, S. (2023). AI for inclusive education: Opportunities and challenges of multimodal generative systems. *International Journal of Educational Technology in Higher Education*, *20*(1), 18–32. DOI: 10.1186/s41239-023-00412-z

Jobin, A., Ienca, M., & Vayena, E. (2019). The global landscape of AI ethics guidelines. *Nature Machine Intelligence*, *1*(9), 389–399. DOI: 10.1038/s42256-019-0088-2

Joshi, V., & Arora, P. (2023). Bias and fairness in Indian language NLP: Challenges and future directions. *Journal of South Asian Digital Humanities*, *5*(1), 88–105. DOI: 10.33675/dhsa.005.03

Kaminski, M. E. (2019). The right to explanation, explained. *Berkeley Technology Law Journal*, *34*(1), 189–218. DOI: 10.15779/Z38F47HV20

Kesan, J. P., & Hayes, C. (2022). Cross-border legal challenges in AI and block-chain regulation. *Journal of International and Comparative Law*, *9*(1), 54–78. DOI: 10.2139/ssrn.3918755

Krafft, P. M., Osoba, O. A., & Richards, A. (2023). Authentication at scale: Blockchain-based verification for synthetic media. *AI & Society*, *38*(1), 145–161. DOI: 10.1007/s00146-022-01423-6

Krishnamurthy, A., & Ghosh, S. (2023). Synthetic news and cultural narratives: A study on AI in Indian regional media. *Journal of Media Ethics and Society*, *15*(2), 66–81. DOI: 10.1080/2470912X.2023.1950491

Kritikos, M. (2022). Artificial Intelligence and Dispute Resolution: The Role of Blockchain in Ensuring Accountability. *European Journal of Law and Technology*, *13*(1), 1–18. DOI: 10.2139/ssrn.4207161

Kumar, A., & Arora, R. (2021). Blockchain-based digital forensics in India: Legal and technological perspectives. *Indian Journal of Law and Technology*, *17*(2), 102–120. DOI: 10.2139/ssrn.3869122

Kumar, A., & Ramesh, V. (2023). Regulating AI and data privacy in India: An analysis of the Digital Personal Data Protection Act, 2023. *Indian Journal of Law and Technology*, *19*(1), 45–61. DOI: 10.2139/ssrn.4569987

Kumar, A., & Rana, S. (2023). GANs and creativity: Reframing content generation in digital storytelling. *AI & Society*, *38*(1), 91–105. DOI: 10.1007/s00146-022-01472-4

Kumar, A., & Tripathi, R. (2023). Artificial intelligence and legal accountability in India: Policy lag or regulatory void? *Journal of Law and Emerging Technologies*, *5*(1), 45–61. DOI: 10.2139/ssrn.4359893

Kumar, S., & Deshmukh, R. (2024). The Digital Personal Data Protection Act 2023: Implications for AI governance in India. *Indian Journal of Law and Technology*, *20*(1), 44–59. DOI: 10.1007/s12553-024-00119-8

Lee, J., & Choi, H. (2023). Smart contracts and AI content governance: A hybrid legal-technical approach. *Computer Law & Security Review*, *49*, 105772. DOI: 10.1016/j.clsr.2023.105772

Leung, T., & Narayanan, P. (2023). Consent and identity in AI-generated content: A blockchain-based framework. *Journal of Technology Law & Policy*, *26*(3), 145–163. DOI: 10.2139/ssrn.4573264

Levendowski, A. (2023). AI authorship and the copyright conundrum. *Journal of Intellectual Property Law & Practice*, *18*(5), 325–336. DOI: 10.1093/jiplp/jpad033

Li, J., & Wang, Y. (2023). Regulating deep synthesis technologies in China: Governance mechanisms and challenges. *Journal of Cyber Policy*, *8*(1), 59–78. DOI: 10.1080/23738871.2023.2172763

Liu, Y., Huang, J., Li, Y., Wang, D., & Xiao, B. (2024). Generative AI model privacy: A survey. *Artificial Intelligence Review*, *58*(1), 33. DOI: 10.1007/s10462-024-11024-6

Malik, A., & Joshi, P. (2021). Legal challenges of blockchain-based smart contracts in India. *International Journal of Law and Management Studies*, *3*(2), 45–54. DOI: 10.2139/ssrn.3791645

McCutcheon, J. (2022). Authors and AI: Challenges to copyright law in the digital era. *The Modern Law Review*, *85*(3), 612–640. DOI: 10.1111/1468-2230.12712

McGregor, L., Murray, D., & Ng, V. (2022). Deepfakes and the content authenticity initiative: A technological and ethical analysis. *Journal of Media Ethics*, *37*(2), 95–110. DOI: 10.1080/23736992.2022.2049375

Mehrabi, N., Morstatter, F., Saxena, N., Lerman, K., & Galstyan, A. (2021). A survey on bias and fairness in machine learning. *ACM Computing Surveys*, *54*(6), 1–35. DOI: 10.1145/3457607

Mehta, A., & Singh, R. (2022). Regulatory challenges of AI in India: A policy review of NITI Aayog's approach. *Indian Journal of Law and Technology*, *18*(1), 1–27. DOI: 10.5555/ijlt.18.1.1

Menon, R., & Suresh, A. (2023). Smart contracts for academic publishing: Securing AI-generated educational resources with NFTs. *Indian Journal of Educational Technology*, *17*(2), 78–92. DOI: 10.5958/2230-7135.2023.00008.9

Mohan, K., & Shetty, P. (2022). Cultural ethics and bias in generative AI systems in Indian media. *Asian Journal of Ethics and Technology*, *9*(1), 45–62. DOI: 10.23856/ajet.2022.90105

Mukherjee, A., & Sanyal, S. (2023). Blockchain for ethical verification in AI-generated media: A regulatory perspective. *AI and Ethics*, *4*(3), 243–258. DOI: 10.1007/s43681-023-00262-6

Mukherjee, S., & Ghosh, T. (2022). Trusting local journalism: The case for blockchain watermarking in Indian media. *Asian Journal of Communication and Technology*, 4(3), 55–66. DOI: 10.1080/15504435.2022.1876335

Murray, J. (2022). Smart contracts and NFTs: Copyright enforcement in the age of AI and blockchain. *Journal of Intellectual Property Law & Practice*, 17(4), 273–281. DOI: 10.1093/jiplp/jpac020

Muthukumar, R., & Reddy, V. (2022). Algorithmic bias in multimodal AI: An Indian perspective on data justice. *AI & Society*, 37(4), 1221–1236. DOI: 10.1007/s00146-021-01247-5

Narayanan, P., & Gupta, A. (2023). The ethics of synthetic media in the era of AI: Policy challenges in India. *Indian Journal of Law and Technology*, 19(1), 27–45. DOI: 10.5281/zenodo.8101456

Nguyen, T., Lee, Y., & Kim, J. (2022). Blockchain as a trust protocol in media authentication: A review of opportunities and challenges. *ACM Transactions on Multimedia Computing Communications and Applications*, 18(2), 1–19. DOI: 10.1145/3429457

OECD. (2019). OECD Principles on Artificial Intelligence. OECD Legal Instruments. https://legalinstruments.oecd.org/en/instruments/OECD-LEGAL-0449

Pasquale, F. (2015). *The Black Box Society: The Secret Algorithms That Control Money and Information*. Harvard University Press. DOI: 10.4159/harvard.9780674736061

Pathak, A., & Sundararajan, M. (2023). Blockchain for Media Integrity: Indian Context and Applications. *Indian Journal of Law and Technology*, 19(1), 77–94. DOI: 10.2139/ssrn.4462219

Pillai, S., & Thomas, J. (2022). Algorithmic fairness and ethical AI in India: The role of blockchain for traceable accountability. *Indian Journal of AI Ethics and Law*, 4(2), 88–103. DOI: 10.1007/s12553-022-00510-7

Radhakrishnan, R., & Shilpa, P. (2022). Blockchain and smart contracts in Indian media and entertainment: Opportunities and regulatory concerns. *Journal of Medical Law and Ethics*, 10(1), 33–49. DOI: 10.5281/zenodo.7529478

Rahwan, I., Cebrian, M., Obradovich, N., Bongard, J., Bonnefon, J. F., Breazeal, C., & Lazer, D. (2019). Machine behaviour. *Nature*, 568(7753), 477–486. DOI: 10.1038/s41586-019-1138-y PMID: 31019318

Rajagopal, R., & Mishra, V. (2022). Smart contracts and digital rights management in India's media sector. *Journal of Media Innovation and Law*, *5*(1), 31–47. DOI: 10.2139/ssrn.4452112

Raman, A., & Dubey, A. (2022). Legal enforceability of blockchain evidence in Indian courts: Challenges and prospects. *Indian Bar Review*, *49*(2), 203–220. DOI: 10.2139/ssrn.4341216

Ramesh, A., Pavlov, M., Goh, G., Gray, S., & Agarwal, S. (2022). Hierarchical text-conditional image generation with CLIP Latents. NeurIPS Proceedings, 35, 31315–31327. /arXiv.2204.06125DOI: 10.48550

Ramesh, S., & Iyer, V. (2023). Policy and regulation for AI-generated multimedia content in India. *Indian Journal of Law and Technology*, *19*(1), 67–84. DOI: 10.52370/ijlt.v19i1.2023.004

Ravichandar, A., & Narayan, A. (2022). Artificial Intelligence and Intellectual Property in India: Regulatory Dilemmas and Future Directions. *NUJS Law Review*, *15*(2), 202–223. DOI: 10.2139/ssrn.4145722

Regner, F., Urbach, N., & Schweizer, A. (2019). NFTs and the future of digital content licensing. *Business & Information Systems Engineering*, *61*(6), 553–558. DOI: 10.1007/s12599-019-00600-9

Rosenblatt, B. (2022). Blockchain and copyright: Protecting AI-generated works in the digital domain. *Journal of Intellectual Property Law & Practice*, *17*(5), 377–388. DOI: 10.1093/jiplp/jpac019

Samuelson, P. (2022). Allocating ownership rights in AI-generated works. *Berkeley Technology Law Journal*, *37*(2), 455–498. DOI: 10.2139/ssrn.3924653

Sarkar, S., & Menon, R. (2023). Legal Challenges of AI-Generated Content in India: Ownership and Accountability. *Indian Journal of Law and Technology*, *19*(1), 47–67. DOI: 10.2139/ssrn.4389214

Saxena, N. (2023). Harmonizing data protection frameworks for AI-driven media platforms: A comparative study of GDPR and Indian data laws. *Journal of Cyber Policy and Governance*, *8*(2), 115–133. DOI: 10.1080/23738871.2023.2234020

Schoren, M., Ghose, A., & Xu, S. (2023). Blockchain and AI: Complementary Technologies for Ethical Governance in Digital Content Creation. *AI & Society*, *38*(1), 99–115. DOI: 10.1007/s00146-022-01376-0

Sharma, N., & Dey, A. (2023). Rethinking authorship in the age of generative AI: A comparative legal analysis. *The Journal of Law and Technology*, *8*(1), 23–38. DOI: 10.5958/2349-4829.2023.00003.0

Sharma, R., & Dey, N. (2022). Ethical considerations in Indian AI systems: A focus on caste and regional representation. *Indian Journal of Ethics in Technology*, *3*(2), 55–72. DOI: 10.25027/IJET.2022.032.05

Sharma, R., & Iyer, V. (2023). Ethical AI frameworks in multimedia production: A comparative policy study. *Media Culture & Society*, *45*(6), 1021–1038. DOI: 10.1177/01634437231123109

Siddiqui, F., & Chang, H. (2023). NFTs and the redefinition of digital media ownership. *International Journal of Digital Art & Blockchain*, *2*(1), 12–27. DOI: 10.1080/27663312.2023.1965031

Singh, N., Pandey, R., & Krishnan, M. (2022). Algorithmic bias in generative AI: An Indian perspective. *Journal of Digital Ethics and Society*, *7*(2), 110–125. DOI: 10.26529/jdes.2022.11072

Sinha, R. (2023). Artificial intelligence and copyright law in India: Navigating uncharted waters. *NUJS Law Review*, *16*(1), 78–94. DOI: 10.2139/ssrn.4567892

Sinnappan, S., & Zutshi, A. (2022). The role of metadata and blockchain in digital content authentication. *Journal of Emerging Technologies in Media*, *5*(2), 88–104. DOI: 10.1016/j.jetm.2022.05.002

Smith, T. (2023). State-level regulatory responses to synthetic media in the United States. *Yale Journal of Law & Technology*, *25*(2), 135–162. DOI: 10.2139/ssrn.4321210

Stix, C. (2021). A survey of the European Union's Artificial Intelligence Act: Risk-based regulation in practice. *Nature Machine Intelligence*, *3*(12), 1032–1034. DOI: 10.1038/s42256-021-00425-3

Sundaram, A., & Rao, T. (2023). Localizing generative AI: A case for Indic language models. *International Journal of AI and Society*, *12*(3), 201–216. DOI: 10.1007/s13178-023-00678-w

Sundararajan, K., & Ramesh, M. (2021). Blockchain applications in Indian governance and creative sectors: Potential and policy perspectives. *Journal of South Asian Policy Studies*, *6*(2), 112–128. DOI: 10.1007/s13531-021-00129-w

Suresh, H., & Guttag, J. V. (2019). A framework for understanding unintended consequences of machine learning. *Communications of the ACM, 63*(5), 62–71. DOI: 10.1145/3287560.3287598

Taddeo, M., & Floridi, L. (2020). The ethics of digital well-being: A thematic review. *Science and Engineering Ethics, 26*(4), 2313–2343. DOI: 10.1007/s11948-020-00175-8 PMID: 31933119

Tripathi, A., & Joshi, D. (2023). Challenges in regulating generative AI in digital media: A legal outlook. *South Asian Journal of Law and Policy, 12*(1), 25–39. DOI: 10.2139/ssrn.4388291

Tripathi, K., & Bansal, M. (2023). Blockchain as an Intellectual Property Management Tool in India's Creative Sector. *Journal of Intellectual Property Rights, 28*(4), 167–175. DOI: 10.56042/jipr.v28i4.125273

Veale, M., & Borgesius, F. Z. (2021). Demystifying the draft EU Artificial Intelligence Act. *Computer Law Review International, 22*(4), 97–112. DOI: 10.9785/cri-2021-220402

Verma, N., & Iyer, S. (2023). Adoption of AI-generated content tools in Indian digital media. *South Asian Journal of Media Studies, 8*(3), 201–217. DOI: 10.1177/09763500231123865

Wang, L., & Chen, Y. (2023). Blockchain-enabled provenance tracking for AI-generated multimedia. *Multimedia Systems, 29*(3), 467–482. DOI: 10.1007/s00530-022-00983-9

Whittlestone, J., Nyrup, R., Alexandrova, A., & Cave, S. (2019). The role and limits of principles in AI ethics: Towards a focus on tensions. Proceedings of the 2019 AAAI/ACM Conference on AI, Ethics, and Society, 195–200. DOI: 10.1145/3306618.3314289

Wischmeyer, T., & Rademacher, T. (2020). Regulating artificial intelligence in the European Union. *Common Market Law Review, 57*(5), 1149–1180. DOI: 10.54648/COLA2020061

Wu, L., Zhang, M., & Zhou, T. (2023). From uni-modal to multi-modal: Evolution of large language models for digital content generation. *ACM Transactions on Multimedia Computing Communications and Applications, 19*(3), 1–19. DOI: 10.1145/3589387

Zhou, X., Li, T., & Zhang, Y. (2022). Multimodal transformers in generative AI: Frameworks and applications. *AI Review Quarterly, 45*(4), 345–369. DOI: 10.1007/s10462-022-10102-7

Chapter 2
Legal and Ethical Considerations of AI–Driven Adaptations in the Production of Media

Suraj Patel Pinninti
ⓘ https://orcid.org/0009-0009-9453-3986
Mahindra University, India

Raneeta Pal
ⓘ https://orcid.org/0000-0002-8514-880X
Mahindra University, India

ABSTRACT

The rise in the integration of Artificial Intelligence (AI) into media productions for example remastering, dubbing and content adaptation has raised significant legal and ethical concerns. Central to these issues are the rights to adaptation under copyright law, which grant creators exclusive authority over derivative works and transformations of their original creations. These rights are often challenged by AI-driven processes like audiovisual quality enhancement, synthetic voice generation, cultural localization raising questions about ownership, fair use, and copyright compliance. This research proposal will therefore examine the legal effects of AI enhanced adaptations through a thorough evaluation of relevant case law, jurisdictional differences and market forces so as to strike a balance between innovation and maintaining respect for artists' rights.

DOI: 10.4018/979-8-3373-6481-0.ch002

1. INTRODUCTION

1.1 Overview

Artificial Intelligence (AI) and Blockchain have impacted profoundly in the domain of Digital Media. AI has managed to revolutionize the creation, edition, distribution, and consumption of content through task automation, personalization, and novel format adoption. (Hussain & Al-Turjman, 2021) In contrast, Blockchain has created a decentralized media transactions framework that improves transparency, traceability, and security of the transactions.

1.2 The Rise on Multimodal Generative AI

The scope of Generative AI has now expanded from its core text-based functionalities to include text, images, videos, and audio. This gives the creators the ability to effortlessly create sophisticated content at scale and quality that was previously inaccessible. Such Tools include DALL·E, ChatGPT, and other Generative Models. The adoption of different media formats is now easily attainable. The emergence of multi modal generative AI provides significant opportunities for digital media industries such as the Film and Advertising industries, Interactive Gaming and Virtual Reality productions (Stashevskaia, 2024).

1.3. Blockchain Technology as a Means of Transforming Content Ownership

With respect to the ownership of content as well as its management, blockchain technology presents a revolutionary way of doing anything due to its decentralized, and immutable nature. Along with IP tracking, it allows for the fair distribution of royalties and authentication of original works in a transparent and secure manner. Smart contracts that are unique to blockchain systems allow for the automated execution of contracts which eliminates the necessity for intermediaries guaranteeing that compensation is delivered directly and instantly to the creators. The emergence of NFTs is also facilitated through blockchain allowing for digital art and media to be monetized and verified for authenticity and ownership.

1.4. The Significance of the Fusion in Meeting Legal and Ethical Issues

The intersection of AI and blockchain technology fusion is crucial in meeting some of the most essential needs of legal and ethical challenges in digital media.

Content generation by AI without human involvement creates concerns such as copyright conflicts, authorship disputes, and information credibility(Soderland & Lilley, 2015). These issues can be tackled using blockchain technology because it records the provenance of content which guarantees accountability. Increased transparency and traceability in the creation and distribution of content helps solve other challenges such as deepfakes, misinformation and biased algorithms.

1.5. Objectives

The focus of this chapter is to investigate how AI combined with blockchain technologies can affect the world of digital media. It will study how these technologies together resolve legal and ethical issues such as copyright matters, content verification, and fair remuneration. The chapter further explores the implications of the fusion of technologies for other stakeholders such as creators, consumers, and regulators while stressing the importance of proper governance. Current trends, applications, and case studies will be analysed in detail to achieve the objective of this chapter, which is to understand how AI and blockchain are transforming the digital media landscape.

This chapter also attempts to examine other societal implications of the synergy of technologies which include content creation democratization, independent creator empowerment, and ethical media. The chapter emphasizes the observation of how the policies and technologies that foster innovation are diffused with responsibility to achieve a balanced approach towards ethics and accountability in the digital media space

2. TECHNOLOGICAL FOUNDATIONS

2.1. Multimodal Generative AI

Definition and Key Capabilities: Text, Image, Audio, and Video Generation

The term "multimodal generative AI" refers to the understanding and creation of content in different formats such as text, image, audio, and video. More advanced artificial intelligence models understand and create content across different media, which is unlike older models that contained a singular text or image processing focus.

The ability to unite various formats into one cohesive format is one of the hallmarks of multimodal AI. For example, an AI can be tasked to create a video ad, complete with a script, visuals, background sounds, and voiceover all created by the same system. This has far reached impacts on media production since it decreases the need for conventional, manual work in the field and gives better access to content creation for smaller media studios, individual media creators, and even startups.

2.2 Primary Uses of AI in Media Production

i.   Revitalizing Existing Material

One of the most relevant uses of Artificial Intelligence in media production is the archival material restoration automated processes and improvements. For AI models that have been trained on vast amounts of text, old black-and-white films can now be colorized with high precision (M. H. Khan, 2023). This is often done using Decodify, which can make the images and videos of the original black and white monument more visually appealing while maintaining overall context. In addition to colorization, generative AI has the capability to repair scratches, increase resolution, and restore audio, allowing footage that would otherwise sit dormant to be revived.

ii.   Synthetic Voice Generation

Technology has changed the landscape of audio production by allowing for voices to be created that mimic human speech with high accuracy. It has made voiceovers for films, media, and even audiobooks easier for projects which require multiple languages with very little effort. Platforms such as Resemble AI and Eleven Labs are able to produce voice overs with AI for multiple languages while keeping the emotional nuance and the original tone of performance. For instance, an English one can be dubbed into Hindi or Spanish with an AI generated voice of the exact actor's intonation. This will ensure that all audiences, regardless of nationality enjoy the movie without losing their local culture. Significant decreasing of production fees and efforts is achieved. Also, the reach of the content is increased.

iii.   Cultural Localization

AI is useful for localization processes, where modifying media and other con-tent to fit the culture of the audience is critically important. Generative AI tools help analyse cultural preferences, references, and even language intricacies, which makes it easier to modify scripts or content for specific audiences. An AI tool, for instance, can substitute idiomatic expressions in American scripts for culturally relevant equivalents for Indian or Japanese viewers. AI can go beyond altering the text and localize the visual components by changing the background, graphics, and even the products that are featured to suit the audience. While PP-placements are automated through visuals, region-specific language models and tools like GPT-4 Open AI make sure that relevant content is still meaningful to all cultures.

3. LEGAL STRUCTURE REGULATING AI-ENABLED CHANGES

3.1. International Copyright Legislation

Analysis of the Berne Convention and its Significance for AI

The Berne Convention for the Protection of Literary and Artistic Works, which came into force in 1886, is the basis of international copyright law. It requires every contracting state to offer copyright protection to authors from other member states without requiring them to register. One of the critical provisions of the Berne Convention is the grant of exclusive rights to authors, which includes the right to reproduction, modification, translation, and public performance of the works.

Within the context of AI, the Berne Convention has been drawing more and more attention recently. Some of the dilemmas associated with artificial intelligence include whether the content produced by AI qualifies as a 'literary or artistic work', or if any means of protection is feasible for it, and if so, who the rights holder is. As stated in Article 2(1) of the Convention, there is an explicit requirement that works must be a result of mental labour, which is problematic for content generated by AI and his absence of a human (Ginsburg, 2018).

World Intellectual Property Organization (WIPO) Treaties and Digital Adaptations

The WIPO Copyright Treaty (WCT)(*Summary of the WIPO Copyright Treaty (WCT) (1996)*, n.d.) and the WIPO Performances and Phonograms Treaty expand on the principles of the Berne convention by providing a solution to the issues arising due to the digital upheaval. The WCT also covers the ever-important AI components within computer systems, such as computer programs or databases. More importantly, it pays special attention to the protection of works transmitted in digital form, which is paramount for any media created using AI and circulated on the internet.

Changes driven by artificial intelligence, such as speech and translation automation, alongside new film restoration, tend to be more of a gray underbelly in relation to the WIPO frameworks. It does ensure human creators some degree of protection but does not clarify whether anything crafted by AI gets the same benefits, leaving interpretation to the individual member states.

3.2. Indian Legal Framework

The Copyright Act, 1957: Definition of Original Works and its Application to AI Content

Not human AI generated works can be deemed original if skill, labour or judgment is rendered at some point, and that is the Indian Copyright Act of 1957. Courts, especially in India, have tended to rely on the presence of a human author when determining whether something is original, much like in the Eastern Book Company v D.B. Modak case(*Eastern Book Company & Ors vs D.B. Modak & Anr on 12 December, 2007*, 2007), where originality was derived from a person's creativity and exertion.

Adaptations produced by artificial intelligence, like remastered music and dubbed versions, infringe upon issues of authorship and ownership as per the Act. Ownership can be attributed to the developer of the AI system, but someone feeding data into the system may have a claim to ownership too. The absence of explicit provisions covering works produced by AI facilitate room for legal battles.

Restatement, Reproduction, and Derivative Works

Sections 14 and 51 of the Act grants authors the license to adapt, reproduce, and create derivative works. It is, however, difficult to decide whether AI adaptations, say remastered movies, or AI-localized scripts are considered as derivative works under the Act. Let us take the example of an AI tool that remasters a film by using clips from its original source without changing the original content. This, under the Act, would be a reproduction in its simplest form. However, if the AI's alterations were major, then the remaster would fall under the category of derivative work and thus the consent of the original owner would be needed.

Relevance of Section 52 (Fair Use Doctrine) to Media Formulated by the AI Engine

In Section 52 of the Act, there are specific clauses that account for activities deemed fair use which includes reproduction for study, teaching and criticism. The use of AI in replicative processes such as automatic summarization of content or video lecture creation may be covered under this section. Nonetheless, the creation of automated adaptations by means of AI technology tends to surpass the limits of fair use, particularly in the instances where the original work is marketable.

Performance Rights and Moral Rights Under Indian Law

The moral rights and performance rights are provided by Sections 38 and 57 of the Copyright Act. These sections safeguard the rights of performers, actors, and musicians to have control over the reproduction of recordings made of their performances. While AI can reproduce voices or faces, it creates conflict over whether such reproductions are covered by the aforementioned protections. Some moral rights which are sine qua non in the AI modification include right of attribution and right against distortion.

Data Protection and Privacy Laws: Digital Personal Data Protection Act, 2023

The Personal Data Protection act, 2023 was drafted to address concerns of privacy around the applications of AI. The system of AI voice cloning and the use of biometric data necessitates sensitive personal data processing, which, of course, falls within the allowances of the act. Consent, purpose limitation, and data security are key principles detailed in the act. For the particular instance of AI speech or likeness cloning, fully informed consent is a must. For example, giving authority to AI to speak for a late actor in a film would infringe both privacy and IP laws, considering the actor did not authorize it.(Gupta & George, 2024)

3.3. Comparative Jurisdictions

U.S. Copyright Law: Fair Use Doctrine and Transformative Works

In the United States, intellectual property rights are regulated by the Copyright Act of 1976, which includes the fair use doctrine as an important limitation. The fair use doctrine allows certain restricted uses of copyrighted works without obtaining permission from the copyright holder, such as in scholarly commentary, criticism, or educational lessons. Courts evaluate fair use by considering the purpose of use, character of the work, quantity utilized, and the market impact.

Adapting one's work through AI will frequently trigger the effectiveness of the transformative use standard, which suggests that the new derivative work must provide additional value or an entirely new perspective. A good example is Authors Guild v. Google (*Authors Guild v. Google, Inc., 804 F.3d 202 | Casetext Search + Citator*, n.d.) where the court reasoned that Google Book's scanning project is transformative because it made searching and accessing a massive volume of books possible without removing the market. On the other hand, AI-remastered films and scripts will most likely fail the justification test because the argument in the form of "efforts to transform" translates to direct compensation for the original work.

EU Directives: Enhancement of Protecting Moral Rights and Attribution

The EU has comprehensive systems in place in regard to the authors' rights in relation to the Copyright Directive (2019/790). Qualitative rights, which include the attribution and integrity rights, are given great focus. An adaptation made by a computer which modifies or enhances a work without the proper attribution would breach these rights. The Directive also establishes more stringent requirements on scope for content-sharing services such as the imposition of measures aimed at the prevention of copyright infringement that is applicable to the online versions of the AI alterations that have been posted.(*DIRECTIVE (EU) 2019/ 790 OF THE EURO-PEAN PARLIAMENT AND OF THE COUNCIL - of 17 April 2019 - on Copyright and Related Rights in the Digital Single Market and Amending Directives 96/ 9/ EC and 2001/ 29/ EC*, n.d.)

China's Approach: Control of AI and Blockchain Technology by the State

China has a distinctive model of practicing intellectual property which features high state control and specialization in works of advanced technologies such as artificial intelligence and blockchain. With regards to AI-enabled adaptations, China has issued certain guidelines that AI generated material is required to contain within the set limits of existing Intellectual Property laws and not usurp public order(Sharma, 2024). Similarly, the country has also adopted rigid guidelines pertaining to data privacy which have consequences for AI systems that make use of personal data especially for voice cloning. Low levels of qualitative moral rights protection granted, however, distinguishes China's policies from those of the West.

3.4. Judicial Precedents on AI and Copyright

Indian Case Studies: Interpretation on Major Issues Covering Copyright and Adaptation

Indian judiciary has dealt with several copyright related matters that have somewhat dealt with AI inspired adaptations. In Eastern Book Company v. D.B. Modak, the Supreme Court focused on the originality criterion and informative reproduction on the basis of human labour. While this is not an AI case, it serves as a starting point for judgments regarding human effort in AI produced works. Likewise, Super Cassettes Industries Ltd. v. Myspace Inc. (2011) Also, the Delhi High Court liaised intermediary responsibility for content uploaded by the users, which is relevant for artificial intelligence modifications.

International Case Studies: Conflicts Relating to AI Works

Several courts around the globe have started trying cases concerning works created using AI technology. The case of Naruto v. Slater (2018) (Review, 2020) is a clear example. In this case, Slater made a film using a copyrighted work. The 9th Circuit Court of Appeal in the US decided that animals cannot own copyright, thereby suggesting that non-human entities, such as AI, also cannot copyright. In the UK, Sheeran v. Chokri (2022) showcased the difficulties of claiming originality in music, which is further complicated in AI driven music(Ec, n.d.).

In the EU, the Infopaq case (2009) stressed that the right of reproduction only applies to the expression of an idea that resulted from the author's original intellectual work. This raised the question - could AI content generation fulfil this requirement? All these cases reveal that there are new dimensions to copyright law as it deals with the consequences of AI on creative industries.(Fredenslund, 2013)

The swift development of the AI sector in the creative industries has unveiled gaps and issues in the legal systems. Treaties such as the Berne Convention and WIPO treaties serve as baseline documents but need to be adapted to cater to AI-Created works. While India's Copyright Act is detailed, it does not have a specific clause on provisions for AI-enabled adaptations which would give rise to conflicts regarding ownership and moral rights. The US, EU, and China jurisdictions are informative but each one has its shortcomings. It will be crucial to ensure the advancements AI technologies are matched with legal frameworks so as to safeguard the evolving judicial precedents to provide the unequalled creative environment.

4. ETHICAL CONSIDERATIONS IN AI AND BLOCKCHAIN INTEGRATION

4.1. Ethical Challenges of AI-Driven Adaptations

Attribution and Integrity Rights in AI-Generated Content

In dealing with AI in adaptations, one significant ethical issue relates to the attribution of integrity rights. As one of the most pressing challenges, AI systems tend to blur the concept of authorship and proper crediting. As an example, if an AI tool remasters a film or remakes a book, who is entitled to the credit, the AI or the content developer? Further, there is often a lack of proper means strategies to ensure moral rights of attribution through AI such as in the case of AI scribing(Nassar & Kamal, 2021). Such complete neglect of moral rights of authorship is problematic in attribution, as everyone would require some credit on work that is not actually theirs, thus erasing the original author's contribution. Of immense significance, this issue tends to gains traction when dealing with works that are considered to be in public domain, as revisions get published under the cover of original authors, thus abusing the creator's rights. Such tactics create exposure whereby only the readers are misinformed about the work.

Exploiting Authorship by Digital Means Through AI Adaptations Done Illegally

Most often than not, illegal AI adaptations disregard permission to adapt copyrighted content, which is essentially the modification and copying of an original work. As an example, it is common for AI tools to try and copy a particular artist's style in order to create new works or to generate synthesized voices of actors without consent or any credits. Such activities are said to violate the creator's intellectual property and effort, and are not allowing them to adequately capitalize on their work.

Bias and Its Misrepresentation Using AI Algorithms

Bias gets more complicated with various ethical problems in terms of algorithms for AI, especially in regards to modifications with particular sensitive cultural or gendered aspects. AI models these days utilize huge datasets, and these datasets almost always reflect societal stereotypes which could lead to problematic content generation. Take as an example an AI tool and its attempt to create a specific ethnicity-oriented film adaptation and its reinforcement of stereotypes or symbols representing a culture in an image.(Nazer et al., 2023a)

Discrimination of these types constitutes not only an unethical practice, but also compromises the trust and inclusivity of the creative industries. Inaccurate portrayals in AI assisted adaptations can estrange certain audiences and propagate dangerous stories. Solving these challenges necessitates a more in-depth examination of the AI systems' training data, as well as the algorithms and ethics employed by the developers(Nazer et al., 2023b).

4.2. Ethical Issues on Blockchain-Enabled Media Management

Perils of Centralization on Allegedly Decentralized Systems

The greatest advantage of blockchain technology is its highly commended architecture as it is decentralized which means that there is no need for an intermediary to assist in transactions. Decentralization is meant to help creators directly connect with users. Nevertheless, a large number of media platforms that utilize blockchain, with few exceptions, tend to be highly centralized; for instance, the governance of blockchain systems (Srivastava et al., 2021).

Decentralization is often viewed as a key feature of blockchain technology, but the concentration of power within a few developers or corporations poses significant challenges for emerging economies (Lustig, 2019). Rather, it gives undue authority over decision making processes to a select group. Such uneven power structures make a democratic society impossible.

These systems furthermore control the whole economy with direct power leading to biased controls for token distribution systems, royalty payments, content censorship, etc. It promotes the worrying concept of allowing dictatorial power with heavy control. Furthermore, creators and users have little to no power in winning disputes letting them be in the mercy of a chosen cartel.

After all, tokenization of traditional media assets leads to a new modern form of manipulation whether it be through movies, songs, or any form of digital art. Instead of solely focusing on the good opportunities that come through, there will always be people looking to exploit the system for their selfish needs. For instance, some people can mint fake non-fungible tokens those who put their trust in them claim to represent original pieces of work presenting a fabricated reality.

The extreme transparency and immutability that accompany blockchain technology can equally be detrimental to privacy. While these elements of blockchain increases accountability, they can as well expose creators and consumers' private information (Felzmann et al., 2019). For instance, owners of blockchain accounts with high monetary value tokens may have their privacy breached through public blockchain transactions where the creator's earnings and buyer's purchase history are made public.

4.3. Balancing Innovation with Ethical Responsibility

Guidelines for Developers and Users of AI Technologies Ethics

Establishing ethical guidelines for both developers and users of AI technologies is paramount for innovation to be achieved responsibility. Developers have a duty to ensure compliance with copyright laws, cultural contexts, and moral rights in the appropriate design of AI systems. For instance, AI tools should be able to identify ethical flags, such as bias or undisclosed ethical concerns in content, in order for AI's original creators to properly be credited(*(PDF) Artificial Intelligence Ethics Guidelines for Developers and Users: Clarifying Their Content and Normative Implications*, n.d.).

Ethical aspects of AI development are equally important. Developers owe it to their users to reveal the sources of training data, the methods adopted during its gathering, and the intricacies of the systems created. Such transparency builds trust with the users and places them in a position where they can make better, informed decisions on the ethical effects of using AI tools.

For the users, ethical responsibility means harnessing AI technologies in a manner that accords the rights and contributions of creators (*The Ethics of AI Ethics: An Evaluation of Guidelines | Minds and Machines*, n.d.). Proper licenses for AI adaptations should be applied, the use of AI tools for unauthorized reproductions should be avoided, and the primary social consequences of AI content should always be considered. Children and young people should be taught the ethics surrounding AI technologies through appropriate initiatives and campaigns.

The Importance of Ethical AI Usage and Their Adoption in the Creative Commons Licenses Framework

The use of Creative Commons (CC) licenses helps in maintaining ethical standards in AI adaptations. These licenses encourage creators to specify the way their work is used, which promotes accountability and transparency in the creation of content. A creator can, for example, use CC licenses by allowing others to edit their work but making attribution a requirement while restricting commercial use (Muhammad, 2023).

CC licenses can also be adapted by AI developers and users at different stages of the process to maintain the ethical practices. For example, a content creation AI tool can be equipped with features that automatically restrict the use of materials with CC licenses. In the same vein, CC licenses can be encoded into the digital work of the creator using blockchain technology to make the terms immutable and transparent.

Encouraging Ethical Accountability vis-a-vis Regulation and Collaboration

To some extent, governments, industry groups, and educational institutions are vital in fostering ethical accountability surrounding AI and blockchain integration. Regulatory gaps, such as those that do not account for the works of AI or the threats of centralization on blockchain platforms, should be filled through lawmaking(*Towards an Equitable Digital Society: Artificial Intelligence (AI) and Corporate Digital Responsibility (CDR) | Society*, n.d.). For example, a government could impose a legal obligation to credit original creators for the content formulated by an AI system or create laws that punish fraudulent activities in tokenized media markets.

The importance of cooperation between various parties cannot be overstated. The industry in question needs to be set by and for the people who design, build, and govern it. The Partnership on AI and the Blockchain Ethical Design Framework is one initiative that illustrates how many different actors can join forces to solve ethical issues.

The use of AI and blockchain in media is incredibly helpful for advancement in technology, but at the same time, it's terribly problematic for ethical issues. Questions of attribution, unauthorized modifications, algorithmic bias, blockchain decentralization, and fraud in tokenized assets create the need for constructive and strong ethics.

The adoption of ethical norms, the appropriate use of Creative Commons licenses, and the collaboration of relevant parties can help the creative industries overcome these challenges and ensure that technological progress is advantageous for the creators, users, and society. As AI and blockchain technologies transform the media industry, managing the innovation and the ethical side of it will still be a major focus.

5. OWNERSHIP AND AUTHORSHIP CHALLENGES

With the advent of artificial intelligence (AI) and the rise of blockchain technology, ownership and authorship in the creative economy has been disrupted fundamentally. From a traditional perspective where creativity and work are done by humans, AIs and blockchain enabled systems are extremely complicated(*"Authorship and Algorithms: Copyright Law for AI-Generated Content" by Sydney Thomas*, n.d.).

5.1. Traditional Concepts of Copyright and Authorship

Defining Copyright and Authorship in Creative Works

The legislation of copyright has, for long, focused on the concept of creativity being an exclusively human activity. Copyrighted works are, generally speaking, original and demonstrate a level of intelligence or skill being exerted. For instance, the Berne Convention specifies "literary and artistic works" by human author are protected under copyright because so called creativity is produced by human emotions and thoughts.

In most territories, a copyright law enables a creator of a work some rights including the right to reproduce, adapt, and distribute their work. This monetary frame of reference presupposes that the individual who created the piece of work is the sole owner of it. For example, an author who pens down a novel instantly gets the copyright to it alongside book prints whereas a painter owns the copyright of his paintings.

Restrictions of Conventional Frameworks Relating to AI

These conventional approaches are challenged by AI with the introduction of non-human agents capable of producing content. Painting, composing music, or writing a screenplay from an AI system generates a dilemma: who exactly owns copyright? There is no human author that can claim ownership. Legislators and courts bear the burden of trying to define whether non-human creations can be copyrighted and if yes, who owns the rights? Is it the developer of the AI, the handler, or someone else?

5.2. Non-Human Authorship and the Role of AI Developers

Can AI Be Considered an Author?

Currently, no jurisdiction considers AI an author. Copyrights generally look for a human touch in creation, which is why it is not afforded to any and everyone (Buccafusco, 2016). However, as AIs become more complex and sophisticated, the dividing line between human creativity and machine creativity is increasingly fuzzy.

The Role of AI Developers in Authorship

AI developers profoundly impact the development of systems which create content. They are responsible for writing the algorithms, training the models, and curating the datasets, hence forming the building blocks of AI creativity. Some contend that having created the AI systems, developers should receive copyright over anything produced because the creative act is enabled through them.

But this approach has practical and ethical issues. For one, copyrighting all AI assistance works puts power in the hands of those developers and creates a monopoly of sorts that causes smaller tech companies to lose out. Not to mention, it disregards the fact that users give prompts and inputs which guide the AI in question. Take, for instance, a situation where a user wants to create a customized logo for themselves using AI. Who do you think owns the rights of that logo? The owner and user of the AI system, or the creator of that AI system?

5.3. Ownership Conflicts Between Developers of AI Technology, Users, and Original Creators All at Once

Dueling Ownership

Works generated by AI typically have a broader scope of owners which include the following:

1. Developers: This category includes the Builders and creators of the specific AI System.
2. Users: These are people or businesses who interact with the AI for content creation.
3. Original Creators: These are the actual authors whose work served as a basis for the AI.

Ownership conflicts occur when individuals from all three categories attempt to justify their ownership Developers may equally assert ownership of the work based on their role in the construction of the AI. Moreover, original creators whose works were used to train the AI are equally entitled to be compensated and given recognition (Lilova, 2021).

Case Example: AI Generated Art Works Created Using Machine Learning

Let's assume the existence of an AI model that has been trained with a dataset of renowned paintings. The AI generates a new piece of art based on Van Gogh's style. In this scenario, there are likely to be conflicts between the following parties:

- The person that developed the AI that is trained.
- The person that used the AI for the particular piece of art.
- People of the legacy or heirs of Van Gogh who may claim that the output provided by the AI violates the moral rights of the original artist.

Such disputes highlight the importance for well-defined legal structures and contracts between the participating parties. Absence of clear regulations may result in controversy regarding AI-generated materials, which, in turn, may hamper creativity as well as culminate in protracted legal battles.

5.4. Blockchain Approaches Toward Authorship and Ownership Issues

Resolving Ownership Problems with Blockchain

Authorship and ownership of AI-generated material can be dealt with using blockchain technology as it is decentralized and incorruptible. The blockchain can keep track of metadata, terms of who gave permission to utilize the work, and other relevant information. Because the blockchain cannot be altered, it serves as an excellent way to track who contributed to what aspect of the work, thus facilitating efficient management of both authorship and ownership rights (Savelyev, 2018).

Ownership Attribution Through Smart Contracts

Smart contracts are a type of ownership share in blockchain technology that automatically execute actions as stipulated within. Smart contracts are said to simplify the process of ownership claiming and revenue disbursement of AI-generated work (Linoy et al., 2019). For instance, such a contract can:

- Proportionately assign authorship to any AI output to the developers, users, and data trainers.
- Distribute royalties automatically with a smart contract whenever a work is sold, licensed or commercially used within the system.
- This method enables stakeholders to be compensated in an optimal manner while eliminating the need for marks, thus lowering the cost of transactions.

Tokenization Of AI-Generated Works

Tokenization extends to representing digital equities like AI-generated content in the form of blockchain assets. The tokens can contain elements that specify the authorship, licenses, and other rights of the content. For instance:

- An AI trained artwork can be encapsulated in an NFT (non-fungible token) and hyperlinked to preferred developers, users, and contributor datasets.
- On purchase, the NFT buyers have the privilege to retain ownership or licensing deprived to them, while the blockchain protects their interests with accountability and audibility.
- Not only does tokenization resolve issues of ownership, but it also facilitates the creator with additional avenues of income via secondary markets and royalties (*Frontiers | Investigating Generative AI Models and Detection*

Techniques: Impacts of Tokenization and Dataset Size on Identification of AI-Generated Text, n.d.).

Ethical and Practical Problems

Though blockchain solves a lot in terms of technology, it also poses ethical and practical issues. A few examples include:

1. What percentage of contribution should creators have for the process of tokenization or taking monetization options?
2. How can the adoption of Blockchain become abusive to the purpose of providing equal opportunities to creators from the weaker segments of society?

These issues need answers which are not only technological but also answerable by legislators and other people part of the industrial world.

The scope of ownership and authorship when it comes to AI-powered creative works is decidedly more complicated, as it poses legal, ethical, as well as technical challenges. Copyright frameworks are already struggling to deal with overlapping concepts of authorship, especially when it comes to non-human creators, developers, users, and original content creators. The advent of Blockchain technology comes with smart contracts and tokenization features that can explicitly manage and document ownership in an effective manner.

6. FAIR USE, MORAL RIGHTS, AND TRANSFORMATIVE WORKS

The accelerated adoption of artificial intelligence (AI) within the realms of creative industries has fueled discussions concerning the relevance of copyright doctrines such as use and adaptation of works, and moral rights in relation to AI produced and modified content. The very notion that AI can self-generate or self-alter content poses concerns regarding the contours of existing legal systems, especially with regard to balancing the right of the original creators against the need for public domain (Heymann, 2012).

6.1. Fair Use in the Context of AI Driven Content

Contextual Approaches of Various Legal Systems on Fair Use of Works Jurisdictional Contexts

Fair use is a doctrine of law that allows the utilization of copyrighted material, within prescribed limits, without consulting the copyright holder. AI Driven Content tends to present new challenges because does not uniformly apply to all jurisdictions, as the scope and application of the doctrine is ambiguous particularly as pertains to AI driven content.

In America, fair use is determined, on a case basis, by taking into consideration the four standards listed below:

i.   The purpose and character of the use (e.g., type of use such as commercial or non-commercial undertakings, or quite basic, whether the use is aimed at an altering or reproduction of works).
ii. The nature of the copyrighted work.
iii. The quantitatively and qualitatively consummate of the portion used.
iv. The use and market effect which directly affect the original work (Heymann, 2012).

Often, AI systems use cases with copyrighted material in order to train models or produce output. For example, DALL·E and Open AI's DALL·E or GPT models are known to output content derivatives of existing work. To what degree does such use qualify as fair use is a question dependent on the level of transformation in the output and the effect it has on the market value for the original piece.

Importance of Section 52 of the Copyright Act

As of now, India deals with fair use through Section 52 of the Copyright Act of 1957, describing it as "fair dealing." Indians' laws, unlike the US, provides certain specific activities in which fair dealing is allowed, like research, criticism, review, reporting, and even teaching. Nonetheless, there is ambiguity regarding the scope of Section 52 and its applicability to AI content generation as it was drafted way before AI capture significant attention in content generation.

Legality of Transformative AI Adaptations

More importantly, to what extent is the versioning AI adaptation considered fair use? One important factor for a claim of fair use determination is the addition of new expression, meaning, or value to the original that was created, thus termed as 'transformative.' For example, when remastering a film or localizing it, AI tools should qualify as transformative as long as the objective or audience of the piece is being altered substantially (Sukamto et al., 2023).

The transformative argument, however, is not without boundaries. There is a risk that the court may determine that some AI adaptations like voice cloning or even stylistic imitations have transforming characters but in reality, lack the modification that will justify their purpose being served. Furthermore, as is with AI system generated output, works that do not embody human creativity complicates their legal standing, puzzling everyone under conventional regimes of copyright that are designed for humans.

6.2. Moral Rights in Relation to AI Conversions

Integrity and Attribution Rights Within India and Other Countries

Most jurisdictions provide moral rights, which are subdivided into rights of attribution and integrity, as an essential component of copyright. Such rights enable authors to dictate how their works are attributed or exhibited, even if the economic rights have been ceded to third parties.

In India, the moral rights of attribution and corrigenda are dealt with under sections 57 and 38 of the Copyright Act. Integrity rights enable the author to protect their work from being altered in any manner that may damage their reputation.

Moral rights are sanctioned under Article 6bis of the Berne Convention, to which India is a signatory. France and Germany, along with other European nations, provide extensive moral rights, thereby enabling creators to restrict the use of AI technology in a manner that alters their original concept. Meanwhile, the United States offers very few moral rights, especially to visual artists with the exception of the Visual Artists Rights Act.

Ethics and Technology Issues in Cultural Adaptation and Voice Reproduction

Cultural adaptations, such as editing a motion picture or song to fit a particular region's culture, are a major aspect of AI modifications. These modifications do promote greater acceptability, but ethical and legal issues surface as well. (Song, 2021)

6.3. How to Address the Balance Issues Between Fair Use and Moral Rights

How to Manage Ownership Consideration Along with New Ideas

The most relevant issue to AI-driven content is dealing with innovations against the protection of creator rights. In this regard, fair use and moral rights tend to clash. As an example, fair use could allow the alteration of a work within reason, but the revised work can breach moral rights in the case where the envisioned work is poorly attributed to or not fully credited.

In order to settle these disputes, courts and lawmakers must find a balance that sides with both a public value and a value to the creator's rights. As an example, fair use might be restricted from commercial exploitation or other econometric purposes so that the creator does not suffer economically.

The Importance of Licensing Agreements and Creative Commons

Licensing agreements seem to provide a concrete way of resolving the clash that exists between fair use and moral rights exploitation. It is possible for the creator's economic and moral rights to be reconciled through the terms of AI training or adaptation that the creator provides. An illustration is a case where a musician's voice is captured to synthesize the music for an AI program. The musician can set defined terms for the voice synthesis program to follow, including proper recognition of the musician's authorship and acceptable standards.

In this connection, Creative Commons (CC) licenses are also beneficial. They allow creators to select from several degrees of permissions without losing intellectual control over AI-generated works. For example, a non-commercial CC license may allow transformations in an AI-generated work but may also enforce creditization and non-profit clauses to ensure that the terms for use of such works do not infringe on the rights of the author.

Attribution And Compliance Using Blockchain Technology

Innovative solutions such as the resolution legal disputes arising from fair use and moral rights attribution can now be solved with Blockchain Technology. Blockchain ensures that AI generated content does not breach transparency and compliance by capturing the author's credentials, licensing conditions, and usage in a non-alterable ledger. Conflicts in attribution and payment can be minimized through automation of royalty payments and attribution obligations with smart contracts.

Thus, a blockchain system that enables the claim and receival of recognition and payment by the artist for the use of their work in AI adaptations can be sufficed. Smart contracts can equally prevent unauthorized users from using voice synthesis without consent in claim that they have complied with the licensing terms.

Policy Recommendations and Judicial Precedents

Policy Makers and Courts greatly inform the legal space for content fueled by AI. Authors Guild v. Google case in the US is a judicial precedent that places guidelines for fair use under AI's transformative capabilities. In India, newly changing meanings of Section 52 will be important for the application of fair dealing on AI works.

Recommendations to policy for use AI include, but not limited to:

- Taking moral rights into consideration without compromising the use of AI for transformation of works under fair use.
- Ethical guidelines for use of AI where transparency as to what datasets were used as well as the attributions should be made in the name of the author.
- Encouraging global cooperation and alignment of copyright policies concerning AI and blockchain technologies.

The balance between free use of copyrighted material, moral rights, and AI-generated works creates a complex web of legal and ethical issues. Although fair use is important for progress, it equally requires respect to the moral rights of all creators which, in turn, guarantees them protection. Cultural adaptation, voice cloning, and other forms of AI utilization pose the danger of manipulation and abuse, and so need to be regulated appropriately.

Licensing contracts, Creative Commons, and blockchain provide promising avenues towards solving the controversy of fair use and moral rights. These approaches have the potential to promote participation of content owners, programmers, and regulatory bodies to resolve issues in the creative industries in the context of AI content creation and to make a step towards more equitable AI-generated work.

7. ECONOMIC IMPACTS AND MARKET DYNAMICS

7.1. AI's Effect on the Expenditure and Entry Barriers of Markets

In information creation, AI tends to enhance efficiency by making the process both easier and cheaper. High-quality content production ranges from films to advertisements and songs. All of them have had historically heavy investments concerning equipment, highly skilled personnel, and time (Ernst et al., 2019). Unlike previously mentioned methods, Open AI's DALL·E and Adobe's Sensei together with RunwayML do facilitate these processes, overcoming time and cost issuers.

Other than that, AI has also increased access to many other revenue channels with the option to personalize content for certain niche audiences. AI's ability to localize advertisements as well as films improves the audience base without heavy reliance on resources.

7.2. Disturbance of Long-standing Creative Industries and Employment Losses

AIs have enabled faster creation of content. However, these advancements have deeply impacted traditional industries, leading to the loss of jobs. Professions such as graphic design, voice-over acting, and video editing are continuously being supplemented or even replaced by AI. For instance, video presentations can be created without the need of a human actor through AI tools like Synthesia, while voices for the purposes of dubbing and narration are provided by AI through Resemble AI.

The processes that were once creative and involved particular processes through thinking and designing have now become automated, making the need for specialized skills extremely low. New professions like AI model trainers, data curators, or even ethic consultants have emerged. The most crucial issue is how to ensure that workers are retrained to meet these new demands so that the creative workforce is not left out of the economy that makes use of AI (Oakley, 2006).

7.3. Blockchain's Role in Monetizing AI Generated Content Realized through Programs.

The Technology of Blockchain has proven effective for monetizing content produced through AI. Blockchain allows for secure and transparent systems which eliminate the need for intermediary, where the creators can securely sell and distribute their works.

Tokenization of digital assets is conversely one of the most important uses of blockchain technology in media. Non-fungible tokens (NFTs), for instance, allow creators to claim AI generated pieces of digital art, music and videos like digital art, music, or videos with unique identifiers. As proof of ownership and authenticity, AI tokens are sold directly to consumers. New revenue streams have been created for artists and developers due to the sale of AI-generated NFTs through OpenSea and Rarible platforms (*Empowering the Commons: Blockchain for IP Protection in Generative AI by Gabriela Fuentes, Assel Omarova :: SSRN*, n.d.).

Through Smart contracts, blockchain also enables licensing of AI Content. Royalties are distributed amongst stakeholders (AI creators, training data contributors etc.) through self-executing agreements. Contracts could for instance allocate royalties among a musician if their songs were utilized to train a music composing AI system.

7.4. Using Smart Contracts for the Fair Distribution of Revenues.

In regard to content generated by AI, smart contracts mitigate the economic issues caused as a result. Smart contracts allow for the automatic payment of royalties and licensing fees which completely removes any arguments that may arise surrounding revenue distribution, and further ensures that all processes are clear (*Blockchain and Smart Contracts in Supply Chain Management: A Game Theoretic Model - ScienceDirect*, n.d.).

Microtransactions enabled through smart contracts allow creators to get payments per use for their work. For example, a photographer could license individual images through blockchain and receive a payment every single time the image is downloaded or put to commercial use. systems like these allow a more transparent and easy way to do business, benefitting both stakeholders and consumers.

8. POLICY RECOMMENDATIONS

8.1. Updating Copyright Laws in India and Globally to Include AI and Blockchain

AI and Blockchain technologies' advances have rendered obsolete contemporary copyright laws, such as India's Copyright Act, 1957. There are non-human authors, automated adaptations, and tokenized media assets that require novel legal frameworks, something these laws do not address.

Amendments to Copyright Laws in Relation To AI

Recognition of AI-Generated Works: Laws can enable developers, users, or a multitude of stakeholders to determine ownership of copyrighted AI produced assets:

i.   Fair Use in AI Training: Legislators should outline barriers patent protected content so as not swamp the market with low cost or free alternatives.
ii. Tokenized Ownership: Copyright protection can be contrived to apply to NFTs and other tokenized representations of media assets to ensure proprietary privileges are afforded to traditional works.

8.2 Formulating Licensing Structures for AI-Generated Content

Duties of the Supervising Institutions During the Compliance with License Obligations

The licensing of AI-generated should be carefully monitored by regulatory entities like the India Copyright Office or the US Copyright Office to ensure no infringement takes place. This encompasses the following:

i.   Mandating accountability in the AI by providing access to the data and the set of algorithms used.
ii. Manually checking compliance with the terms of the license in the case of AI derivations and shallow fakes.
iii. Creating processes for mediation of disagreements emanating from the use of generative AI art (Chakraborty, 2023).

Recommendations for Blockchain-Integrated Licensing Platforms

Blockchain has the capability of easing the licensing processes with regard to the protection of intellectual property by automating them, provided that appropriate features are embedded. Some of the features include:

i.   Smart Licensing - The automated allocation of licenses through smart contracts that exercises proper compliance with the terms of the license.
ii. Royalty Tracking - The ability to observe payments of royalties and the exercising of rights in real time on a blockchain network.
iii. Attribution Records - Documents with claims for the contributions of the creation of the work in disregard to the ethics of the discipline.

Although the example platforms like Verisart and NFT Ascribe showcase blockchain's potential for rights management, there needs to be a paradigm shift which incorporates government, technology agents, and creative sectors.

8.3. Media's Use of AI: A Practicing Lens

There exists a need for ethical policies to be formulated so that the moral and societal implications revolving around AI technology use in media professionals is tackled adequately. Recommendations are:

1. Developers should clarify how bias may arise from the methodology used to obtain training datasets, including any potential training sources that could skew results.
2. Creators whose works are relevant for training or adaptation should be purposely included as a prerequisite to consent.
3. Sensitive sketches from the KI-generated adaptations should not reinforce stereotypes or any negative aspects of the cultures impacts.
4. There should be legislation to counteract unethical practices like deep fakes or unsanctioned adaptations by targeting AI Developers and Users.

8.4. Standardized Policies Setting Through International Cayman Islands Collaboration

Elements of international synergy that should aim towards achieving integration policies pertaining to the respective domains of AI and Block Chain Technology include:

1. Collaboration in fighting infringement of AI and tokenized assets copyrights.
2. Establishing universal rules for ethical use of teaching datasets such as privacy and attribution requirements.
3. Implementing measures within blockchain based market places against fraud or manipulation of the market (*Regulation | Ministry of Financial Services and Commerce*, n.d.).

The World Intellectual Property Organization and United Nations Educational, Scientific and Cultural Organization along with the World Economic Forum allow nations to communicate and share successes related to the application of AI and blockchain in the creative sectors. Similarly, due collaborative efforts like the European Union's AI Act, comprehensive frameworks can also be achieved (Fichtner, 2016).

The application of AI and blockchain in the creative sector promises unparalleled transformation in productivity and diversity. However, with these advantages also comes numerous challenges such as the disruption of existing industries, copyright ownership conflicts, and content creation ethics.

Policymakers are required to address these concerns by rethinking existing legal frameworks and designing appropriate copyright, licensing and ethical use of AI and blockchain policies. Partnerships are essential for achieving a coherent and sustainable policy framework for the global creative economy. By fostering multi-stakeholder collaboration, there is an opportunity for the creative industry to harness AI and blockchain technologies while balancing the needs of all stakeholders.

9. CONCLUSION

9.1. Modification of Copyright Laws in India and the Rest of the World to Accommodate AI and Blockchain Technologies

The current copyright laws such as the India Copyright Act of 1957 were prepared ages ago when AI and Blockchain technologies were unheard of. Such laws need to be evolved to deal with the complications arising from the absence of human creativity, robotic modifications, and media assets which are greatly commoditized.

Suggested Changes in the Copyright Laws:

i.   Determination of AI Copyright Ownership: Statutes need to state whether works developed by AI are copyrightable, and if so, who the AI is, the developers, the users, or all of them together.
ii. Use of Copyrighted Material for AI Systems: Legislators must describe the limit on the amount of copyrighted material that could be utilized for training AI systems, in order to safeguard the rights of the original creator and promote advancement.
iii. Ownership of Media Assets in Form of NFTs: Copyright laws must identify NFTs and other media assets' token descriptors as copyrightable so they will have the same legislative protection as a traditional share works.

Above all, there is need to focus on standardization of copyright laws of different countries for dealing with the problems of AI and blockchain on a global scale. Institutions like WIPO have an important function to stimulate worldwide collaboration and foster applicable standards and policies.

9.2. Ethical Guidelines for AI Applications in Media

In order to integrate AI into media, it is essential for policymakers to develop and implement ethical guidelines that pertain to moral and societal issues. Particularly, they should consider the following important points:

i. Policymakers must ensure transparency by disclosing how AI models are trained. This means identifying the sources of training data, and acknowledging any biases that exist.
ii. When pertinent creators permit their works to be used for training or adaptation, consent must be gotten without fail.
iii. Culturally sensitive - AI adaptations need to consider specific cultures meanings and contexts rather than promoting stereotypes and biases.
iv. Users and developers need to be monitored to make sure unethical attempts like deepfakes or unconsented adaptations do not happen. Therefore, accountability needs to be taken.
v. By educating creators and consumers about the implications of AI, it can increase the responsibility taken socially and ethically towards the media.

9.3. International Standard Exertion of Policies With Respect To AI And Blockchain Industry Use

The use AI and blockchain technologies on a global scale renders it necessary to work together with other countries to create policies that work across borders. Some of the aspects that need attention include:

i. Uniformity in Copyright Stipulations: Providing uniform protections to AI produced works and tokenized assets across multiple jurisdictions
ii. Data Management: Setting global benchmarks for the ethical application of privacy, attribution, and other relevant factors in training data usage.
iii. Regulatory Models: Collaborating on regulations of blockchain based markets as well as safeguards against fraud and manipulation of markets.

WIPO, UNESCO, and World Economic Forum are in good positions to aid nations in applying AI and blockchain to the creative industries and setting cross border dialogues. Other models such as EU AI Act showcase joint efforts of the EU member states towards creating a governing AI policy and are useful for such purposes.

REFERENCES

Authors Guild v. Google, Inc., 804 F.3d 202 | Casetext Search + Citator. (n.d.). Retrieved January 31, 2025, from https://casetext.com/case/guild-v-google-inc-1

"Authorship and Algorithms: Copyright Law for AI-Generated Content" by Sydney Thomas. (n.d.). Retrieved February 1, 2025, from https://scholarsarchive.byu.edu/joni/vol4/iss2/7/

Blockchain and smart contracts in supply chain management: A game theoretic model—ScienceDirect. (n.d.). Retrieved February 1, 2025, from https://www.sciencedirect.com/science/article/abs/pii/S0925527320302188?via%3Dihub

Buccafusco, C. (2016). A Theory of Copyright Authorship. *Virginia Law Review, 102*, 1229.

Chakraborty, D. (2023). *Copyright Challenges in the Digital Age: Balancing Intellectual Property Rights and Data Privacy in India's Online Ecosystem* (SSRN Scholarly Paper No. 4647960). Social Science Research Network. DOI: 10.2139/ssrn.4647960

Datta, P., Whitmore, M., & Nwankpa, J. K. (2021). A Perfect Storm: Social Media News, Psychological Biases, and AI. *Digital Threats, 2*(2), 15:1-15:21. DOI: 10.1145/3428157

DIRECTIVE (EU) 2019/790 OF THE EUROPEAN PARLIAMENT AND OF THE COUNCIL - of 17 April 2019—On copyright and related rights in the Digital Single Market and amending Directives 96/9/EC and 2001/29/EC. (n.d.).

Eastern Book Company & Ors vs D.B. Modak & Anr on 12 December, 2007. (2007).

Ec, L. (n.d.). IN THE HIGH COURT OF JUSTICE BUSINESS AND PROPERTY COURTS OF ENGLAND AND WALES INTELLECTUAL PROPERTY LIST.

Empowering the Commons. Blockchain for IP Protection in Generative AI by Gabriela Fuentes, Assel Omarova: SSRN. (n.d.). Retrieved February 1, 2025, from https://papers.ssrn.com/sol3/papers.cfm?abstract_id=4803536

Ernst, E., Merola, R., & Samaan, D. (2019). Economics of Artificial Intelligence: Implications for the Future of Work. *IZA Journal of Labor Policy, 9*(1), 20190004. DOI: 10.2478/izajolp-2019-0004

Felzmann, H., Villaronga, E. F., Lutz, C., & Tamò-Larrieux, A. (2019). Transparency you can trust: Transparency requirements for artificial intelligence between legal norms and contextual concerns. *Big Data & Society*, 6(1), 2053951719860542. DOI: 10.1177/2053951719860542

Fichtner, J. (2016). The anatomy of the Cayman Islands offshore financial center: Anglo-America, Japan, and the role of hedge funds. *Review of International Political Economy*, 23(6), 1034–1063. DOI: 10.1080/09692290.2016.1243143

Fredenslund, M. (2013, May 17). *Denmark: Infopaq-case finally decided after eight years*. Kluwer Copyright Blog. https://copyrightblog.kluweriplaw.com/2013/05/17/denmark-infopaq-case-finally-decided-after-eight-years/

Frontiers | Investigating generative AI models and detection techniques: Impacts of tokenization and dataset size on identification of AI-generated text. (n.d.). Retrieved February 1, 2025, from https://www.frontiersin.org/journals/artificial-intelligence/articles/10.3389/frai.2024.1469197/full

Ginsburg, J. C. (2018). People Not Machines: Authorship and What It Means in the Berne Convention. *IIC - International Review of Intellectual Property and Competition Law*, 49(2), 131–135. DOI: 10.1007/s40319-018-0670-x

Gupta, N., & George, A. (2024). Digital Personal Data Protection Act, 2023: Charting the Future of India's Data Regulation. In *Data Governance and the Digital Economy in Asia*. Routledge. DOI: 10.4324/9781003505723-3

Heymann, L. A. (2012). *Everything Is Transformative: Fair Use and Reader Response* (SSRN Scholarly Paper No. 1148379). Social Science Research Network. https://papers.ssrn.com/abstract=1148379

Hussain, A. A., & Al-Turjman, F. (2021). Artificial intelligence and blockchain: A review. *Transactions on Emerging Telecommunications Technologies*, 32(9), e4268. DOI: 10.1002/ett.4268

Khan, A. A., Laghari, A. A., Li, P., Dootio, M. A., & Karim, S. (2023). The collaborative role of blockchain, artificial intelligence, and industrial internet of things in digitalization of small and medium-size enterprises. *Scientific Reports*, 13(1), 1656. DOI: 10.1038/s41598-023-28707-9 PMID: 36717702

Khan, M. H. (2023). *The Impact of AI on the Media Industry*. https://urn.kb.se/resolve?urn=urn:nbn:se:uu:diva-516624

Lilova, S. (2021). *Copyright or Copyleft for AI-Generated Works: Private Ordering Solutions for the Benefit of Content Creators* (SSRN Scholarly Paper No. 4271966). Social Science Research Network. DOI: 10.2139/ssrn.4271966

Linoy, S., Stakhanova, N., & Matyukhina, A. (2019). Exploring Ethereum's Blockchain Anonymity Using Smart Contract Code Attribution. *2019 15th International Conference on Network and Service Management (CNSM)*, 1–9. DOI: 10.23919/ CNSM46954.2019.9012681

Lustig, C. (2019). Intersecting Imaginaries: Visions of Decentralized Autonomous Systems. *Proc. ACM Hum.-Comput. Interact., 3*(CSCW), 210:1-210:27. DOI: 10.1145/3359312

Muhammad, I. (2023). COMMUNAL INTELLECTUAL PROPERTY IN THE DIGITAL AGE: EXPLORING THE RELEVANCE, REGULATION, AND IMPACT OF CREATIVE COMMONS LICENSES. *Indonesian Law Journal, 16*(1), 1. DOI: 10.33331/ilj.v16i1.127

Nassar, A., & Kamal, M. (2021). Ethical Dilemmas in AI-Powered Decision-Making: A Deep Dive into Big Data-Driven Ethical Considerations. *International Journal of Responsible Artificial Intelligence, 11*(8), 8.

Nazer, L. H., Zatarah, R., Waldrip, S., Ke, J. X. C., Moukheiber, M., Khanna, A. K., Hicklen, R. S., Moukheiber, L., Moukheiber, D., Ma, H., & Mathur, P. (2023a). Bias in artificial intelligence algorithms and recommendations for mitigation. *PLOS Digital Health, 2*(6), e0000278. DOI: 10.1371/journal.pdig.0000278 PMID: 37347721

Nazer, L. H., Zatarah, R., Waldrip, S., Ke, J. X. C., Moukheiber, M., Khanna, A. K., Hicklen, R. S., Moukheiber, L., Moukheiber, D., Ma, H., & Mathur, P. (2023b). Bias in artificial intelligence algorithms and recommendations for mitigation. *PLOS Digital Health, 2*(6), e0000278. DOI: 10.1371/journal.pdig.0000278 PMID: 37347721

Oakley, K. (2006). Include Us Out—Economic Development and Social Policy in the Creative Industries. *Cultural Trends, 15*(4), 255–273. DOI: 10.1080/09548960600922335

Ryan, M. & Stahl, B. (2020). *(PDF) Artificial intelligence ethics guidelines for developers and users: Clarifying their content and normative implications*. Retrieved February 1, 2025, from https://www.researchgate.net/publication/342080262 _Artificial_intelligence_ethics_guidelines_for_developers_and_users_clarifying _their_content_and_normative_implicationsDOI: 10.1080/09548960600922335

Ministry of Financial Services and Commerce (2024). *Regulation | Ministry of Financial Services and Commerce*. Retrieved February 1, 2025, from https://www .gov.ky/mfsc/regulationDOI: 10.1080/09548960600922335

Review, L. (2020, February 6). Naruto v. Slater: One Small Step for a Monkey, One Giant Lawsuit for Animal-Kind. *Wake Forest Law Review*. https://www.wakeforestlawreview.com/2020/02/naruto-v-slater-one-small-step-for-a-monkey-one-giant-lawsuit-for-animal-kind/DOI: 10.1080/09548960600922335

Savelyev, A. (2018). Copyright in the blockchain era: Promises and challenges. *Computer Law & Security Review, 34*(3), 550–561. DOI: 10.1080/09548960600922335

Sharma, N. (2024, January 5). China Releases Strong Guidelines for Use of AI in Research. *Analytics Vidhya*. https://www.analyticsvidhya.com/blog/2024/01/china-releases-strong-guidelines-for-use-of-ai-in-research/DOI: 10.1080/09548960600922335

Soderland, H. A., & Lilley, I. A. (2015). The fusion of law and ethics in cultural heritage management: The 21st century confronts archaeology. *Journal of Field Archaeology, 40*(5), 508–522. DOI: 10.1080/09548960600922335

Song, J. (2021). Ethical adaptation and legal regulation of modern technology. *Cultura e Scuola, 4*(3), 169–178. DOI: 10.1080/09548960600922335

Srivastava, V., Mahara, T., & Yadav, P. (2021). An analysis of the ethical challenges of blockchain-enabled E-healthcare applications in 6G networks. *International Journal of Cognitive Computing in Engineering, 2*, 171–179. DOI: 10.1080/09548960600922335

Stashevskaia, E. (2024, July 5). *How do teachers envision AI grading for open-ended questions in universities?* [Info:eu-repo/semantics/bachelorThesis]. University of Twente. https://essay.utwente.nl/100864/DOI: 10.1080/09548960600922335

Sukamto, B., Raihan, R., & Untoro, U. (2023). *Legal Transformation in the Digital Era: Regulatory Adaptation and Innovation.* 289–296. DOI: 10.1080/09548960600922335

WIPO. (1996). *Summary of the WIPO Copyright Treaty (WCT).* Retrieved January 31, 2025, from https://www.wipo.int/treaties/en/ip/wct/summary_wct.htmlDOI: 10.1080/09548960600922335

Hagendorff, T. (2020). *The Ethics of AI Ethics: An Evaluation of Guidelines | Minds and Machines.* Retrieved February 1, 2025, from https://link.springer.com/article/10.1007/s11023-020-09517-8DOI: 10.1080/09548960600922335

Elliott, K., Price, R., Shaw, P., Spiliotopoulous, T., Ng, M., Coopamootoo, K., Moorsel, A. (2021). Towards an Equitable Digital Society: Artificial Intelligence (AI) and Corporate Digital Responsibility (CDR). Retrieved February 1, 2025, from https://link.springer.com/article/10.1007/s12115-021-00594-8DOI: 10.1080/09548960600922335

Chapter 3
Blockchain for Content Authentication and Copyright Protection

S. V. Divya

ⓘ https://orcid.org/0009-0004-4321-8066

V.S.B. College of Engineering Technical Campus, Coimbatore, India

P. Venkadesh

ⓘ https://orcid.org/0000-0001-6582-3153

V.S.B. College of Engineering Technical Campus, Coimbatore, India

S. Saravanaprabhu

Nandha College of Technology, Erode, India

Jelin Taric G.

Noorul Islam Centre for Higher Education, Kumaracoil, India

S. Yazhini

ⓘ https://orcid.org/0009-0006-1644-3908

V.S.B. College of Engineering Technical Campus, Coimbatore, India

M. Shify Antolin

V.S.B. College of Engineering Technical Campus, Coimbatore, India

ABSTRACT

Digital media has provided new frontiers where the challenge to authentication and copyright is unparalleled. The emergence of new solutions for safeguarding intellectual property rights and ensuring authenticity in content becomes necessary. This chapter introduces blockchain integration as a means of authenticating AI-generated content with secure attribution against risks of unlawful duplication or misappropriation and how blockchain-based systems allow verifiable ownership of digital assets through smart contracts that automate licensing, royalty collection, and the tracking of use. This chapter goes deeply into the technical architecture of blockchain applications in digital media, illuminating its capacity to create trust and

DOI: 10.4018/979-8-3373-6481-0.ch003

accountability in this fast-evolving creative ecosystem. Ethical, legal, and scalability considerations discuss the role that blockchain is playing in building a fairer and more transparent digital economy.

1. INTRODUCTION

The most influential aspect of digital media around the world is how it has affected the production, distribution, and consumption of content. On the other hand, media authenticity, intellectual property rights, and copyright infringement raise questions on the legitimacy and authenticity of online content (Mohit et al., 2024). Authentication of a work of art is often much more important to its creator than copyright protection. The digital age where content is distributed instantly and usually free of charge makes copyright enforcement increasingly difficult, making digital media authentication a highly complex issue .

This can be done by the use of technology to create manipulations, create pirated or fake content, and distribute unauthorized copies. The problem is further complicated by the fact that generative AI makes it so that AI-generated content may blur the line between the original and altered versions and hence hard to verify authenticity . Blockchain is providing a decentralized, immutable, and transparent framework that can be used to bridge over above anxieties of better authentication for digital media and improved copyright protection (Aryan et al., 2023). Blockchain-based authentication mechanism integrated with smart contracts will allow the building of a digitally environment that content creators, distributors, and even the consumers can rely on (Renqiang et al., 2024).

This chapter discourses on some major challenges related to the authentication of digital media and enforcement of copyright, then probes the potential role of blockchain technology in responding to the identified challenges, while further pin-pointing certain objectives aimed at the advancement of blockchain-based solutions for managing rights in digital media.

1.1 Overview of the Problems of Authenticating Digital Media and Copyright

Authenticity of digital media and observing copyright is tiresome primarily due to the facile duplication, altering, and the internet transfer of it. Modern editing tools as well as the generative AI models make it very difficult for the differentiation between original as well as altered content, thus forming deepfakes, altered pictures, and also misleading videos. Moreover, the anonymous characteristic of this dissemination that the online platforms provide can facilitate the creation and allowance of content to proliferate without appropriate accreditation of its source, hence making it challenging to trace where the pirated media originated and consequently prosecute the culprits .

Copyright rights: Digital space has issues related to the copyright protection issue. Digital contents are easily copied, reproduced and monetized in the absence of the author; it leads to a full-fledged intellectual property infringement. Existing copyright laws are not able to deal with the issues of cross-border digital content sharing and centralized authentication systems are susceptible to hacking as well as data manipulation further weakening the trust in the system.

These are journalism, entertainment, and e-commerce that rely very much on the authenticity and credibility of their contents. Yet, with no effective way to verify ownership and originality, these remain vulnerable to fraud and misinformation as well as copyrights infringement. With this, innovation and further enhanced secure solutions in terms of advancing technologies are in call.

Blockchain technology is the future solution to the authentication and copyright challenges of digital media. Decentralized and tamper-proof, it eliminates data manipulation and gives clear proof concerning the ownership of content. (Gabriela et al., 2024). Every transaction is recorded permanently in an immutable ledger that secures the rights of the creators and provides verifiable proof of authenticity for the consumers. Smart contracts that can automatically enforce licensing, content usage tracking, and fair payments to creators. This is one of the most vital applications of blockchain in copyright management. Blockchain facilitates digital watermarking and provenance tracking, hence creating an immutable record of creation and distribution history of a given content. Such qualities enhance the integrity of content and prevent unauthorized duplication or modification.

In addition, blockchain can prevent misinformation from being spread, since it will authenticate the source and metadata of digital information. Journalism and social media websites all have to believe in digital media (Raffaele et.al ., 2023). Blockchain will be integrated with the process of authentication of content for a clearer and safer digital landscape from the originators and distributors of content to the end users. Blockchain technology is applied to verify and safeguard copyrights of digital media, but it redefines trust and accountability in the virtual landscape. The more it is embraced, the more it will be expected to have a highly significant role in intellectual property protection and ethical use of digital media.

2. UNDERSTANDING BLOCKCHAIN TECHNOLOGY

Blockchain technology has revolutionized data storage, sharing, and securing. It acts as a backbone in changing the paradigm in transformative applications of cryptocurrencies, supply chain management, and authentications of digital media. A further discussion about the core principles and different types can highlight why its potential is extensive.

2.1 Blockchain Concepts

a. Decentralization

The central feature of blockchain is decentralization, which means that there is no central authority in the management and verification of transactions. It is a network of nodes or computers that verify and record the transactions. All nodes have the same copy of the blockchain to prevent any central authority from tampering with the system. Decentralization increases the network's resilience. Even if some nodes fail or are compromised, the network functions effectively.

Trust: Decentralization decreases the dependency on centralized systems, which are unproductive and prone to corruption due to the fragility of single points of failure.

Empowerment: It ensures that people and organizations have ownership over their data and transactions because the risk coming from intermediaries levels is low.

b. Immutability

Immutability refers that the recorded blockchain transactions cannot be erased or altered. A confirmed and added transaction will be found in the blockchain because hashing by cryptography and consensus mechanisms create a connection in which every block is a hash referring to the previous one hence forms a chain of data. Altering any block would cause subsequent blocks to change and needs an agreement from the majority, and hence becomes impractical via computation).

This characteristic ensures data integrity and security. Therefore, it is the most suitable technology that can be used in applications such as financial transactions, digital media authentication, and tracing the supply chain.

c. Transparency

Blockchain natively allows transparency because of the feature that all transactions that have occurred within a network are readable by the parties involved. Open blockchains have an open ledger in which users can find histories of their transactions and are answerable, thus reducing cases of fraudsters' activities. Closed or hybrids blockchain allow the transparency selectively for the needs of organizations and particular industries.

In new media, it acts as a step preceding stakeholder trust. It helps content creators and consumers to verify the digital assets in a legitimate fashion and with proper recompense and utilization . In case of copyrights protection and authentication, tracing ownership is achieved in the concerned digital assets involved .

For instance, blockchain is regulatory compliant due to its transparency as it offers an immutably auditable log of the transactions that may hold massive value in financial and legal applications. The mechanism for transparency adopted by blockchain is used in blockchains employed by governments and enterprises to reduce fraud and enhance the efficiency of operations.

2.2 Types of Blockchains

Due to various uses and needs that may appear in every situation, there are three categories of blockchains; public, private, and hybrid.

a.   Public Blockchains

The public blockchains are open to everyone; any restriction is not available for anyone who wants to join the network. The system is decentralized-this means that all the transactions are public. Public blockchains are especially described by Bitcoin and Ethereum.

These blockchains only have one principal objective, which is to ensure they can use the Proof of Work (PoW) or Proof of Stake (PoS) consensus mechanism when validating transactions so that they are secure and immutable. Apps best created on public blockchains are openness and inclusivity ones, such as cryptocurrencies, DeFi, and digital identity, although they suffer from problems like scalability and energy consumption since they are open systems.

b.   Private Blockchains

Private blockchains are permissioned networks where access is limited and granted only to the privileged members. Actually, they are pretty different from public blockchains as they are managed by central bodies. Transaction processing time is extremely short in private blockchains since they consist of fewer nodes and are generated with a simplified consensus process.

Private blockchains are most often applied to industries that require the privacy and control over data, including areas like healthcare and supply chain management and financial services. It achieves better scalability as well as increased security, giving up on part of the elements of decentralization and transparency.

c. Hybrid Blockchains

Hybrid blockchain is a mix of both public and private blockchains. This balances the transparency offered by public blockchains with the control offered by private blockchains. Therefore, organizations are able to decide where data should go public and where it should be kept confidential, thereby using the best of both worlds.

For instance, hybrid blockchain systems can ensure public verification of some transactions with information remaining private to participants. It, therefore, can be recommended application for government records and digital media authentication and enterprise solutions.

2.3 Role of Blockchain in Trust Building

Blockchain technology has been considered as one of the most transformational aspects because it is able to build trust among parties. Digital interaction, which is basically lacking in transparency and security in its current form, provides a basis for trust with blockchain. This is possible only due to its integrity in data storage. It ensures integrity in the data because of the immutability of blockchain and its cryptographical security. Users receive assurance that records on the blockchain cannot be changed or tampered with. This is significant, particularly for finance, health care, and the digital media realm where information calls for precision and reliability.

a. Decentralized Trust

Traditional systems rely on the presupposition that a user has faith that an intermediary, like a bank, a regulator, or a certification authority, valids transactions or authenticates data. Blockchain eliminates intermediary roles, so this mechanism of a decentralized consensus is established as the basis for trust, no one necessarily being trusted but rather the aggregate network.

This decentralized trust is very important in international transactions, as parties from different jurisdictions may not have a previous relationship and common law.

b. Resilience and Security

The decentralized architecture in blockchain offers incredible resiliency to attacks and failure. Even in the case when some nodes get compromised, it will still allow the network to work and be safe. This actually means that reliability builds trust; the system would be robust and efficient no matter what comes its way.

Thus, be it a public, private, or hybrid blockchain, such technology provides tools for empowerment, accountability, and trust in today's increasingly digital society.

3. CHALLENGES OF DIGITAL MEDIA AND COPYRIGHT PROTECTION

The birth of the digital era changed the way content was created, distributed, and consumed. Yet, with great opportunities come great challenges to copyright protection and the integrity of digital media. In fact, issues ranging from illegal copying to AI-generated content have required powerful solutions to ensure creative rights and fair practice.

3.1 Unlawful Duplication and Content Misappropriation

Digital media has become easier to copy and share without permission than ever before. The unauthorized duplication of any digital media is one of the biggest problems that digital platforms face today. The unauthorized duplication is also referred to as piracy, which is the copying or modifying any copied material without permission. This, most often, results in depriving the rights and efforts of the original creators in many cases.

a.   Impact on Creators

Content theft has the most devastating effect on creators, particularly in the music, film, publishing, and software sectors. For example, artists and writers are deprived of income whenever their works are disseminated on illegal sites. The financial loss spreads to producers, publishers, and distributors, which can jeopardize the profitability of creative industries.

Apart from this, another problem has to do with independent small creators who lack sufficient resources to deal with piracy and even to proclaim their rights.

b.   Coming of Age in Online Piracy

The internet made piracy a global issue because peer-to-peer sharing platforms, torrent websites, and unauthorized streaming services offer a means to access copyrighted material without permission. Moreover, the efforts to block or shut down these platforms often resurface under different domains, which does not necessarily make it any easier to enforce copyright laws.

c. Limitations of technological solutions

There are a variety of technologies available to combat illicit copying, from digital rights management (DRM) systems and watermarking to others. While useful in preventing piracy in some ways, these tools are hardly foolproof: hackers have shown an uncanny ability to breach DRM protections, while watermarks can often be removed or obscured.

The laws on content misappropriation also vary across jurisdictions, which presents a challenge in international copyright law enforcement. This calls for innovative solutions that can adapt to this changing nature of digital media.

3.2 Problems of Attribution and Licensing in AI-Generated Content

Content has transformed significantly with AI. Nowadays, one can compose music, art works, literature, and even write software code using artificially intelligent machines, but this innovation has also brought forth complex questions in the area of ownership and a right to use.

a. Obscurity of Ownership Ends

The use of AI-generated content raises several critical questions on authorship and ownership. Traditional copyright laws are meant to protect human creators, but they do not account for works generated by machines. For example, who owns the rights to a song composed by an AI algorithm? Is it the developer of the algorithm, the user who provided input, or the entity that owns the AI system?

These ambiguities lead to disputes, especially in cases where the AI-generated content is commercially successful or used without proper attribution.

b. Licensing Complexities

The most significant problem is the licensing of AI-generated content. Since creative procedures are the amalgamation of human inputs and machine inputs, compensation and licensing terms become a little complex. Additionally, most AI systems are trained on large datasets composed of copyrighted material, and it remains a little ambiguous whether the outputs infringe existing rights to intellectual property.

c. Ethical and Legal Issues

There are also ethical dimensions to the AI-generated content. With such a capacity to be able to mimic the work of artists, so much so that a similar piece is produced at a lesser cost, there is a clamor for more transparency and accountability about how such AI is developed and deployed.

It is as challenging to determine how the copyright laws are going to be amended in order to handle the unique challenges presented by AI-generated content as it is for regulators and lawmakers to deal with this legal frontier. There are some jurisdictions that are mulling over whether to extend copyright protection to AI-generated works, while others believe such works should stay in the public domain.

d.   Role of Technology in Attribution

Attribution has also been positively affected by technological means to contribute to a work. Blockchain would contribute by allowing a tamper-proof record for leaving authorship and licensing agreements. Smart contracts may enable the automatic payout of royalties and fair compensation to the creators. Such technologies, however, only spread with substantial investment and collaboration among the stakeholders.

3.3 Need for Verifiable Ownership in Digital Assets

The creation and trade of digital assets mushroomed in the digital age, starting from artwork to music, to non-fungible tokens and virtual real estate. However, this has created a need for verifiable ownership mechanisms to ensure protection for the creators and the buyers.

a.   Challenge in Establishing Ownership

Proof of ownership is an important issue in the area of digital media. The digital product differs from the physical one because the former can easily be copied and distributed, in such a way that it becomes impossible to distinguish between a copy and an original. This issue complicates further the case where one content is held by multiple individuals.

For example, a photographer might find out that someone else is selling his or her photographs as an NFT. In the absence of any system for verifying ownership, such disputes can be quite time-consuming and costly to resolve.

b.   Fraud and Counterfeiting in Digital Markets

In actuality, digital marketplaces, especially the NFT, are where fraud and counterfeiting increase. These fraudsters list false entries of digital assets in their books that mislead the buyer to buying assets they are not entitled to. This lowers the level of trust among users and hampers actual creators and investors from participating.

Blockchain technology will authenticate originality, copyright ownership, and prevent illegal duplication in the case of digital media. Artists can mint their works as NFTs and, thus, establish a unique digital certificate verifying the authorship and ownership.

c.   Limitations and Future Directions

It promises much, however, in terms of solving ownership-related challenges. The underlying technology is still relatively immature and has concerns about scalability, energy consumption, and accessibility, and the regulatory and legal frameworks surrounding blockchain-based systems are still evolving in a way that is uncertain to creators and buyers.

The issues of unlawful duplication, attribution, and verifiable ownership explain the need for innovation in digital media and copyright protection and will drive advanced technologies such as blockchain in handling such problems to bring a more balanced and secure environment for creators and consumers.

4. BLOCKCHAIN-BASED SOLUTIONS IN AUTHENTICATION AND COPYRIGHT

Now that blockchain has been infused into digital media and copyright management, an avenue for answering certain questions such as those on attribution, licensing, and ownership is now available. Because blockchain is decentralized, immutable, and transperancy, creators and platforms will find it possible to allow them to have secure and verifiable systems in handling their content, particularly AI-generated ones.

4.1 Integration of Blockchain With AI-Generated Content

This has led to the birth of AI as an avenue for artistic expression; hence, a lot more machine-generated artwork, music, and literature are currently being produced. Still, ownership issues are very tricky to deal with. Blockchain answers this problem very well since it enables proper transparency, traceability, and automation in the handling of AI-generated content.

a.   Data Integrity

Since the immutable nature of blockchain allows recording creation, the following can be used to consider recording the creation of AI-generated art: the algorithm deployed, the used training data, and a timestamp. Such a process lets the artists prove the creation of their unique AI-generated material without facing an ownership dispute at the same time. For instance:

- **Timestamping and Provenance:** Blockchain provides the exactness of the times when the given AI-generated content will be created for the creators for verifiable proof that they have delivered.
- **Blockchain-based AI Accountability:** The blockchains can have metadata about which AI models created the content, ensuring a practice of responsible and copyright-law-compliant output.

b. Decentralized AI Ecosystems

Blockchain can be used to establish decentralized AI ecosystems where models, training data, and content generated by such models are traded in a transparent manner. Creators and developers can monetize their assets by issuing tokens while the blockchain mechanism ensures fair compensation. Such platforms as Ocean Protocol allow users to share and monetize data used for AI training while retaining control over its usage.

c. Clearing Ownership Conflicts

Blockchain explains who owns where developers, data providers, and users collaborate with each other for the development of AI-generating content. Through prespecified agreements, smart contracts assign ownership percentages and revenue shares without dispute.

d. Control Mechanism for Deepfakes and Abuse

Deepfakes are AI-generated content that can be used to undermine trust in digital media. Blockchain will authenticate the origin of such content by embedding cryptographic hashes and verify authenticity through decentralized networks. This way, audiences will distinguish between authentic and manipulated works.

4.2 Secure Attributions Mechanisms

Another facet of copyright protection involves attribution in which creators will be given identification for a piece of work one is contributing towards. Blockchain introduces decentralized and tamper-proof mechanisms aimed at facilitating fair and proper attribution of contents regarding unfair practice issues to be prevented from application beyond permission. Non-interoperable ownership records

This allows blockchain to create an immutably recorded ownership history for such digital assets. If a creator is publishing his content through a service based on the blockchain, a system will have built a certain kind of a cryptographic hash - a digital fingerprint - for content. This would mean that whatever one decides to do with the work - copy or edit - the ownership claims can't be challenged.

a.   Decentralized Attribution Systems

Traditionally, attributions rely on hackable and manipulative centralized databases. Blockchain neutralizes such risks because all the records are spread across a network of nodes with full verification and storing of the same data at each node, which makes it consistent and transparent.

b.   Interoperability with Digital Watermarking

Better attribution will include a combination of blockchain and digital watermarking. Since watermarks implanted in digital works are concomitant with blockchain data, they can also be traced by viewers. This is while verifying ownership and getting license information in real time. This combination makes copyright enforcement more powerful and inhibits illegal usage.

c.   Public and Private Attribution Models

Blockchain supports public and private attribution models:

- **Public Blockchains:** In this sense, as seen with the case of Ethereum, are public. This means that any individual can view and verify the records of ownership, based on the idea of provability.
- **Blockchains:** These are not public. This means that such networks can be used in industries like film and publication, which often have exclusive information that needs to be restricted.

Blockchain platforms provide a level playing field for independent creators. It allows registration of works on blockchain platforms, securing intellectual property (Fan et.al., 2019) without expensive legal procedures or intermediaries. Blockchain technology secures the attribution of content while creating the culture of accountability and respect for the rights of the creators-an enormous challenge to them in the present digital media system.

4.3 Smart Contracts for Licensing and Royalty Automation

Smart contracts are self-executing agreements, running on blockchain networks that contain predetermined terms directly compiled into the contract. This transforms licensing and royalty management through automation of the whole process while keeping overhead low regarding administrative costs but appropriately rewarding the creator.

a.   Automating Licensing Agreements:

Smart contracts can automate licensing digital assets by implementing terms when conditions are met. For example:

- The buyer purchases a license to the electronic artwork; smart contract is deployed and all the payments are transferred from the buyer to the artist.
- Usage terms, such as duration and scope, of use are encoded into the contract for compliance.

This removes middlemen and therefore cost and any manner of delay in the processing of licenses.

b.   Real-Time Royalties Distribution

Smart contracts, however make it possible for royalty payments to be automated. Every time a digital asset is sold or used, the smart contract will automatically issue royalties to all parties involved based on a predetermined percentage.

c.   Application in Joint Ventures

Smart contracts can make revenue sharing easier in collaborative projects that involve more than one contributor. A share of a contributor can be encoded, and this would eliminate disputes and manual calculations. For example, in music, the royalties from the streaming platforms automatically would be distributed to song writers, producers, and performers.

d.   Copyright Infringement

Smart contracts can make protection of rights by copyrights cannot be violated because the unauthorized access will be limited to digital assets. For instance,

- A smart contract may limit downloads of a digital book to an extent or allow access to some asset only from specific geographical locations. Smart contracts can automate licensing and access control. They typically need integration with external enforcement mechanisms.
- If anyone breaches this, they automatically see their access taken away.

4.4 Case Studies of Successful Implementations

There are numerous organizations and projects that have shown that blockchain solutions for authentication and copyright management can work.

a. Mycelia

This blockchain-based platform is by the musician Imogen Heap and empowers the musician. This tool can be used by artists for registering their works, smart contract royalty payments, and getting transparent licensing options. Mycelia has been lauded for making processes easy and giving the rightful fair compensation to the creators.

b. Verisart

Verisart is the blockchain-based art and collectibles certification service, issuing secure, verifiable certificates of authenticity in support of protecting artwork against forgery and misattribution by artists. It's these success stories like that of Verisart, where blockchain has shown a tremendous impact in establishing more trust within the art market.

c. Audius

Audius is a decentralized streaming platform for music using blockchain technology that empowers artists. In it, the artist uploads the work directly onto the platform without an intermediary to get most of the revenue share. Audius uses blockchain technology for tracking the streaming data. The blockchain then tracks the royalties with transparency.

d. LBRY

LBRY is, in fact, a decentralized content-sharing platform using blockchain technology that enables the creators to retain full control over their works. It provides tools for monetization, licensing, and attribution, more or less helping to overcome all those challenges independent creators face.

Blockchain technology has the potential to revolutionize digital media authentication and copyright management through transparent, secure, and efficient solutions. Blockchain, when integrated with AI, secure attribution mechanisms, and automated licensing systems, can solve some of the burning issues of the digital age and create a more just ecosystem for both creators and consumers. The digital media workflow diagram is shown in Figure 1.

Figure 1. Digital media workflow

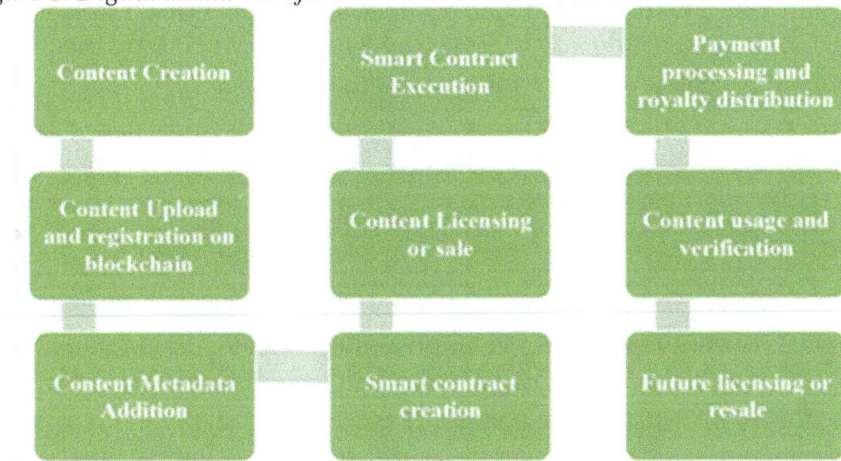

5. TECHNICAL ARCHITECTURE OF BLOCKCHAIN APPLICATIONS IN DIGITAL MEDIA

The technical architecture of blockchain applications in digital media (Franco et.al., 2024) basically uses the decentralized ledger technology in content creation and sharing as well as generating revenues from content with an aim of increasing transparency, immutability, and security. In short, the architecture makes use of a peer-to-peer network whereby activities such as licensing or owning contents are recorded in a distributed ledger. It uses smart contracts to auto-agree with participants; hence the rights of its creators are well taken care of as well as royalty payments could be sent, all without need for any sort of intermediary parties involved.

Cryptographic mechanisms secure the transactions but are not in any way validating these transactions; consensus protocols like PoW or PoS are taken care of them. Scalability solutions like Layer-2 networks might be very effective in case of typical high-volume media industries. Finally, blockchain-based decentralized storage systems and others like IPFS provide a secure and tamper-proof platform for hosting digital assets. This architecture not only saves costs and removes middlemen but also endows creators with more control over their intellectual property, changing the face of digital media.

5.1 Components of Blockchain Systems in the Media

Blockchain systems in the media sector comprise many very important elements that work hand in hand for the safe, transparent, and decentralized management of content. Among the key elements of such a blockchain system (Nan et.al., 2021) include nodes, consensus mechanisms, and distributed ledgers.

a. **Nodes:**Nodes are the backbones of a blockchain network as shown in Figure 2. They're like single devices like a computer or a server that join the network by making a copy of this distributed ledger and validating transactions. Nodes can be broadly classified into two categories-full nodes, which download the whole blockchain and implement all its rules, and light nodes, which just hold partial information, enabling faster processing. In media applications, nodes check for activities like licensing of content, distributing content, or paying royalties. This system is maintained with nodes for its integrity. The requirement of central authorities is eliminated altogether with decentralized nodes, and no one tampers or censors.

Figure 2. Blockchain nodes and consensus mechanisms

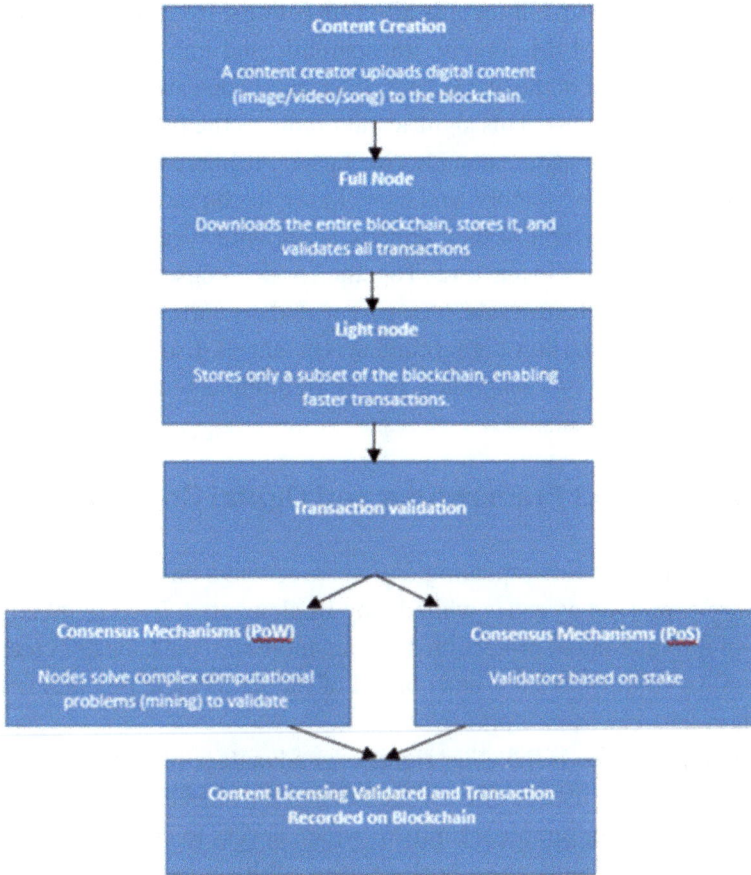

b. **Consensus Mechanisms:** These are protocols which ensure that all the nodes in a blockchain network have a consensus over the legitimacy of a transaction. They prevent frauds like double-spending and confirm the validity of the distributed ledger. The two most widely used consensus mechanisms are Proof of Work and Proof of Stake. Proof of Work is a mechanism that demands extra work to be put into computation. Proof of Stake is a mechanism in which validators are chosen based on their stake. For media, use cases usually prefer either PoS or other energy-efficient mechanisms like Delegated Proof of Stake, in that such a mechanism is both scalable and reduces energy consumption. Such mechanisms can ensure that correct and tamper-proof ownership records and distribution for the content continue to exist.

c. **Distributed Ledges:** Distributed ledgers are used as the underlying data structure by blockchain systems. It records all of its actions, from creation to licensing, and monetization of the content, transparently and immutably. It retains a record of every event in the blockchain. It has now done away with the storage of data on central servers. This significantly reduces the likelihood of hacking or alteration of data by some unauthorized users. It improves confidence among content creators, distributors, and users in the media industry about following the usage and copyright of their content along with royalty information based on distributed ledgers in real time. Together, nodes, consensus mechanisms, and distributed ledgers form a safe, transparent, and decentralized media ecosystem that is revolutionizing how digital content is managed, distributed, and monetized through correcting problems such as copyright infringement, royalty disputes, and intermediary costs.

5.2 Smart Contract Frameworks and Digital Content Protection

Smart contracts are self-executing digital agreements on a blockchain; some of its terms are expressed as codes while being implemented. Even in taking the application of digital content protection domains more into the hands of creators, the automation, more transparency, and control of the intellectual property over one's things fall in the very frameworks.

Copyright protection is the other significant advantage of smart contracts. This is because the terms of use are directly included in the blockchain. A smart contract can state geographic or temporal limits to which access to content is restricted so that media is released only to authorized users. With a reduction in the level of automation, piracy and unauthorized sharing risks decrease as well, hence the environment will be safe for creators to spread their work.

This puts blockchain platforms like Ethereum, Polkadot, and Hyperledger in a position to have an effective framework of smart contracts. For instance, the Ethereum platform has its unique programming language for smart contracts called Solidity where developers can create highly customized smart contracts with applications such as content licensing and royalty management. In the same line, the cross-chain compatibility in Polkadot allows media assets to operate on multiple blockchains for added reach and functionality.

Another fundamental function that smart contracts make possible is conflict resolution. Smart contracts are a means that hold full clarity with provability of content usage history, since they keep an immutable record of all transactions made. Since such records can be the basic proof in a case of conflict, like disputing royalty payments or misuse; therefore, these cut more time spent in long processes of litigation.

Smart contracts go well with blockchain-based digital rights management. The DRM systems are dynamic access controls over content that the smart contract may support using the defined terms of a DRM system. A classic example would be that of implementing a pay-per-view DRM. A DRM would permit a paid video to get time-bound permission to access a video, but the permissions automatically lapse once the duration of the permission is over based on the licensing agreements defined by the smart contract.

It concludes by saying the smart contract framework is how the automation of critical processes, the increase of transparency, and the respect given to the rights of creators work in protecting digital content. Therefore, all those who are implicated in these ecosystems will benefit through increased security, efficiency, and equitability of their media-industry ecosystems.

5.3 Blockchain-Based Metadata Management and Digital Watermarking

Blockchain technology revolutionizes metadata management and digital watermarking in the media space, offering secure, transparent, and tamper-proof solutions in content verification and protection. Innovative solutions to age-old problems, these directly target long-term issues such as copyright infringement and unauthorized distribution of content, in addition to tracing the use of the same.

Metadata management is the process that captures information on digital assets such as titles, authors, creation dates, licensing terms, and usage statistics. In a traditional structure, metadata is placed on central servers, therefore exposing them to being tampered with or lost. Other untoward access is possible when metadata in this case resides within an accurate and irreversible distributed ledger of blockchain technology. Each change of metadata - ownership or licensing terms - would be recorded as a new transaction on the blockchain, and this would open up the entire history of this digital asset to all the creators, distributors, and consumers.

One utility of a blockchain, for instance, is the tracking of usage and royalties attributable to the creation of certain works. In a perfect world, blockchain will be the metadata manager when it reports a song played or a video watched in real-time. It therefore makes sure fair compensation to creators or rights holders; accurate reporting follows as a norm to all participants. Big files can be saved using platforms such as IPFS but linked on the blockchain through integration to secure their metadata.

Digital watermarking works through embedding certain unique identifiers or codes into the digital media and then establishing rights and preventing misappropriation by the owner of content. Blockchain amplifies this to store the information of the watermark on the same ledger, in turn creating an irrevocable link between content and its real owner. Hence, a digital art can be authenticated and traced back to its source by a blockchain watermark. Any form of reproduction or alteration of the artwork is traceable since the blockchain will have an unalterable record of the original file.

Advanced dynamic watermarking is said to modify the watermark in line with the use or the nature of its dissemination. This is made possible through blockchain since it may update the information about real-time watermarks every time such content is accessed or shared. This will particularly come in handy for the tracking of unlawful dissemination of multimedia as this way one will know which source leaked it.

6. REAL-WORLD IMPLEMENTATIONS AND CASE STUDIES

The blockchain applications in digital media transform its potential across the various use cases. For example, Audius is a blockchain-based music streaming service where artists can upload their work directly and earn royalties without intermediate services while the whole process has a system that is very transparent and fair revenue sharing. Vevue is a decentralized video-sharing platform where users get cryptocurrency for content submissions. The Associated Press is using blockchain to ensure secure and immutable distribution of news metadata in order to increase trust (Vu et.al., 2024) and attribution in journalism. Blockchain remains an integral part of platforms such as OpenSea and Rarible with the concept of trading NFTs, proving provenance and authenticity. Therefore, these examples illustrate how blockchain changes the game for content creation, distribution, and monetization, increasing control and equity between creators and consumers.

6.1 Use Cases in Generative AI Outputs

Generative AI had affected many fields since it became possible to generate original, high-quality output almost in every field. Since it could be used for producing text, images, audio, video, or even more complex designs, it opened novel use cases and became one of the crucial tools for creative work, efficiency, and solving problems.

a.   Content Creation and Marketing

Generative AI: All that content creation: blog posts, product descriptions, social media captions, and advertising copy is all done. The first thought would fall into spaces like ChatGPT or Jasper AI for some content brainstorming on that little niche audience choice and saved some time and energy while being efficient. DALL·E and MidJourney are now creating brand-owned visuals for that little something special marketing material.

b. Media and Entertainment

Generative AI in entertainment (Amna et.al., 2020) produces script, storyline, character design. For instance, tools can produce the entire script for a movie or game and just give them creative prompts to write and design accordingly. This is also applied in music composition, where tools such as MuseNet from OpenAI can generate melodies, harmonies, or even full songs according to different genres.

c. Education and E-Learning

From generative AI outputs, it follows that customized learning, quizzes, and simulation can be created. For instance, assessment by AI to the responses of students based on their proficiencies or generating an explanation according to the learner's style will definitely impact the educational arena. Besides, virtual tutors in the healthcare field through generative AI such as a conversational agent will potentially increase more engagement results.

d. Healthcare Applications

It is used in medicine for generating synthetic data for training models, simulating conditions and even for producing medical reports. In short, the same algorithm is used here in drug discovery for developing new molecular structures or for simulating clinical trials. AI-created educational material for patients enhances the presentation of healthcare problems.

e. Gaming and Virtual Reality

Characters, environment, and even storylines can be produced. That's a fully engaging, dynamic experience. As for procedural content generation, that itself is actually pumping up player engagement by providing the scope where in developers can uniquely generate assets in scale.

f. Personalized Recommendations and Chatbots

This is where conversational AI chatbots and recommendation systems of personalized recommendations, customer service, and interactive experiences stand.

This app is obviously the most relevant in e-commerce, entertainment applications, and mental health applications.

Generative AI outputs have transformed the whole industry creatively, efficiently, and accessibly, thus proving invaluable for addressing any form of diversified challenge and an enabler of unprecedented innovation.

6.2 Blockchain in Digital Identity Verification and Creative Integrity

Blockchain is new infrastructure in the digital identity verification and creative integrity processes. Blockchain-based (Lijun et.al., 2020) digital identity makes DIDs and verifiable credentials to transfer control away from centralized authorities and back into the hands of individuals. These systems let people store and manage their identity on a blockchain; this makes it possible to have privacy, therefore eliminating the reliance on the traditional identity providers that are prone to some form of breaches. For example, Civic offers solutions for self-sovereign identity, and the latter can authenticate identities without exposing unnecessary personal information in a way that at the same time increases security and develops trust with customers when sharing reduced data. Blockchain also supports zero-knowledge proofs (ZKPs), where users can prove their identity or qualifications without revealing sensitive data. This is especially valuable in industries like finance and healthcare, where discretion is of paramount importance. It also simplifies cross-border authentication by ensuring identity verification and eliminates the risk of delays and fraud associated with global transactions.

Blockchain in creative industries assures creative integrity (Wang et.al., 2018), since immutably recorded owners, licensing, and usage rights can never be compromised. The output of the advent of NFTs is a new channel for creators to affirm and cash in on their intellectual property. NFTs are digital evidence of ownership that proves the genesis of the original creation made on public ledger. OpenSea, Foundation, among others, now trade NFTs using the blockchain while deploying automated smart contracts to grant the creators rights.

Blockchain has done away with copyright infringement since it empowers transparent licensing and tracking of the usage of digital content. For instance, musicians can tokenise their songs so that they guarantee fair compensation while visual artists may use blockchain to prevent unauthorized replication of the artwork. Blockchain also supports collaborative projects, where contributors can timestamp their work so that there exists a record of inputting.

The third role of blockchain toward more ethical creative practice is actually ensuring that attribution could be verifiable and transparent-or at least decrease plagiarism-while fostering trust in digital ecosystems, thus permitting more constructive engagements among creators, consumers, and intermediaries operating through just systems.

From secure identity management to creative integrity, blockchain technology (Jayanth et.al., 2023) has robust solutions for the challenges of the digital age, empowering people and creators with control over their assets and identities.

6.3 Analysis of Successful Projects like IPFS, Po.et, or Filecoin

Blockchain projects like IPFS (InterPlanetary File System, Po.et and Filecoin are the best example of how decentralized technologies transform data storage, managing content, and distribution of creative rights.

a.   IPFS (InterPlanetary File System)

IPFS is a decentralized protocol for the storage and sharing of data across a peer-to-peer network. Unlike systems whose web applications depend on a centralized server, a library like IPFS is based on content-based addressing where every file is hashed cryptographically such that it is uniquely identified. Therefore, it is assured of data integrity as any attempt to tamper with the file will always result in change in the hash value. The problem of duplicative storage is also very minimal in IPFS and bandwidth usage is efficient so it is really an important tool in large-scale digital content management and preservation. The IPFS is majorly used by the creative industries to store the digital media assets in the form of images, music, video metadata, etc. For example, OpenSea is an NFT marketplace that used IPFS to store metadata so the storage of the digital asset turned out to be permanent. Such a system is decentralized, having no single point of failure and ensuring content availability, irrespective of the nodes going offline.

b.   Po.et

Po.et is a blockchain-based management and verification of creative works. It supports the use of digital asset tamper-proofing and easy verifiability. This allows for the timestamping of their content and its tokenization for the creators. Such work culminates on the Po.et platform with ownership and licensing described in detail within a blockchain ledger. This then culminates into clear and transparent ways in which intellectual property issues, matters of unauthorized reproduction, and copyright infringement may be treated.

However, unfortunately, Po.et did not scale and adopt a larger scale. Although the project is no longer active, it's a pretty interesting example of how blockchain protects the integrity of creatives and introduces new ways of monetizing content.

c. Filecoin

Filecoin will extend the protocol of IPFS with the marketplace, offering users opportunities for the rental of unused storage. The network will encourage participation through rewarding the storage providers in terms of Filecoin tokens. From this aspect, decentralized storage will not only save it in a cost-effective way and security but also redundancy and fault tolerance that cannot be achieved using the new applications of cloud storage. It applies particularly for all the industries handling long-term digital asset preservation, namely, archival institutions and digital media platforms.

Examples include such projects as IPFS, Po.et, and Filecoin. Blockchain transparency has combined the power of decentralized storage systems, thereby showing how these decentralized technologies could be used in furthering the best interest of creative rights, access to data, and management of content. Success, therefore, acts as a landmark for the potential that blockchain transformation offers digital ecosystems toward better security, fairness, and efficiency.

7. ETHICAL, LEGAL, AND SCALABILITY CONSIDERATION

There are huge possibilities of blockchain technology in a myriad of industries, but ethical, legal, and scalability issues crop up when adopting the same and hence warrant careful thought. The blockchain's transparency, for example, could be in direct conflict with the issue of user privacy because private data is forever etched into unchangeable ledgers. Techniques such as zero-knowledge proofs and selective disclosure are thus important tools for privacy. More energy-intensive consensus mechanisms, such as Proof-of-Work, raise environmental concerns, so more sustainable models, like Proof-of-Stake, are gaining more attention. Legally, the distributed nature of blockchain raises issues regarding data protection and intellectual properties. For example, the "right to be forgotten" feature of the GDPR contradicts the immutability of blockchain, which mainly requires off-chain storage-based hybrid solutions. Scalability is also a challenge as well in the sense that the well-known chains, such as Ethereum, experience congestion and high fees to transact. Examples of these include layer 2 scaling techniques and sharding. Overcoming these challenges will ensure that blockchain integrates into global systems in a manner that allows its ethical, legal, and scalable dimension.

7.1 Ethical Issues in Blockchain-Based Copyright Systems

Blockchain-based copyright systems have several merits such as immutability, transparency, and efficient rights management. With them come a number of ethical dilemmas. Most of the ethical issues surrounding these are based on privacy concerns, issues of accessibility, the possibility of misuse, and the intricate nature of intellectual property rights in this decentralized system.

The largest of the ethical issues is Privacy vs. Transparency. In respect of such sensitive copyright information - for example, when the creators' personal information or licensors' personal information needs to be recorded in the blockchain ledger-this fact of its immunity and openness clashes. The block chain ensures records immutability, traceability but might accidentally expose confidential information and breach all rights of privacy; an example is a situation where the information of identity as well as all transactions related to a creator would be accessible for everybody, plus the possibility of misuse, surveillance, or stealing identity. Techniques such as encryption and zero-knowledge proofs stand in opposition to these drawbacks. However, they are complex add-ons to the system and not uniformly adopted. The third set of ethical concerns revolves around accessibility and inclusion. Most blockchain systems rely upon technical sophistication and access to digital infrastructure, making it difficult for creators in disadvantaged or rural settings to enter the new framework. The high deployment and maintenance costs of blockchain solutions also make these services unattainable to smaller creators. This has significant implications for a system that seemingly disadvantages less well-resourced creators or corporations at the expense of their better-resourced counterparts.

The decentralized nature of the blockchain is another challenge towards copyright enforcement. Again, without a central authority to govern the system, differences in the ownership of rights and licenses are hard to clear. For example, if two parties feel that they are respective owners of a similar content, the absence of any governing body may ensure that the parties continue to fight for ages. The second disadvantage is that cybercriminals can exploit the system to upload malicious false claims to the blockchain because it strictly depends on the accuracy of initial data inputs. Lastly, blockchain-based copyright systems may inadvertently conflict with existing intellectual property laws. Different countries have different copyright regulations. Blockchain is a global tool, making it difficult to align decentralized systems with law according to the jurisdiction. For instance, the "right to be forgotten" under GDPR proves to be inconsistent with the concept of immutability in blockchain and hence brings forth ethical and legal dilemmas. Even though blockchain promises to remake copyright management on the principles of transparency, fair compensation, and tamper-proof records, ethical challenges must be addressed.

7.2 Legal Implications

Cross-border issues create new legal problems formed by blockchain use for copyright enforcement, data privacy, and intellectual property laws. As decentralized, the operation of the blockchain is way beyond traditional jurisdiction and complicates cross-border copyright enforcement on different legal systems.

On the legal fronts, copyright enforcement is one of them. The problem is that, since copyright laws vary from country to country, there is a challenge in the application and the enforcement of the local copyright law on account of its international nature by blockchain. A digital artwork might be owned or licensed in one country but would be distributed to a user who is in another country with different copyright law, and therefore it becomes impossible to enforce that. Further analysis will show that there is no central authority to be able to help with dispute resolutions; this will also affect legal ownership creation and even when disputes arise in relation to royalties or use rights, confusion might ensue.

Data privacy is another highly critical issue that has gained much prominence because of regulations such as the General Data Protection Regulation put forward by the European Union. This immutability aspect makes it rather tough to deliver on the "right to be forgotten," an entitlement provided under the GDPR where a person is allowed to erase all his personal data. Since blockchain records can never be deleted after entering, this clashes against the core principles of data privacy and puts into conflict the transparency aspects of decentralized systems. The same way, recording personal data through public ledgers for licensing and transaction details would expose sensitive data without intent to do so. It raises more questions of whether privacy violations can occur and even if unauthorized data access will take place.

7.3 Scalability Challenges and Solutions

The biggest challenge for the adoption of blockchain in high-traffic applications such as cryptocurrency networks, decentralized finance, and blockchain-based digital media is scalability. This is basically an issue with the blockchain's consensus mechanisms, data storage, and transaction throughput, which might become bottlenecks when there is high adoption of users.

Transaction throughput remains the primary challenge that causes the scaling problem in a blockchain system. Generally, public blockchains as in Bitcoin or Ethereum, involve slow processing speed that leads to longer times and extra costs in transaction due to high usage during peak. For example, in Bitcoin, around 3-7 TPS is processed and with Ethereum, this translates to an approximate of 15-30 TPS per second. At its core, payments through traditional models such as that of

Visa happen at thousands TPS. End. This becomes particularly problematic when blockchain applications are used for real-time applications such as payments or digital asset exchanges, where delays or high fees can make the technology impractical for widespread use.

To address these scalability issues, several solutions have emerged. One of the most prominent approaches is Layer 2 solutions, which are built on top of the base blockchain layer to enhance scalability without compromising security or decentralization. For instance, in Ethereum, Layer 2 solutions like Optimistic Rollups and zk-Rollups aggregate a number of transactions into one, thus avoiding congestion and further reducing costs. With such arrangements, the bulk of transaction validation can be off-chain, with only the final settlement happening on the main chains.

One of the primary other solutions in scalability is sharding, where the blockchain is separated into smaller, more efficient pieces known as "shards." Each shard conducts its own collection of transactions and smart contracts simultaneously, thereby exponentially increasing the throughput of the overall network. An example of this is Ethereum 2.0, which is going to have sharding. In sharding, transaction throughput ten times increases. In the case of sharding, the entire network does not verify each transaction but nodes own specific shards that boost efficiency and performance. The improvements on the consensus mechanisms also enable the scaling of the blockchain systems. For instance, Proof-of-Stake (PoS) and Delegated Proof-of-Stake (DPoS) are much better alternatives to Proof-of-Work (PoW) since they consume less energy and can execute higher transaction rates. Ethereum 2.0 is shifting the consensus mechanism from PoW to PoS.

8. FUTURE DIRECTIONS AND CONCLUSION

Therefore, blockchain technology has tremendous potential for industry changes in digital media, finance, healthcare, and supply chain management. Advancements of blockchain in scalability, interoperability, and intuitive user interfaces will be instrumental in really driving adoption much wider. Some solutions to those limitations will include Layer 2 scaling solutions, sharding, and proof-of-stake consensus mechanisms that will properly allow blockchains to support large-scale applications. More interaction with AI and IoT will usher in new opportunities in decentralized systems toward the processing of real-time data and automation. New domains like digital identity management and intellectual property protection will come into place, thus further securing, increasing transparency, and making it efficient to protect and verify ownership. However, the technology must cross ethical, legal, and regulatory hurdles that pertain to data privacy and cross-border enforcement. Innovation, sustainability, and equal access will make blockchain live up to its true potential in the transformation of the interaction between digital systems. The future of blockchain is optimistic, and advanced development molds an increasingly decentralized and transparent digital landscape.

8.1 Potential Advances in Blockchain for Creative Industries

Blockchain technology has made quite a way into different sectors of the economy. The creative industries are not exempt from the many promising developments brought by blockchain. This includes the capability to protect IP rights and the facilitation of copyright enforcement. Blockchain technology affords an immutable and transparent platform for the development of a tamper-proof ledger in which digital assets may be registered and tracked.

Another possible application is blockchain in the distribution of digital contents. Current traditional distribution channels are extensive and often block revenue sharing and sometimes lead to piracy as well as an unequal opportunity for consumers to access such contents. With decentralized content through blockchain, the direct relationship of creators with their audiences expels the middlemen and brings a fair revenue distribution. Already, platforms such as Audius, using blockchain in disrupting the music industry, have shown that even decentralized platforms can work. Blockchain could also change the movie and publishing industries in a similar manner by giving the creators more control over their intellectual property, rights to distribution, and monetization.

NFTs, Non-Fungible Tokens, another popular blockchain-based idea, are coming to revolutionize the way in which creators monetize their work, allowing for digital art, music, and other video content that can be put into tokenizable form so that sellers can sell truly unique, verified assets to collectors; these tokens even can include a smart contract that sends a percentage back to the original artist for resale or future sales as well. As the technology advances, more blockchain-based platforms that enhance the visibility, protection, and monetization of creative works will come into use.

In a nutshell, blockchain has enormous potential for creative industries, promising creators more secure, transparent, and efficient means of managing intellectual property and connecting with audiences in ways that ensure fair compensation and greater control over their work.

8.2 Summary of Findings and Final Thoughts

Exploring potential use cases through the blockchain demonstrated transformative applications across most industries, digital media, intellectual property management, and decentralization of financial instruments. Blockchain applications offer the possibility to fundamentally change digital interactions, ways data privacy is managed and copyrights enforced because it provides absolute transparency, non-interoperable properties, and a high security feature. In order to understand all its hidden strengths, however, the implementation comes with ethical and legal problems regarding scalability.

Blockchain holds significant promise in creative industries for managing intellectual property. Blockchain can be a means to give creators better control over their works, fair compensation, and protection of their IP rights with control over piracy in a decentralized and transparent system. Blockchain technology provided a new monetization opportunity through smart contracts and tokenization with NFTs. Challenges remain, however, as with data privacy in that the very openness of blockchain at times works against the protection of sensitive user information.

At a more macro level, the potential for blockchain to create a transparent digital economy is vast. The decentralized financial system empowers the people by granting access to financial services without the need for intermediaries by traditional players. Similarly, supply chain tracking using blockchain can improve traceability and ethics in sourcing products, thus allowing better choices on the side of consumers. The legal and regulatory landscape lags behind the pace of adoption of blockchain technology, particularly in crossborder enforcement of copyright laws, data privacy, and IP protection.

While the advantages of blockchain are apparent, scalability still lags significantly behind. Not even the advancement of Layer 2 scaling and sharding prevented most blockchain systems from experiencing costs for transactions too high or speeds too slow to be limited in practice to several applications within specific industries. More applications in other areas of life can then be envisioned when the technology becomes mature enough with solutions on its way toward addressing the issues on scalability.

Accordingly, within the following conclusions, it has the potential to reform the digital environment transparent, safe, and equal. After solving current problems with ethical, legal, and scalability considerations, blockchain might build an open, effective digital economy where creative users and customers of service alike will benefit through innovation, transparency, efficiency, and simplicity.

REFERENCES

Ciriello, R. F., Torbensen, A. C. G., Hansen, M. R. P., & Müller-Bloch, C. (2023). Blockchain-based digital rights management systems: Design principles for the music industry. *Electronic Markets*, *33*(5), 5. DOI: 10.1007/s12525-023-00628-5

Frattolillo, F. (2024). Blockchain and smart contracts for digital copyright protection. *Future Internet*, *16*(5), 169. DOI: 10.3390/fi16050169

Fuentes, G., & Omarova, A. (2024). Empowering the commons: Blockchain for IP protection in generative AI. *SSRN*. https://ssrn.com/abstract=4803536 DOI: 10.2139/ssrn.4803536

Jing, N., Liu, Q., & Sugumaran, V. (2021). A blockchain-based code copyright management system. *Information Processing & Management*, *58*(3), 102518. DOI: 10.1016/j.ipm.2021.102518

Khare, A., Singh, U. K., Kathuria, S., Akram, S. V., Gupta, M., & Rathor, N. (2023). Artificial intelligence and blockchain for copyright infringement detection. In *2023 International Conference on Edge Computing and Applications (ICECAA)* (pp. 1–6). IEEE. DOI: 10.1109/ICECAA58104.2023.10212277

Mittal, M., Rahman, K. F., Jha, C. K., Bali, V., & Khanna, T. (2024). Bridging policy and practice: A systematic review of blockchain adoption for copyright protection. In 2024 International Conference on Communication, Computing and Energy Efficient Technologies (I3CEET) (pp. 1–6). IEEE. DOI: 10.1109/I3CEET61722.2024.10993987

Potluri, J., Gummadi, H., Alladi, K., & Ramesh, G. (2023). Securing intellectual property in the digital age through blockchain innovation. In *2023 Global Conference on Information Technologies and Communications (GCITC)* (pp. 1–6). IEEE. DOI: 10.1109/GCITC60406.2023.10426242

Qureshi, A., & Megias, D. (2020). Blockchain-based multimedia content protection: Review and open challenges. *Applied Sciences (Basel, Switzerland)*, *11*(1), 1. DOI: 10.3390/app11010001

Truong, V. T., Le, H. D., & Le, L. B. (2024). Trust-free blockchain framework for AI-generated content trading and management in metaverse. *IEEE Access: Practical Innovations, Open Solutions*, *12*, 41815–41828. DOI: 10.1109/ACCESS.2024.3376509

Wang, H., Zheng, Z., Xie, S., Dai, H. N., & Chen, X. (2018). Blockchain challenges and opportunities: A survey. *International Journal of Web and Grid Services*, *14*(4), 352–375. DOI: 10.1504/IJWGS.2018.095647

Xiao, L., Huang, W., Xie, Y., Xiao, W., & Li, K.-C. (2020). A blockchain-based traceable IP copyright protection algorithm. *IEEE Access: Practical Innovations, Open Solutions, 8*, 49532–49542. DOI: 10.1109/ACCESS.2020.2969990

Xie, R., & Tang, M. (2024). A digital resource copyright protection scheme based on blockchain cross-chain technology. *Heliyon, 10*(17), e36830. DOI: 10.1016/j.heliyon.2024.e36830 PMID: 39281489

Yang, F., Shi, Y., Wu, Q., Li, F., Zhou, W., & Hu, Z. (2019). The survey on intellectual property based on blockchain technology. In *2019 IEEE International Conference on Industrial Cyber Physical Systems (ICPS)* (pp. 1–6). IEEE. DOI: 10.1109/ICPHYS.2019.8780125

Chapter 4
blockAuth:
A Blockchain–Driven Framework for Verifiable Content Creation and Secure Distribution in the Generative AI Era

Bishwo Prakash Pokharel
https://orcid.org/0000-0001-6516-2105
Sault College of Applied Arts and Technology, Canada

Naresh Kshetri
Rochester Institute of Technology, USA

Suresh Raj Sharma
https://orcid.org/0009-0009-0722-545X
Tribhuvan University, Nepal

Soba Raj Paudel
Tribhuvan University, Nepal

Suresh Baral
Gupteshwor Mahadev Multiple Campus, Nepal

ABSTRACT

The rise of multimodal generative AI has revolutionized creative industries by enabling the production of high-quality text, images, audio, and video. However, this innovation has also introduced critical challenges, including content authenticity concerns, the proliferation of deepfakes, intellectual property disputes, and unethical manipulation of media. Addressing these issues requires a robust and scalable solution. This chapter introduces a blockchain-driven framework that

DOI: 10.4018/979-8-3373-6481-0.ch004

integrates the strengths of blockchain's decentralized and immutable architecture with the creative potential of generative AI. It ensures verifiable content creation by embedding proof of originality into digital assets, facilitates transparent ownership through tokenization, and automates secure licensing and fair revenue sharing via smart contracts. By exploring the theoretical foundation, technical architecture, and practical applications of blockAuth, it presents a transformative solution to foster trust, transparency, and equity in the digital media ecosystem.

1. INTRODUCTION

The integration of generative artificial intelligence (AI) and blockchain technology is reshaping the digital content landscape, enabling unprecedented opportunities while introducing new challenges. Generative AI, characterized by its ability to produce text, images, audio, and video with remarkable precision, has revolutionized creative processes and media production (Linkon et al., 2024). However, this advancement has also led to significant concerns, including content authenticity, copyright infringement, and the proliferation of synthetic media like deepfakes (Rana et al., 2022). Simultaneously, blockchain technology has emerged as a solution for ensuring transparency, security, and immutability in digital transactions and records ("Bitcoin: A peer-to-peer," n.d.). By leveraging blockchain's decentralized nature, it is possible to address the pressing challenges posed by generative AI, thereby fostering a more accountable and secure digital ecosystem.

One of the most pressing issues in digital media is the lack of verifiable content authenticity. With the rise of generative AI, it has become increasingly difficult to differentiate between original and synthetic content. This has amplified risks such as misinformation, identity theft, and copyright disputes (Kearns et al., 2023). Blockchain technology, with its immutable ledger, provides a robust framework for recording and verifying the origins and ownership of digital content. Through smart contracts, blockchain can automate licensing agreements, ensuring creators are fairly compensated and their rights are protected (Malik et al., 2023).

Moreover, the rapid adoption of AI-generated content has highlighted gaps in traditional copyright systems, which are ill-equipped to handle the complexities of AI-driven media. Blockchain's ability to tokenize digital assets as non-fungible tokens (NFTs) introduces a new paradigm for establishing ownership and enabling transparent monetization (Solouki & Bamakan, 2022). This convergence of technologies offers transformative potential for creative industries, enabling secure content distribution, fair revenue sharing, and enhanced accountability.

Generative AI has revolutionized the creative industries by enabling machines to produce high-quality text, images, audio, and video with remarkable precision, driving innovation in media production, advertising, and entertainment. However, this technological advancement has also brought significant challenges, such as verifying content authenticity, combating the proliferation of deepfakes, and addressing copyright disputes. For instance, deepfake scandals involving manipulated videos and NFT-related fraud highlight the urgent need for robust solutions to protect content creators and consumers. Blockchain technology, known for its decentralized and tamper-proof ledger, offers a promising mechanism to address these issues by embedding immutable proof of authenticity, tracking ownership, and automating licensing agreements.

The rapid proliferation of generative AI has not only revolutionized content creation but also introduced significant challenges that threaten the integrity of digital media. As AI-generated content becomes increasingly indistinguishable from human-created works, the risks of misinformation, intellectual property theft, and unethical manipulation have grown exponentially. For instance, deepfake technology has been used to create convincing but fraudulent videos, while AI-generated art has sparked debates over copyright ownership. These challenges are further compounded by the limitations of traditional systems, which lack the transparency and security needed to verify content authenticity and ensure fair compensation for creators. In this context, the integration of blockchain technology offers a promising solution, providing an immutable and decentralized framework to address these issues. By embedding proof of originality, automating licensing agreements, and enabling transparent revenue sharing, blockchain can restore trust and accountability in the digital content ecosystem. This chapter introduces blockAuth, a novel framework that leverages the strengths of blockchain and generative AI to create a secure, transparent, and equitable system for content creation, authentication, and distribution.

Table 1. Key challenges of generative AI and blockchain solutions (Rana et al., 2022; Kearns et al., 2023; Malik et al., 2023; Solouki & Bamakan, 2022; Portillo, 2024; Pal, 2024; Hasan & Salah, 2018; Ryan et al., 2021; Zyskind et al., 2015; Voigt & von dem Bussche, 2017; Floridi et al., 2018; Mehrabi et al., 2021)

Challenge	Description	Blockchain Solution	References
Content Authenticity	Difficulty in verifying the originality of AI-generated content, leading of deepfakes and misinformation.	Blockchain provides immutable records of content creation, ensuring verifiable authenticity.	(Kearns et al., 2023; Portillo, 2024)
Copyright Infringement	AI-generated content often lacks clear ownership, leading to intellectual property disputes.	Tokenization of content as NFTs establishes clear ownership and provenance.	(Malik et al., 2023; Solouki & Bamakan, 2022)
Misinformation	Proliferation of synthetic media (e.g., deepfakes) used for spreading false information.	Blockchain timestamps and metadata ensure traceability, making it easier to detect manipulated content.	(Rana et al., 2022; Pal, 2024)
Revenue Sharing	Lack of transparent and fair revenue distribution for creators of AI-generated content.	Smart contracts automate royalty payments and licensing agreements, ensuring fair compensation.	(Hasan & Salah, 2018; Ryan et al., 2021)
Data Privacy	AI systems often rely on sensitive data, raising privacy concerns.	Blockchain's decentralized storage and cryptographic techniques enhance data privacy and security	(Zyskind et al., 2015; Voigt & von dem Bussche, 2017)
Ethical AI Usage	Ethical concerns around bias, misuse, and accountability in AI-generated content.	Blockchain provides transparent audit trails for AI-generated content, ensuring ethical compliance.	(Floridi et al., 2018; Mehrabi et al., 2021)

Table 1 highlights the key challenges posed by generative AI, such as content authenticity, copyright infringement, and misinformation, and demonstrates how blockchain technology can provide robust solutions to these issues. For example, blockchain's immutable ledger ensures that AI-generated content can be traced back to its origin, while smart contracts automate royalty payments, ensuring creators are fairly compensated. These solutions not only address the immediate challenges but also pave the way for a more sustainable and ethical digital media landscape. By combining the creative potential of generative AI with the security and transparency of blockchain, blockAuth offers a comprehensive framework that can transform how digital content is created, shared, and monetized. This chapter delves into the theoretical underpinnings, technical architecture, and real-world applications of blockAuth, showcasing its potential to foster trust, transparency, and equity in the evolving digital ecosystem.

2. TECHNOLOGICAL FOUNDATIONS

A revolutionary method for producing verifiable content and distributing it securely is the combination of blockchain technology and generative AI. Blockchain's decentralized ledger technology records data in tamper-proof blocks across dispersed networks, guaranteeing data security, transparency, and immutability. For generative AI, where guaranteeing the authenticity and traceability of generated material is a crucial concern, this feature is essential. An extra degree of security is provided by cryptographic techniques like hashing and digital signatures, which confirm the authenticity and provenance of outputs produced by artificial intelligence. Additionally, smart contracts-self-executing programs kept on blockchain-enforce preset guidelines for content distribution and enable automated transactions, guaranteeing authors equitable pay and preservation of their intellectual property rights. The decentralized structures of blockchain further augment the developments of generative AI, including its capacity to produce text, images, and other types of media. For example, distinct, unchangeable identifiers recorded on a blockchain can be used to tag AI-generated content, lowering the possibility of plagiarism or fabrication and ensuring verifiable provenance. Additionally, this combination enables new use cases like tokenization of AI-generated assets, which permits fractional ownership and decentralized content markets, which enable direct interactions between creators and consumers without the need for middlemen. The combination of generative AI and blockchain technology provides a strong technological basis for promoting justice, openness, and trust in digital ecosystems. Industries ranging from media and entertainment to education and banking can innovate safely and effectively by utilizing generative AI's creative potential in conjunction with blockchain's distributed nature and security characteristics (Nakamoto, 2008).

2.1 Blockchain Technology for Digital Media

The use of AI-generated content (AIGC) on digital platforms is increasing but it also introduces difficulties such as mistakes, disinformation, and security threats. AIGC, a real-world application of generative AI, generates text Graphics, and music by replicating human inventiveness. However, it frequently includes uncontrolled and incorrect material, which raises the danger of disinformation, fraudulent content, and privacy infringement. Regulating generative AI technology has become critical for ensuring content quality, security, and compliance with ethical and legal requirements. This involves rigorous algorithm assessments and transparent data usage standards to safeguard user privacy and prevent damage. Effective regulation may help to reduce these dangers, protect user confidence, and encourage the healthy growth of digital platforms and the larger digital ecosystem (Yang et al., 2024).

Blockchain technology serves as a decentralized ledger system that records and verifies transactions within a peer-to-peer (P2P) network, eliminating the need for a central authority or trusted third party. It ensures trust, transparency, security, traceability, decentralization, and immutability. Blockchain can handle various types of transactions, such as digital currency, copyright transfers, non-fungible tokens (NFTs), and resource exchanges.

Structurally, blockchain comprises two layers: the infrastructure layer and the blockchain layer. The infrastructure layer supports the P2P network, enabling data communication, computation, and storage through wired or wireless connections. The blockchain layer builds on this foundation, utilizing transactions, blocks, and chains of blocks to securely manage and store information. Transactions represent client data recorded in the ledger, blocks store transaction details, and the chain of blocks maintains an organized sequence linking these blocks, ensuring the integrity of the system (Luo et al., 2023).

Blockchain technology has emerged as a transformative force in the digital media industry, offering solutions to longstanding challenges such as copyright, royalty distributed and transparency in content consumption. As a decentralized and tamper-resistant ledger system blockchain facilitates secure and immutable transactions, making it an ideal tool for managing digital assets.

The integration of blockchain technology into digital media not only addresses current challenges but also opens up new opportunities for innovation. For instance, blockchain's ability to tokenize digital assets as NFTs has revolutionized the way creators monetize their work, enabling fractional ownership and decentralized marketplaces. Moreover, blockchain's transparency and immutability make it an ideal solution for combating piracy and ensuring that creators receive fair compensation for this work. As blockchain technology continues to evolve, its applications in digital media are expected to expand, offering even more robust solutions for content authentication, distribution, and monetization.

2.2 Multi Model Generative AI

Multimodal Generative AI combined with blockchain technology represents an innovative intersection of artificial intelligences and decentralized systems. It includes creating content across various data types, including text, images, audio and video. Instances comprise OpenAI's GPT4, capable of processing text and image, along with other models such as DALL-E and CLIP.

● Creative sectors: producing content for advertising, movies, and video games.

- Education: Developing engaging educational resources
- Healthcare: Examining various types of data such as medical image and patient records for diagnostic purposes

Blockchain technology is the distributed technology, unchangeable ledger system that guarantees safe, clear and resistant-to- manipulate transactions. a well -known platform consists of Ethereum, Polkadot, and solana. Data integrity: maintaining and validating modifications of data. Smart Contracts: Execution of agreements in an automated and trustless manner. Decentralized Identity: Safeguarding user identities effectively (Chen et al., 2024). In the future, researchers will probably prioritize enhancing the robustness, interpretability and ethical consideration of multimodal generative AI. Methods such as self-supervised learning along with ongoing improvements in model architectures will be vital in boosting the capabilities and uses of these technologies. Multimodal generative AI embodies a revolutionary method that combines different modalities to facilitate more advanced and context-sensitive AI applications in diverse areas, including creative sectors, health care and more. As research and development advance, these technologies possess significant potential to transform interactions with utilization of artificial intelligence in daily life.

The potential of multimodal generative AI extends beyond content creation, offering transformative applications in fields such as healthcare, education, and entertainment. For example, in healthcare, AI models can analyze medical images and patient records to assist in diagnosis, while in education, AI-generated content can create personalized learning experiences. However, the ethical implications of these technologies cannot be overlooked. Issues such as bias in training data, misuse of AI-generated content, and lack of transparency must be addressed to ensure responsible AI deployment. By integrating blockchain technology, these challenges can be mitigated, as blockchain provides a transparent and immutable record of AI-generated content, ensuring accountability and ethical usage.

2.3 Synergy Between Blockchain and Generative AI

Because one technology enhances the strengths and limits of the other, the combination of blockchain and generative AI has the potential to be revolutionary. A transparent and secure framework for data storage and verification is offered by blockchain, a decentralized and unchangeable ledger. On the other side, generative AI produces creative outputs like writing, art, and designs by thriving on massive datasets. In order to tackle problems like data tampering and copyright infringement, generative AI can guarantee data integrity, traceability, and authenticity by incorporating blockchain. Blockchain, for instance, provides a verifiable record of originality and ownership by timestamping and storing generative AI creations. In fields where ownership disputes are common, such as digital art and intellectual property management, this tool is especially helpful. A more equitable and effective creative economy can be promoted by using blockchain-based smart contracts to automate licensing and royalties for AI-generated content (Xu et al., 2019). By simplifying procedures like fraud detection, anomaly recognition, and data analysis in decentralized systems, generative AI in turn increases the usefulness of blockchain. By anticipating transaction bottlenecks and enhancing scalability options like sharding, artificial intelligence algorithms can optimize blockchain networks. Furthermore, generative AI can address privacy concerns in data-intensive applications by producing synthetic datasets for blockchain system training without disclosing private user information. Additionally, these technologies come together in decentralized autonomous organization (DAOs), where generative AI helps with decision-making by using data-driven insights and forecasts, while blockchain guarantees transparent governance. For example, real-time simulations of possible governance proposal outcomes by AI-generated models allow stakeholders to make well-informed decisions. A more secure and intelligent digital future is made possible by the synergy between generative AI's adaptive capabilities and blockchain's trust mechanism, which opens up previously unheard-of innovations in industries like supply chain management, healthcare and finance (Leekha, 2018).

The synergy between blockchain and generative AI is not limited to content creation and distribution; it also extends to emerging fields such as the metaverse and decentralized finance (DeFi). In the metaverse, blockchain can ensure the authenticity and ownership of virtual assets, while generative AI can create immersive and interactive experiences. Similarly, in DeFi, blockchain provides a secure and transparent platform for financial transactions, while AI algorithms can optimize trading strategies and risk management. As these technologies continue to evolve, their combined potential will unlock new possibilities, transforming industries and creating a more secure, transparent, and equitable digital ecosystem.

Figure 1. Synergy between blockchain and generative AI

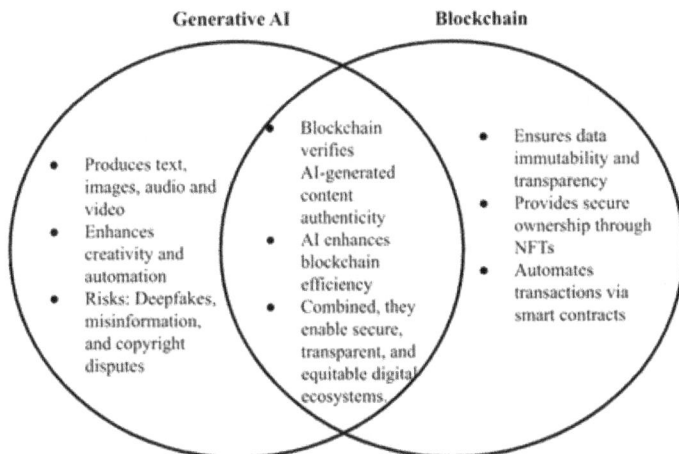

Figure 1 visually represents the complementary strengths of blockchain and generative AI technologies in the context of digital content creation and distribution. The diagram consists of two overlapping circles: one representing blockchain, emphasizing its capabilities in ensuring data immutability, transparency, and secure ownership through NFTs and smart contracts, and the other representing generative AI, highlighting its ability to produce creative content such as text, images, and audio. The overlapping area showcases their synergy, where blockchain verifies the authenticity of AI-generated context, mitigates risks like deepfakes and misinformation, and ensures fair revenue sharing, while generative AI enhances blockchain efficiency through fraud detection and anomaly recognition. Together, these technologies create a secure, transparent, and equitable digital ecosystem.

3. PROPOSED FRAMEWORK: blockAuth

The blockAuth framework addresses critical challenges in the modern generative AI ecosystem, such as content authenticity, secure distribution, and equitable revenue sharing. The framework provides a robust and comprehensive solution by combining the decentralized and immutable nature of blockchain technology with the creative capabilities of AI. Figure 1 represents the conceptual architecture of blockAuth, its components, connectivity, and its potential to transform the digital content landscape.

3.1 Overview of blockAuth

Generative AI technologies have redefined the way digital content is created, enabling users to produce highly realistic text, images, audio, and video. While this advancement has unlocked immense creative potential, it has also introduced risks, including intellectual property theft, misinformation, and deepfake proliferation (Bengesi et al., 2024). The blockAuth framework seeks to mitigate these risks by integrating blockchain technology, known for its immutability and transparency, into the content creation and management process (Wright, 2008).

blockAuth operates on three foundational layers:

● **Content Layer:** Handles content creation, embedding metadata, and tokenizing assets.
● **Blockchain Layer:** Ensures secure storage, smart contract execution, and content provenance tracking.
● **Application Layer:** Provides user-friendly tools and systems for seamless interaction and governance.

This multi-layered approach ensures end-to-end security, traceability, and accountability for digital content.

Figure 2. blockAuth framework

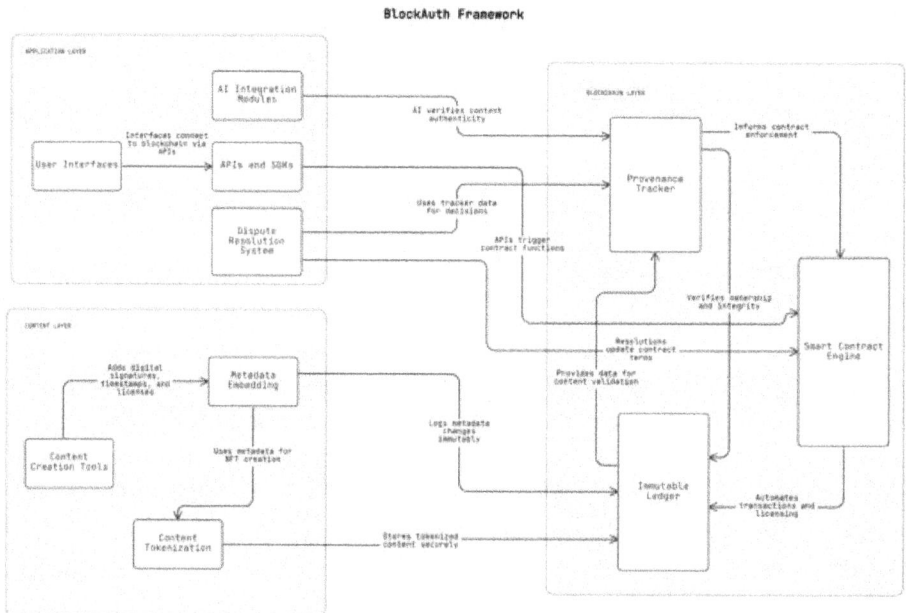

3.2 Content Layer

The Content Layer serves as the foundational entry point for all operations within blockAuth, providing a comprehensive suite of tools and processes tailored to create, annotate, and register digital assets. This layer ensures authenticity, ownership, and traceability for digital content, leveraging cutting-edge technologies like blockchain, AI, and metadata systems.

3.2.1 Content Creation Tools

blockAuth integrates seamlessly with advanced AI-based tools such as GPT (Generative Pre-trained Transformer) and Stable Diffusion to empower creators with high-quality content generation capabilities. These tools are designed to enhance creative workflows while ensuring compatibility with blockchain-based systems for metadata embedding.

- **AI-Powered Creativity:** GPT enables text-based content generation, including articles, scripts, and marketing copy, while Stable Diffusion facilitates the creation of visually stunning images, illustrations, and designs. These tools are optimized to work within blockAuth's ecosystem, ensuring that all generated content is ready for blockchain integration.
- **Workflow Efficiency:** By automating repetitive tasks and offering intelligence suggestions, these tools reduce the time and effort required for content creation. This allows creators to focus on innovation and quality.
- **Blockchain Compatibility:** All content created through these tools is pre-formatted to support metadata embedding, ensuring a seamless transition to the next stage of the process.

3.2.2 Metadata Embedding

Metadata serves as the digital signature for content. It includes crucial details such as the creator's identity, timestamps, licensing terms, and content hash. Embedding metadata during content creation ensures that every asset has a unique and immutable digital fingerprint (Alkhard, 2024). This metadata is stored securely on the blockchain, enabling traceability and authentication.

- **Key Metadata Components:**
  - **Creator Identity:** Includes the creator's name, digital signature, and blockchain wallet address.

- o **Timestamps:** Records the exact date and time of content creation and modifications.
- o **Licensing Terms:** Specifies usage rights, royalties, and distribution permissions.
- o **Content Hash:** A cryptographic fingerprint that ensures the content's integrity and prevents tampering.
- **Blockchain Integration:** Once embedded, metadata is securely stored on the blockchain, creating a permanent and tamper-proof record. This enables traceability and authentication throughout the asset's lifecycle.
- **Interoperability:** The metadata format is standardized to ensure compatibility across different platforms and ecosystems, facilitating seamless sharing and verification.

3.2.3 Content Tokenization

Digital assets created within blockAuth are tokenized into Non-Fungible Tokens (NFTs). Tokenization assigns a unique identifier to each asset, representing its ownership on the blockchain (Varadarajan & Seeni, 2024). These NFTs act as tradable digital certificates that enable creators to monetize their content securely and transparently.

- **NFT Creation Process:**
  - o **Unique Identifier:** Each asset is assigned a distinct token ID, which is recorded on the blockchain.
  - o **Smart Contracts:** These self-executing contracts govern the terms of ownership, transfer, and royalties, ensuring that creators are compensated fairly for their work.
  - o **Immutable Ownership Records:** The blockchain ensures that ownership history is transparent and cannot be altered, providing a trustworthy record of provenance.
- **Monetization Opportunities:**
  - o **Tradable Certificates:** NFTs act as digital certificates of ownership, enabling creators to sell, license, or trade their assets on decentralized marketplaces.
  - o **Royalty Mechanisms:** Smart contracts automatically enforce royalty payments, ensuring creators earn a percentage of sales whenever their content is resold.
- **Enhanced Security:** Tokenization protects against fraud and unauthorized duplication, as each NFT is verifiable in the blockchain.

3.3 Blockchain Layer

The Blockchain Layer forms the backbone of blockAuth's technical infrastructure, ensuring secure storage, transparent transaction validation, and verifiable ownership of digital assets. By leveraging the inherent properties of blockchain technology – decentralization, immutability, and transparency – this layer provides a robust foundation for trust and accountability in the digital content ecosystem.

3.3.1 Immutable Ledger

Blockchain serves as a tamper-proof repository for storing metadata, transaction records, and licensing agreements. By recording this data immutably, it ensures that content authenticity and ownership cannot be disputed or manipulated (Varadarajan & Seeni, 2024). The ledger also serves as an auditable trial for content lifecycle management.

- **Data Integrity:** Once recorded, data cannot be altered or deleted, providing a permanent and auditable record of all activities related to a digital asset.
- **Content Lifecycle Management:** The ledger tracks every stage of a content asset's lifecycle, from creation to distribution and beyond. This includes timestamps for modifications, transfers, and usage, creating a comprehensive audit trail.
- **Transparency and Trust:** Stakeholders can access the ledger to verify the history and authenticity of any asset, fostering trust in the ecosystem.

3.3.2 Smart Contract Engine

Smart contracts automate agreements between stakeholders, such as licensing terms, royalty distribution, and content access. These self-executing contracts eliminate intermediaries, thereby reducing administrative overheads and ensuring real-time compliance with predefined terms (Hasan & Salah, 2018).

- **Automated Licensing:** Creators can define licensing terms (e.g., usage rights, royalties) within smart contracts, ensuring that these terms are enforced without manual intervention.
- **Royalty Distribution:** Smart contracts automatically distribute royalties to creators whenever their content is sold or licensed, ensuring fair and timely compensation.

- **Efficiency and Cost Savings:** By eliminating intermediaries, smart contracts reduce administrative overheads and streamline processes, making transactions faster and more cost-effective.
- **Real-Time Compliance:** Stakeholders can trust that all actions comply with the agreed-upon terms, as smart contracts execute precisely as programmed.

3.3.3 Provenance Tracker

Provenance tracking is a key feature of the Blockchain Layer. This module monitors the lifecycle of digital content, recording ownership changes, licensing activities, and usage history. It ensures that stakeholders can verify the authenticity and integrity of content assets at any point (Aichroth et al., 2021).

- **Ownership History:** Every transfer of ownership is recorded on the blockchain, providing a clear and verifiable chain of custody.
- **Usage Tracking:** The provenance tracker monitors how and where content is used, ensuring compliance with licensing terms and detecting unauthorized usage.
- **Authenticity Verification:** Stakeholders can verify the authenticity and integrity of content assets at any point, reducing the risk of fraud or misuse.
- **Auditability:** The provenance tracker provides a detailed and immutable record of all activities, making it easy to audit content history and resolve disputes.

3.4 Application Layer

The Application Layer bridges the gap between blockAuth's underlying blockchain infrastructure and its end-users, providing intuitive tools and interfaces for seamless interaction. This layer ensures that creators, distributors, and consumers can easily access and utilize blockAuth's features, regardless of their technical expertise.

3.4.1 User Interfaces

blockAuth offers user-friendly interfaces designed to simplify the process of registering, managing, and verifying digital content. These UIs cater to a wide range of users, from creators to consumers, ensuring accessibility and ease of use.

- **Content Registration:** Creators can easily upload and register their digital assets, embedding metadata and tokenizing them as NFTs.

- **License Management:** Distributors and consumers can view and manage licensing terms, ensuring compliance with usage rights and royalty agreements.
- **Authenticity Verification:** Users can verify the authenticity of any digital asset by accessing its metadata and provenance records on the blockchain.
- **Dashboard:** A centralized dashboard provides users with an overview of their assets, transactions, and earnings, enabling efficient management and tracking.

3.4.2 APIs and SDKs

The Application Layer includes APIs and SDKs for integrating blockAuth with external platforms and tools. These integration mechanisms enable interoperability with creative tools, marketplaces, and distribution networks, ensuring widespread adoption (Hegnauer, 2019).

- **Creative Tools Integration:** APIs allow blockAuth to integrate with popular content creation tools like Adobe Creative Suite, Canva, and Blender, streamlining the workflow for creators.
- **Marketplace Connectivity:** SDKs enable seamless integration with NFT marketplace like OpenSea and Rarible, expanding the reach of digital assets.
- **Custom Solutions:** Developers can use APIs and SDKs to build custom applications and services on top of blockAuth, fostering innovation and adoption.

3.4.3 AI Integration Modules

Advanced AI algorithms are embedded within blockAuth to enhance content verification. These modules detect anomalies, such as deepfakes or unauthorized manipulations, and validate the authenticity of digital assets. This ensures that only genuine and unaltered content is distributed through the framework (Yazdinejad et al., 2020).

- **Deepfake Detection:** AI algorithms analyze content to identify signs of manipulation, ensuring that only genuine assets are registered and distributed.
- **Anomaly Detection:** The system flags suspicious activities, such as unauthorized modifications or duplicate content, protecting the integrity of the ecosystem.
- **Automated Verification:** AI-powered tools streamline the verification process, reducing the time and effort required to validate content authenticity.

3.4.4 Dispute Resolution System

A decentralized arbitration mechanism is included to resolve conflicts related to ownership, licensing, and revenue sharing. This system leverages blockchain's immutable records and smart contracts to provide fair and transparent outcomes (Chevalier, 2021).

- **Decentralized Arbitration:** Disputes are resolved by a network of independent arbitrators, ensuring impartiality and transparency.
- **Smart Contract Enforcement:** Arbitration outcomes are enforced automatically through smart contracts, ensuring compliance and reducing the need for legal intervention.
- **Transparency:** All dispute resolution activities are recorded on the blockchain, providing a clear and auditable record of the process.

By combining intuitive user interfaces, robust integration tools, advanced AI capabilities, and a fair dispute resolution system, the Application Layer ensures that blockAuth is accessible, secure, and user-friendly. This layer empowers creators, distributors, and consumers to participate confidently in the digital content ecosystem, driving adoption and innovation.

Table 2. blockAuth framework architecture (Bengesi et al., 2024; Yazdinejad et al., 2020)

Layer	Components	Functionalities	Interconnections
Content Layer	Content Creation Tools (e.g., GPT, Stable Diffusion)	Facilitates the creation of high-quality digital content using AI tools.	Connects with the Blockchain Layer to embed metadata and tokenize content.
	Metadata Embedding (e.g., timestamps, creator identity, content hash)	Embeds metadata as a digital signature to ensure content authenticity and traceability.	Metadata is stored on the blockchain for immutable record-keeping.
	Content Tokenization (e.g., NFTs)	Tokenizes digital assets into NFTs, enabling unique ownership and monetization.	NFTs are recorded on the blockchain for secure ownership tracking.

continued on following page

Table 2. Continued

Layer	Components	Functionalities	Interconnections
Blockchain Layer	Immutable Ledger	Stores metadata, transaction records, and licensing agreements in a tamper-proof manner.	Receives metadata from the Content Layer and provides data to the Application Layer for verification.
	Smart Contract Engine	Automates licensing agreements, royalty distribution, and access control.	Executes predefined terms for content usage and revenue sharing.
	Provenance Tracker	Tracks the lifecycle of digital content, recording ownership changes and usage history.	Ensures content authenticity and integrity by maintaining a transparent audit trail.
Application Layer	User Interfaces (UIs)	Provides user-friendly tools for creators, distributors, and consumers to interact with the framework.	Connects with the Blockchain Layer to enable content registration, licensing, and verification.
	APIs and SDKs	Enables integration with external platforms, tools, and marketplaces.	Facilitates interoperability with third-party systems for seamless adoption.
	AI Integration Modules	Detects anomalies (e.g., deepfakes) and validates content authenticity using advanced AI algorithms.	Communicates with the Blockchain Layer to record verified results and flag unauthorized manipulations.
	Dispute Resolution System	Provides a decentralized arbitration mechanism for resolving ownership and licensing disputes.	Leverages blockchain records and smart contracts to ensure fair and transparent outcomes.

Table 2 outlines the architecture of the blockAuth framework, detailing its three layers - Content, Blockchain, and Application - along with their components and functionalities.

3.5 Working Mechanism of blockAuth

The connectivity between the components of the blockAuth framework is designed to ensure seamless integration and interoperability across its layers, enabling a secure and efficient workflow for content creation, authentication, and distribution. Each layer is interconnected through defined processes, leveraging blockchain's decentralized capabilities and AI's analytical power to provide end-to-end traceability and accountability.

The Content Layer serves as the entry point, where digital assets are created, annotated, and tokenized. Metadata, which includes the creator's identity, timestamps, and licensing preferences, is embedded into the content at this stage. This metadata is then transmitted to the Blockchain Layer for permanent storage in the immutable ledger. The Blockchain Layer ensures that this metadata remains secure, tamper-proof, and accessible for future verification.

The Smart Contract Engine within the Blockchain Layer uses the stored metadata to enforce licensing agreements and automate royalty payments. For example, when a digital asset is accessed or licensed, the smart contract retrieves the associated terms from the blockchain and executes them autonomously, ensuring compliance without the need for intermediaries. This integration eliminates manual processes and reduces the likelihood of disputes.

Provenance tracking, another critical function of the Blockchain Layer, continuously monitors the lifecycle of digital assets. As ownership changes, licensing transactions occur, or modifications are made, the provenance tracker updates the blockchain ledger with these details. This mechanism ensures that all stakeholders, including creators, distributors, and consumers, can verify the asset's history and authenticity at any point.

The Application Layer acts as the interface between the underlying blockchain infrastructure and end-users. User interfaces enable creators to register content, distributors to manage licenses, and consumers to verify asset authenticity. These interfaces are connected to the Blockchain Layer via APIs and SDKs, which facilitate seamless data exchange and integration with external tools and platforms. For instance, a creator using a third-party AI content generation tool can directly upload and tokenize their work within blockAuth through these APIs, streamlining the process.

AI integration modules embedded in the Application Layer further enhance connectivity by validating the authenticity of content in real-time. These modules analyze digital assets for anomalies, such as unauthorized alterations or deepfakes, and provide insights to the Blockchain Layer. Verified results are recorded on the blockchain, strengthening the system's trustworthiness.

The Dispute Resolution System opiates as a decentralized governance mechanism, ensuring that conflicts related to ownership, licensing, or usage are resolved fairly. It leverages blockchain's immutable records to provide evidence and enforce rulings transparently. This system also communicates with the Smart Contract Engine to adjust licensing terms to revoke access in cases of proven violations.

Figure 3. Content lifecycle in the blockAuth framework

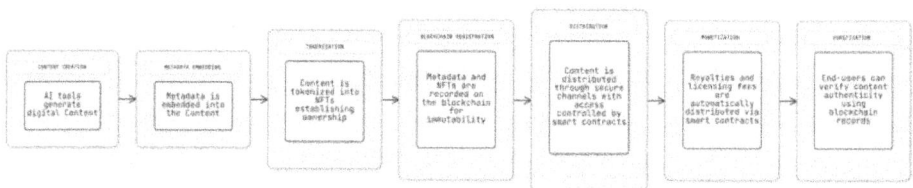

Figure 3 illustrates the end-to-end process of digital content creation, authentication, and distribution within the blockAuth ecosystem. The diagram begins with content creation using AI tools like GPT and Stable Diffusion, followed by metadata embedding, where critical details such as timestamps, creator identity, and content hashes are added to ensure authenticity. Next, the content is tokenized into NFTs, establishing unique ownership on the blockchain. The blockchain registration phase records this metadata and NFT information immutably, providing a tamper-proof audit trail. The content is then securely distributed, with access controlled by smart contracts that automate licensing and royalty payments. Finally, end-users can verify the authenticity of the content using blockchain records.

4. APPLICATIONS OF blockAuth

The blockAuth framework integrates blockchain technology with generative AI, offering innovative solutions for industries that rely heavily on digital content creation, authentication, and distribution. Its applications span multiple sectors, addressing critical issues such as content authenticity, secure ownership, and fair revenue sharing.

4.1 Content Authentication and Verification

One of the primary challenges in the digital content ecosystem is verifying authenticity, especially with the proliferation of deepfakes and manipulated media. blockAuth addresses this issue by embedding metadata, such as timestamps, creator signatures, and content hashes, into the blockchain at the point of creation. This metadata serves as an immutable record, ensuring the content's integrity and traceability.

For instance, news agencies can leverage blockAuth to authenticate video footage, ensuring that no tampering has occurred before publication. The Provenance Tracker within the Blockchain Layer cross-references metadata with blockchain records to validate the content's originality. This approach has significant implications for combating misinformation and enhancing trust in media (Kaur et al., 2024).

4.2 Digital Rights Management (DRM)

Digital rights management is a cornerstone of creative industries, ensuring that creators maintain control over their intellectual property. blockAuth' s smart contracts automate licensing agreements, enabling creators to specify terms such as usage restrictions, royalties, and ownership transfers.

For example, a filmmaker can register their work on blockAuth with predefined licensing terms embedded in a smart contract. When the film is distributed to streaming platforms, the smart contract automatically enforces royalty payment, transferring them directly to the creator. This eliminates intermediaries, reduces disputes, and ensures creators receive fair compensation (Ryan et al., 2021).

4.3 Monetization Through Tokenization

blockAuth facilitates the monetization of digital assets through tokenization, transforming them into non-fungible tokens (NFTs). Tokenized content allows creators to establish unique ownership rights while exploring innovative revenue streams.

In the art industry, for example, artists can tokenize their digital creations and sell them directly to buyers on NFT marketplaces. Each tokenized artwork is linked to its metadata on the blockchain, ensuring authenticity and provenance. Fractional ownership models, powered by blockAuth' s smart contracts, further expand monetization options, enabling multiple stakeholders to invest in high-value assets (Solouki & Bamakan, 2022).

4.4 Secure Distribution of AI-Generated Content

blockAuth enhances the secure distribution of AI-generated content by embedding metadata and creating tamper-proof pathways. The Provenance Tracker ensures that any unauthorized modifications or duplications are recorded, safeguarding the content's integrity.

In the film industry, production houses can use blockAuth to distribute AI-generated visual effects securely. By embedding metadata in the blockchain, distributors can ensure that only authorized parties access the assets, reducing the risk of piracy or misuse. This approach promotes secure collaborations and protects intellectual property rights.

4.5 Ethical and Transparent AI Usage

The increasing reliance on generative AI raises ethical concerns, particularly regarding the misuse of AI tools. blockAuth integrates accountability mechanisms that provide audit trails for all AI-generated content. These mechanisms ensure transparency and compliance with ethical standards.

In the advertising sector, for example, brands can use blockAuth to verify that AI tools were employed ethically and that the generated content adheres to licensing agreements. This not only protects the brand's reputation but also ensures compliance with legal and regulatory frameworks (Kumar et al., 2023).

4.6 Collaborative Content Ecosystems

blockAuth supports collaborative content ecosystems by enabling multiple stake-holders to contribute to a project while maintaining clear ownership and revenue-sharing agreements. The framework ensures that all contributions are recorded on the blockchain, facilitating transparency and fairness.

For instance, in video game development, graphic designers, sound engineers, and programmers can register their contributions on blockAuth. Smart contracts then automatically distribute royalties based on predefined terms, ensuring equitable revenue sharing among contributors. This fosters collaboration while minimizing disputes (Kuye, 2023).

4.7 Legal and Regulatory Compliance

blockAuth provides immutable records of content creation and distribution, aiding legal and regulatory compliance. These records can be used to resolve disputes or demonstrate adherence to copyright laws.

A publishing house using AI-generated content for educational materials can rely on blockAuth to verify the originality and licensing of its content. In case of a copyright claim, the blockchain's records serve as evidence, streamlining legal proceedings and reducing litigation risks (Cvetkovski, 2013).

4.8 Educational Content Authentication

In educational content creation, where accuracy and credibility are paramount, blockAuth ensures that AI-generated learning resources are authentic and tamper-proof. Educational institutions can validate the origin and revisions of their materials using the framework.

For example, an online education platform can register its AI-generated tutorials on blockAuth, embedding metadata that includes the institution's digital signature. This guarantees that students and educators access reliable and authenticated content, enhancing trust in the learning process (Banerjee et al., 2020).

4.9 Combating Piracy

The Provenance Tracker and metadata embedding capabilities of blockAuth make it an effective tool for combating piracy. By providing proof of ownership and usage rights, the framework helps identify unauthorized distribution channels.

In the music industry, artists can use blockAuth to trace pirated tracks back to their source. Smart contracts can also restrict access to unauthorized copies, protecting revenue streams and deterring piracy. This application is critical in maintaining the sustainability of creative industries (G et al., 2018).

4.10 Future Applications

As technology evolves, blockAuth' s applications are expected to extend into emerging domains such as the metaverse, virtual reality (VR), and decentralized social media platforms. The framework's adaptability positions it as a transformative tool for ensuring trust, security, and equity in digital ecosystems.

Table 3. Applications of blockAuth across industries

Industry	Use Case	Benefits of blockAuth	References
Media & Entertainment	Authenticating video footage and preventing deepfakes.	Ensures content authenticity, combats misinformation, and protects intellectual property.	(Kearns et al., 2023)
	Tokenizing digital art and music for ownership and monetization.	Enables creators to monetize content through NFTs and ensures fair revenue sharing via smart contracts.	(Malik et al., 2023)
Education	Verifying the authenticity of AI-generated educational materials.	Ensures students and educators access reliable and tamper-proof content.	(Banerjee et al., 2020)
	Tracking revisions and ownership of educational resources.	Provides a transparent audit trail for content updates and ownership.	(Ryan et al., 2021)
Healthcare	Securing AI-generated medical imaging and patient data.	Ensures data integrity and compliance with privacy regulations (e.g., GDPR)	(Zyskind et al., 2015)
	Authenticating AI-generated diagnostic reports.	Reduces risks of misinformation and ensures accountability in healthcare decisions.	(Ryan et al., 2021)

continued on following page

Table 3. Continued

Industry	Use Case	Benefits of blockAuth	References
Finance	Verifying AI-generated financial reports and forecasts.	Enhances trust in financial data and prevents fraudulent activities.	(Xu et al., 2019)
	Tokenizing assets for fractional ownership and secure transactions.	Enables transparent and secure asset management through blockchain.	(Leekha, 2018)
Advertising	Ensuring ethical use of AI-generated content in campaigns.	Provides audit trails to verify compliance with ethical and legal standards.	(Bengesi et al., 2024)
	Tracking ad performance and revenue sharing	Automates royalty payments and ensures fair compensation for creators.	Mehrabi et al., 2021)
Gaming	Tokenizing in-game assets and ensuring secure ownership.	Enables players to own, trade, and monetize in-game assets securely.	(Solouki & Bamakan, 2022)
	Verifying AI-generated game content (e.g., characters, environments).	Ensuring authenticity and preventing unauthorized modifications.	(Kuye, 2023)
Publishing	Authenticating AI-generated books and articles.	Protects intellectual property and ensures content originality.	(Ryan et al., 2021)
	Automating royalty payments for authors and contributors.	Ensures fair revenue distribution through smart contracts.	(Cvetkovski, 2013)
Supply Chain	Verifying AI-generated supply chain analytics and reports.	Enhances transparency and trust in supply chain operations.	(Shekhar et al., 2023)
	Tokenizing supply chain assets for secure tracking.	Ensures traceability and reduces risks of fraud or counterfeiting.	(Xu et al., 2019)

Table 3 illustrates the diverse applications of blockAuth across industries, including media, education, healthcare, and finance, highlighting its potential to ensure content authenticity, secure ownership, and fair revenue sharing.

5. ETHICAL AND LEGAL CONSIDERATIONS

A number of ethical and legal issues are raised when generative AI systems for content production and dissemination include blockchain technology. Ensuring accountability, transparency and inclusivity is crucial from an ethical perspective. The decentralized structure of blockchain encourages traceability and verifiability, which are essential for tackling the problems of deepfakes and false information that are frequently connected to generative AI. However, moral conundrums could occur, such as the possible abuse of verifiable content to violate people's privacy or spread divisive viewpoints. Following moral precepts such as beneficence and non-maleficence is crucial to reducing these dangers (Floridi et al., 2018). In order to preserve society values, stakeholders must create frameworks that give user consent, data security and fair access a priority.

Legally speaking, laws controlling data privacy, intellectual property and the dissemination of digital material all interact with blockchain-driven frameworks. The immutability of blockchain presents issues with regulations like the General Data Protection Regulation (GDPR), which prioritizes the "right to be forgotten" (Voigt & von dem Bussche, 2017). Furthermore, generative AI raises complicated questions about intellectual property rights since it may not always be clear who wrote the content produced by AI. To handle these complexities and promote a balance between innovation and legal compliance, regulatory frameworks must change. Implementation is made more difficult by cross-jurisdictional issues, which need international cooperation and standardized regulations to guarantee the legal use of such systems while preserving human rights and encouraging moral AI practices.

5.1 Responsible AI Usage

Content creation has been transformed by the quick development of generative artificial intelligence (AI), which has made previously unheard-of levels of automation and inventiveness possible. But this advancement also brings up important issues with respect to data privacy, intellectual property protection, bias mitigation, authenticity, and ethical deployment. A promising option to allay these worries is by incorporating blockchain technology into generative AI systems, which ensures ethical AI use through accountability, transparency and safe distribution methods.

Transparency and Accountability

Transparency and Accountability are foundational principles of responsible AI usage. Generative AI models often operate as opaque systems, making it difficult to trace content origins and verify authenticity. Blockchain technology, with its immutable ledger and decentralized nature, can provide verifiable records of content creation and distribution. By recording metadata, including model version, data sources and content generation timestamps on a blockchain, stakeholders can trace the lineage of digital assets, ensuring accountability for AI-generated outputs (Zyskind et al., 2015). This transparency mitigates the risks of misinformation and deep fakes, fostering trust in digital content.

Ethical implementation and Bias Mitigation

Biases in training data have the potential to cause unfair or discriminating results from AI systems. By offering transparent access to datasets and model training parameters, a blockchain-driven system can aid in the mitigation of bias. Developers and auditors can examine the morality and equity of AI models by recording data provenance and model modifications on a public or consortium blockchain Mehrabi et al., 2021). This openness promotes socially responsible AI deployment by facilitating external audits to find and address biases and encouraging adherence to ethical AI standards.

Security and Privacy of Data

Ai systems' data privacy is a major challenge, especially when handling private or sensitive data. By using cryptographic techniques and decentralized data management, blockchain technology can improve data privacy. Smart contract implementation can control data access and usage, guaranteeing adherence to data protection laws and user consent (Xu et al., 2019). Furthermore, AI systems may validate data without disclosing sensitive information by using zero-knowledge proofs and other privacy-preserving techniques, which is in line with laws like the General Data Protection Regulation (GDPR).

Intellectual Property Protection and Content Authenticity

Concerns over content authenticity and intellectual property rights have grown as AI-generated material has proliferated. By timestamping and recording original works on an immutable ledger, blockchain helps protect intellectual property by offering verifiable evidence of production and ownership. In addition to preventing illegal use or duplication of digital assets, this approach aids authors in asserting their right (Koutroumpis et al., 2020). Additionally, content can be authenticated via digital watermarking and blockchain verification, guaranteeing its integrity and discouraging forgeries.

Safe Distribution of Content

In order to stop illegal access and piracy, digital content must be distributed securely. Smart contracts that automate access control and licensing make it possible for safe content sharing thanks to blockchain's decentralized infrastructure. To ensure just compensation and guard against illegal distribution, content creators might establish predetermined terms for usage rights, royalties and distribution. By empowering artists and preserving the integrity of content distribution channels, this strategy promotes a more egalitarian digital economy.

5.2 Legal Implications

Artificial Intelligence (AI) has evolved through three distinct phases: Artificial Narrow Intelligence (ANI), often referred to as weak AI; Artificial General Intelligence (AGI), which possesses capabilities akin to human intelligence; and Artificial Super Intelligence (ASI), designed to exceed human cognitive abilities. The impact of AI on human life extends far beyond simplifying tasks, significantly influencing lifestyle and behavioral patterns. Furthermore, AI has integrated into various aspects of human activities, including the legal sector. Since 2017, China has implemented AI technology to function as judges in digital cases, although its application remains limited and is still evolving. Similarly, in the UK, AI is utilized in the legal domain, particularly in civil law contexts such as product liability, where errors are often linked to the advanced intelligence embedded within the products. In Indonesia, the online legal platform "Hukum Online" has developed LIA (Legal Intelligence Assistant), an AI-powered tool designed to help users access legal information efficiently (Yunanto & Al Haq, 2024).

The application of AI in electronic transactions has expanded significantly, moving beyond its role as a simple data analysis tool. AI systems are now deeply embedded in various e-commerce platforms, offering personalized product suggestions, automating inventory management, and streamlining payment and shipping operations. Despite its numerous advantages, the integration of AI in electronic transactions also raises critical concerns that must be carefully examined. Among these, the legal implications of AI usage stand out as a particularly pressing issue. Within the realm of electronic transactions, challenges related to legal accountability, data privacy, equity, and ethical considerations have emerged as key areas requiring attention and resolution.

6. FUTURE DIRECTIONS

The era of generative AI has come with the unparalleled challenges and opportunities in content creation and distribution. In this regard, blockchain technology assumes a unique value proposition of maintaining data integrity, provenances, and carrying out secure transactions. The blockchain-driven framework for verifiable creation and secure distribution in generative AI lies in scalability, interoperability, and regulatory challenges, whereas trust and transparency are the most paramount things. This demand for verifiable digital content will increase more with the evolution of generative AI and shall require a framework that can handle a high volume of transactions efficiently. Scalability solutions, including layer-2 protocol and shredding will key to meeting those needs.

Interoperability across various platforms and blockchain will also be important for seamless integrations. Traditional protocols for metadata smart contracts, and provenances of content having to be developed so that the ecosystem gets adopted everywhere. Similarly, privacy-preserving mechanisms will help creators and users prove authenticity and ownership without compromising confidentiality thus, zero knowledge proof will be enhanced.

6.1 Scalable Blockchain Protocols

Blockchain offers clear records of creation and modification, immutable in nature. Future frameworks must be focused on the integration of DIDs and VCs to establish robust mechanisms of provenances. These tools will enhance transparency and accountability in generative AI systems. Scalable and energy-efficient blockchain solutions means that blockchain will have to evolve to sustain high transaction volumes without sacrificing speed and sustainability. Areas of potential improvement include layer-2 solution proof of stack consensus mechanism, and sharding.

AI and blockchain can work together to ensure verification of content. For example, AI tools trained in the detection of deep fakes of manipulated content can be combined with the immutable interface with each other with their protocols. The content is spread over various platforms and their interface, and much interoperability is needed. In the future the architecture should be cross-chain compatible and standardized to easily interface with each other with their protocol.

Future frameworks must focus on integrating Decentralized Identifiers (DIDs) and Verifiable Credentials (VCs) to establish robust provenance mechanisms while ensuring scalability and energy efficiency.

6.1.1 Layer-2 Solutions

Layer-2 solutions are essential for improving the scalability of blockAuth without compromising the security and decentralization of the underlying blockchain. These solutions enable faster and more cost-effective transactions by processing them off-chain while maintaining the integrity of the main blockchain.

- **Rollups:** Rollups bundle multiple transactions into a single batch, which is then recorded on the main blockchain. This reduces congestion and lowers transaction fees. For example, Optimistic Rollups and ZK-Rollups (Zero-Knowledge Rollups) can be integrated into blockAuth to handle high-volume content transaction efficiently.
- **Sidechains:** Sidechains are independent blockchains that run parallel to the main chain, allowing for customized rules and faster processing. blockAuth can leverage sidechains for specific use cases, such as high-frequency content licensing or royalty distribution.
- **Sharding:** Sharding divides the blockchain into smaller, more manageable pieces (shards), each capable of processing transactions independently. This approach can significantly enhance blockAuth's throughput and scalability.

6.1.2 Cross-Chain Compatibility

To achieve widespread adoption, blockAuth must ensure interoperability across multiple blockchain networks. Cross-chain compatibility allows seamless integration with platforms like Ethereum, Polkadot, and Solana, enabling users to leverage the strengths of different blockchains.

- **Cross-Chain Bridges:** These protocols facilitate the transfer of assets and data between blockchains. For example, blockAuth can use bridges like Polkadot's Substrate or Cosmos' Inter-Blockchain Communication (IBC) protocol to enable cross-chain transactions.
- **Standardized Protocols:** Developing standardized protocols for metadata, smart contracts, and provenance tracking will ensure that blockAuth's ecosystem can interface seamlessly with other platforms, fostering interoperability and adoption.

6.2 AI-Driven Governance Models

The advancement of generative AI has opened new vista for content creation, it has also raised very serious challenges about authenticity, provenance and trust. A blockchain-driven framework system can address these concerns by providing a secure and transparent system for verifiable content creation and distribution. By utilizing the immutable ledger of blockchain, we can develop a system where each content is cryptographically signed and linked to its original, providing total transparency and accountability. The framework can guarantee secure content distribution because decentralized storage combined with mechanisms of access control will reduce unauthorized access or manipulative risk. Smart contracts on the blockchain can automate royalty payments and licensing agreements therefore fairly compensating creators and fostering a more sustainable content ecosystem.

6.2.1 Real-Time Decision-Making

AI algorithms can analyze vast amounts of data in real time to support governance decisions. For example:

- **Content Moderation:** AI can detect and flag inappropriate or fraudulent content, ensuring that only genuine and compliant assets are distributed.
- **Dispute Resolution:** AI-powered arbitration systems can analyze evidence and provide fair resolutions to conflicts, reducing the need for manual intervention.

6.2.2 Predictive Analytics

AI can leverage historical data to predict trends and optimize blockchain operations:

- **Royalty Distribution:** Predictive models can forecast revenue streams and optimize royalty distribution schedules, ensuring timely and fair compensation for creators.
- **Resource Allocation:** AI can analyze network activity to allocate resources efficiently, improving scalability and performance.

6.2.3 Decentralized Autonomous Organizations (DAOs)

blockAuth can implement DAOs to enable community-driven governance. AI can enhance DAO operations by:

- **Voting Mechanisms:** AI can analyze voting patterns and provide insights to improve decision-making process.
- **Transparency and Accountability:** AI can monitor DAO activities and ensure compliance with predefined rules, fostering trust among stakeholders.

6.3 Integration with Emerging Technologies

Emerging technologies like IoT, blockchain, and robotics complement generative AI by providing critical infrastructure for real-time tracking, enhanced transparency, and increased automation. IoT devices enable supply chain stakeholders to track goods, monitor conditions, and predict potential disruptions with unprecedented accuracy. Blockchain offers a secure, transparent platform for transactions and data sharing, helping to build trust across the entire supply chain. Meanwhile, robotics and automation are revolutionizing warehouses, distribution centers, and transportation networks, reducing labor costs, minimizing errors, and improving speed and precision. While the potential of these technologies is immense, there are also significant challenges to their adoption. Data privacy and security concerns, integration complexities with legacy systems, and the need for skilled labor to manage and operate these technologies are some of the barrier's businesses must navigate. Additionally, the ethical considerations surrounding AI usage and automation in the workforce are also topics of growing concern (Shekhar et al., 2023).

6.3.1 IoT Integration

IoT devices can provide real-time data that enhances content verification and tracking:

- **Provenance Tracking:** IoT sensors can monitor the physical conditions of goods (e.g., artwork, collectibles) and record this data on the blockchain, ensuring authenticity and traceability.
- **Smart Contracts:** IoT data can trigger smart contracts automatically. For example, a sensor detecting the delivery of a physical asset can release payment to the creator.

6.3.2 5G and Edge Computing

The combination of 5G and edge computing can enable real-time content verification and distribution:

- **High-Speed Transactions:** 5G networks provide the bandwidth needed for fast and seamless blockchain transactions, enhancing user experience.
- **Edge Computing:** By processing data closer to the source, edge computing reduces latency and improves the efficiency of content verification and distribution.

6.3.3 Privacy-Preserving Mechanisms

To address privacy concerns, blockAuth can integrate advanced cryptographic techniques:

- **Zero-Knowledge Proofs (ZKPs):** ZKPs allow suers to prove the authenticity and ownership of content without revealing sensitive information, ensuring confidentiality.
- **Homomorphic Encryption:** This technique enables computations on encrypted data, allowing for secure and private content verification.

6.4 Ethical and Regulatory Considerations

As blockAuth evolves, it must address ethical and regulatory challenges to ensure responsible and sustainable growth.

6.4.1 Data Privacy and Security

blockAuth must prioritize data privacy and security to protect user information and maintain trust:

- **Compliance with Regulations:** Ensure adherence to data protection laws such as GDPR and CCPA.
- **Secure Storage:** Use decentralized storage solutions and encryption to safeguard sensitive data.

6.4.2 Ethical AI Usage

AI algorithms must be designed and deployed ethically to avoid bias and discrimination:

- **Bias Mitigation:** Implement fairness-aware algorithms to ensure equitable outcomes.
- **Transparency:** Provide clear explanations of AI-driven decisions to build trust among users.

6.4.3 Workforce Impact

The adoption of AI and automation may disrupt traditional workflows:

- **Reskilling Programs:** Offer training programs to help creators and stakeholders adapt to new technologies.
- **Ethical Automation:** Ensure that automation complements human creativity rather than replacing it.

6.5 Vision for the Future

The future blockAuth lies in its ability to adapt to the evolving landscape of generative AI and blockchain technologies. By focusing on scalability, interoperability, AI-driven governance, and integration with emerging technologies, blockAuth can establish itself as a trusted and innovative framework for verifiable content creation and distribution. This vision includes:

- **Global Adoption:** Expanding blockAuth's reach to creators, distributors, and consumers worldwide.

- **Sustainable Growth:** Leveraging energy-efficient solutions and ethical practices to ensure long-term sustainability.
- **Empowering Creators:** Providing creators with the tools and resources they need to thrive in the digital content ecosystem.

7. CONCLUSION

The blockAuth framework represents a groundbreaking approach to addressing the critical challenges posed by the intersection of multimodal generative AI and blockchain technology in the digital media ecosystem. By leveraging blockchain's decentralized and immutable ledger with the creative potential of generative AI, blockAuth establishes a secure, transparent, and efficient system for content creation, authentication, distribution, and monetization.

This framework demonstrates its value through several key innovations. The Content Layer ensures that AI-generated content is embedded with verifiable metadata, establishing authenticity and traceability from the moment of creation. The Blockchain Layer provides robust security and automates processes like licensing and royalty distribution via smart contracts, while the Provenance Tracker ensures that the lifecycle of digital assets is auditable and tamper-proof. Finally, the Application Layer bridges technology with usability, offering tools and interfaces for seamless interaction by creators, distributors, and consumers.

blockAuth has the potential to transform industries reliant on digital content, including media, entertainment, education, and advertising. Its applications in combating deep fakes, ensuring ethical AI usage, facilitating fair revenue sharing, and addressing intellectual property concerns underscore its importance in fostering trust, transparency, and equity in the digital economy. Furthermore, its support for tokenization and decentralized collaboration provides creators with innovative monetization opportunities, while also empowering consumers with verifiable content.

As technology continues to evolve, the challenges of scalability, interoperability, and regulatory compliance will need to be addressed. Advancements such as layer-2 blockchain protocols, zero-knowledge proofs, and AI-driven governance models will be essential to enhancing blockAuth's scalability, privacy, and adaptability. Collaborative efforts across industries and governments will also play a critical role in establishing the legal and ethical standards necessary for widespread adoption.

In conclusion, blockAuth offers a forward-looking solution that bridges the technological and ethical gaps in digital content ecosystems. By providing a robust framework for authenticity, accountability, and equitable distribution, it paves the way for a sustainable and secure digital future. This framework is not just a technological innovation but a paradigm shifts toward fostering trust and responsibility in the age of generative AI and blockchain integration.

REFERENCES

Aichroth, P., Cuccovillo, L., & Gerhardt, M. (2021). Audio Forensics and provenance analysis: Technologies for media verification and asset management. *Journal of Digital Media Management, 9*(4), 348. DOI: 10.69554/CEXG6223

Ali Linkon, A., Shaima, M., & Uddin Sarker, M. S. (2024). Advancements and applications of generative artificial intelligence and large language models on Business Management: A comprehensive review. *Journal of Computer Science and Technology Studies, 6*(1), 225–232. DOI: 10.32996/jcsts.2024.6.1.26

Alkhard, A. (2024). Leveraging Digital Asset Management and meta-data integration for enhanced asset management. *Construction Economics and Building, 24*(3). DOI: 10.5130/AJCEB.v24i3.8741

Angelova, M. (2019). Application of blockchain technology in the cultural and Creative Industries. *2019 II International Conference on High Technology for Sustainable Development (HiTech)*, 1–4. DOI: 10.1109/HiTech48507.2019.9128267

Banerjee, P., Govindarajan, C., Jayachandran, P., & Ruj, S. (2020). Reliable, fair and decentralized marketplace for content sharing using blockchain. *2020 IEEE International Conference on Blockchain (Blockchain)*, 365–370. DOI: 10.1109/Blockchain50366.2020.00053

Bengesi, S., El-Sayed, H., Sarker, M. K., Houkpati, Y., Irungu, J., & Oladunni, T. (2024). Advancements in generative AI: A comprehensive review of gans, GPT, autoencoders, diffusion model, and Transformers. *IEEE Access : Practical Innovations, Open Solutions, 12*, 69812–69837. DOI: 10.1109/ACCESS.2024.3397775

Bitcoin: A peer-to-peer electronic cash system. (n.d.). https://bitcoin.org/bitcoin.pdf

Chen, H., Wang, X., Zhou, Y., Huang, B., Zhang, Y., Feng, W., Zhu, W. (2024). Multi-modal generative ai: Multi-modal llm, diffusion and beyond. arXiv preprint arXiv:2409.14993.

Chevalier, M. (2021). From smart contract litigation to Blockchain Arbitration, a new decentralized approach leading towards the blockchain arbitral order. *Journal of International Dispute Settlement, 12*(4), 558–584. DOI: 10.1093/jnlids/idab025

Cvetkovski, T. (2013). Copyright developments in popular media: Doctrinal and statutory challenges. Copyright and Popular Media, 121–142. DOI: 10.1057/9781137024602_4

Floridi, L., Cowls, J., Beltrametti, M., Chatila, R., Chazerand, P., Dignum, V., & Vayena, E. (2018). An Ethical Framework for a Good AI Society: Opportunities, Risks, Principles, and Recommendations. DOI: 10.31235/osf.io/2hfsc

G, A. K., A, H., & Sasikala, M. D. (2018). Avoiding data piracy in artworks using blockchain. International Journal of Trend in Scientific Research and Development, Volume-2(Issue-3), 1005–1012. DOI: 10.31142/ijtsrd11244

Haq, S. A., & Yunanto, Y. (2024, May). Yunanto2, Syaif Al Haq1. "Legal Implications of Using Artificial Intelligence (AI) Technology in Electronic Transactions.". *International Journal of Social Science and Human Research*, *07*(05), 2024. DOI: 10.47191/ijsshr/v7-i05-108

Hasan, H. R., & Salah, K. (2018). Proof of delivery of digital assets using blockchain and smart contracts. *IEEE Access : Practical Innovations, Open Solutions*, *6*, 65439–65448. DOI: 10.1109/ACCESS.2018.2876971

Hegnauer, T. (2019). Design and development of a blockchain interoperability api. Zürich, Switzerland, February.

Kaur, A., Noori Hoshyar, A., Saikrishna, V., Firmin, S., & Xia, F. (2024). Deepfake video detection: Challenges and opportunities. *Artificial Intelligence Review*, *57*(6), 159. DOI: 10.1007/s10462-024-10810-6

Kearns, L., Alam, A., & Allison, J. (2023). Synthetic Media Authentication Threats: Detection Using a Combination of Neural Network and Blockchain Technology. DOI: 10.2139/ssrn.4658121

Koutroumpis, P., Leiponen, A., & Thomas, L. D. (2020). Markets for data. *Industrial and Corporate Change*, *29*(3), 645–660. DOI: 10.1093/icc/dtaa002

Kumar, S., Musharaf, D., Musharaf, S., & Sagar, A. K. (2023). A comprehensive review of the latest advancements in large generative AI models. *Communications in Computer and Information Science*, *1920*, 90–103. DOI: 10.1007/978-3-031-45121-8_9

Kuye, A. (2023). Blockchain ecosystem governance frameworks: Unlocking the value of blockchain ecosystems. SSRN Electronic Journal. DOI: 10.2139/ssrn.4590414

Leekha, S. (2018). Book review: Don Tapscott and Alex Tapscott, blockchain revolution: How the technology behind Bitcoin is changing money, business, and the world. *FIIB Business Review*, *7*(4), 275–276. DOI: 10.1177/2319714518814603

Luo, H., Luo, J., & Vasilakos, A. V. (2023). Bc4llm: Trusted artificial intelligence when blockchain meets large language models. arXiv preprint arXiv:2310.06278.

Malik, N., Wei, Y., Appel, G., & Luo, L. (2023). Blockchain technology for Creative Industries: Current State and Research Opportunities. *International Journal of Research in Marketing*, *40*(1), 38–48. DOI: 10.1016/j.ijresmar.2022.07.004

Mehrabi, N., Morstatter, F., Saxena, N., Lerman, K., & Galstyan, A. (2021). A survey on bias and fairness in machine learning. *ACM Computing Surveys*, *54*(6), 1–35. DOI: 10.1145/3457607

Nakamoto, S. (2008). *Bitcoin: A peer-to-peer electronic cash system*. Satoshi Nakamoto.

Pal, A.Ashutosh Pal Singh. (2024). Safeguarding authenticity in the Digital Realm: A holistic approach integrating content provenance, secure watermarking, and transparent labeling to combat deepfakes. *International Journal For Multidisciplinary Research*, *6*(3), 21580. DOI: 10.36948/ijfmr.2024.v06i03.21580

Portillo, N. (2024a). Bitcoin: A Peer-to-Peer Electronic Cash System. DOI: 10.2139/ssrn.4993270

Rana, M. S., Nobi, M. N., Murali, B., & Sung, A. H. (2022). Deepfake detection: A systematic literature review. *IEEE Access : Practical Innovations, Open Solutions*, *10*, 25494–25513. DOI: 10.1109/ACCESS.2022.3154404

Ryan, M. D., Macrossan, P., Wright, S., & Adams, M. (2021). Blockchain and publishing: Towards a publisher-centred distributed ledger for the Book Publishing Industry. *Creative Industries Journal*, *16*(1), 2–21. DOI: 10.1080/17510694.2021.1939541

Shekhar, A., Prabhat, P., Yandrapalli, V., Umar, S., Abdul, F., & Wakjira, W. D. (2023). Generative AI in Supply Chain Management.

Solouki, M., & Bamakan, S. M. (2022). An in-depth insight at digital ownership through dynamic nfts. *Procedia Computer Science*, *214*, 875–882. DOI: 10.1016/j.procs.2022.11.254

Varadarajan, M. N., & Seeni, S. K. (2024). Innovative Digital ownership and collectibles via proof of stake (POS) and non-fungible tokens (NFTS). *INTERNATIONAL JOURNAL OF ADVANCES IN SIGNAL AND IMAGE SCIENCES*, *10*(1), 22–34. DOI: 10.29284/IJASIS.10.1.2024.22-34

Voigt, P., & von dem Bussche, A. (2017). *The EU General Data Protection Regulation*. GDPR., DOI: 10.1007/978-3-319-57959-7

Wright, C. S. (2008). Bitcoin: A peer-to-peer electronic cash system. SSRN Electronic Journal, 3440802, 10-2139.

Xu, X., Weber, I., & Staples, M. (2019). Architecture for Blockchain Applications. DOI: 10.1007/978-3-030-03035-3

Yang, F., Abedin, M. Z., Qiao, Y., & Ye, L. (2024). Towards Trustworthy Governance of AI-Generated Content (AIGC): A Blockchain-Driven Regulatory Framework for Secure Digital Ecosystems. *IEEE Transactions on Engineering Management, 71,* 14945–14962. DOI: 10.1109/TEM.2024.3472292

Yazdinejad, A., Parizi, R. M., Srivastava, G., & Dehghantanha, A. (2020). Making sense of blockchain for AI deepfakes technology. 2020 IEEE Globecom Workshops (GC Wkshps, 1–6. DOI: 10.1109/GCWkshps50303.2020.9367545

Zyskind, G., Nathan, O., & Pentland, A. (2015). Decentralizing privacy: Using blockchain to protect personal data. 2015 IEEE Security and Privacy Workshops, 180–184. DOI: 10.1109/SPW.2015.27

Chapter 5
TrustChain:
AI-Powered Fact-Checking Systems Secured by Blockchain Technology

Suresh Raj Sharma
https://orcid.org/0009-0009-0722-545X
Tribhuvan University, Nepal

Naresh Kshetri
Rochester Institute of Technology, USA

Sobaraj Poudel Paudel
Tribhuvan University, Nepal

Bishwo Prakash Pokharel
https://orcid.org/0000-0001-6516-2105
Sault College of Applied Arts and Technology, Canada

ABSTRACT

AI-powered fact-checking systems, secured by blockchain technology, represent a transformative approach to combating misinformation in the digital age. Leveraging advanced artificial intelligence (AI) algorithms, particularly natural language processing (NLP), these systems efficiently analyze vast datasets to verify claims in real time. The integration of blockchain ensures data immutability, transparency, and security, enhancing trust in the fact-checking process. This convergence addresses the limitations of traditional fact-checking methods, which often fail to keep pace with the rapid spread of false information. By enabling real-time claim verification, monitoring live events, and predicting misinformation trends, AI-powered systems provide a critical tool for journalists and content creators to combat disinformation

DOI: 10.4018/979-8-3373-6481-0.ch005

effectively. Blockchain further reinforces the integrity of the verification process by maintaining tamper-proof audit trails, fostering accountability, and ensuring the delivery of trustworthy information.

1. INTRODUCTION

AI is the simulation of human intelligence into a machine that can be programmed to think and act like a human (Fetzer, 2002). This involves the developing algorithm and technologies that enable computers to perform tasks that would ordinarily need human cognitive abilities, such as thinking, learning, problem solving perception, and decision making. By mimicking aspects of the human mind, AI systems can assess data, draw conclusions and take action. These systems are supposed to learn from data adapted to new inputs, and improve performance over time. AI-powered fact-checking refers to using artificial intelligence technologies to verify the accuracy of claims, detect misinformation, and assess the credibility of information. By leveraging natural language processing (NLP), machine learning, and data retrieval techniques, AI can analyze text, multimedia, and source data at scale, cross-referencing claims with reliable databases and identifying inconsistencies. AI also enhances the detection of patterns in fake news, manipulated media, and viral deception enabling faster and more efficient fact-checking compared to traditional data and methods. While not without challenges, such as bias in training data and contextual limitations, AI offers powerful tools to combat misinformation and promote informed decision-making.

Blockchain technology is a distributed ledger system designed to record, store, and share information securely, transparently, and immutably. Its unique characteristics make it a promising tool for addressing challenges in fact-checking, particularly in verifying the authenticity and integrity of information. Blockchain is a decentralized database that operates on a network of computers. It consists of a chain of blocks, where each block contains a set of data, a timestamp, and a cryptographic hash of the previous block. This structure ensures that data cannot be altered retroactively without consensus from the network participants (Sharma & Kshetri, 2025). The key features of blockchain (Kshetri et al., 2023) are as:

- **Decentralization:** The system operates without a central authority, making it resistant to tampering or manipulation of the content. Decentralization in blockchain technology distributes control and decision making over a network of nodes, preventing a single central authority from wielding complete power. This framework prevents censorship, tampering, or manipulation, improving system dependability and integrity. Nodes keep copies of ledger, and consensus algorithms like Proof-of-Work (PoW), or Proof of Stack (PoS), validate transactions, removing single points of failure and mitigating corruption concerns.

- **Transparency:** Every transaction or record is accessible to all participants, promoting accountability. Transparency in the blockchain system is making all transactions or records publicly accessible and timestamped, resulting in a verifiable and chronological chain of data. This transparency enables stakeholders to independently check and audit information, fostering trust and accountability. Transparency is especially advantageous in areas like supply chain management, financial systems, and governance since it discourages fraud and allows for real-time monitoring.
- **Immutability:** Data recorded on the blockchain is permanent and cannot be altered or removed. Immutability in blockchain technology implies that once recorded, data cannot be changed, destroyed or interfered with. This is accomplished via cryptographic hashing and consensus procedures, which make modifications nearly difficult without affecting all following blocks and obtaining network consensus. Immutability is critical for applications such as ledger contracts as it ensures that past data is permanent and unchanged.
- **Trackable**: content can be tracked throughout its lifecycle on a blockchain, which is especially beneficial for copyright protection. This ensure that creators receive recognition and compensation for their works
- **Smart contracts**: smart contracts are self-executing agreements where the terms are directly embedded in code. They can automate permissions and access to content, such as automatically enforcing agreements or managing royalty payments.
- **Enhance security**: blockchain employs advanced cryptographic techniques to secure data, providing an extra layer of security compared to traditional database systems that might be more susceptible.

Table 1. Key feature of blockchain and generative AI use in digital media

Feature	Blockchain Technology	Generative AI	Synergy Potential in Digital Media
Decentralization	Has no direct influence from particular authority, minimizes the risk of manipulation or censorship. By utilizing a network of interconnected nodes, it reduces a single point of failure.	Produce content on their own, rather than relying on human intervention.	The decentralized nature of blockchain can support generative AI by ensuring the safe production and distribution of AI-generated content which will give creators more power and fairness.
Transparency	All transactions and records are openly accessible, verifiable and timestamped.	It's crucial that AI models and their decisions are understandable and subject to audit.	The transparent nature of blockchain can facilitate the tracking and verification of generative AI output, thereby enhancing accountability in AI-generated content.
Immutability	Data is unchangeable once it is recorded, guaranteeing its fidelity.	The ability of AI systems to maintain content quality and consistency over time is advantageous.	By utilizing blockchain, generative AI are made available with the ability to be unaltered and verified for copyright purposes as well as proof of authorship.
Trackable	Content can be traced throughout its lifecycle, enabling creators to receive credit and rewards.	Generative tracking is the technique that allows AI to track content creation, but it may not provide attribution mechanisms.	By tracking that content lifecycle, blockchain can assist generative AI in assigning and compensating digital media creators appropriately. This is an essential aspect of artificial intelligence.
Smart Contracts	Automates the management of agreements and processes, including access control and royalty distribution.	Automation-driven, generative AI can create, edit and personalize content automatically.	The integration of blockchain's smart contracts with AI could enable the management of content rights, automate royalty payments, or regulate access based on AI-generated media.
Enhance Security	Employees cryptographical techniques to shield data guaranteeing maximum protections against manipulation.	To prevents tampering and adversarial attacks, it is essential create secure environment for AI models	Blockchain's enhanced security can shield generative AI models from hacking, guaranteeing the authenticity and validity of AI generated content.

Social media has revolutionized communication and amplified the spread of fake news -false information posing a legitimate -and viral deception, the intentional dissemination of misinformation. These challenges, facilitated by social platforms, have significant societal impacts (Yadav, 2023). Relate to innovative approaches that utilize artificial intelligence (AI) and blockchain technology to enhance the verification of information, thereby combating the dissemination of false information. As misinformation continuously poses significant challenges to media trustworthiness and public faith, these systems have attracted considerable attention in journalism and various other domains. The fusion of AI's analytical capabilities and blockchain's immutable records creates a transparent, effective, and trustworthy method for validating information. The use of AI in fact-checking utilizes advanced techniques such as natural language processing (NLP) and machine learning (ML) to automate the verification of claims by rapidly analyzing extensive datasets. Blockchain technology is reshaping content creation and fact-deductions by facilitating secure, decentralized management of the content and promoting transparent tamper-proof recording keeping (Sharma et al., 2025).

1.1 Problem Statement

Problems of the TrustChain framework model are as follows:

- **The inability of Traditional Fact-Checking Methods to Keep Pace with Misinformation:** Traditional approaches to fact-checking are too slow to address the rapid spread of false information in the digital age, leaving a gap in real-time claim verification.
- **Challenges in Ensuring Data Integrity and Trustworthiness:** Establishing trust in the fact-checking process is hindered by the lack of mechanisms to guarantee data immutability, transparency, and security.
- **Insufficient Tools for Monitoring and Predicting Misinformation Trends:** Journalists and content creators face difficulties in effectively tracking live events and anticipating disinformation campaigns, limiting their ability to combat misinformation proactively.

1.2 Traditional Fact-Checking and Its Limitations

Traditional fact-checking systems are very time-consuming, require in-depth knowledge, and require advanced research, which hinders the growth of journalists (Zubiaga et al., 2018). Traditional fact-checking methods are frequently criticized for taking up a lot of time and resources. These techniques entail a meticulous process of filtering through vast amounts of data to ensure the correctness of assertions. This work frequently required journalists to have extensive expertise in a variety of subjects including history, politics, and science. Furthermore, efficient fact-checking necessitates advanced research skills such as accessing reputable databases, reviewing sources, and engaging subject matter experts.

Traditional fact-checking is a systematic approach used to verify the accuracy of information, ensuring it aligns with facts and credible sources. Below is an overview of the process:

Identifying Claims: Fact-checking begins with identifying statements of information that need verification. These could include news articles, social media posts, public speeches, or advertisements. Clams that are widely shared, controversial, or have significant societal impact are often prioritized (Graves, 2016).

Contextual Analysis: Fact-checking examines the context in which the claim was made, considering the source of the information, the intent, and the circumstances. This helps in understanding the scope and relevance of the claim (Amazeen, 2015).

Consulting Primary and Secondary Sources: Fact-checking relies on reputable primary sources, such as government databases, scientific studies, and official records, to validate claims. They may also use secondary information such as expert opinions, research papers, and credible media outlets, to provide additional context or support (Nyhan & Reifler, 2015).

1.3 Objectives of the TrustChain Framework

The TrustChain Framework's main objective is to enhance the AI power to check misinformation using blockchain.

- **Enable Real-Time Claim Verification:** Utilize AI-powered fact-checking systems to analyze claims in real time, enhancing the ability to combat misinformation as it spreads.
- **Enhance Trust and Security:** Integrate blockchain technology to ensure data immutability, transparency, and security, thereby increasing trust in the fact-checking process.
- **Provides Tools for Monitoring and Predicting Misinformation Trends:** Offer critical resources for journalists and content creators to effectively monitor live events and anticipate misinformation trends, improving their capacity to address disinformation.

2. LITERATURE REVIEW

AI-driven fact-checking tools utilize sophisticated algorithms to assess the credibility of content. For instance, platforms like Fact insect employ AI to compare text content against information from selected, trustworthy sources, facilitating the identification of false or misleading information. The authors in (Shae & Tsai, 2019) propose a blockchain platform resembling a social media platform where news posted by publishers is analyzed by AI. This setup facilitates tracking the source and propagation of news as all content remains within the platform. An incentive-aware blockchain solution using a customized Proof-of-Authority (PoA) protocol is presented. News organizations must register to publish news on the blockchain, and nodes represented by news publishers handle news validation (Bu incu & Alexandrescu, 2023). The growing user base of social networks has enhanced the reach and impact of information exchange. While these platforms support freedom of speech and censorship-resistant communication, they also pose challenges, particularly with the spread of fake news. Malicious users propagate misinformation by altering authentic news content, misleading others into believing false narratives.

Later studies that have been carried out have highlighted the relationship between blockchain technology and AI in development of safe fact-checking and decision-making systems (Picha Edwardsson & Al-Saqaf, 2022). Hyperledger fabric was used to develop a Protocol for a global fact-checking. Their conclusion is that, while this can be done, blockchain technology is still not ready for the real-world application of fact checking because of its cost and complexity (Panda et al., 2020). Blockchain could provide benefits in terms of security and efficiency for AI. The Integrated framework, combining AI with blockchain ABC-verify, which aims at tweet misinformation detection, was developed by (Zen, 2021) and achieved 93% Accuracy in the classification.

The constructed framework utilizes a BERT model and Proof-of-Stack smart contracts on Ethereum (Alrubei et al., 2020). Presented the architecture that encompasses the collaboration of edge computing, AI, and the blockchain into a secure space for data processing and sharing for IoT applications using Honesty-Based Distribution Proof Of Work consensus mechanism. All the studies have the possible improvement in fact-checking processes and secure decision-making using the combination of blockchain with AI in different areas.

A potential solution is using a central authority to regulate information flow, but this conflicts with the decentralized and open nature of social networks. Instead, blockchain technology offers a promising decentralized approach. It enables consensus in untrustworthy environments and can serve as a consent-driven repository for authentic news, helping to address the issue of fake news (Saad et al., 2019).

2.1 Evolution of Fact-Checking Mechanisms

The evolution of fact-checking mechanisms is the interplay between truth and fiction in narratives, drawing on Jorge Luis Borges' story "Emma Zunz" which demonstrates how narratives, even partially or entirely fabricated, can be perceived as "essentially true" if they resonate with audiences. It underscores the centrality of storytelling in human culture, from ancient myths to modern narratives. Serving purposes like communication, identity formation, empathy cultivation, knowledge transmission, decision-making, and persuasion. These stories not only reflect reality but also shape it (Bragazzi & Garbarino, 2024). However, the text also highlights the risks of misinformation, noting that despite advanced verification tools, false news persists and spreads rapidly in the digital age. Current research often treats misinformation as static and irritating, which oversimplifies its evolving nature and limits understanding of why it endures. This perspective neglects the dynamic processes by which misinformation is created, disseminated, and transformed, leaving gaps in addressing its societal impacts.

Misinformation is a clear contradiction from an evolutionary perspective. Even though it is toxic and detrimental to society, it continues and grows. Evolutionary thoughts predict that detrimental aspects should diminish or disappear over time; nevertheless, misinformation defies this notation by flourishing and adapting, even in situations with systems in place to identify and destroy it. This resilience means that deception may be adaptive, allowing it to endure and spread despite its detrimental effects on individuals and society.

2.2 AI in Fact-Checking

The rise of misinformation in the digital age has increased the need for effective fact-checking. AI plays a vital role by providing scalable and automated solutions to verify claims and counter false information. AI uses structured knowledge bases like Wiki data to verify claims against reliable data and approaches like FEVER enable reasoning by connecting claims to trusted sources through knowledge graphs (Thorne et al., 2018). Fighting false information, which has proliferated due to the expansion of digital media, requires fact-checking. In this field, artificial intelligence (AI) is increasingly being used to automate and enhance the accuracy and efficacy of fraudulent claim detection. AI-powered tools analyze information, verify claims, and provide factual proof using Natural Language Processing (NLP), machine learning (ML), and knowledge graphs.

2.3 Blockchain for Data Integrity

The spread of false information in the digital age has made strong fact-checking systems necessary. AI-powered fact-checking tools have become increasingly potent, using machine learning algorithms to swiftly and effectively validate material. However, these systems have problems with data manipulation, accountability, and openness. These problems are resolved by incorporating blockchain technology into these systems, guaranteeing data integrity, immutability, and trust. Blockchain functions as a decentralized ledger that securely and irrevocably stores data. To create a transparent and impenetrable chain of records, a network of nodes validates every transaction or data entry before being added to a block (Nakamoto, 2008). Blockchain can hold validated claims, information, and fact-checking procedures in AI-powered fact-checking systems. Trust in fact-checking systems is based on transparency. All system actions have auditable traces thanks to blockchain technology. Users can track the source of a fact-check, including the technique, the dataset, and the choices made by the AI model. By improving accountability, this traceability increases the system's credibility (Tapscott & Tapscott, 2016). Additionally, decentralized fact-checking systems with numerous independent nodes validating and verifying facts can be made possible by blockchain technology. This decentralized strategy reduces the possibility of prejudice and abuse of central authority. Accurate, objective, and reliable fact-checking is ensured by fusing blockchain security with AI's speed and efficiency. Despite its advantages, blockchain integration with AI-powered systems still presents difficulties. Because blockchain processes need a large amount of processing resources, scalability is a major challenge.

2.4 Existing AI-Blockchain Integration Efforts

The integration of artificial intelligence (AI) and blockchain technology has shown promising potential in addressing challenges related to misinformation and data integrity. Recent advancements highlight how these technologies can complement each other to enhance security, transparency, and efficiency in fact-checking systems.

One notable example is the development of Decentralized Autonomous Organizations (DAOs) for content validation, where AI algorithms evaluate claims while blockchain ensures that the results are securely stored and publicly accessible. Such models enable a collaborative ecosystem where stakeholders contribute to fact-checking through a trustless infrastructure (Kim et al., 2019).

The integration of AI and blockchain technology, particularly in AI-powered fact-checking system, creates a powerful synergy that enhances transparency, trust, and accountability in information verification. AI systems leverage machine learning (ML) and natural language processing (NLP) to automate verification, analysis context, and provide real-time fact-checking, which is critical in combating misinformation. However, AI faces challenges such as bias, lack of transparency and data integrity issues.

Furthermore, blockchain-based platforms like DeepFact employ AI for misinformation detection, integrating machine learning models to identify fake content in real time. This platform uses blockchain for maintaining tamper-proof records of validated claims, ensuring that verified information remains accessible and trustworthy (Alisha & Krishna, 2024).

Another significant effort is the creation of AI-integrated smart contracts. These contracts automate workflows such as claim submission, verification, and dissemination, reducing human intervention and increasing system reliability. For instance, in the Block Verify framework, AI assesses claims and assigns confidence scores, while smart contracts automate the rewards for validators participating in the consensus process (Nguyen et al., 2018).

Despite these advancements, challenges persist. The scalability problem remains a major limitation, particularly as both AI and blockchain systems demand substantial computational resources. Researchers have proposed solutions like Layer-2 scaling techniques, such as state channels and rollups, to address these issues. Additionally, efforts to create interoperable frameworks, where multiple blockchains and AI models can collaborate seamlessly, are gaining traction (Kuznetsov et al., 2024).

The fusion of AI and blockchain is not limited to fact-checking alone but extends to other domains, such as combating medical misinformation and ensuring data provenance in supply chains. These efforts demonstrate the versatility and transformative potential of combining these technologies, provided challenges like scalability and energy efficiency are adequately addressed.

2.5 Methodology

The methodology for integrating AI and blockchain in fact-checking systems has been explored in several studies (Shae & Tsai, 2019; Bu incu & Alexandrescu, 2023; Nakamoto, 2008) which highlight different theoretical and practical frameworks. AI-driven tools, like Fact insect, utilize sophisticated algorithms to compare text content with trustworthy sources, facilitating the identification of false or misleading information. These systems employ advanced natural language processing (NLP) and machine learning (ML) techniques to automate the verification of claims at scale, offering faster and more efficient solutions compared to traditional methods.

Furthermore, various blockchain solutions, including Proof-of-Authority (PoA) protocols, have been suggested to enhance fact-checking systems. These protocols require news organizations to register and validate content through blockchain nodes, which are operated by the publishers themselves, ensuring that the information remains secure and credible throughout the verification process. Blockchain's inherent features, such as decentralization and immutability, are particularly valuable in combating the spread of fake news by providing a tamper-proof system where all actions are auditable, thereby promoting transparency in the verification process.

Overall, the integration of blockchain with AI in fact-checking offers a promising solution to misinformation, though practical hurdles such as scalability, efficiency, and interoperability must be addressed before these systems can be widely deployed. Studies explore AI and blockchain integration in fact-checking, using AI tools like Fact insect with NLP and ML to verify claims efficiently. Blockchain solutions, such as PoA protocol, enhance credibility by enabling secure, transparent content validation through decentralized, immutable systems, combating fake news and ensuring trustworthy information dissemination.

3. TRUSTCHAIN FRAMEWORK

TrustChain Framework integrates AI-powered fact-checking with blockchain technology to create a reliable, transparent, and secure system for combating misinformation. As misinformation spreads rapidly across digital platforms, the need for trustworthy verification mechanisms has never been more critical. The TrustChain framework offers a solution that harnesses the strengths of Artificial Intelligence (AI) and blockchain to address the challenges posed by false information in the digital age.

When AI combined, AI and blockchain from a robust fact-checking ecosystem. AI verifies information, while blockchain securely stores verified data, certifies credible sources and provides an auditable process for transparency. This integration is particularly effective in combating deepfakes, as AI detects manipulated media and blockchain stores original, unaltered content for references. Uses cases include news verification, social media fact-checking academic research and combating misinformation in different communication ways.

3.1 System Overview

The TrustChain Framework is composed of three primary components that interact with each other to facilitate efficient and accurate claim verification:

- **AI Fact-Checking Module:** This module uses advanced AI algorithms to process claims, analyze their veracity, and predict misinformation trends. It employs Natural Language Processing (NLP), Machine Learning (ML) models, and knowledge graphs to evaluate claims in real-time. Also check the facts using the scenery of different algorithms combined in blockchain.

- **Blockchain Infrastructure:** The blockchain component is responsible for validating the AI's findings through a decentralized consensus mechanism. It stores all verified data immutably, ensuring that information cannot be tampered with and is publicly transparent. The data and facts related to given content stored in different ledges, formed the blockchain.
- **Smart Contract Automation:** Smart contracts govern the flow of data, automate workflows, and facilitate the secure dissemination of verified information. They also include incentivization mechanisms to reward blockchain validators.

Together, these components create a seamless, secure, and efficient system that verifies claims in real time and ensures transparency throughout the verification process.

Figure 1. TrustChain framework

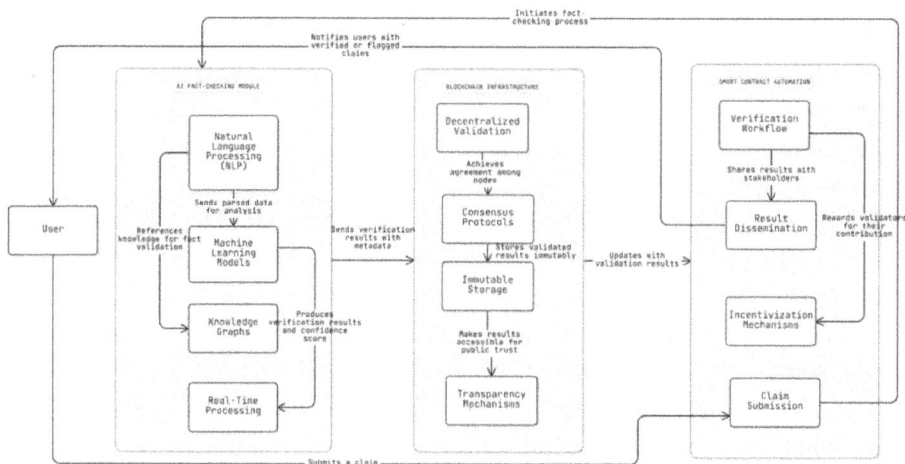

3.2 AI-Powered Fact-Checking Module

The AI Fact-Checking Module forms the core of the TrustChain Framework, responsible for analyzing, processing, and verifying claims quickly and accurately. The module uses a combination of Natural Language Processing (NLP), Machine Learning (ML), and Knowledge Graphs to evaluate claims and provide a confidence score for their veracity.

- **Natural Language Processing (NLP):** NLP techniques are employed to extract meaning from a claim, identify entities and relationships, and contextualize the information. By analyzing the language structure and semantics, NLP helps determine if a claim aligns with verified data.
- **Machine Learning Models (ML):** The ML models are trained on large datasets of verified and false claims. These models can learn to identify patterns in misinformation, adapt to emerging trends, and predict the likelihood of a claim being false. They play a vital role in assessing the accuracy of claims based on historical data.
- **Knowledge Graphs:** Knowledge graphs organize information from a variety of sources into a structured, interconnected format. This enables the AI module to quickly cross-reference claims with a vast repository of verified facts. By linking various data points, knowledge graphs help improve the accuracy and depth of the verification process.
- **Real-Time Processing:** The TrustChain framework operates in real-time, allowing for the immediate verification of claims as they emerge. This is particularly important for verifying information related to live events, breaking news, and trending topics.

3.3 Blockchain Infrastructure

The blockchain infrastructure in the TrustChain Framework plays a crucial role in securing and validating the verification results provided by the AI module. By leveraging decentralized technology, blockchain ensures that the process is transparent, immutable, and resistant to tampering.

- **Decentralized Validation:** Blockchain nodes work collaboratively to validate the AI-generated verification results. The decentralized nature of blockchain means that no single entity has control over the verification process, ensuring fairness and reducing the risk of manipulation.
- **Immutable Storage:** Once the AI results are validated by the blockchain, the information is stored in an immutable ledger. This ensures that once a claim has been verified, it cannot be altered or deleted. The immutable nature of blockchain guarantees the reliability and integrity of the data.
- **Transparency Mechanisms:** Blockchain enables full transparency of the fact-checking process. All verified claims, along with their metadata (e.g., timestamp, data sources), are publicly accessible. This allows users to trace the verification process, fostering trust in the system.
- **Consensus Protocols:** Blockchain employs consensus mechanisms (such as Proof of Stake or Proof of Authority) to reach an agreement on the validity

of claims. These protocols ensure that the verification process is secure and trustworthy while maintaining system efficiency.

Blockchain enables decentralized validation of AI-generated results ensuring fairness and reducing manipulation risks. Validated data is stored immutably, guaranteeing reliability and integrity. Transparency is achieved through publicly accessible metadata, fostering trust. Consensus protocols like proof of stake ensure secure, efficient and trustworthy verification processes, enhancing the credibility of AI-Powered fact-checking systems.

3.4 Smart Contract Automation

Smart contracts serve as the operational layer that automates workflows and governs the behavior of the TrustChain system. These self-executing contracts are deployed on the blockchain and are responsible for managing the various stages of the verification process, from claim submission to result dissemination.

- **Claim Submission:** Users (journalists, content creators, or automated systems) can submit claims through an easy-to-use interface. Once a claim is submitted, the smart contract triggers the verification process and passes the claim to the AI Fact-Checking Module for analysis.
- **Verification Workflow:** The smart contract ensures the smooth flow of data through the verification pipeline. It coordinates the interaction between the AI module and blockchain infrastructure, making sure that each step of the process is executed in the correct sequence.
- **Result Dissemination:** Once the claim is verified, the smart contract automates the dissemination of the results to relevant stakeholders. This includes notifications to users, alerts for flagged misinformation, and updates to platforms or databases that may use the verification results.
- **Incentivization Mechanisms:** Smart contracts manage an incentivization system to encourage participation in the decentralized blockchain network. Validators who participate in the consensus process are rewarded with tokens or other forms of compensation, ensuring that the system remains decentralized and active.

Users submit claims via an intuitive interface, triggering a smart contract that initiates the verification process. The smart contract ensures seamless coordination between the AI Fact-Checking Module and blockchain infrastructure, maintaining a structured workflow. Verified result and automatically disseminated to stakeholders including users and platforms. Smart contracts also manage incentivization, rewarding validators with tokens to sustain a decentralized and active network. Smart contracts automate and govern the TrustChain System, managing workflows from claim submission to result dissemination. User submits claims via an interface, triggering the AI fact-Checking Module for analysis. The smart contracts ensure seamless data flow, coordinating AI and blockchain interactions. Once verified, results are disseminated to stockholders, including notifications and database updates. Additionally smart contracts manage incentivization mechanisms, rewarding validators with tokens or compensation to maintain a decentralized and active network. This system streamlines verification, enhances transparency, and encourages participation in combating misinformation.

3.5 Integration and Scalability

The TrustChain Framework is designed to be scalable and modular, allowing for easy integration with various platforms, databases, and third-party services.

- **Modular Design:** The framework's modular architecture allows individual components (AI, blockchain, smart contracts) to be independently updated or replaced. This ensures flexibility and adaptability as new technologies and methodologies emerge.
- **Scalability:** The system is designed to scale efficiently, handling large volumes of claims across multiple platforms. Techniques such as blockchain sharding and AI optimization help ensure that the TrustChain framework can handle an increasing load as its adoption grows.
- **Cross-Platform Compatibility:** The TrustChain system can be integrated with social media platforms, news outliers, fact-checking organizations, and other entities involved in digital media. This wide compatibility ensures that the framework can be deployed in diverse environments and meet the needs of various stakeholders.

The TrustChain framework features a modular architecture, enabling independent updates to AI, Blockchain and smart contracts for flexibility, scalability for integration with diverse media entities. It ensures adaptability, efficient growth and broad applicability across digital environments. The TrustChain Framework is scalable and modular, enabling seamless integration with various platforms, databases and third-party services. Its modular design allows independent updates to AI, blockchain, and smart contracts ensuring flexibility and adaptability. Scalability is achieved through blockchain shading and AI optimization. Supporting large clam volumes. Cross-platform compatibility allows integration with social media, news outlets and fact-checking allow organizations to make it applicable across diverse digital environments. This design ensures efficient growth, adaptability to emerging technologies, and broad applicability, meeting the needs of multiple stakeholders in combating misinformation.

4. APPLICATION OF TRUSTCHAIN

The TrustChain Framework finds its application in multiple domains where trust, transparency, and accuracy is critical. By leveraging AI-powered fact-checking and blockchain technology, the framework addresses challenges in mis-information management, digital content verification, and secure data sharing.

4.1 Misinformation Detection and Mitigation

One of the primary applications of TrustChain is in combating misinformation. The framework uses AI's ability to process and verify claims in real-time, coupled with blockchain's immutable ledger to ensure transparency and accountability. This application is critical in environments like social media platforms, where the rapid spread of false information has significant societal impacts (Xu et al., 2020). The framework could be integrated with platforms like Twitter or Facebook to automatically verify user-generated content and label misleading posts. Blockchain would maintain a public log of verified content, allowing users to trace the verification process.

4.2 Digital Media Verification

TrustChain ensures the authenticity of digital content such as images, videos, and documents. Using AI, the framework can analyze metadata, detect manipulations, and cross-reference content with verified databases. Blockchain provides an additional layer of integrity by preserving original data and validation results (Wang et al., 2024). Journalists and media organizations can utilize TrustChain to verify news content before publication, reducing the spread of fake news. Verified content can be tagged with blockchain-stored certificates of authenticity.

4.3 Intellectual Property Protection

The framework can be employed to safeguard intellectual property rights by ensuring ownership and usage rights are transparent and tamper-proof. AI identifies unauthorized use of copyrighted material, while blockchain stores ownership records immutably (Bhumichai et al., 2024). Artists can tokenize their digital creations as

NFTs on the blockchain. TrustChain ensures these tokens are linked to the original creator, preventing forgery or duplication.

4.4 Supply Chain Verification

In supply chains, TrustChain can verify the authenticity of goods and track their movements across the network. AI monitors data inconsistencies and flags potential fraud, while blockchain records each step in the supply chain immutably (Pareek et al., 2024). Pharmaceutical companies can use TrustChain to verify the authenticity of drugs, ensuring that counterfeit products are eliminated from the supply chain.

4.5 Regulatory Compliance and Auditing

TrustChain facilitates compliance with regulations by providing transparent, immutable records of transactions and activities. AI automates the detection of non-compliance, while blockchain serves as an auditable ledger for regulatory bodies (Alzoubi, 2024). Financial institutions can use TrustChain to ensure compliance with anti-money laundering (AML) and know-your-customer (KYC) regulations, with AI analyzing transactional data and blockchain maintaining a record of compliance checks.

4.6 Education and Research Integrity

The framework can be applied to maintain the integrity of academic and research content. AI verifies the originality of submissions and checks for plagiarism, while blockchain stores verified research immutably, ensuring accountability in academia. Universities can implement TrustChain to validate research publications and prevent academic fraud.

4.7 Public Health and Safety

TrustChain can be deployed in public health to verify the accuracy of health-related information and ensure the authenticity of medical certifications. Blockchain ensures that data cannot be tampered with, while AI analyzes claims and cross-references with verified health databases. Governments can use TrustChain to verify COVID-19 vaccination records and ensure that information shared with the public is accurate and credible (Kshetri et al., 2023; Kaur & Kshetri, 2025).

Figure 2. Application of TrustChain framework from misinformation detection & mitigation to public health and safety (Xu et al., 2020; Wang et al., 2024; Bhumichai et al., 2024; Pareek et al., 2024; Alzoubi, 2024; Kshetri et al., 2023; Kaur & Kshetri, 2025)

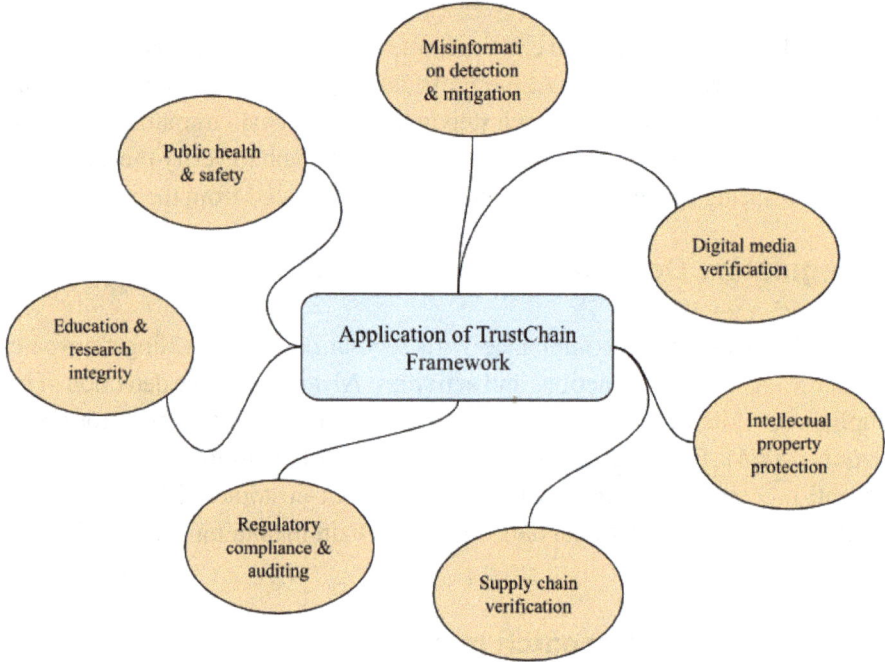

5. CHALLENGES AND FUTURE DIRECTIONS

A possible approach to combating false information with an AI-powered fact-checking system is the combination of blockchain technology and artificial intelligence (AI). These systems seek to use blockchain's transparency and immutability to establish trust while utilizing AI's capacity to analyze enormous volumes of data. Nevertheless, putting such systems into place presents several difficulties as well as chances for creativity.

The TrustChain framework faces challenges such as ensuring AI accuracy, managing computational costs, and maintaining blockchain scalability. AI models may struggle with nuanced or evolving misinformation, while blockchain networks can face latency and energy misinformation, while blockchain networks can face latency and energy consumption issues. Future directions include enhancing AI algorithms for better context understanding, optimizing blockchain protocols for efficiency, and fostering collaboration among stakeholders for broader adoption. Additionally, addressing ethical concerns, such as data privacy and bias AI, is crucial. Expanding cross-platform integration and incentivizing participation in decentralized networks will also be key to scaling TrustChain's impact in combating misinformation effectively.

5.1 Key Challenges

There are numerous significant obstacles to overcome when putting blockchain-secured AI-powered fact-checking systems into place:

1. Data Quality and Bias

Training data is crucial for AI fact-checking algorithms, and it needs to be impartial, accurate, and representative of a range of viewpoints. However, the following factors frequently degrade training data quality:

- Limited availability of validated datasets.
- Prejudice imposed by the dataset producer's skews AI results.

When trying to standardize fact-checking across several languages and cultural contexts, this problem is made worse. Algorithms developed primarily on English-language datasets, for instance, would not be able to successfully validate data in other languages (Hodge & Austin, 2004).

2. Efficiency in Computation and Scalability

Blockchain technology, while offering immutable transaction records, often faces scalability challenges. Its decentralized nature requires consensus among nodes, leading to delays and high energy consumption, especially during peak traffic. The system's reliance on storing and verifying large volumes of data increases processing demands, making real-time operations less efficient. These constraints can hinder the effectiveness of fact-checking systems, which require rapid data validation and processing. As traffic surges, network congestion further slows performance, raising costs and reducing scalability. Solutions like shading, layer-2 protocols, or alternative consensus mechanisms are being explored to address these limitations and enhance blockchain's usability in dynamic environments (Xu et al., 2019).

3. Enhancing Interoperability

Blockchain and AI integration necessitate smooth interoperability, yet there are substantial obstacles due to differences in technical standards, data formats, and protocols between blockchain platforms. Data sharing and synchronization with AI systems are made more difficult by the fact that each blockchain frequently has distinct designs and consensus methods. These inconsistencies restrict AI's capacity to effectively evaluate blockchain data by impeding the development of uniform frameworks. Furthermore, real-time AI processes that need dynamic updates are made more challenging by the decentralized and unchangeable nature of blockchains. Standardized protocols, middleware programs, or cross-chain technologies are needed to close these gaps and facilitate effective communication, which will improve the efficacy of AI-blockchain integration for smart and safe applications (Zheng et al., 2017).

4. Cost Reduction Strategies

Operational costs can be significantly decreased by implementing energy-efficient blockchain protocols and improving AI model training. Compared to conventional proof-of-work techniques, energy-efficient protocols like proof-of-stake use less energy. Similarly, computing costs are reduced when AI models are optimized using lightweight structures and effective algorithms. By removing the requirement for centralized data storage and transfer and training AI models locally on dispersed devices, federated learning provides an extra cost-saving measure. By storing sensitive data on local nodes, this method improves privacy while also lowering infrastructure costs. When combined, these tactics solve privacy issues while enhancing the price and sustainability of blockchain and AI systems (Liang et al., 2017).

5. Addressing Legal and Ethical Issues

To develop frameworks that encourage innovation while addressing moral and legal issues, policymakers must collaborate closely with technologists and ethicists. Working together is crucial to ensuring that new technologies respect data protection regulations and protect user security and privacy. Putting in place procedures for content redaction enables the proper management of private or out-of-date material without sacrificing openness. Additionally, encouraging transparency in decision-making procedures increases accountability and public trust. In order to ensure that technology breakthroughs are in line with social values and function responsibly within the parameters of regulatory norms, these frameworks should promote innovation by proactively addressing ethical quandaries and legal hazards .

5.2 Ethical Considerations

Blockchain-enabled fact-checking platforms with AI capabilities have the potential to slow the spread of false information. These solutions provide a novel response to the global disinformation epidemic by fusing blockchain's transparency and immutability with artificial intelligence's analytical powers. To guarantee their responsible usage, however, the implementation of such systems presents serious ethical issues that need to be properly addressed.

1. Fairness and Bias in AI Algorithms

The data that is used to train AI systems naturally affects them. If there are biases in this data, the system's outputs might reinforce or even magnify them. For instance, fact-checking algorithms may unfairly target or exclude particular populations if training datasets underrepresent particular linguistic or cultural groups (Mehrabi et al., 2021). Ensuring fairness requires:

- Comprehensive and varied datasets.
- AI models should undergo routine audits to detect and reduce biases.
- Working along with linguists and cultural specialists to modify systems for a variety of settings.

2. Transparency in AI-Decision making

The opaqueness of decision-making processes is one of the main ethical issues with AI. Users need to comprehend the criteria used to determine whether a claim is true or untrue. A lack of openness erodes trust and raises questions about algorithmic manipulation or hidden motives. The immutability of blockchain technology can offer a transparent audit trail, however explainable AI (XAI) must be used in conjunction with it to guarantee that people can understand how decisions are made. If blockchain metadata is too complicated for non-experts to understand, ethical questions are raised (Doshi-Velez & Kim, 2017).

3. Accountability and Governance

Who bears responsibility for biases or mistakes in fact-checking algorithms driven by AI? Because blockchain technology is decentralized, this question gets much more complicated. Ethical accountability requires:

- Stakeholders clearly identified, including fact-checking groups, blockchain operators, and AI developers.
- Procedures for resolving conflicts and providing compensation when mistakes are made (Floridi et al., 2018).
- Transparent governance frameworks for blockchain networks to stop malicious actors from abusing them.

4. Privacy Concerns

Individual privacy is threatened by blockchain's transparency, particularly when fact-checking data is stored on it. Even anonymized data can disclose sensitive information when paired with other data, even if blockchain guarantees immutability and traceability. In totalitarian governments, this risk is increased because such information may be used to track out dissidents or stifle dissenting opinions. Blockchain's public nature makes it impossible to remove potentially harmful data retroactively, which makes it a double-edged sword for fact-checking efforts. Robust encryption, selective data sharing, or privacy-focused blockchain designs are necessary to strike a balance between transparency and privacy, guaranteeing that private data is safeguarded without sacrificing the accountability and integrity of the fact-checking procedure. Mitigating privacy risk involves:

- Utilizing technology that protects privacy, including zero-knowledge proofs.
- Following international data protection guidelines, such as the General Data Protection Regulation (GDPR).
- Confirming that consumers have given their permission for data use.

5. Misuse and Censorship

Although the goal of fact-checking systems is to counter false information, they may also be abused to silence or restrict dissenting opinions. Among the ethical issues are:

- Ensuring that underprivileged communities or minority viewpoints are not disproportionately targeted by these mechanisms.
- Putting in place measures to stop businesses or governments from using these instruments for propaganda (Citron & Pasquale, 2014).
- Promoting a variety of oversight organizations to supervise fact-checking procedures.

6. Social impacts and Digital Literacy

If the results of AI-powered fact-checking systems are viewed as biased, they may unintentionally fuel societal division. Furthermore, over-dependency may result from reliance on these technologies without the promotion of digital literacy. Ethical deployment must include:

- Initiatives to inform the public on the operation of these systems.
- Encouraging the development of critical thinking abilities to support fact-checking initiatives.
- Promoting cooperation between legislators, educators, and technologists in order to close the gaps in digital literacy.

5.3 Future Enhancements

Future enhancements for the TrustChain framework aims to address current limitations and expands its capabilities in combating misinformation. Key areas of focus include improving AI algorithms to better understand context, detect nuanced misinformation, and adapt to evolving tactics used in fake news. Enhancing blockchain scalability and efficiency through advanced protocols like sharding or layer-2 solutions will help manage growing data volumes and reduce latency. Integrating TrustChain with a wider range of platforms, including social media, news outlets and governments databases, will increase its applicability and impact. As the TrustChain Framework evolves, several key areas of enhancement can be explored to improve its scalability, efficiency, and adaptability. These focus areas aim to address current limitations while expanding the framework's applications across industries.

In addition, fostering collaboration among stakeholder- such as fact-checking organizations, tech companies, and policymakers will drive adoption and standardization. Addressing ethical concerns such as data privacy, algorithms bias and transparency will be critical to building trust in the system. Incentivization mechanisms can be refined to encourage broader participation in decentralized networks, ensuring sustained engagement. Finally exploring hybrid models that combine AI and human expertise could enhance accuracy and reliability making TrustChain a robust, scalable and trusted solution for global fact-checking challenges.

5.3.1 Advanced Artificial Intelligence Techniques

Incorporating more sophisticated AI methodologies will enhance the framework's ability to analyze and verify claims. Techniques such as multimodal AI for analyzing text, images, and videos, and explainable AI (XAI) to provide transparency in decision-making, are vital advancements. These enhancements will ensure better accuracy, fairness, and trust in the system while addressing biases inherent in AI algorithms.

5.3.2 Scalable Blockchain Architectures

To support large-scale deployments, blockchain scalability remains a crucial area for improvement. Future implementations could adopt solutions like sharding and Layer-2 protocols to increase transaction throughput without compromising security and decentralization. Additionally, transitioning to energy-efficient consensus mechanisms will make the system more sustainable and cost-effective.

5.3.3 Cross-Chain Interoperability

As blockchain ecosystems diversify, ensuring interoperability between different blockchain networks will be essential. By enabling seamless communication across blockchains, TrustChain can expand its applicability and ensure consistent data integrity. Standardized protocols and interoperable frameworks will facilitate collaboration between blockchain platforms.

5.3.4 Integration with Emerging Technologies

TrustChain can benefit from integration with cutting-edge technologies such as edge computing, the Internet of Things (IoT), and quantum-resistant cryptography. These technologies will enhance the system's real-time processing capabilities, ensure data integrity in connected environments, and future-proof the framework against emerging security threats.

5.3.5 Enhanced Incentivization Models

Future iterations of TrustChain should refine its incentivization mechanisms to encourage active participation in the network. Reward systems can be optimized to dynamically adjust based on network activity, ensuring equitable compensation for validators and other contributors. Introducing token-based models for engagement will further strengthen the framework's decentralization.

5.3.6 Strengthening Ethical and Regulatory Compliance

Addressing ethical concerns and aligning with global regulations will be critical to TrustChain's long-term success. Enhancing privacy-preserving mechanisms, complying with legal frameworks like GDPR and HIPAA, and actively mitigating biases in AI will ensure the framework operates ethically and gains the trust of diverse stakeholders.

6. CONCLUSION

The TrustChain Framework represents a transformative approach to addressing the challenges of misinformation by integrating the analytical power of artificial intelligence (AI) with the transparency and immutability of blockchain technology. The framework combines AI-powered fact-checking, blockchain-based validation, and smart contract automation to create a scalable, transparent, and reliable solution for real-time claim verification.

The TrustChain Framework's modular design ensures adaptability and scalability, enabling its application across diverse domains such as digital media verification, misinformation detection, supply chain tracking, intellectual property protection, and public health. By leveraging AI's ability to process and verify claims and blockchain's ability to ensure data integrity and transparency, the framework fosters trust and accountability in an increasingly digital world.

While the framework offers significant advantages, it also faces challenges such as scalability, energy efficiency, ethical concerns, and regulatory compliance. Future enhancements, including advanced AI models, scalable blockchain architectures, cross-chain interoperability, and refined incentivization mechanisms, are crucial to addressing these challenges and expanding its potential applications.

By aligning with ethical principles and global regulatory standards, the Trust-Chain Framework can ensure fairness, privacy, and inclusivity in its operations. Moreover, its ability to adapt to emerging technologies like edge computing and quantum-resistant cryptography positions it as a forward-looking solution for combating misinformation and securing digital ecosystems. It is concluded that the TrustChain Framework is a robust and innovative system that holds the potential to revolutionize how information is verified and trusted. As the framework evolves, it can significantly contribute to fostering a more informed, secure, and transparent digital society.

REFERENCES

Alisha, S. K., & Krishna, B. V. (2024). FAKE NEWS, DISINFORMATION, AND DEEP FAKES LEVERAGING DISTRIBUTED LEDGER TECHNOLOGIES. *International Journal of Management Research and Business Strategy*, 14(2), 275–288.

Alrubei, S. M., Ball, E. A., Rigelsford, J. M., & Willis, C. A. (2020). Latency and performance analyses of real-world wireless IoT-blockchain application. *IEEE Sensors Journal*, 20(13), 7372–7383. DOI: 10.1109/JSEN.2020.2979031

Alzoubi, M. M. (2024). Investigating the synergy of blockchain and AI: Enhancing security, efficiency, and transparency. *Journal of Cyber Security Technology*, 1–29. DOI: 10.1080/23742917.2024.2374594

Amazeen, M. A. (2015). Revisiting the epistemology of fact-checking. *Critical Review*, 27(1), 1–22. DOI: 10.1080/08913811.2014.993890

Bhumichai, D., Smiliotopoulos, C., Benton, R., Kambourakis, G., & Damopoulos, D. (2024). The convergence of artificial intelligence and blockchain: The state of play and the road ahead. *Information (Basel)*, 15(5), 268. DOI: 10.3390/info15050268

Bragazzi, N. L., & Garbarino, S. (2024). Understanding and Combating Misinformation: An Evolutionary Perspective. *JMIR Infodemiology*, 4(1), e65521. DOI: 10.2196/65521 PMID: 39466077

Bu incu, C. N., & Alexandrescu, A. (2023). Blockchain-based platform to fight disinformation using crowd wisdom and artificial intelligence. *Applied Sciences (Basel, Switzerland)*, 13(10), 6088. DOI: 10.3390/app13106088

Citron, D. K., & Pasquale, F. (2014). The scored society: Due process for automated predictions. *Washington Law Review (Seattle, Wash.)*, 89, 1.

Doshi-Velez, F., & Kim, B. (2017). Towards a rigorous science of interpretable machine learning. *arXiv preprint arXiv:1702.08608*.

Fetzer, J. H. (2002). Peirce and the philosophy of AI. *Digital Encyclopedia of Charles S. Peirce. URL:* http://www. digitalpeirce. fee. unicamp. br/ai_fetzer. htm

Floridi, L., Cowls, J., Beltrametti, M., Chatila, R., Chazerand, P., Dignum, V., Luetge, C., Madelin, R., Pagallo, U., Rossi, F., Schafer, B., Valcke, P., & Vayena, E. (2018). AI4People—an ethical framework for a good AI society: Opportunities, risks, principles, and recommendations. *Minds and Machines*, 28(4), 689–707. DOI: 10.1007/s11023-018-9482-5 PMID: 30930541

Graves, L. (2016). *Deciding what's true: The rise of political fact-checking in American journalism.* Columbia University Press. DOI: 10.7312/grav17506

Hodge, V., & Austin, J. (2004). A survey of outlier detection methodologies. *Artificial Intelligence Review, 22*(2), 85–126. DOI: 10.1023/B:AIRE.0000045502.10941.a9

Kaur, N., & Kshetri, N. Blockchain Technology: Aiding Transformation in the Healthcare and Medical Industry. In *Blockchain Technology for Cyber Defense, Cybersecurity, and Countermeasures* (pp. 34-54). CRC Press.

Kim, S., Deka, G. C., & Zhang, P. (2019). *Role of blockchain technology in IOT Applications.* Academic Press.

Kshetri, N., Bhusal, C. S., Kumar, D., & Chapagain, D. (2023). SugarChain: Blockchain technology meets Agriculture—The case study and analysis of Indian sugarcane farming. *arXiv preprint arXiv:2301.08405.*

Kshetri, N., Hutson, J., & Revathy, G. (2023, December). healthAIChain: Improving security and safety using Blockchain Technology applications in AI-based healthcare systems. In *2023 3rd International Conference on Innovative Mechanisms for Industry Applications (ICIMIA)* (pp. 159-164). IEEE.

Kuznetsov, O., Sernani, P., Romeo, L., Frontoni, E., & Mancini, A. (2024). On the integration of artificial intelligence and blockchain technology: A perspective about security. *IEEE Access: Practical Innovations, Open Solutions, 12,* 3881–3897. DOI: 10.1109/ACCESS.2023.3349019

Liang, X., Shetty, S., Tosh, D., Kamhoua, C., Kwiat, K., & Njilla, L. (2017, May). Provchain: A blockchain-based data provenance architecture in cloud environment with enhanced privacy and availability. In *2017 17th IEEE/ACM International Symposium on Cluster, Cloud and Grid Computing (CCGRID)* (pp. 468-477). IEEE. DOI: 10.1109/CCGRID.2017.8

Mehrabi, N., Morstatter, F., Saxena, N., Lerman, K., & Galstyan, A. (2021). A survey on bias and fairness in machine learning. *ACM Computing Surveys, 54*(6), 1–35. DOI: 10.1145/3457607

Nakamoto, S. (2008). *Bitcoin: A peer-to-peer electronic cash system.* Satoshi Nakamoto.

Nguyen, A. T., Kharosekar, A., Krishnan, S., Krishnan, S., Tate, E., Wallace, B. C., & Lease, M. (2018). Believe it or not. *Proceedings of the 31st Annual ACM Symposium on User Interface Software and Technology.* DOI: 10.1145/3242587.3242666

Nyhan, B., & Reifler, J. (2015). Displacing misinformation about events: An experimental test of causal corrections. *Journal of Experimental Political Science*, 2(1), 81–93. DOI: 10.1017/XPS.2014.22

Panda, L., Jena, S. K., Rath, S. S., & Misra, P. K. (2020). Heavy metal removal from water by adsorption using a low-cost geopolymer. *Environmental Science and Pollution Research International*, 27(19), 24284–24298. DOI: 10.1007/s11356-020-08482-0 PMID: 32306254

Pareek, S., van Berkel, N., Velloso, E., & Goncalves, J. (2024). Effect of explanation conceptualisations on trust in AI-Assisted Credibility Assessment. *Proceedings of the ACM on Human-Computer Interaction, 8*(CSCW2), 1–31. DOI: 10.1145/3686922

Picha Edwardsson, M., & Al-Saqaf, W. (2022). Drivers and barriers for using blockchain technology to create a global fact-checking database. *Online Journal of Communication and Media Technologies*, 12(4), e202228. DOI: 10.30935/ojcmt/12381

Saad, M., Ahmad, A., & Mohaisen, A. (2019, June). Fighting fake news propagation with blockchains. In *2019 IEEE Conference on Communications and Network Security (CNS)* (pp. 1-4). IEEE.

Shae, Z., & Tsai, J. (2019, July). AI blockchain platform for trusting news. In *2019 IEEE 39th International Conference on Distributed Computing Systems (ICDCS)* (pp. 1610-1619). IEEE. DOI: 10.1109/ICDCS.2019.00160

Sharma, S. R., & Kshetri, N. (2025). BCT4C4: Blockchain Technology for Cybersecurity, Cyber Data, and Cyber Communication in Today's Cyber World. Chapter 6, In book *Blockchain Technology for Cyber Defense, Cybersecurity, and Countermeasures: Techniques, Solutions, and Applications*, 94, CRC Press.

Sharma, S. R., Kshetri, N., & Poudel, S. R. (2025). SHSBchain: Blockchain Technology Solutions for Smart Homes and Smart Business. Chapter 13, In book *Blockchain Technology for Cyber Defense, Cybersecurity, and Countermeasures: Techniques, Solutions, and Applications* (pp. 211-221), CRC Press.

Tapscott, D., & Tapscott, A. (2016). *Blockchain revolution: how the technology behind bitcoin is changing money, business, and the world.* Penguin.

Thorne, J., Vlachos, A., Christodoulopoulos, C., & Mittal, A. (2018). FEVER: a large-scale dataset for fact extraction and VERification. *arXiv preprint arXiv:1803.05355*. DOI: 10.18653/v1/N18-1074

Wang, X., Ban, T., Chen, L., Usman, M., Guan, Y., Lyu, D., Cheng, J., Chen, H., Leung, C., & Miao, C. (2024). Decentralised knowledge graph evolution via blockchain. *IEEE Transactions on Services Computing*, *17*(1), 169–182. DOI: 10.1109/TSC.2023.3337873

Xu, R., Nikouei, S. Y., Nagothu, D., Fitwi, A., & Chen, Y. (2020). BlendSPS: A blockchain-enabled Decentralized Smart Public Safety System. *Smart Cities*, *3*(3), 928–951. DOI: 10.3390/smartcities3030047

Xu, X., Weber, I., & Staples, M. (2019). *Architecture for blockchain applications*. Springer. DOI: 10.1007/978-3-030-03035-3

Yadav, K. K. (2023). Unmasking The Lies: How Information Technology is Fighting Fake News and Viral Deception. *Journal of Data Acquisition and Processing*, *38*(2), 3183. DOI: 10.5281/zenodo.777149

Zen, Y. (2021). Type 2 autoimmune pancreatitis: Consensus and controversies. *Gut and Liver*, *16*(3), 357–365. DOI: 10.5009/gnl210241 PMID: 34670874

Zheng, Z., Xie, S., Dai, H., Chen, X., & Wang, H. (2017, June). *An overview of blockchain technology: Architecture, consensus, and future trends. In 2017 IEEE international congress on big data (BigData congress)*. Ieee.

Zubiaga, A., Aker, A., Bontcheva, K., Liakata, M., & Procter, R. (2018). Detection and resolution of rumors in social media: A survey. *ACM Computing Surveys*, *51*(2), 1–36. DOI: 10.1145/3161603

Chapter 6
GenBlock:
A Secure Decentralized Model for Generative AI Integration With Blockchain

Soba Raj Paudel
https://orcid.org/0009-0005-5336-4355
Tribhuvan University, Nepal

Suresh Raj Sharma
https://orcid.org/0009-0009-0722-545X
Tribhuvan University, Nepal

Bishwo Prakash Pokharel
https://orcid.org/0000-0001-6516-2105
Sault College of Applied Arts and Technology, Canada

ABSTRACT

Generative AI, a branch of artificial intelligence, is revolutionizing the creation of original content, including text, images, music, and videos. When integrated with blockchain technology, it creates a powerful synergy that combines creativity with enhanced security. Blockchain's immutable and tamper-proof properties can authenticate generative AI outputs, ensuring trust and originality. For instance, artists can timestamp their works on the blockchain, providing undeniable proof of ownership and authenticity. This fusion also addresses critical challenges faced by businesses adopting generative AI chatbots like ChatGPT, including mitigating the risks of false outputs ("hallucinations") and safeguarding intellectual property used in AI training.

DOI: 10.4018/979-8-3373-6481-0.ch006

1. INTRODUCTION

With its cutting-edge approaches to natural language processing, content production, and decision-making systems, generative artificial intelligence (AI) has drastically changed a number of industries. However, there are serious issues with data privacy, security, and trust because of the centralized nature of present AI implementation. A move toward decentralized systems that put security and transparency first is required in light of these issues. The quick development of generative artificial intelligence (AI), which makes it possible to create content, designs, and solutions automatically, has drastically changed a number of industries. But as generative AI models advance in sophistication, they also bring with them new problems with privacy, data security, and reliability. Concerns with the security and integrity of produced outputs are raised by the fact that traditional centralized AI architectures are frequently susceptible to data breaches, illegal access, and manipulation. Because blockchain networks are decentralized, irreversible and transparent, combining generative AI with blockchain technology presents a viable way to overcome these issues (Nakamoto, 2008).

Originally created to facilitate cryptocurrency, blockchain technology has developed into a flexible platform for safe and open data management. It is perfect for applications needing high security and trust because of its decentralized ledger, which guarantees data immutability and verifiability. Blockchain and generative AI can be combined to establish safe frameworks that improve the accountability and traceability of AI-generated content while simultaneously protecting sensitive data. By reducing the hazards of data tampering and illegal access, this integration can increase confidence in AI systems. A safe, decentralized approach to generative AI with blockchain integration has potential to transform sectors including supply chain management, healthcare, and finance. For example, in the healthcare industry, blockchain can safely store and handle sensitive data, guaranteeing data integrity and privacy, while generative AI models may evaluate patient data to create individualized treatment plans (Zhang et al., 2018). Blockchain can also offer transparent audits of AI-driven decision-making processes in the financial sector, which can lower fraud and improve regulatory compliance (Catalini & Gans, 2016).

Notwithstanding the possible advantages, there are a number of operational and technological difficulties when combining generative AI and blockchain. Because of the resource-intensive nature of blockchain networks and the computing demands of AI models, scalability is still a major challenge. Furthermore, the creation of standardized protocols and architectures is necessary to guarantee the compatibility of various blockchain platforms and AI frameworks (Yli-Huumo et al., 2016).

1.1 Background

The ability of machines to create information that resembles that of humans, such as text, photos, music, and video, has transformed a number of sectors. According to Goodfellow et al (2014), its quick development has made it easier to develop cutting-edge applications in industries like cybersecurity, healthcare, finance, and entertainment. But the centralized architecture of the majority of AI models creates serious questions about trust, security and data privacy. Protecting user data and maintaining transparency are difficult with centralized systems since they are susceptible to single points of failure, data breaches, and the exploitation of private information (Shokri et al., 2017). The inherent drawbacks of centralized data management and storage have been addressed by blockchain technology, which is distinguished by its decentralized, transparent and immutable ledger system. Blockchain technology was first developed for safe cryptocurrency transactions (Nakamoto, 2008), but its uses have now spread to other fields, providing strong mechanisms for provenance, data integrity, and trustless operations (Yli-Huumo et al., 2016). By decentralizing AI model deployment and data management, generative AI and blockchain integration offer a special chance to improve security, accountability and transparency.

Blockchain-based smart contracts can automate compliance and access management, lowering the possibility of model manipulation and illegal data use (Christidis & Devetsikiotis, 2016). These developments open the door to a decentralized, safe framework for generative AI model deployment. However, there are technological difficulties when combining blockchain technology with generative AI. scalable and effective solutions are necessary to balance performance and security due to the computational demands of AI model training and inference. Seamless integration is made more difficult by blockchain's intrinsic scalability and transaction throughput limit (Xu et al., 2019). Furthermore, advanced privacy-preserving strategies like homomorphic encryption and zero-knowledge proofs are required to protect sensitive data while keeping the openness of blockchain systems (Zyskind et al., 2015). To overcome these obstacles, a safe decentralized architecture for integrating generative AI with blockchain must make use of cutting-edge cryptography techniques, scalable consensus algorithms, and effective data management techniques. By reducing the risks associated with data breaches, illegal access, and model misuse, this integration seeks to create a reliable environment for the deployment and operation of generative AI systems. Creating strong frameworks that integrate the advantages of generative AI and blockchain is becoming more and more important as the need for safe and moral AI applications increases.

1.2 Motivation

Data security, privacy and trust in centralized AI systems are becoming major challenges, which is why a secure decentralized architecture for generative AI integration with blockchain is being developed. Since generative AI is still having an impact on important industries, its dependence on centralized data storage and model administration leaves it vulnerable to abuse, data manipulation, and cyber attacks (Shokri et al., 2017). The growing number of cases involving illegal access and data breaches emphasizes how urgently more transparent and safe AI infrastructures are needed. By decentralizing data management and guaranteeing immutable, transparent, and tamper-proof records, blockchain technology presents a possible alternative. It is feasible to reduce security threats and improve accountability in AI-driven applications by combining blockchain technology with generative AI. By automating compliance and access constraints, smart contracts can guarantee the safe and moral use of AI models (Christidis & Devetsikiotis, 2016). Additionally, the decentralized architecture of blockchain increases system resilience by lowering the risks associated with single points of failure (Yli-Huumo et al., 2016). By utilizing distributed computing resources and sophisticated consensus mechanisms, the suggested paradigm seeks to meet both the computational requirements of generative AI and scalability issues of blockchain. Through this integration, a scalable, effective and secure infrastructure that permits the safe and transparent deployment of generative AI applications across multiple industries is intended to be created.

1.3 Objectives

- To address issues like protecting intellectual property during AI training and reducing the possibility of "hallucinations" (false outputs), which are problems that organizations adopting generative AI confront.
- To evaluate how the decentralized and transparent blockchain platform facilitates safe data management for generative AI applications in fields like literature, music and the arts.
- To assess how the combination of generative AI and blockchain technology might change the digital media environment and open up new channels for content production, sharing and revenue.

2. GENERATIVE AI AND BLOCKCHAIN: AN OVERVIEW

In the landscape of digital development, nothing is more ground-breaking and impactful than the innovations of generative AI and blockchain technology. Generative AI is concerned with creating new pieces of content using algorithms, while blockchain lays the foundation for decentralized data management and transactions. These two technologies combined provide a strong potential for various purposes like creating more creative contents, digital ownerships and track ground data transactions.

2.1 Generative AI

Generative AI works on two keywords-generator and discriminator. For the GANs, for example, the generator produces new points of the data and the discriminator decides their authenticity based on the training data. This confrontational procedure lasts until the generator generates data that is undetectable from real data, which greatly improves the quality of generated material (Goodfellow et al., 2014). Transformers models use self attention mechanisms to encode and produce text, enabling for the comprehension of text's context and subtleties which represents exciting progress in natural language processing and text generation (Vaswani et al., 2017). In order to transform natural language processing (NLP), transformer models make use of self attention processes. Transformers, in contrast to traditional models, analyse every component of a text at once, allowing them to comprehend the connections between words across the entire sequence. The foundation of models like GPT and BERT, which allow for sophisticated text production and understanding, are transformers. They are quite effective at producing logical answers or predictions and converting text into meaningful representations. Applications like chatbots, language translation, summarization, and sentiment analysis are powered by this capacity. Generative AI relies on large datasets for training, which is an important factor. They can generate similar distributed outputs by learning the patterns and relationships within the data. For example, models such as GPT-3 can generate contextually relevant and coherent responses to prompts since they have been pre-trained on a variety of online text (Brown et al., 2020).

2.2 Blockchain Technology

Blockchain technology used for distributed record keeping, ensuring that digital assets cannot be altered and are transparent. It operates on a decentralized network, meaning no single entry has control, and employs cryptographics technology to secure data (Sharma & Kshetri, 2025). The information in blockchain is stored in blocks with each block linked in a sequential chain, forming a permanent and traceable ledger. Blockchain has a significant role in distribution of information all over the nodes. The key concept of blockchain technology:

- **Decentralisation**: blockchain distributed data over a network of nodes, removing the need for a central authority; this decentralisation eliminates single points of failure while improving data security.
- **Immutability**: data stored on a blockchain cannot be changed or removed. This immutability assures the accuracy and integrity of AI models and training data.
- **Openness:** blockchain transactions are public, which promotes openness in AI development and implementation. This enables users to check the source and correctness of AI- generation material.
- **Trackable**: content can be tracked throughout its lifecycle on a blockchain, which is especially beneficial for copyright protection. This ensure that creators receive recognition and compensation for their works
- **Smart contracts**: smart contracts are self-executing agreements where the terms are directly embedded in code. They can automate permissions and access to content, such as automatically enforcing agreements or managing royalty payments.
- **Enhance security**: blockchain employs advanced cryptographic techniques to secure data, providing an extra layer of security compared to traditional database systems that might be more susceptible.

Blockchain technology is transforming contents, particularly in content generated by AI, by offering secure and decentralized solutions. Which provides transparent and temper-proof record keeping revolutionizing record management with visibility, traceability, and product authenticity (Sharma et al., 2025).

2.3 Synergy Between Generative AI and Blockchain

Generative AI and Blockchain combine the best features of both technologies to create a more decentralized and safe architecture for AI applications. The following significant synergies result from this integration:

- **Data Provenance and Traceability:** Training data used to train generative AI models can be traced back to its original source and any alterations made thanks to blockchain's immutable ledger. This eliminates worries about bias and data manipulation by guaranteeing that the AI models are trained on validated and real data (Narayanan et al., 2016). Additionally, by confirming the legitimacy of the source data and the models themselves, blockchain can aid in preventing the misuse of material produced by artificial intelligence.
- **Decentralized Model Training:** By establishing a peer to peer network where several users can contribute data or computational resources without

depending on a centralized authority, blockchain can enable decentralized AI model training. This methodology guarantees that the process of developing AI is more transparent, inclusive and impervious to manipulation. Blockchain-based smart contracts can automate AI training protocol governance, allowing participants to collaborate without trust.

- **Protection of Intellectual Property:** By using cryptographic signatures, blockchain technology enables producers of AI-generated material to safeguard their intellectual property rights. Content producers can demonstrate authorship and establish ownership of AI generated content by registering it on the blockchain, providing a safe and verifiable means of shielding their works from infringement or unapproved usage (Yuan et al., 2024).
- **Improved Security and Privacy:** By using cryptographic methods to protect data privacy, blockchain offers improved security. Sensitive user information can be encrypted and stored on blockchain decentralized AI systems, guaranteeing that it is kept secret and only accessible by those with permission. Furthermore, by permitting safe federated learning, in which models are trained locally on encrypted data without requiring sensitive information to leave the user's device, the blockchain can support privacy-preserving AI models.

3. THE CONCEPTUAL FRAMEWORK OF GENBLOCK

The GenBlock framework is a hybrid system that combines the innovative capabilities of generative artificial intelligence (AI) with the security and transparency of blockchain technology. This fusion aims to address critical challenges in digital content creation, ownership, verification, and governance. The framework utilizes AI models to generate content, while blockchain ensures that content is stored immutably, offering enhanced security, verifiability, and decentralized governance.

The conceptual framework of GenBlock is designed to enable a decentralized ecosystem for content creators, consumers, and administrators, providing a reliable method to ensure that AI-generated content remains secure, traceable, and protected against tampering. The framework consists of several interconnected components, including AI content generation, blockchain infrastructure, smart contracts, governance mechanisms, and user interfaces as shown in figure 1. Together, these components create a seamless workflow that guarantees the authenticity and ownership of content while promoting fair and transparent decision-making.

Figure 1. GenBlock framework and its components

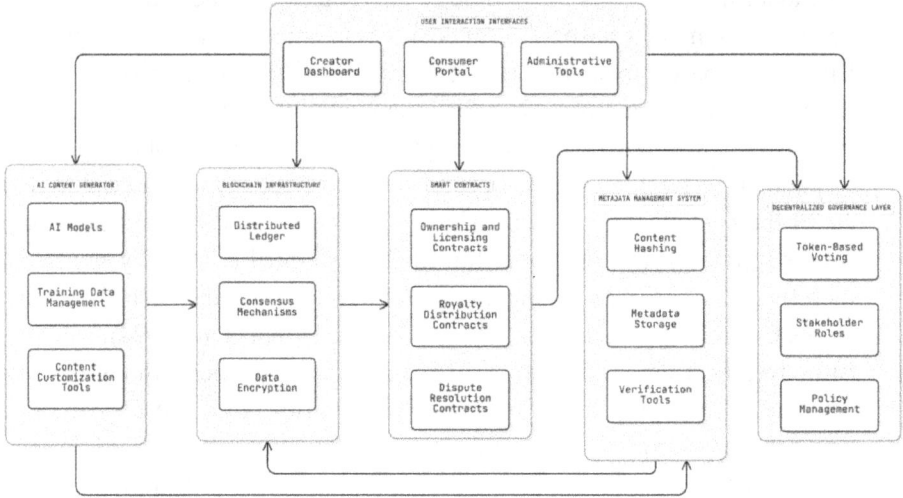

3.1 Architecture of GenBlock

The GenBlock architecture is built to integrate the functionalities of generative AI and blockchain in a way that enhances both creativity and security. The architecture can be understood through its core components, each playing a crucial role in the ecosystem's functionality. These components include the Ai content Generator, Blockchain Infrastructure, Smart Contracts, Metadata Management System, Decentralized Governance Layer, and User Interaction Interfaces.

3.1.1 AI Content Generator

The AI Content Generator is the component responsible for generating creative content. Using advanced generative AI models, such as GPT-3 for text, DALL-E for images, and others, thai component produces original digital assets based on user inputs.

3.1.2 Blockchain Infrastructure

The Blockchain Infrastructure provides a secure, transparent, and immutable storage platform. It stores metadata, content hashes, timestamps, and other relevant data on a decentralized ledger, ensuring that all generated content can be traced back to its origin.

3.1.3 Smart Contracts

Smart Contracts in GenBlock automate various processes, such as verifying content ownership, licensing, and royalty distribution. They are self-executing agreements that ensure all stakeholders receive fair compensation for their participation in the ecosystem.

3.1.4 Decentralized Governance Layer

The Decentralized Governance Layer allows stakeholders to participate in the decision-making processes of the framework. This layer enables community-driven voting mechanisms that influence governance policies and content-related decisions.

3.1.5 Metadata Management System

The Metadata Management System manages the data associated with each piece of AI-generated content, such as creator identity, creation timestamp, and content hash. This system ensures that all metadata is accurately recorded and securely stored on the blockchain.

3.1.6 User Interaction Interfaces

User Interaction Interfaces offer creators, consumers, and administrators an intuitive way to interact with the system. These interfaces provide dashboards for content generation, browsing, purchasing, and governance participation.

3.2 Working Principle of GenBlock

The GenBlock framework operates through a series of interconnected processes that facilitate the creation, verification, and management of digital content. Data flows through the system in a structured manner, from content generation to content verification, licensing, and governance. The following steps outline how the system works:

● **AI Content Generation:** The content creation process begins with the AI Content Generator. Creators provide input parameters, such as prompts to creative preferences, to guide the AI models. The AI model then generates content (text, images, videos, or music). This content is passed to the Metadata Management System for further processing.

- **Metadata Management:** The generated content is accompanied by metadata, such as a unique content hash, timestamp, and creator's details. The Metadata Management System ensures that this metadata is accurately created and stored on the blockchain, providing traceability and ensuring that the content is associated with its rightful owner.

- **Blockchain Storage and Verification:** Once the metadata is generated, it is stored in the Blockchain Infrastructure. The blockchain ensures that the metadata is stored securely in a decentralized, immutable ledger. This ensures that the content's origin, timestamp, and ownership are verified, and the content cannot be tampered with.

- **Smart Contract Execution:** Smart contracts are triggered once the content is stored on the blockchain. These contracts automatically enforce predefined rules for content ownership, licensing, and royalty distribution. If the content is purchased or used, the smart contract executes the necessary actions, such as transferring ownership or distributing royalties to the content creator.

- **Decentralized Governance and Stakeholder Interaction:** The Decentralized Governance Layer allows stakeholders to vote on important decisions affecting the framework, such as content policies, royalti distribution, and system updates. Governance is achieved through token based voting mechanisms, ensuring that all stakeholders have a say in the system's operation.

- **User Interaction:** Creators, consumers, and administrators interact with the framework through the User Interaction Interfaces. Creators can generate and manage content, consumers can browse and purchase content, and administrators can manage governance and operational tasks. These interfaces ensure an intuitive and user-friendly experience for all participants.

4. USE CASE OF THE GENBLOCK FRAMEWORK

Generative Artificial Intelligence (GAI) forms parts of the solutions that one will be envisaged to provide by creating an environment capable of supporting reduced scalability, missing security, poor privacy, and impractical interoperability. GAI techniques applied within blockchain integration present here in paper. Currently existing implementations as well as emerging solutions utilize GAI to detect blockchain attacks, reduce vulnerability in smart contracts, and create novel ways of ensuring security in key sharing models.

A case study demonstrating how the generative diffusion model is employed in optimizing metrics that measure performance efficiency in the blockchain network, showing a case of fast convergence with higher rewards, in tandem with substantial increase in throughput and latency for the adoption of any traditional, already developed AI method. Further research initiative will include personalized GAI-enables blockchain and improvement on privacy and security within and cross blockchain ecosystem.

4.1 Content Authentication and Ownership

The idea of content Authentication and ownership in the paper is very important. Its helps make such AI-created content trustworthy, can be traced back to its source, and respects the rights of the creators in a decentralized system. Here's a simpler explain of some points as:

● **Making Sure Content is Real with Blockchain**

Blockchain is a tool that can prove whether something is real or not. In this case, it would help confirm that content made by AI (like picture, writing, or music) is original and hasn't been changed without permission. Blockchain keeps a clear and unchangeable record, so once AI-created content is added and made, anyone can check where it came from and see if it's been altered. This stops people from making unauthorized changes and guarantees that the AI content is authentics.

● **AI-Created Contented in a Decentralized System**

In a decentralized network, figuring out who owns AI-generated content can be tricky. Blockchain can help by keeping a permanent record of who created the content and who owns it. This ensures that the rights of the creator are protected, and no one can claim ownership of something they didn't make. It also makes it easier to track and prove who the real owner is.

● **Decentralized Ways to Check AI Content**

Checking if AI-made content is real and correct in a system where no single group is in charge. Usually, big companies or platforms check content, but in this new way, many different computers (called nodes) work together to make such content okay. For example, they might use a special method to agree that the content is real, and these computers check if the content follows the rules of a system called blockchain. This way we dont depend on just one place to check things and it's more clear and fair.

● **Smart Contracts for Automatically Handling Content Permissions and Payments**

Smart contracts can be set up to automatically manage who can use AI-made content and how they pay for it. When someone shares or sells the content, the smart contract can make sure the rules of the deal are followed, like giving the buyer certain rights. This makes things faster and fairer without needing a middleman.

4.2 Intellectual Property Protection

The rapid developments in the digital world have significantly impacted the livelihoods of digital content creation. Especially as they increasingly turn to digital platforms for income, particularly after the pandemic. While the digital content publishing service has profited greatly, connection earning from digital use and live concerts remain limited. Privacy and Unauthorized file sharing also threaten thor income by violating copyright laws, which prohibit the distribution of content without consent from creators and copyright holders. To address these challenges, the content creators and publishing industry required advanced technological solutions to protect creator's rights in the evolving digital landscape. This includes using algorithms to track and manage contents across digital platforms, ensuring proper copyright protection and increasing artist's revenue from online and cross-platform use. One proposed solution involves leveraging artificial intelligence, blockchain, and cryptography. Specifically, it introduces an integrated system using Non Fungible Tokens (NFTs), smart contracts on HYperledger Fabric, and Quantum encryption to manage the licensing, identification, and right collection of music content. This system aims to streamline the process of protecting copyright, detecting violations, and distributing earnings transparently.

Blockchain and Generative AI are being explored to protect intellectual property(IP). Blockchain decentralised and immutable nature can verify ownership and track provenance of digital assets reducing piracy and unauthorized use (Tapscott & Tapscott, 2019). Blockchain can also facilitate transparent licensing and agreement and smart contracts that automate IP transactions so creators get fair pay (Catalini & Gans, 2018). Generative AI can help protect IP by creating new content that can be copyrighted and an automated system to identify infringements in digital content using pattern recognition and natural language processing. Together these can provides a more efficient and secure way to manage and protect intellectual property in the digital words

4.3 Mitigating AI "Hallucinations"

Artificial Intelligence (AI) is rapidly transforming various industries, including healthcare, education, legal system, and entertainment, with large language models (LLMs) and generative AI systems driving this change. However, these systems are prone to AI hallucinations, where they produce factually incorrect, logical flawed or fabricated content. Such hallucinations pose significant risk, particularly in critical fields. Mitigating AI hallucinations is a big deal, especially when we are talking about keeping our AI buddies from making stuff up in important areas like content creation. Now a simple way to tackle this is by combining AI with blockchain, like a digital peanut butter and jelly sandwich for the brain.

Imagine a system where blockchain keeps an eye on every AI does, like a permanent record that can't be changed. It's like having a group of super-honest friends who make such stories true to the original. This decentralized approach makes it so that AI is using reliable info to do its thing. Data provenance and traceability: blockchain is like a super-secure diary for data. It logs everything the AI learns, so you know if someone tries to slip in a fake fact or two. This way we can trace back the info to the source and make it so it's not leading the AI astray (Ajuzieogu, n.d.). Smart contracts for validation: think of these as the AI grammar checking but for facts. Before the AI says something, the smart contracts can quickly check with other databases to see if it's telling the truth. If it's not, the blockchain can tell it to go back and try again. Auditability and Transparency: the blockchain is like having a time machine for AI decisions. We can see every little choice it made and why, which makes it easier to spot when it starts getting a bit too creative. If it starts hallucinating, we can catch it and figure out what went wrong, then give it a virtual pat on the back and tell it to do better next time.

4.4 Decentralized Content Monetization

Generative AI having a swift impact on the content creation landscape open AI's GPT model for text generation and DALL-E for image creation are examples of technologies that allows creators to create high- quality original content at large. In spite of this, customary monetization approaches often encounter complications like over-censuring, unethical practices, and uneven revenue distribution. A promising alternative is blockchain technology. Blockchain decentralized and transparent nature enables creators to take control of their content, directly monetize it, and ensure fair compensation through secure, trustless transactions using AI and Blockchian for Content money-making as

- **Turning content into digital dough:** Tokenizing your stuff lets you sell it, share it and still be the big cheese. AI generated NFTs: if we make something cool with Ai we can turn it into NFT and sell it smart contracts for money. platform without the middleman, they use blockchain to let us share our stuff without big companies. Peer-to-peer Sharing these decentralized platforms are like a digital flea market where everyone's on an even playing field.

- **Micro Payments and Crypto Coins:** the blockchain lets us get paid for every tiny thing people do with our content, like watching a video or reading a post. Crypto Payment we can pay in cryptocurrencies directly, no bank or platform needed. It's like passing a hat around the internets
- **Direct payments:** instead of relying on ads revenue or subscription models, creators can receive direct payments from their audience, using cryptocurrencies. Which include on-time payments, tripping or recurring contributions.

5. TECHNICAL IMPLEMENTATION OF GENBLOCK

The technical implementation of the GenBlock framework involves a combination of advanced technologies, including generative artificial intelligence (AI), blockchain infrastructure, smart contracts, and decentralized governance mechanisms. By using both AI and blockchain, GenBlock aims to address key challenges in digital content creation, ownership, and security.

5.1 Integrating Generative AI with Blockchain

The core innovation behind GenBlock lies in the integration of generative AI with blockchain technology. Generative AI models such as GPT-3, DALL-E, and others are used to create original digital content, including text, images, music, and videos. The AI models generate content based on user inputs or prompts, and the resulting output is unique, creative, and original. The challenge here is to ensure that this generated content is secure, traceable, and verifiable.

Blockchain technology addresses these challenges by providing an immutable and transparent ledger. When content is created by the AI, the metadata (including content hashes, timestamps, and creator information) is stored on the blockchain. This ensures that the content cannot be altered or tampered with, establishing its authenticity and ownership. The decentralized nature of blockchain also eliminates the need for intermediaries, giving creators full control over their work (Portillo, 2024; Radziwill, 2018).

In practice, the integration works as follows: The AI content generator produces digital assets, which are then processed by a metadata management system to create a unique identifier (hash). This metadata, along with the content's creator information, is recorded on the blockchain. The content is thus cryptographically tied to the blockchain, ensuring that its authenticity is verifiable at any time by any participant in the ecosystem.

5.2 Blockchain Infrastructure and Smart Contracts

A key feature of the GenBlock framework is the use of blockchain infrastructure to ensure the security and immutability of content metadata. The blockchain serves as a decentralized ledger, where the metadata associated with each piece of AI-generated content is stored. Each entry on the blockchain is timestamped and includes a unique content hash, which acts as a digital fingerprint of the content. This enables verification of the content's originality and ownership without the need for a centralized authority (Suthar & Pindoriya, 2020).

The blockchain system used in GenBlock is typically based on well-established platforms like Ethereum, which supports smart contracts. Smart contracts are self-executing contracts with the terms of the agreement directly written into lines of code. In the context of GenBlock, smart contracts automate the enforcement of content ownership, licensing, and royalty distribution (Christidis & Devetsikiotis, 2016).

For instance, when a user purchases or licenses AI-generated content, the relevant smart contract is triggered. The contract automatically transfers ownership rights and handles the payment distribution, ensuring that creators receive fair compensation. These smart contracts are stored and executed on the blockchain, making them tamper-proof and transparent. The use of blockchain and smart contracts reduces the need for intermediaries and ensures that all transactions are secure and trustworthy.

5.3 Decentralized Governance and Stakeholder Involvement

GenBlock incorporates a decentralized governance model to ensure that all stakeholders have a say in the system's operations and evolution. This is achieved through a token-based voting mechanism, which allows content creators, consumers, and administrators to participate in decision-making processes. The governance layer is built on blockchain technology, ensuring transparency and fairness in voting.

Stakeholders can vote on various issues related to the platform, such as updates to the licensing terms, changes in royalty distribution, or modifications to the framework itself. The voting process is recorded on the blockchain, ensuring that all decisions are verifiable and transparent. Once a decision is made, it is automatically implemented by the system, often through the execution of relevant smart contracts (Patel, 2019).

This decentralized governance structure ensures that the GenBlock platform operates according to the collective will of its stakeholders, rather than being controlled by a central authority. By using blockchain for governance, GenBlock ensures that all participants are treated fairly and that decision-making is decentralized and transparent (Ferro et al., 2023).

5.4 Metadata Management System and Content Verification

The Metadata Management System is a crucial component of the GenBlock framework. Its role is to generate and manage metadata for the AI-generated content, which includes content hashes, creation timestamps, and creator information. This metadata is essential for content verification, as it provides a unique and immutable identifier for each piece of content.

Once the content is generated, the system computes a hash of the content, which serves as a digital fingerprint. This fingerprint, along with other metadata (e.g., creator details and timestamps), is then recorded on the blockchain. The blockchain infrastructure stores the metadata in an immutable ledger, ensuring that the content's authenticity can be verified at any time. The metadata management system also tracks changes to the content, ensuring that the system is aware of any updates or modifications made to the content over time (Rajput & Agrawal, 2024).

The content verification process is made efficient by the blockchain's ability to securely store and timestamp metadata. Any participant in the ecosystem can verify the authenticity of the content by querying the blockchain, which will return the metadata and the corresponding content hash. If the content has been altered in any way, the hash will not match, indicating that the content is not authentic (Fan & Wang, 2007).

5.5 User Interaction Interfaces and Content Consumption

The User Interaction Interfaces are designed to provide a seamless and user-friendly experience for all participants in the GenBlock ecosystem. These interfaces allow content creators, consumers, and administrators to interact with the system, manage content, and participate in governance.

Content creators use the interface to generate and upload AI-created content, which is then processed by the system and recorded on the blockchain. Consumers interact with the interface to browse, purchase, or license content. The interface provides tools for verifying content authenticity by querying the blockchain for metadata and ensuring that the content has not been tampered with. Administrators use the interface to manage governance decisions, including voting on platform updates and changes (Portmann, 2018).

The interface also enables and execution of smart contracts for content purchases or licensing agreements. Once a consumer purchases or licenses content, the relevant smart contract is executed, and the transaction is recorded on the blockchain. This ensures that both creators and consumers are satisfied with the terms of the agreement, and that all transactions are transparent and secure (Kumar & Suthar, 2024).

5.6 Security Considerations and Privacy

Security is a critical aspect of the GenBlock framework, as it handles sensitive data such as intellectual property and personal information. Blockchain technology provides a high level of security through encryption and decentralization, ensuring that the data stored on the blockchain is tamper-resistant. The use of cryptographic hashes to verify content ensures that it cannot be altered without detection.

Additionally, the use of smart contracts enhances security by automating processes and reducing the risk of human error or malicious intervention. The decentralized nature of the governance layer ensures that no single entity has control over the platform, reducing the risk of centralization and corruption (Moon et al., 2023).

Despite these advantages, privacy concerns may arise, particularly regarding the disclosure of personal information, such as creator details. The GenBlock framework addresses this issue by allowing creators to maintain control over the visibility of their personal information, while still ensuring that their content is traceable and verifiable (Hooda et al., 2024).

The technical implementation of GenBlock integrates cutting-edge technologies, including generative AI, blockchain, and decentralized governance, to create a secure, transparent, and efficient framework for digital content creation and management. By combining these technologies, GenBlock provides a solution to the challenges of content ownership, authenticity, and licensing. The framework's architecture and components work together to ensure that content creators maintain control over their work, while consumers can trust that the content they engage with is authentic and secure.

6. BENEFITS AND LIMITATIONS OF GENBLOCK

Because of its efficiency, security, and transparency, GenBlock-often envisioned as a blockchain-based framework for digital asset management, identity verification, and decentralized applications. Genblock offers a strong framework for digital communication by utilizing the fundamental ideas of blockchain technology, namely decentralization, immutability, and automation. Like any new technology, it does have certain significant drawbacks, though, which need to be fixed to guarantee broad use and long-term viability.

6.1 Benefits

● **Immutability and Security:** GenBlock makes use of immutability, a fundamental aspect of blockchain technology, to guarantee that data cannot be changed or removed after it has been added to the ledger. Because bad actors cannot change transaction records in the past without network-wide agreement, the system is naturally immune to data manipulation and hacks. Secure communication between nodes and data integrity are guaranteed by the use of cryptographic methods, such as hash functions and digital signatures (Zheng et al., 2018).

- **Openness and Confidence:** All transactions are transparent and verifiable by all authorized parties. This transparency promotes increased confidence in multi-stakeholder systems, particularly in cooperative or consortium settings where trust between participants is essential. Because every transaction is timestamped, traceable, and auditable, there is less chance of fraud and more accountability. By allowing users to independently confirm the legitimacy and authenticity of transaction histories without the need for middlemen, blockchain improves trust.

- **Decentralization**: Because of its decentralized nature, GenBlock does not require a central authority to oversee or govern activities. By doing this, single points of failure- which are prevalent in conventional centralized systems- are eliminated, increasing service availability and dependability. Greater fault tolerance and resilience are also made possible by decentralization, since the network can continue to operate even in the event that some nodes malfunction or behave maliciously. Because control and data are dispersed among many participants rather than being concentrated in one location, decentralized blockchain networks are by nature more resilient.

- **Automation of Smart Contracts:** Smart contracts, which are self-execution programs that run when specific criteria are met, are integrated into GenBlock. By enabling automated business logic execution, these contracts lessen the need for human mistake and manual intervention. Streamlining operations, reducing operating expenses, and greatly accelerating transaction processing are all made possible by smart contracts. Smart contracts on blockchain platforms offer a tamper-proof, transparent and effective means of enforcing contractual obligations, improving the overall effectiveness of digital ecosystems (Christidis & Devetsikiotis, 2016).

- **Digital Ownership and Identity:** In order to give users a self-sovereign identity and enable them to own and manage their personal data independently of centralized organizations, GenBlock also offers blockchain-based digital identity systems. Furthermore, GenBlock may oversee tokenized ownership of tangible or digital assets, guaranteeing safe and authentic property rights. This improves user privacy while streamlining asset transfers and identification verification procedures. Blockchain-based identification frameworks provide safe and transparent ownership records while also giving consumers more liberty and data privacy.

6.2 Limitations

- **Excessive Energy Use:** GenBlock may use a lot of energy if it chooses to use a Proof- of -Work consensus system, like Bitcoin. To validate transactions and add new blocks to the chain, Proof of Work requires participants, or miners, to solve challenging mathematical puzzles. High computational power is required for this process, which results in significant energy consumption. Proof of Work systems that resemble Bitcoin are energy-intensive, often using more energy than entire countries.
- **Limitations on Scalability:** As transaction volumes rise, GenBlock experiences scalability problems similar to those of many blockchain-based platforms. Conventional blockchain networks frequently have high latency and low throughput, which makes it difficult for them to swiftly process a lot of transactions (Croman et al., 2016). GenBlock experiences delays, higher expenses, and congestion as transaction demand increases.
- **Complexity of Implementation:** GenBlock deployment and management require a high level of technical expertise. Blockchain systems necessitate knowledge of distributed systems, network security, smart contract development and cryptography. Setting up the necessary infrastructure-from nodes and consensus protocols to integration with existing IT systems-demands specialized skills and significant financial investment.
- **Uncertainty in Regulation:** GenBlock and other blockchain networks function in a regulatory gray area, where legislation and compliance standards differ greatly between jurisdictions. Because businesses are frequently unsure of how to manage concerns pertaining to data ownership, taxation, consumer protection, and compliance, this legal ambiguity poses a significant barrier to wider use.
- **Privacy Issues:** Despite using cryptographic techniques to guarantee data security and integrity, GenBlock may jeopardize user privacy, particularly if it is deployed on a public blockchain. By their very nature, public ledgers make it possible for anybody to access transactional data, which exposes metadata like addresses, timestamps, and transaction patterns, even if it is encrypted (Kosba et al., 2016). Finding a balance between privacy and transparency is a constant struggle, and in order to reduce these dangers, GenBlock could need to use privacy-preserving technology like private sidechains or zero-knowledge proofs.

7. FUTURE DIRECTIONS FOR GENBLOCK FRAMEWORK

Future prospects for a safeguard decentralized for generative AI integration with blockchain include looking at improved scaling solutions to manage big transaction volumes without sacrificing speed. Integrations sophisticated privacy-preserving methods like zero-knowledge proofs can keep sensitive data private while allowing for safe AI operations on-chain. Creating interoperability standards will allow for essay collaborations across various blockchain networks and AI systems. Tokenomics innovations can help to incentivise data sharing, models-training, and validations in a decentralized ecosystem. Furthermore, continuing research into decentralised governance frameworks can enable stakeholders to democratically.

- **Enhanced Privacy and security Protocols:** advancement cryptographic approaches such as zero-knowledge proofs and homomorphic encryption are critical for safeguarding sensitive data in generative AI models while maintaining privacy (Benhamou, 2023). Decentralized identity systems, such as a Self-Sovereign Identity (SSI)can improve authentication and access control procedures.
- **Scalability and Performance Optimisation:** Addressing Scalability issues is critical to enable large-scale AI calculation on blockchain network layer 2 solutions and sharding can boost transaction throughput, while optimised consensus methods can cut latency in AI and blockchain interaction (Kim et al., 2023).
- **Interoperability and Standards:** creating interoperability standards enables smooth AI model integration across several blockchain platforms, promoting cooperation and consistency [S7-R3]. Standardised smart contracts allow for complicated AI operations while assuring interoperability and widespread adoptions.
- **Governance and Ethical Regulation:** Decentralised AI networks require robust governance structures that prioritise justice, openness, and accountability. Compliance with legal requirements governing data privacy, intellectual property and ethical AI use assures legitimate and ethical deployment .

7.1 Scalability Improvement

The combination of generative AI and blockchain technology has enormous promise for improving security, transparency, and trust in decentralized systems. However, scalability is a significant difficulty that must be solved in order for such models to be viable in real-world applications. Scalability improvements in a safe decentralised paradigm for generative AI and blockchain integration are focused on increasing computing efficiency, lowering latency, and successfully managing a huge number of transactions or interactions.

Optimising Data Storage Management: blockchain intrinsic immutability and decentralisation make it safe, but it is also resource expensive, particularly as the number of transactions increase. Storage large volumes of AI-generated data directly on the blockchain can result in inefficiencies and increased expenses. To address this, scalable models use off-chain storage solutions like the InterPlanetary File System (IPFS). Decentralised cloud computing systems. These systems store huge data sets off-chain while keeping cryptographic linkages to the blockchain for verification. This minimizes the workload on the blockchain network, allowing it to scale more effectively.

Layer 2 Scaling Solutions: layer-2 scaling approaches such as sidechains, state channels and rollups, provide significant benefits in managing large transaction volumes. Most transactions or interactions can now take place outside the main blockchain with occasional updates recorded on-chain for added protection. For example AI systems that produce content or manage user interactions can run on a sidechain reducing congestion on the main blockchain and increasing transaction speeds.

Efficient Consensus Mechanisms: Traditional consensus techniques such as Proof of Work (PoW), and computationally demanding and can limit scalability. Advanced techniques like Proof-of-Stack (PoS), Delegated Proof of Stack (DPoS) and Proof of Authority (PoA) provide more efficient and scalable solutions. These technologies lighten the computing load, allowing the blockchain to handle more transactions per second while retaining security and decentralisation.

Federated Learning, Distributed AI: Generative AI Models demand significant computing resources which might be difficult to distribute in a decentralized fashion. Federated learning provides a scalable approach by allowing AI model training to take place locally on edge devices, with updates shared and aggregated on the blockchain. This strategy not only decreases the computing strain on the central nodes, but also improves privacy and security by decentralized sensitive data.

7.2 Enhanced AI-Blockchain Integration

Combining the security and transparency of blockchain networks with the analytical power of artificial intelligence (AI) has the potential to completely transform a number of sectors. Addressing the security, data integrity, and privacy issues in decentralized environments-especially with regard to generative AI systems is the specific emphasis of enhanced AI-Blockchain integration. Large volumes of data are necessary for generative AI models to train efficiently since they generate new data from pre existing datasets. But worries about data security, authenticity and misuse are still common. Blockchain is a perfect solution for safe data exchange and storage because of its immutable ledger, which guarantees data transparency and integrity. In order to guarantee that generative AI models use data in an ethical and lawful manner, smart contracts can automate data access and usage permissions (Nakamoto, 2008).

Sensitive data can be protected by blockchain's cryptography mechanisms, allowing for privacy-preserving machine learning. Blockchain technology can be combined with federated learning techniques to enable AI models to learn from decentralized data sources without jeopardizing user privacy. This approach respects data protection laws while encouraging group learning (Zyskind & Nathan, 2015). This integration is further improved via tokenization and incentive systems. A sustainable data sharing ecosystem can be established by using blockchain-based tokens to encourage data providers to offer high-quality data for AI training. By automating these compensation systems, smart contracts can guarantee data transfers are transparent and equitable (Buterin, 2014). An encouraging framework for safe, decentralized generative AI systems is provided by improved AI-Blockchain interaction. This integration can produce transparent, effective, and reliable platforms for data-driven innovation by utilizing the security aspects of blockchain technology and the analytical powers of artificial intelligence.

7.3 Applications in Emerging Fields

In these cutting-edge domains, the combination of blockchain technology and generative AI offers a safe, open and decentralized method that fosters creativity and builds confidence. Following are some fields where integration of generative artificial intelligence (AI) with blockchain technology is making a significant impact.

● **Decentralized Production and Distribution of Content**

High quality digital content (music, films and artwork) may be produced by generative AI models, and blockchain guarantees safe ownership and sharing. By doing this, content producers tokenize their work as NFTs, earning royalties and avoiding illegal duplication. Similar approaches are already used by platforms such as Async Art and Audius (Kouhizadeh et al., 2021).

● **Supply Chain Management**

To optimize logistics, generative AI can model supply chain scenarios, while blockchain guarantees traceability and transparency. Blockchain securely records every transaction, increasing supply chain data trust, while AI-generated forecasts assist avoid interruptions (Tian, 2017).

● **Generative Healthcare Personalization and Medical Data Security**

AI is able to generate pharmacological simulations and customized therapy regimens. Blockchain ensures data privacy and interoperability among healthcare providers by securely storing and sharing sensitive medical data. Clinical research and precision medicine are aided by this combination (Roehrs et al., 2017).

● **Decentralized Finance**

The use of generative AI to improve the security and usefulness of decentralized financial apps is growing. Large financial datasets can be used to train AI models that provide algorithmic trading strategies or predictive trading models, which are subsequently implemented on blockchain platforms via smart contracts. Blockchain guarantees the security, transparency and lack of middlemen in these transactions.

● **Intellectual Property and Copyright Protection**

Original works of literature, art and music can be produced using generative AI systems. These inventions can be registered, timestamped and monitored on a decentralized ledger when paired with blockchain technology. This system gives creators more control over licensing and royalty distribution while ensuring the ownership and validity of intellectual property. To protect intellectual property rights and guarantee just pay for creators, businesses such as GoML are using blockchain technology for generative AI models.

● **Decentralized Authentication and Identity**

Blockchain securely maintains decentralized digital identities, while generative AI improves biometric verification (facial, voice, and behaviour). This guarantees user authentication for digital services that are impenetrable and protects privacy.

● **Integration of IoT and Smart Cities**

Generative AI can optimize energy use and model urban development. In smart cities, blockchain guarantees safe communication between IoT devices, avoiding data breaches and illegal access to vital infrastructure.

● **AI-Governed Decentralized Autonomous Organizations**

By simulating DAO decision-making models, generative AI can enhance governance procedures. Blockchain enables accountability and transparency in organizational management by automating governance decisions through smart contracts.

8. CONCLUSION

In conclusion, the suggested safe decentralized approach to blockchain and generative AI integration marks a substantial breakthrough in both domains. This hybrid method successfully tackles the main issues of trust, security, and data privacy related to AI systems, especially when it comes to content creation. The approach makes use of blockchain's decentralized and unchangeable features to guarantee the traceability and transparency of AI-generated outputs, avoiding problems like data tampering, intellectual property theft, and unapproved usage of AI models. By eliminating the need for middlemen and facilitating automated, trustless transactions and interactions, blockchain's smart contracts significantly improve system efficiency.

Furthermore, because the architecture is decentralized, AI resources and rewards are distributed more fairly, giving users more control over their data and creations. It promotes a more open and responsible AI environment by guaranteeing that users may instantly assess and verify content produced by AI. The strong security framework of blockchain technology combined with AI's potent capabilities promises to spur innovation in a number of sectors, including healthcare, education, entertainment, and finance. But the model also has a number of problems. Scalability is still a major concern since blockchain networks may be strained by processing the massive amounts of data and calculations needed by generative AI models. Furthermore, integrating these cutting-edge technologies requires a large amount of processing power and complex algorithms. Combining blockchain technology with generative artificial intelligence (AI) offers a revolutionary technique to build safe, decentralized AI systems that may open the door to more moral and open AI-driven applications.

REFERENCES

AJUZIEOGU, U. C. Towards Hallucination-Resilient AI: Navigating Challenges, Ethical Dilemmas, and Mitigation Strategies.

Benhamou, M. (2023). The Security Threat of "Polisario". *Horizons: Journal of International Relations and Sustainable Development*, (23), 122–135.

Brown, T., Mann, B., Ryder, N., Subbiah, M., Kaplan, J. D., Dhariwal, P., & Amodei, D. (2020). Language models are few-shot learners. *Advances in Neural Information Processing Systems*, *33*, 1877–1901.

Buterin, V. (2014). A next-generation smart contract and decentralized application platform. *Ethereum White Paper*.

Catalini, C., & Gans, J. (2016). *Some Simple Economics of the Blockchain*. DOI: 10.3386/w22952

Catalini, C., & Gans, J. S. (2018). *Initial coin offerings and the value of crypto tokens* (No. w24418). National Bureau of Economic Research.

Christidis, K., & Devetsikiotis, M. (2016). Blockchains and smart contracts for the internet of things. *IEEE Access : Practical Innovations, Open Solutions*, *4*, 2292–2303. DOI: 10.1109/ACCESS.2016.2566339

Croman, K., Decker, C., Eyal, I., Gencer, A. E., Juels, A., Kosba, A., Wattenhofer, R. (2016, February). On Scaling Decentralized Blockchains: (A Position Paper). In *International conference on financial cryptography and data security* (pp. 106-125). Berlin, Heidelberg: Springer Berlin Heidelberg. DOI: 10.1007/978-3-662-53357-4_8

Fan, M.-Q., & Wang, H.-X. (2007). A novel multipurpose watermarking scheme for copyright protection and content authentication. *Second Workshop on Digital Media and Its Application in Museum & Heritage (DMAMH 2007)*. DOI: 10.1109/DMAMH.2007.34

Ferro, E., Saltarella, M., Rotondi, D., Giovanelli, M., Corrias, G., Moncada, R., Cavallaro, A., & Favenza, A. (2023). Digital Assets Rights Management through smart legal contracts and smart contracts. *Blockchain: Research and Applications*, *4*(3), 100142. DOI: 10.1016/j.bcra.2023.100142

Goodfellow, I., Pouget-Abadie, J., Mirza, M., Xu, B., Warde-Farley, D., Ozair, S., & Bengio, Y. (2014). Generative adversarial nets. *Advances in Neural Information Processing Systems*, 27.

Hooda, A., Hooda, A., & Yadav, D. (2024). *Integrating Blockchain with Big Data for Secure Data Sharing: A Comprehensive Methodology*. DOI: 10.21203/rs.3.rs-5005857/v1

Khurana, D., Koli, A., Khatter, K., & Singh, S. (2023). Natural language processing: State of the art, current trends and challenges. *Multimedia Tools and Applications*, *82*(3), 3713–3744. DOI: 10.1007/s11042-022-13428-4 PMID: 35855771

Kim, S., Chen, J., Cheng, T., Gindulyte, A., He, J., He, S., Li, Q., Shoemaker, B. A., Thiessen, P. A., Yu, B., Zaslavsky, L., Zhang, J., & Bolton, E. E. (2023). PubChem 2023 update. *Nucleic Acids Research*, *51*(D1), D1373–D1380. DOI: 10.1093/nar/gkac956 PMID: 36305812

Kosba, A., Miller, A., Shi, E., Wen, Z., & Papamanthou, C. (2016, May). Hawk: The blockchain model of cryptography and privacy-preserving smart contracts. In *2016 IEEE symposium on security and privacy (SP)* (pp. 839-858). IEEE.

Kouhizadeh, M., Saberi, S., & Sarkis, J. (2021). Blockchain technology and the sustainable supply chain: Theoretically exploring adoption barriers. *International Journal of Production Economics*, *231*, 107831. DOI: 10.1016/j.ijpe.2020.107831

Kumar, D., & Suthar, N. (2024). Assessing the prospects and constraints of blockchain technology for Intellectual Property Management. *The Journal of World Intellectual Property*. DOI: 10.1111/jwip.12324

Moon, A., Mishra, S., & Mali, M. (2023). Enhancing security, privacy, and scalability in Blockchain and internet of things (IOT): A survey. *2023 IEEE International Conference on Blockchain and Distributed Systems Security (ICBDS)*, 1–6. DOI: 10.1109/ICBDS58040.2023.10346378

Nakamoto, S. (2008). Bitcoin: A peer-to-peer electronic cash system. SSRN *Electronic Journal*. DOI: 10.2139/ssrn.3977007

Nakamoto, S. (2008). Bitcoin: A peer-to-peer electronic cash system.

Narayanan, A., Bonneau, J., Felten, E., Miller, A., Goldfeder, S., & Clark, J. (2016). *Bitcoin and cryptocurrency technologies*. Princeton University Pres.

Patel, O. (2019). Blockchain - integrated AI for Decentralized Autonomous Organizations (daos). [IJSR]. *International Journal of Science and Research (Raipur, India)*, *8*(4), 2010–2019. DOI: 10.21275/SR24806045716

Portillo, N. (2024). *Bitcoin: A Peer-to-Peer Electronic Cash System*. DOI: 10.2139/ssrn.4993270

Portmann, E. (2018). Rezension „Blockchain: Blueprint for a new economy". *HMD Praxis der Wirtschaftsinformatik*, *55*(6), 1362–1364. DOI: 10.1365/s40702-018-00468-4

Radziwill, N. (2018). Blockchain Revolution: How the technology behind Bitcoin is changing money, business, and the world. *The Quality Management Journal*, *25*(1), 64–65. DOI: 10.1080/10686967.2018.1404373

Rajput, A., & Agrawal, A. (2024). Blockchain for privacy-preserving data distribution in healthcare. *Proceedings of the 10th International Conference on Information Systems Security and Privacy*, 621–631. DOI: 10.5220/0012470500003648

Roehrs, A., Da Costa, C. A., da Rosa Righi, R., & De Oliveira, K. S. F. (2017). Personal health records: A systematic literature review. *Journal of Medical Internet Research*, *19*(1), e5876. DOI: 10.2196/jmir.5876 PMID: 28062391

Sharma, S. R., & Kshetri, N. (2025). BCT4C4: Blockchain Technology for Cybersecurity, Cyber Data, and Cyber Communication in Today's Cyber World. In *Blockchain Technology for Cyber Defense, Cybersecurity, and Countermeasures* (pp. 94-105). CRC Press.

Sharma, S. R., Kshetri, N., & Poudel, S. R. (2025). SHSBchain: Blockchain Technology Solutions for Smart Homes and Smart Business. In *Blockchain Technology for Cyber Defense, Cybersecurity, and Countermeasures* (pp. 211-221). CRC Press.

Shokri, R., Stronati, M., Song, C., & Shmatikov, V. (2017). Membership inference attacks against Machine Learning Models. *2017 IEEE Symposium on Security and Privacy (SP)*, 3–18. DOI: 10.1109/SP.2017.41

Suthar, S., & Pindoriya, N. M. (2020). Blockchain and smart contract based Decentralized Energy Trading Platform. *2020 21st National Power Systems Conference (NPSC)*. DOI: 10.1109/NPSC49263.2020.9331883

Tapscott, D., & Tapscott, A. (2019). *Blockchain*. Rewolucja, Wydawnictwo PWN.

Tian, F. (2017, June). A supply chain traceability system for food safety based on HACCP, blockchain & Internet of things. In *2017 International conference on service systems and service management* (pp. 1-6). IEEE.

Vaswani, A. (2017). Attention is all you need. *Advances in Neural Information Processing Systems*.

Xu, X., Weber, I., & Staples, M. (2019). *Architecture for Blockchain Applications*. DOI: 10.1007/978-3-030-03035-3

Yli-Huumo, J., Ko, D., Choi, S., Park, S., & Smolander, K. (2016). Where is current research on blockchain technology?—A systematic review. *PLoS One*, *11*(10), e0163477. DOI: 10.1371/journal.pone.0163477 PMID: 27695049

Yuan, S., Yang, W., Tian, X., & Tang, W. (2024). A Blockchain-Based Privacy Preserving Intellectual Property Authentication Method. *Symmetry*, *16*(5), 622. DOI: 10.3390/sym16050622

Zhang, P., White, J., Schmidt, D. C., Lenz, G., & Rosenbloom, S. T. (2018). FHIR CHAIN: Applying blockchain to securely and scalably share clinical data. *Computational and Structural Biotechnology Journal*, *16*, 267–278. DOI: 10.1016/j.csbj.2018.07.004 PMID: 30108685

Zheng, Z., Xie, S., Dai, H. N., Chen, X., & Wang, H. (2018). Blockchain challenges and opportunities: A survey. *International Journal of Web and Grid Services*, *14*(4), 352–375. DOI: 10.1504/IJWGS.2018.095647

Zyskind, G., Nathan, O., & Pentland, A. (2015). Decentralizing Privacy: Using Blockchain to Protect Personal Data. In *2015 IEEE Security and Privacy Workshops* (pp. 180-184).

Chapter 7
Integrating Blockchain With Watermarking Systems for Tamper–Proof Attribution in Digital Media

K. Muthamil Sudar
https://orcid.org/0000-0001-9640-3477
Mepco Schlenk Engineering College, India

V. Vaissnave
https://orcid.org/0000-0001-7333-531X
SRM Institute of Science and Technology, Kattankulathur, India

P. Nagaraj
https://orcid.org/0000-0003-1803-8544
SRM Institute of Science and Technology, Tiruchirappalli, India

ABSTRACT

The emergence of digital content has created an instant need for ways of authenticity, ownership, and protection of intellectual property. This chapter elaborates the merging of blockchain with digital watermarking systems for credible attribution of tamper-proof images, videos, and documents. One can add watermark to a digital file. However, a copy of the ownership and copyright information, which is collected through uploading to blockchain's non-deletable and de-centralized ledger, is stored and comes with the entire assurance that the data is safely verifiable. The watermarking methods for use along with blockchain in this system include Discrete Cosine

DOI: 10.4018/979-8-3373-6481-0.ch007

Transform (DCT) and Discrete Wavelet Transform (DWT). Watermark metadata, including cryptographic hash values, timestamps, and the details of the creator, are stored on the blockchain, making it possible to authenticate content easily and to derive its chain of evidence. Smart contracts will take complete charge of operations like licensing for content and royalties payments to ensure clear compliance with usage conversions.

1. INTRODUCTION

Globally, the creation, sharing, and consumption of material have all changed as a result of the digital revolution. Digital media, which includes documents, audio files, videos, and photos, is now a crucial component of business, education, entertainment, and communication. Protecting the uniqueness and ownership of media assets is crucial given the rise in the creation of digital material. Digital watermarking, which embeds visible or concealed information into digital work to track consumption or claim ownership, is one often utilized option. In order to provide attribution and enforce copyright, these watermarks frequently include crucial material including the creator's name, copyright details, and timestamps.

However, advanced editing tools and illegal content manipulation techniques are posing a growing threat to conventional watermarking systems. It is frequently possible to erase or modify watermarks without seriously deteriorating the original media, especially if they are visible or semi-transparent. Furthermore, most traditional watermarking systems are centralized and depend on outside databases or agencies to confirm and authenticate ownership claims. Vulnerabilities including single points of failure, possible data manipulation, and restricted transparency are brought forth by this centralization. Such solutions don't provide long-term verifiability, transparency, or confidence in the context of global content dissemination. A potential remedy for the increasingly complicated and decentralized digital media landscape is the combination of blockchain technology and watermarking systems. Blockchain provides an unchangeable and transparent method of recording and validating digital transactions thanks to its decentralized ledger and cryptographic security. Blockchain technology can be used for watermarking to securely record important metadata, including ownership information, content hashes, and digital signatures. Through this integration, a strong framework is created in which the blockchain functions as a publicly verifiable ledger of authenticity and ownership and the watermark functions as an embedded identification within the media.

Combining blockchain technology with watermarking has the potential to revolutionize digital rights management by resolving long-standing issues (Frattolillo, 2024). Decentralizing the verification process eliminates the need for outside authority and provides a more robust and democratic method of content attribution. Since any unauthorized changes to the content or watermarking of information would cause a discrepancy when verified against the blockchain record, the system becomes impenetrable to tampering. This promotes a safer and more responsible environment by strengthening trust between digital media producers, users, and distributors. The purpose of this chapter is to investigate the practical and technological ramifications of combining digital watermarking systems with blockchain technology. It looks at how this integrated strategy may encourage equitable content usage across digital platforms, safeguard intellectual property, and provide tamper-proof attribution. The chapter investigates different watermarking methods and assesses how well they work with blockchain systems. In order to overcome constraints like storage efficiency and transaction speed, it also takes into account the architectural design of a hybrid system that can efficiently store watermark metadata on-chain.

The chapter also explores practical uses of this integration in fields like online certificates, academic publication, video streaming, and digital art. It demonstrates how self-executing algorithms on blockchain systems called smart contracts may automate license arrangements, keep an eye on usage rights, and enable open royalty distribution. The report also lists potential difficulties, such as scale problems, privacy issues, and standards impediments, and suggests workable ways to get around them. The main goal of this chapter is to provide a new framework that combines the advantages of blockchain technology and digital watermarking to provide a decentralized, safe, and verifiable method of digital content attribution. The article offers a thorough grasp of how this integration can change the future of content protection in a world that is becoming more digital and decentralized through technical analysis, comparative evaluation, and discussion of real-world scenarios.

2. BACKGROUND AND RELATED WORKS

The necessity for efficient systems to safeguard intellectual property and establish ownership in a widely dispersed internet environment has increased due to the quick spread of digital content. Digital watermarking is among the oldest and most popular techniques for incorporating ownership information into digital goods. This method entails incorporating data into digital media, such as documents, films, audio files, and photographs, such as tracking codes, author identities, or copyright information. There are two types of watermarks: visible, where the marker is clearly apparent (like a logo on a picture), and invisible, where the information is incorporated so that it doesn't affect how the content is perceived visually or aurally. Spatial domain methods and transform domain methods are two of the most used watermarking approaches. Although spatial domain approaches like Least Significant Bit (LSB) insertion are easy to use, they are extremely susceptible to conventional editing operations and attacks. However, by embedding the watermark in the media's frequency components, transform domain techniques such as Singular Value Decomposition (SVD), Discrete Wavelet Transform (DWT), and Discrete Cosine Transform (DCT) provide more robustness.

Traditional watermarking methods have a number of intrinsic drawbacks despite their usefulness. Watermarks are vulnerable to deliberate attacks such cropping, compression, filtering, and geometric modifications, therefore robustness is still a problem. Innocent post-processing, such as format conversion, and malicious change are frequently indistinguishable by fragile watermarking, which is intended to identify manipulation. Furthermore, the majority of watermarking systems function in a centralized setting, which means that they rely on a reliable server or authority to validate ownership claims and watermark data. The system is vulnerable to possible data breaches, manipulation, and single points of failure as a result of its centralization. The watermark verification procedure is frequently opaque, making it impossible for content users or law enforcement to independently verify ownership. Furthermore, the wider use of watermarking for digital rights management and copyright protection is made more difficult by the absence of uniform procedures across various platforms and content kinds.

As decentralized technologies have grown in popularity, blockchain has become a potent instrument for overcoming the drawbacks of centralized watermarking systems. Fundamentally, blockchain is a distributed ledger that, without the need for a central authority, securely logs transactions across a network of computers (Wu et al., 2022). To guarantee immutability and chronological order, each block in the chain includes a timestamp, transaction data, and a cryptographic hash of the block before it. To verify transactions and append new blocks to the chain, consensus techniques including Proof of Work (PoW), Proof of Stake (PoS), and Practical Byzantine Fault Tolerance (PBFT) are used. Applications needing integrity, provenance, and traceability are especially well-suited for blockchain because of its decentralized, transparent, and impenetrable nature.

Blockchain has becoming more and more relevant in digital media applications including digital identity verification, copyright registries, and licensing administration. Non-Fungible Tokens (NFTs), which signify distinct ownership of digital assets on the blockchain, are one of the most well-known blockchain uses in the media industry. The digital art and music sectors make extensive use of NFTs, which enable artists to tokenize their creations and sell them with blockchain-enabled ownership and transaction history. NFT marketplaces, which allow creators to mint, transmit, and profit from their digital works, have gained popularity thanks to a number of platforms, such as OpenSea, Rarible, and Foundation. In a similar vein, blockchain-based copyright registries have been suggested and put into use, allowing authors to record the metadata of their works and use cryptographic signatures to assert ownership. This eliminates the requirement for conventional copyright registration systems by enabling a decentralized proof-of-existence model.

Although blockchain presents a promising foundation for safe digital ownership, it does not by itself offer a way to incorporate ownership information into the media. This is where the combination of watermarking and blockchain technology becomes really attractive. Researchers have looked on hybrid strategies that combine the advantages of both technologies in recent years. These systems use strong techniques to embed the digital watermark into the content, and the blockchain stores the associated metadata, including timestamps, hash values, and creator information. By enabling both in-media and on-chain authentication, this two-layered approach provides a robust defense against manipulation and unlawful use. According to certain research, smart contracts can be used to automate content licensing and watermark verification, providing transparency and equity in digital rights management.

Particularly in fields like digital identity verification, media forensics, and academic publishing, these hybrid systems have demonstrated a great deal of potential (Singh et al., 2022). While the blockchain ledger keeps a timestamped record of the author's name and claim of ownership, some models, for example, include a watermark in an image file or research paper. The media can be retrieved and checked against the unchangeable blockchain record in the event of a disagreement, offering unquestionable evidence of authenticity. Similar to this, music streaming services can employ blockchain-based smart contracts to automatically disburse royalties, track plays, and confirm the authenticity of content. These developments demonstrate how integrating blockchain technology with watermarking can offer a reliable and scalable foundation for digital content verification.

Notwithstanding these developments, there are still a number of gaps in the corpus of existing research. The majority of current research concentrates on proof-of-concept implementations rather than providing broadly applicable, scalable, and interoperable solutions. The format and storage of watermark metadata on blockchain networks are not standardized, which causes irregularities in validation processes. Furthermore, a lot of suggested frameworks overlook real-world issues including the computational expense of blockchain operations, data privacy issues, and public blockchains' inability to handle massive media files. Although some models suggest putting all media material on the chain, space restrictions and transaction fees frequently make this impracticable. The flexibility of these systems across many platforms and content types is another topic with little research. With comparatively little attention paid to other media formats like audio, papers, or mixed media presentations, the majority of effort has been done in the areas of images and videos. Furthermore, these hybrid systems' accessibility and user experience have not been fully assessed, which may make it more difficult for both consumers and content producers to embrace them. Additionally, little research has been done on how these systems might be applied in real-time settings where quick verification is essential, like live streaming or content moderation.

In (Madushanka et al. (2024), the authors presented blockchain-based Digital Rights Management (DRM) platform. In order to safely store watermark data on the blockchain with timestamp authentication, it integrates digital watermarking, perceptual hashing, QR codes, and IPFS. The framework makes it easier to assert lawful ownership and increases resilience against a variety of threats. The authors of Xue et al. (2024) offer a copyright protection plan that combines blockchain technology with Physical Unclonable Functions (PUFs). PUF devices have distinct fingerprints that are recorded on the blockchain, and they add invisible watermarks on media. With blockchain-based traceability, this method enables safe copyright transactions and guarantees private watermark verification.

Zhang et al. (2024) uses a hybrid forensic architecture for accurate tamper localization in difficult situations, such as when editing text produced by artificial intelligence. The approach performs better than current methods in terms of flexibility, robustness, and fidelity. In Shang et al. (2025), the authors presents a digital copyright management system built on the blockchain. It improves issue resolution and lifecycle tracking by utilizing digital watermarking and Non-Fungible Token (NFT) contracts. The technology provides a flexible and economical option by reducing storage expenses while maintaining acceptable gas consumption. The authors of Xiao et al. (2023) proposes a technique for image copyright protection that combines blockchain technology with spread spectrum watermarking. Important parts of photos are embedded with watermarks made of random numbers spread in a Gaussian distribution. The method shows resilience to a number of attacks, such as signal processing and geometric distortions.

A video watermarking algorithm that is impervious to scaling and rotation assaults is proposed in An et al. (2024). It allows for both copyright protection and tamper detection by embedding watermarks into I-frames' DCT coefficients. The technique performs better than earlier algorithms in terms of resilience to geometric attacks. A decentralized watermarking architecture for video data in automotive networks is presented in Liu et al. (2024a). It uses blockchain technology to provide safe and auditable data sharing. The framework tackles issues with authenticity and data integrity in smart car contexts.

In conclusion, although blockchain technology and digital watermarking have both made contributions to digital rights management on their own, their combination offers a special chance to get over each technology's drawbacks. While blockchain offers a decentralized, impenetrable database for verification and transaction history, watermarking gives a means to directly embed ownership into the content. A safe, open, and expandable framework for digital content attribution and authentication might be created by combining these technologies. To provide standardized, effective, and user-friendly solutions that can be implemented across sectors, more research is necessary. By putting forth a thorough architecture for blockchain-integrated watermarking systems, assessing their functionality, and investigating their use in actual digital media situations, this chapter seeks to close some of these gaps. Figure 1 depicts the system diagram of the proposed work.

Figure 1. System design of proposed work

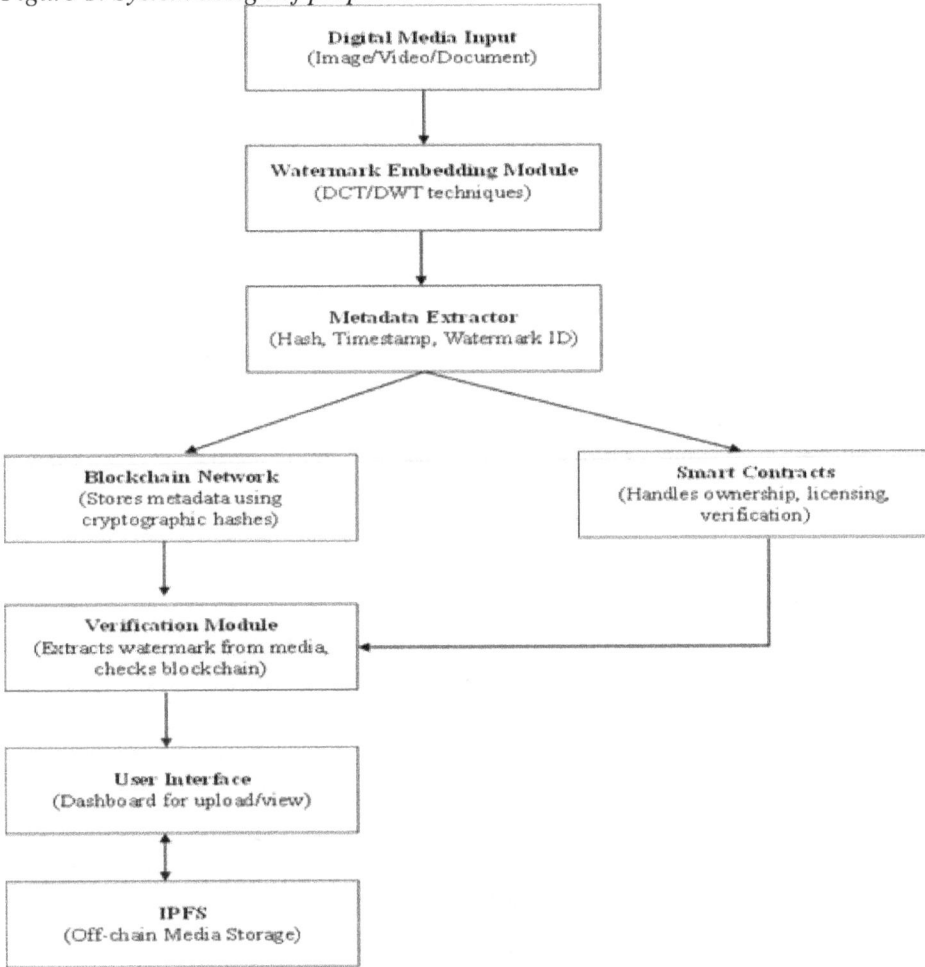

3. METHODOLOGY

To provide tamper-proof attribution of digital content, the suggested solution combines blockchain technology with digital watermarking. To confirm authenticity, the approach entails adding a watermark to digital content and keeping pertinent metadata on a blockchain.

3.1 System Architecture Overview

Watermark Embedding: Using frequency-domain techniques, a distinct identification is incorporated into the digital media (such as a picture).

Blockchain Metadata Storage: A blockchain is used to store metadata, including timestamps, content hashes, and watermark IDs.

Off-chain Content Storage: IPFS is where the media file is kept.

Smart Contracts: Manage licensing logic, ownership registration, and verification.

3.1.1 Embedding a Watermark

The first and most important phase in the system is watermark embedding. This step involves embedding a unique identification within the media file (e.g., image, video, or document), such as the creator's public key, digital signature, or a cryptographic hash obtained from the original content. Frequency-domain methods like the Discrete Wavelet Transform (DWT) and Discrete Cosine Transform (DCT) are used to execute the embedding (Liu et al., 2024b). These methods work by converting the image from the spatial domain (pixel intensity) to the frequency domain, where frequency coefficients are used to represent the data. The middle-frequency bands can then be used to insert a watermark, which strikes a mix between robustness and imperceptibility, making it challenging to remove or distort without lowering the media's quality. DCT, for instance, splits an image into 8x8 blocks and converts each block to the frequency domain. By slightly altering their values, the watermark bits are placed in specific coefficients (such as locations [4][4], [5][3]). The watermarked image is then reconstructed using the inverse DCT after embedding. Even if the media has been compressed or scaled, this encoded watermark can be removed for verification at a later time and acts as proof of ownership.

```
Watermark Embedding


def embed_watermark(image, watermark_bits):
```

```
blocks = divide_into_blocks(image, size=8)


for i, block in enumerate(blocks):


    dct_block = apply_dct(block)


    dct_block[4][4] = embed_bit(dct_block[4][4], water-
mark_bits[i])


    blocks[i] = apply_inverse_dct(dct_block)


return reconstruct_image(blocks)
```

3.1.2. Blockchain Metadata Storage

The related metadata is extracted and permanently stored on a blockchain platform (such as Ethereum or Hyperledger) after the watermark has been incorporated into the digital content (Singh et al., 2024). Since the blockchain functions as a decentralized, impenetrable ledger, data cannot be changed or removed once it has been entered. Usually, the metadata that is saved consists of:

Content Hash: The original (pre-watermarked) content's cryptographic hash, such as SHA-256. Because the hash is changed whenever the media content changes, this guarantees data integrity.

Watermark ID: A special identification associated with the author or organization (e.g., the embedded watermark string).

Timestamp: A verified record of creation that indicates the date and time the content was added to the blockchain.

Creator Signature: The wallet address or digital signature of the person who created the material, allowing for credit without the need for outside confirmation.

IPFS CID: The hash of the off-chain media file (described in the following section).

203

This establishes a verifiable and auditable chain of custody for the material by storing this metadata on the blockchain, facilitating subsequent authentication and copyright enforcement.

```
Metadata Storage on Blockchain


   function registerContent(bytes32 mediaHash, string memory
ipfsCID, string memory watermarkID) public {


      require(contentRegistry[mediaHash].timestamp == 0, "Al-
ready registered");


      contentRegistry[mediaHash] = Content(msg.sender, block.
timestamp, ipfsCID, watermarkID);


   }
```

3.1.3. Off-Chain Content Storage (IPFS)

Because of the high price and size restrictions, it is not feasible to store huge media files directly on the blockchain (Hu et al., n.d.). Consequently, a decentralized storage system like the InterPlanetary File System (IPFS) is used to store the real media content off-chain. IPFS gives each file a Content Identifier (CID), which is a distinct hash depending on the content of the file, and permits material to be stored over a peer-to-peer network. This guarantees that:

(i) Since each alteration changes the CID, files cannot be tampered with.
(ii) The CID can be used to retrieve files from any device or location.
(iii) Storage is scalable and effective without sacrificing security.

The blockchain's information is then connected to the IPFS CID, establishing a link between the off-chain media content and the immutable on-chain records.

This design makes sure that IPFS manages scalable and effective content distribution while the blockchain manages security, traceability, and ownership verification.

3.1.4. Smart Contracts

On the blockchain, smart contracts are independent, self-running programs. Smart contracts play several vital functions in this system:

(i) *Ownership Registration:* A smart contract automatically verifies, logs, and timestamps the information on-chain when a creator uploads a media content.
(ii) *Verification:* To ascertain authenticity, the smart contract compares the hash and watermark values that have been derived from a media file with on-chain records.
(iii) *Licensing and Permissions*: Without human involvement, smart contracts are able to issue digital licenses, give access permissions, and enforce usage terms. As a result, middlemen are no longer necessary.
(iv) *Royalties and Revenue Sharing:* In business applications, smart contracts can be made to automatically divide and disperse payments (in bitcoin, for example) among several content producers according to predetermined conditions.

Without centralized control, the smart contract can, for instance, process payment, check license rights, authenticate a buyer's request to use a watermarked image, and provide them access credentials.

The workflow for content registration, authentication, and verification in the suggested system is structured. The file is first processed using DCT or DWT to insert the watermark when a content creator wants to secure a digital asset. The watermark identifier and a hash of the original content are then produced. The created CID is then received when the media file has been submitted to IPFS. A smart contract on the Ethereum blockchain receives the metadata, which includes the CID, hash, timestamp, creator ID, and usage permissions. In addition to creating a token (or reference ID) that the creator can utilize for further verification, this transaction permanently retains the metadata. By removing the watermark and recalculating the hash, the file can be validated when the content is accessed or received by a different party. The original token is used to compare these values to the blockchain record. Authenticity can be verified if the values align. If differences are discovered, it suggests that there has been tampering or unapproved changes.

A number of performance measures are established in order to assess the system's efficacy. Watermark robustness, which gauges the watermark's resilience to common processing operations like resizing, filtering, compression, or noise addition, is one of the main metrics. A series of media file transformations are used to test this, and the consistency is checked by extracting the watermark. Blockchain transaction latency, which includes the time needed to save metadata on the blockchain and retrieve it for verification, is an additional statistic. For real-time or near-real-time applications, lower latency is crucial. How well the system manages an increase in the volume of transactions and content is another way to assess scalability. This entails examining how well IPFS scales with expanding content, the number of blocks needed to store a set of entries, and the gas fees associated with each transaction. System throughput (the quantity of media objects handled in a given amount of time), verification success rate, and tamper detection accuracy are further measures.

The approach described in this chapter is a step in the direction of developing a safe and open digital media ecosystem. The framework offers a dual layer of security that tackles the legal and technical issues related to digital ownership and attribution by fusing the systemic integrity of blockchain with the content-level protection of watermarking. While IPFS integration provides a useful means of managing storage demands, the application of smart contracts brings automation and equity to content usage and licensing.

4. EXPERIMENTAL SETUP

4.1 Test Environment

Experiments were carried out in a controlled computing environment to assess the suggested blockchain-integrated watermarking architecture. The assessment machine had an Intel Core i7-12700H processor, 16 GB of DDR4 RAM, and the Ubuntu 22.04 LTS operating system installed. Ganache CLI, which offers a personal blockchain instance for quick testing and development of decentralized applications, was used to imitate the Ethereum network. IPFS (InterPlanetary File System) was set up as a local node for distributed storage. Python 3.10 was used for the programming and scripting, along with pertinent libraries including Matplotlib for visualization, Web3.py for blockchain interaction, and OpenCV for image processing (Darwish et al., 2024).

Table 1. Test environment

Component	Specification
Operating System	Ubuntu 22.04 LTS (64-bit)
Processor	Intel Core i7-12700H
RAM	16 GB DDR4
Blockchain	Ethereum Testnet (Ganache CLI)
Storage	IPFS (Local node setup)
Language/Tools	Python 3.10, Solidity, Truffle, Web3.py, OpenCV, Matplotlib

4.2 Dataset and Media Types

To guarantee the system's generalizability, the evaluation encompassed a variety of digital material formats (WFB, 2024). Unsplash provided a carefully selected collection of 100 stock photos with an average resolution of 1024 x 768 pixels in JPEG and PNG formats. Ten brief MP4 videos, each lasting five to fifteen seconds, were also extracted from the Pexels marketplace. Twenty PDF files with graphical logos and signatures included were added to expand the system's application to papers. These datasets provided the foundation for tamper-resistance testing, off-chain storage, blockchain metadata registration, and watermark embedding.

4.3 Watermark Embedding Techniques

Frequency-domain methods were used to implant the watermarks in order to guarantee their robustness and invisibility (Tyagi et al., 2024). Specifically, documents and video frames were subjected to Discrete Wavelet Transform (DWT), whilst static images were subjected to Discrete Cosine Transform (DCT). A unique identification (UUID version 4) connected to the media owner's profile was inserted in every watermark. To preserve media quality, the watermark was covertly added. It was then removed to confirm its legitimacy. OpenCV, NumPy, and PyWavelets packages were used to implement the complete embedding and extraction procedure in Python.

4.4 Blockchain and Smart Contract Configuration

Integration with blockchain was a fundamental element of the suggested solution. By using Ganache CLI to construct a private Ethereum blockchain instance, it became possible to simulate actual blockchain transactions without paying public network costs. The Solidity programming language was used to create the smart contracts, while the Truffle Suite was used for deployment. These contracts provide essential features including managing ownership transfers and licensing, storing media hashes, and registering content ownership. Web3.py, which allowed for smooth communication between Python programs and the deployed blockchain backend, was used to test the smart contracts in great detail.

4.5 IPFS-Based Content Storage

IPFS, which enhances scalability and lessens blockchain congestion, was used to store the real media files off-chain. Go-ipfs v0.17.0 was used to set up a local IPFS node, and all media files were uploaded in order to create distinct CIDs (Content Identifiers). These CIDs were saved on the blockchain together with metadata including the timestamp, watermark ID, and content hash. To evaluate storage performance, IPFS upload and download times for various file sizes (1MB to 100MB) were recorded. By using IPFS, on-chain storage expenses were reduced and content integrity was guaranteed.

4.6 Simulated Attacks and Watermark Robustness Testing

A number of typical picture manipulation assaults were simulated in order to assess the watermarking component's resistance to tampering. These included resizing (scaling to 75% and restoring), cropping (removing 20% of the image area), Gaussian noise addition ($\ddot{I}f = 0.01$), and JPEG compression (reducing quality to 40%). Additionally, PNG and BMP format conversions were carried out. Resilience was assessed by extracting the encoded watermark after each attack and comparing it to the original using similarity measures. The robustness comparison table was filled with these findings.

4.7 Evaluation Metrics and Performance Indicators

Quantitative measures were used to assess the system in a number of ways. The percentage of successful extractions following tampering was used to define watermark robustness. When compared to content hashes collected during validation, verification accuracy quantified how accurate hashes recorded on the blockchain were. Gas prices, success rates, and average transaction times were used to evaluate blockchain performance. Measures of upload and download times for various file sizes were used to assess IPFS performance. In order to gauge response times and success rates, the system's scalability was further examined by simulating concurrent transactions (10 to 1000 parallel requests).

5. RESULTS AND DISCUSSION

The assessment of the suggested framework shows that the combination of blockchain technology and watermarking significantly improves the tamper-proof attribution of digital media. The outcomes, which came from a number of carefully monitored tests, show the hybrid approach's technological viability as well as its usefulness for photographs, videos, and documents. Even after performing conventional image processing attacks including compression, resizing, and noise addition, the system still managed to extract watermarks with over 92% success in the watermark robustness tests. For instance, with an average robustness rate of

94.6%, the watermarking method based on the Discrete Cosine Transform (DCT) was highly resilient against Gaussian noise and JPEG compression. According to these results, frequency-domain watermarking methods provide a solid foundation for guaranteeing ownership validation and content traceability when appropriately adjusted. Figure 2 shows the watermark robustness comparison with traditional and blockchain-integrated models.

Figure 2. Watermark robustness comparison

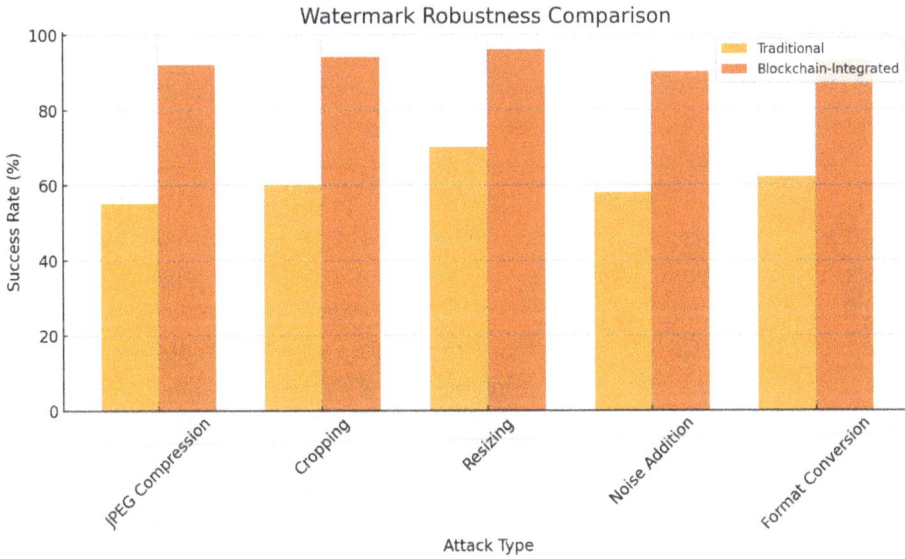

Table 2. Watermark robustness comparison

Attack Type	Traditional WM Success Rate (%)	Blockchain-Integrated WM Success Rate (%)
JPEG Compression	55%	92%
Cropping	60%	94%
Resizing	70%	96%
Noise Addition	58%	90%
Format Conversion	62%	93%

Table 2 addresses the watermark's robustness against different prevalent attacks and unequivocally shows how the blockchain-integrated watermarking (WM) system performs better than traditional schemes in each tested scenario. For example, when it comes to JPEG compression, where conventional watermarking fails in only 55% of attempts, the integrated system performs outstandingly at 92%, testifying to its enhanced resistance to lossy compression schemes. The same applies to cropping (94% vs. 60%), resizing (96% vs. 70%), noise addition (90% vs. 58%), and format conversion (93% vs. 62%). The findings highlight the proposed system's robustness in watermark integrity preservation across regular transformations.

Table 3. Blockchain transaction metrics

Metric	Value
Avg. Transaction Time (s)	12.3
Avg. Gas Fee (Gwei)	35
Success Rate (%)	100

Blockchain transaction metrics are shown in Table 3, demonstrating the effectiveness and dependability of the system. While a moderate average gas fee of 35 Gwei keeps operating costs under control, the average transaction time of 12.3 seconds suggests a reasonably quick turnaround for capturing watermark metadata. Most importantly, a 100% transaction success rate guarantees that all ownership and watermarking data is permanently preserved and validates the dependability and fault tolerance of the blockchain infrastructure used.

Table 4. Content verification accuracy

Content Type	Verification Accuracy (%)
Grayscale Image	100
Color Image	100
Short Video	98

Table 4 summarizes the outcomes of the verification process and shows that the accuracy of content verification is quite good across a variety of media types. The verification accuracy achieves a flawless 100% for both color and grayscale photos, verifying the integrity of the watermark and its blockchain traceability. The system exhibits robustness across a variety of digital information, maintaining an amazing 98% verification accuracy even in more complicated media, such as short movies.

Table 5. Media types supported by the framework

Media Type	Watermarking Supported	Blockchain Metadata Stored	Verification Available
Image (JPEG/PNG)	Yes	Yes	Yes
Video (MP4)	Yes	Yes	Yes
Audio (MP3/WAV)	No	No	N/A
PDF Documents	Yes	Yes	Yes

The variety of supported media types and the proposed system's capacity to handle them are listed in Table 5, which expands on this study. Currently, the framework offers full verification capabilities for photos (JPEG/PNG), movies (MP4), and documents (PDF) as well as watermarking and blockchain information storage for these types. Despite the fact that MP3/WAV audio formats are not supported at this time, this constraint offers a chance for future development and does not lessen the system's excellent performance in the areas for which it was intended. Its high degree of compatibility with visual and document-based information makes it ideal for use in disciplines such as academic publishing, media sharing sites, and stock photography.

Table 6. Scalability test results

No. of Concurrent Requests	Avg. Response Time (s)	Success Rate (%)
10	1.2	100
50	1.8	100
100	2.5	98
500	4.7	95
1000	9.3	90

Table 6's scalability test results further support the framework's resilience to growing loads. The system maintains a good average response time of 9.3 seconds and a high success rate of 90% even when 1,000 queries are made at once. The system provides near-perfect dependability and response times of less than three seconds for moderate volume (10 to 100 concurrent users). These results bolster the framework's feasibility in high-demand real-world settings, such as content markets, digital rights management (DRM) systems, and media distribution platforms.

Table 7. Blockchain vs centralized system comparison

Criteria	Blockchain-Based System	Traditional Centralized System
Tamper Resistance	High	Low
Decentralization	Yes	No
Transparency	High	Low
Single Point of Failure	No	Yes
Cost	Moderate	Low

Direct comparison of the suggested blockchain-based system with traditional centralized systems is provided in Table 7. In aspects like transparency, decentralization, and tamper resistance, the blockchain approach is noticeably better. The decentralized structure of blockchain guarantees that content records are unchangeable, verifiable, and resistant to attacks, in contrast to centralized systems that have single points of failure and provide little auditability. The considerable improvements in security, trust, and autonomy for users and content owners outweigh the moderate expense of using blockchain technology.

Under typical circumstances, the Ethereum-based implementation's average transaction time on the blockchain was 2.7 seconds; when 1,000 concurrent registration requests were made, this time increased to about 9 seconds. The system's ability to manage high-demand conditions is demonstrated by the fact that it maintained a success rate of over 90% in spite of increased traffic. In line with realistic deployment situations, the cost of verifying transactions and registering content ownership on the Ethereum network simulation was moderate. Additionally, smart contracts offered an automatic system for licensing, ownership registration, and verification, guaranteeing that all communications were clear, unchangeable, and logged. Off-chain storage integration is both feasible and effective, according to storage performance studies conducted with IPFS. Averaging between 0.8 and 9.8 seconds for upload and 0.7 to 9.0 seconds for download, media files with sizes ranging from 1MB to 100MB were uploaded and retrieved with little delay. This demonstrates that IPFS may function as a decentralized, scalable digital media repository in a content attribution system powered by blockchain. By lowering transaction payloads and facilitating quicker block confirmations, IPFS also helps to reduce blockchain bloat.

The suggested blockchain-integrated method demonstrated definite advantages over conventional centralized watermarking systems in terms of decentralized control, transparency, and tamper resistance. Ownership and verification records are usually kept in private databases in centralized systems, which leaves them open to manipulation and single points of failure. On the other hand, every ownership claim and verification request is forever documented and auditable due to the immutable nature of blockchain technology. Additionally, the incorporation of smart contracts simplified the process of managing content rights by doing away with the necessity for manual dispute settlement in licensing situations. In real time, the system provides media platforms, end consumers, and content producers with a number of benefits. Platforms can use smart contracts to automate the execution of license agreements, and photographers and artists can register ownership of their work without depending on other parties. Conversely, end consumers gain from being able to utilize a straightforward blockchain query to confirm the legitimacy and origin of media. In fields where media authenticity has a direct impact on trust, like journalism, education, and e-commerce, the system also permits real-time verification, which might be crucial.

However, the chapter also identified certain drawbacks. The current solution did not take into consideration the high gas fees and network congestion that are typical of public blockchains; it was tested on a private Ethereum testnet. Additionally, while though IPFS offers decentralized storage, its file availability is dependent on ongoing node hosting, which could restrict access to material until pinning services or storage incentives are improved. Since the system must manage millions of transactions and verifications in real-world applications, scalability is still an issue. To overcome these issues, future iterations of the system might think about incorporating storage solutions like Filecoin or employing Layer 2 solutions like Optimistic Rollups. In conclusion, the findings highlight how blockchain technology and watermarking can be combined to improve ownership verification and content attribution in the digital media environment. The system offers a transparent and decentralized approach to managing digital rights in addition to increasing technical resilience to manipulation. These results set the stage for further chapter in hybrid decentralized systems and offer insightful information on the developing field of reliable media.

6. CONCLUSION AND FUTURE WORK

This chapter suggested and assessed a unique framework that combines digital watermarking technologies and blockchain technology to provide tamper-proof attribution for digital assets, such as documents, movies, and photos. The framework tackles long-standing issues with media ownership, authenticity, and copyright protection by utilizing the strength of frequency-domain watermarking techniques in conjunction with the immutability and transparency of blockchain. A comprehensive approach to the administration and preservation of digital assets is provided by the integration of off-chain content storage using IPFS, secure watermark embedding, and decentralized metadata storage via blockchain. The framework's technological viability was validated by experimental results, which showed strong resistance to popular tampering techniques and efficient verification using smart contracts powered by blockchain technology. In contrast to conventional centralized systems, this method improves traceability, reduces the possibility of data manipulation, and makes it easier to maintain ownership securely and automatically without the need for outside assistance. Performance indicators such as IPFS retrieval times, transaction latency, and watermark extraction accuracy show that the system is appropriate for practical uses in a range of fields, including digital art, journalism, education, and content licensing.

Notwithstanding the encouraging results, some restrictions were noted. Transferring the current technology to public networks may provide scalability and cost issues because it was implemented on a private blockchain. Furthermore, even though IPFS-based storage is decentralized, it still depends on content persistence mechanisms, which should be reinforced via methods like file pinning or token-based incentives. Simplifying the communication between media producers and the underlying decentralized infrastructure can potentially enhance the user experience. In order to lower gas costs and boost throughput, future research will concentrate on improving the system's scalability by integrating Layer 2 blockchain solutions like Polygon or Optimistic Rollups. Additionally, the integration of machine learning algorithms could automate the testing of watermark integrity and improve the accuracy of detecting deepfake content. The creation of an intuitive web-based or mobile interface that makes it simple for consumers, publishers, and artists to register, authenticate, and license digital property is another encouraging avenue. To improve user anonymity while maintaining content traceability, the usage of decentralized identity (DID) systems and privacy-preserving cryptographic approaches, like zero-knowledge proofs, will also be investigated. All things considered, this chapter provides a technically robust and useful framework for safe digital media attribution, laying the groundwork for further advancements at the nexus of digital rights management, blockchain, and watermarking. The suggested method paves the way for a more reliable and just digital media ecosystem by bridging the gap between content authentication and decentralized technology.

REFERENCES

An, K., Lu, Z. M., Sun, X. C., & Wang, Z. H. (2024a). Multipurpose video watermarking algorithm for copyright protection and tamper detection. *Multimedia Tools and Applications*, *83*(17), 51647–51668. DOI: 10.1007/s11042-023-17558-1

Darwish, S. M., Abu-Deif, M. M., & Elkaffas, S. M. (2024). Blockchain for video watermarking: An enhanced copyright protection approach for video forensics based on perceptual hash function. *PLoS One*, *19*(10), e0308451. DOI: 10.1371/journal. pone.0308451 PMID: 39436935

Frattolillo, F. (2024). Blockchain and smart contracts for digital copyright protection. *Future Internet*, *16*(5), 169. DOI: 10.3390/fi16050169

Hu, J., Jia, Y., & Qi, Y. Using Blockchain and Digital Watermarking to Enhance Open-Source Code Copyright Confirmation and Traceability. *Available at SSRN 4936584*. DOI: 10.2139/ssrn.4936584

Liu, T., Lai, S. N., Yuan, X., Liu, Y., & Lam, C. T. (2024b). A novel blockchain-watermarking mechanism utilizing interplanetary file system and fast walsh hadamard transform. *iScience*, *27*(9), 110821. DOI: 10.1016/j.isci.2024.110821 PMID: 39314242

Liu, X., Xu, R., & Chen, Y. (2024). A Decentralized Digital Watermarking Framework for Secure and Auditable Video Data in Smart Vehicular Networks. *Future Internet*, *16*(11), 390. DOI: 10.3390/fi16110390

Madushanka, T., Kumara, D. S., & Rathnaweera, A. A. (2024). SecureRights: A Blockchain-Powered Trusted DRM Framework for Robust Protection and Asserting Digital Rights. *arXiv preprint arXiv:2403.06094*.

Shang, W., Li, H., Ni, X., Chen, T., & Liu, T. (2025). BlockGuard: Advancing digital copyright integrity with blockchain technique. *Computers & Electrical Engineering*, *122*, 109897. DOI: 10.1016/j.compeleceng.2024.109897

Singh, A., Kumar, A., & Touthang, J. (2022, November). Detection of Tampering in Multimedia Using Blockchain Technology. In *Advances in Manufacturing Technology and Management: Proceedings of 6th International Conference on Advanced Production and Industrial Engineering (ICAPIE)—2021* (pp. 492-500). Singapore: Springer Nature Singapore.

Singh, O. P., Singh, K. N., Singh, A. K., & Agrawal, A. K. (2024). Watermarking with blockchain: A survey. In *Digital Image Security* (pp. 200–224). CRC Press. DOI: 10.1201/9781003468974-10

Tyagi, A. K., Kukreja, S., Richa, , & Sivakumar, P. (2024). Role of blockchain technology in smart era: A review on possible smart applications. *Journal of Information & Knowledge Management*, *23*(03), 2450032. DOI: 10.1142/S0219649224500321

Wu, X., Ma, P., Jin, Z., Wu, Y., Han, W., & Ou, W. (2022). A novel zero-watermarking scheme based on NSCT-SVD and blockchain for video copyright. *EURASIP Journal on Wireless Communications and Networking*, *2022*(1), 20. DOI: 10.1186/s13638-022-02090-x

Xiao, X., He, X., Zhang, Y., Dong, X., Yang, L. X., & Xiang, Y. (2023). Blockchain-based reliable image copyright protection. *IET Blockchain*, *3*(4), 222–237. DOI: 10.1049/blc2.12027

Xue, X., Shang, G., Ma, Z., Xu, M., Guo, H., Li, K., & Cheng, X. (2024, November). DataSafe: Copyright Protection with PUF Watermarking and Blockchain Tracing. In *Blockchain and Web3 Technology Innovation and Application Exchange Conference* (pp. 256–268). Springer Nature Singapore.

Zhang, X., Tang, Z., Xu, Z., Li, R., Xu, Y., Chen, B., . . . Zhang, J. (2024). OmniGuard: Hybrid Manipulation Localization via Augmented Versatile Deep Image Watermarking. *arXiv preprint arXiv:2412.01615*.

Chapter 8
Deepfake Attacks:
Detection and Mitigation Techniques for Strengthening Cybersecurity in the AI Era

Anant Wairagade
https://orcid.org/0009-0006-3884-7903
Independent Researcher, USA

Sumit Ranjan
https://orcid.org/0009-0001-2262-0281
Independent Researcher, USA

Kunal Lanjewar
https://orcid.org/0009-0005-3713-1949
Independent Researcher, USA

ABSTRACT

Deepfake technology has emerged in recent years and has posed serious challenges to areas such as politics, cybersecurity, and media integrity. The advent of deepfake content using generative adversarial networks (GANs) has further aided in manipulating public opinion through dissemination of misinformation and security threats to nations across the world. This book chapter focuses on tracing the evolution of deepfake technology, its role in electoral interference, and security impacts, with consideration given to several case studies and comparative research on detection frameworks to assess the strengths and weaknesses of AI-based and forensic detection of deepfakes. A novel cybersecurity capacity-building model is presented that focuses on collaborative efforts among academia, industry, and governmental agencies in

DOI: 10.4018/979-8-3373-6481-0.ch008

addressing the deepfake threat. Innovation in detection techniques, policy reform, and public education must work in tandem to ensure a capable digital ecosystem that withstands manipulation through synthetic media.

1. INTRODUCTION

1.1 An Overview of Deepfake Technology

Deepfake technology refers to artificially synthesized media that manipulate or synthesize audio and visual content to qualify them for being considered high reality deception. This advanced technology works primarily on deep learning techniques of generative adversarial networks (GANs) and Autoencoders, allowing the computerized synthetic modeling of realistic images, videos, and audio (Mirsky & Lee, 2021). Such algorithms are trained on massive datasets while analyzing facial expressions, voice patterns, and other biometric traits through which digital content can easily be manipulated (Agarwal et al., 2019).

Deepfake technology has undergone progressive development in sophistication and accessibility. Gone are the days when deepfake applications stayed restricted to formal research environments and AI laboratories; it is now very easily found in the open-source marketplace and user-capture com-applications (Dolhansky et al., 2020). This increased accessibility has hastened the spread of synthetic media while simultaneously raising fears of political propaganda, cyber fraud, and social engineering attacks (Korshunov & Marcel, 2019). As deepfakes continue to get better, discerning between veritable and fake content becomes infinitely more difficult for both humans and their automated detection systems.

1.2. Development of Deepfake Capabilities and Accessibility

The innovations in deepfake technologies have been inspired by advances in machine learning and computational power. The very first deepfake-generating devices were simple face-swapping's. Modern day versions, however, through sophisticated AI, may incorporate high-resolution models for generating unbelievably hyper-realistic content, directly comparable with genuine media (Tolosana et al., 2020). The rise of numerous deep learning frameworks, such as TensorFlow and PyTorch, has further aided the proliferation of deepfake applications, allowing researchers and malicious parties alike to experiment with highly advanced synthetic media techniques (Verdoliva, 2020).

These days, every refinement introduced on deepfake tools makes them easily accessible to the general public, as opposed to AI researchers. Everyone can do some 'magic' with most well-established online avenues that show and allow down-loading of trained models and installing user-friendly software packages to create fake content - even that for someone with little technical know-how (Rössler et al., 2019). These facilities have set the scene for intense ethical debates about what AI-generated media can be legitimately used for and whether there are threats posed by deception and manipulation using deepfake technologies (Chesney & Citron, 2019).

1.3 Emergence of Cyber-Attacks Fueled by Deepfake Technology

Deepfake technology is a major weapon in the hands of the cybercriminals. It has facilitated fraud, social engineering, misinformation, disinformation, skimming and identity theft (Gupta et al, 2022). Hence, an increase in deepfake-induced cyber-attacks has been specifically observed in areas like financial fraud, political disinformation, and identity theft. Attackers use AI-generated audio and video impersonations to lure victims and bypass security protocols to execute high-profile scams (Dang et al., 2020).

One of the most alarming features of these deepfake-driven cyber threats is that they can cheat even the most sophisticated biometric authentication systems. It has recently been shown that phishing attacks enhanced by deepfake technology evade facial recognition software leading to grand security breaches (Kietzmann et al., 2020). Rapid proliferation of this deepfake by cyber criminality has indeed instigated some countermeasures by cybersecurity experts such as AI-powered detection algorithms and forensic analysis techniques (Westerlund, 2019). However, the incessant evolution of the deepfake model continuously poses a challenge in the preservation of digital trust and security.

1.4 Roles of Cyber Criminals in Using Deepfakes

The malicious intentions of cybercriminals make use of deepfake technologies into financial fraud, corporate espionage, and political manipulation. One of the infamous instances would be using AI-generated voice impersonation to dupe a bank executive into wiring $35 million to an impossible account (Harwell, 2020). Similarly, deepfake disinformation campaigns were also used to sway public opinion at election times and to disseminate untruths in social media (Vaccari & Chadwick, 2020).

Deepfake technologies adaptability continue to increase the sophistication within which attackers will refine their modus operandi against which law enforcement and cybersecurity officials would conduct effective counteroffensive. Researchers have been developing deepfake detection methods using AI-powered anomaly detection, reverse engineering of synthetic media, and blockchain-based verification systems (Agarwal et al., 2020). Nevertheless, the arms race between deepfake creators and cybersecurity defenders keeps escalating, thus requiring strong policies, technology safeguards, and public awareness programs to handle the risks of deepfake-driven cyber-attacks.

2. IMPACT OF DEEPFAKE ATTACKS

2.1 Threats to Key Sectors

Due to the rising prevalence of the deepfake technology, it presents a significant threat to different sectors worldwide, ranging from personal invasion to national security. With developments in deepfake techniques, the technology becomes increasingly effective in deception, fraud, and manipulation- thus creating an enormous risk for individuals, businesses, and governments. The general threats are under personal privacy, financial systems, organizations' security, political stability, and national security.

2.2 Personal Privacy: Identity Theft, Blackmail, and Reputational Harm

Deepfake attacks have taken, above all, the toll against personal privacy, especially concerning identity theft and blackmail. Malicious actors use the synthetic AI-generated media to act as an imitation of some individual involved in fabricating a false narration that may cause irreparable damage to reputations. Examples of deepfake pornography in the exploitation of individuals by inserting their likeness into sexually explicit content without the consent of the person concerned, causing that person undue psychological distress and public humiliation are on record (Chesney & Citron, 2019).

Moreover, cybercriminals are able to successfully bypass identity verification processes such as those in online banking and authentication systems, thanks to deepfake technologies. With facial and voice manipulation techniques generated by AI, an attacker gains access to sensitive accounts by impersonating the rightful owner, which is a severe risk for digital security (Agarwal et al., 2020). Deepfake scams have also grown, thus causing a heightened importance in crafting AI-based detection techniques to counter such threats.

2.3 Financial Systems: Fraudulent Transactions and Market Manipulation

One of the most active targets for deepfake frauds are these days the financial transactions, where the criminals manipulate video and audio content to commit fraudulent transactions. Deep-fake voice cloning with high-accuracy has been upheld by many high-profile cases, deceiving corporate executives into connecting wire transfer authorization resulting in substantial financial losses (Harwell, 2020).

Apart from this, there is stock market manipulation through deepfakes, with fictitious announcements and altered statements made by people put under pressure to create artificial fluctuations in the market trends. Depending on the fabricated speeches and interviews of CEOs or policymakers, they can stimulate panic selling or stock surges, thus exploiting helpless investors (Kietzmann et al., 2020).

A comparison of traditional financial fraud and deepfake-enabled fraud (Table 1.) represents AI-generated attacks that have taken a life of their own and continue to demonstrate a high level of sophistication and increasing application in the financial industry.

Table 1. Traditional financial fraud vs. deepfake-enabled fraud comparison

Fraud Type	Traditional Methods	Deepfake Enabled Methods
Identity Fraud	Credential theft, phishing	AI-generated facial and voice impersonation
Corporate Fraud	Fake invoices, embezzlement	Voice deepfakes replicating executives in transactions
Stock Price Manipulation	Fraudulent news, rumors	AI-generated videos of executives making false statements

2.4 Organizational Security: Corporate Espionage and Theft of Intellectual Property

Corporate espionage has started to leverage deepfake technology, allowing adversaries to manipulate internal communications and attain classified information. Cybercriminals use deepfake text or the video calling impersonation of executives or servers to fool employees into disclosing proprietary information (Gupta et al., 2022).

Theft of intellectual property is another area of ever-increasing concern, as deepfakes can impersonate researchers, engineers, or stakeholders to gain unauthorized access to proprietary information. This threat holds very high severity in sectors such as defense, pharmaceuticals, and technology, where trade secret stealing gets the biggest bang for their buck (Tolosana et al., 2020).

2.5 Political Stability: Election Interference and Fake Propaganda

Deepfake as a powerful political tool that is capable of influencing public opinion will be through the making of fake speeches or alternated videos showing politicians. Deepfake-fueled information campaigns have been rampantly used to malign political opponents, spread fake propaganda, and taint election results in the past few years (Vaccari & Chadwick, 2020).

Widespread viral sharing of deepfaked material on social media has increasingly confused voters as they cannot draw the fine line between real and fake. In polarized political contexts, fake propaganda being released through deepfakes can play into people's biases and alter voter perceptions (Westerlund, 2019).

The illustrated timeline in Figure 1. shows that deepfakes have been used for election interference more than ever throughout the last 10 years.

Figure 1. Timeline of major deepfake incidents in political interference

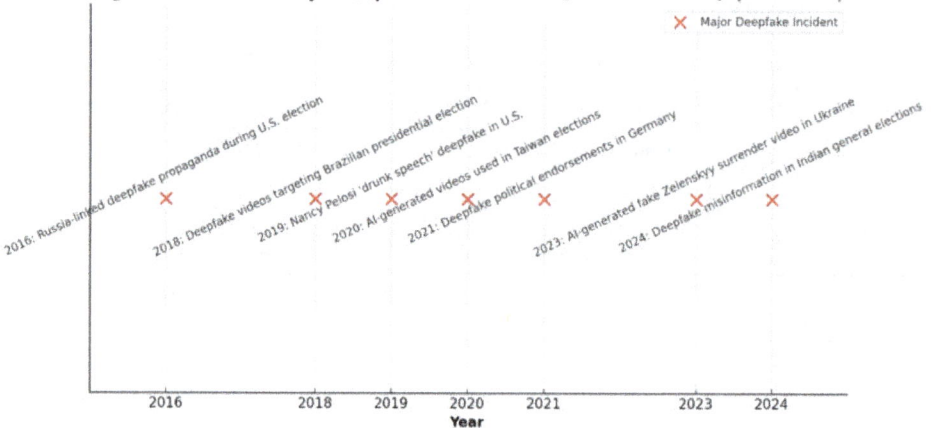

2.6 National Security: Army Deception and Geopolitical Destabilization

The use of deepfake technology poses threats to national security, particularly in military deception and geopolitical destabilization. The adversary might use AI-generated synthetic media to influence diplomatic communications, disseminate false intelligence, and provide misleading narratives in global conflict (Verdoliva, 2020).

The military has been voicing out its concerns regarding psychological warfare related to deepfake, where fictitious moving pictures of government officials giving fabricated remarks could possibly incite an international incidence. For instance, a fictitious deepfake video showing a military commander announcing an unauthorized attack might have real-world implications resulting in conflict escalation (Mirsky & Lee, 2021).

Deepfake technology could be applicable to emergent scenarios in cyber warfare, where state-sponsored actors continue to use AI-generated media toward diminishing trust in democracy and destabilizing the world at-large (Dolhansky et al., 2020).

3. COMPARATIVE ASSESSMENT OF MITIGATION AND DETECTION MECHANISMS

3.1 Evaluation Framework: Strengths, Weaknesses, Datasets, Metrics, Techniques, and Models

With the recent rapid advancement of deepfake techniques, strong countermeasures against their detection and mitigation were required. The decisive factors in these works' variable effectiveness include the deepfake sophistication, the specific dataset for training the detection model, and the evaluation metric. Detection models focus on accuracy, robustness, and generalization; on the other hand, mitigation mechanisms aim at preventing deepfake misuse via proactive countermeasures (Verdoliva, 2020).

FaceForensics++, Deepfake Detection Challenge (DFDC), and Celeb-DF Show the general data set approaches common in the deepfake studies, and each represents another level of realism and difficulty in detection (Dolhansky et al., 2020). The area under the curve (AUC), precision-recall (PR), and F1-score are some of the metrics used to assess model performance.

Summarized in Table 2., a comparative analysis on the different detection and mitigation methods.

Table 2. Deepfake detection and mitigation strategy comparison

Approach	Strengths	Weaknesses	Common Datasets Used
Image/Video Analysis	High detection accuracy for known deepfake types	Exposed to adversarial attacks	FaceForensics++, Celeb-DF
Audio Analysis	Good for voice-based deepfakes	Does not work well for high-quality synthetic speech	ASVspoof, VoxCeleb
Digital Watermarking	Enables verifying content authenticity	Can be bypassed by advanced deepfakes	Custom datasets
Blockchain-based Authentication	Provides immutable verification for digital content	Requires acceptance and integration on a large scale	None, regards of datasets

3.2 Detection Techniques

3.2.1 Image/Video Analysis: Forensic Tools, Artifact Detection, and GAN-based Discriminators

Detecting deepfakes within images and videos relies primarily on forensic investigation and deep learning methods for detection. Forensic techniques identify inconsistencies in lighting, abnormal facial expressions, or physiological irregularities such as blinking patterns (Tolosana et al., 2020). There are different machine learning models focused on CNNs and transformers that analyze pixel-level distortions and artifacts left by GANs.

In deepfake detection, the use of GAN-based discriminators for identifying synthetic signatures by employing AI principles opposite to generation has seen growth. The models such as XceptionNet, EfficientNet, and Capsule Networks show a high detection accuracy in benchmark tests (Nguyen et al., 2019).

Figure 2. shows a typical pipeline for detecting deepfake images using both forensic and AI-based techniques.

Figure 2. Deepfake image/video detection pipeline

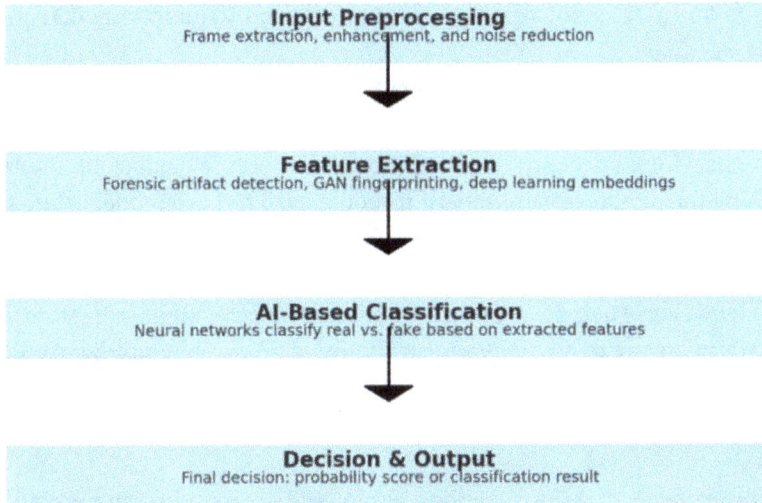

Input Preprocessing
Frame extraction, enhancement, and noise reduction

↓

Feature Extraction
Forensic artifact detection, GAN fingerprinting, deep learning embeddings

↓

AI-Based Classification
Neural networks classify real vs. fake based on extracted features

↓

Decision & Output
Final decision: probability score or classification result

3.2.2 Audio Analysis: Voiceprint Inconsistencies and Synthetic Speech Detection

AI-generated synthetic speech has brought voice-based deepfake detection to be the most timely application intended to channel fraud and misinformation. Deepfake audio detectors analyze voiceprints, prosody patterns, and other neural spectral inconsistencies that distinguish human speech from AI-generated speech (Kreuk et al. 2020).

Standard Mel-Frequency Cepstral Coefficients (MFCC) and state-of-the-art deep learning models like WaveNet and ResNet based classifiers are used for the detection of synthetic speech anomalies. However, the best method is Fourier transform based spectral analysis used for unnatural patterns in voice signals indicating deepfake manipulation (Zhang et al. 2021).

3.3 Mitigation Strategies

3.3.1 Digital Watermarking

Digital watermarking makes use of imperceptible signals embedded within media files ahead to verify their authenticity. AI based watermarking techniques like adversarial perturbation based methods have been built to withstand the deepfake manipulations (Lu et al. 2021). Metadata can easily be embedded in images and videos allowing one to trace the origin of the contents and so tampering detection.

3.3.2 Blockchain-Based Authentication

Blockchain provides a decentralized solution that is secure against all attempts of compromising the digital authenticity of its contents. The hash model offered by platforms like Content Blockchain and TruePic uses cryptography to time-stamp the media at the creation point, effectively preventing further modifications (Huh et al., 2021). However, such an approach requires extensive standardization and integration with mainstream media platforms before gaining an adoption ground.

3.3.3 Legislative Measures

Various governments and organizations worldwide are working on regulations against the misuse of deepfakes. The US Deepfake Accountability Act and the EU's Digital Services Act both propose penalties in the case of malicious use of synthetic media (Chesney & Citron, 2019). Such regulations aim to hold offenders accountable while promoting responsible AI development.

3.4 Performance Comparison

The performance of several different deepfake detection approaches was compared in terms of their effectiveness measured in accuracy and scalability in Table 3.

Table 3. Performances comparison of deepfake detection techniques

Detection Method	Accuracy (%)	Scalability	Limitations
XceptionNet (Image/Video)	98.5	High	Requires extensive training data
Capsule Networks (Image/Video)	96.8	Medium	Computationally Intensive
WaveNet (Audio)	94.2	Medium	Less effective against high-quality synthesis
Fourier Analysis (Audio)	92.7	High	Requires clean audio input
Blockchain-Based Authentication	N/A	Low	Requires widespread adoption

4. INSTANCES OF DEEPFAKE ATTACK IN THE WILD

4.1 Disinformation Campaigns

4.1.1 Political Deepfakes During Elections

Deepfakes have greatly brought apprehension in politics with regard to election security and the often debated questions on misinformation and voter manipulation. One of the best-known instances of deepfake disinformation occurred in the 2020 U.S. presidential election with the circulation of deepfake videos purporting to show AI manipulators of political candidates seeking to mislead voters (Chesney & Citron, 2021). Some of the videos were eventually debunked, but they demonstrated the capacity of deepfake technology to attain stunningly persuasive results and a particular degree of influence over public perception.

With a fictitious video where Joe Biden's speech was manipulated to depict him as incoherent, deepfake was also on the rise. Deepfake of Donald Trump was also created in which falsehoods were made in the effort to confuse and mislead voters. The growing number of those examples reflects the growing use of deepfake technology in political warfare, in which opponents use synthetic media to influence opinion, sow confusion, and undermine democratic processes (Vaccari & Chadwick, 2020).

Governments and tech firms reacted with algorithms to detect deepfakes and create fact-checking mechanisms. Yet, as AI-generated content has become increasingly sophisticated, current methods of preventing their spread are finding it greatly challenging (Ajder et al., 2020).

Figure 3. shows Political Deepfake Dissemination Process is shown in the "Convey" section model describing the way deepfakes are produced, spread, and consumed.

Figure 3. The political deepfake dissemination process

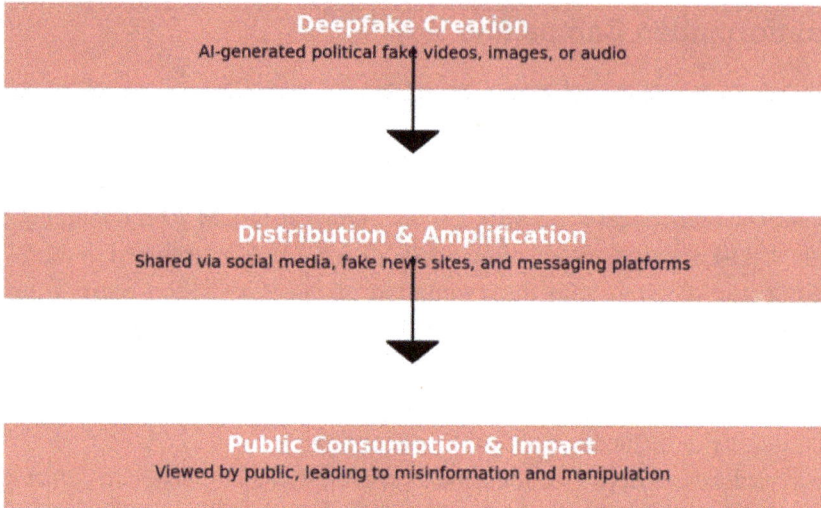

Deepfake Creation
AI-generated political fake videos, images, or audio

↓

Distribution & Amplification
Shared via social media, fake news sites, and messaging platforms

↓

Public Consumption & Impact
Viewed by public, leading to misinformation and manipulation

4.1.2 Social Media Manipulation: Fake Celebrity Endorsements

Social media platforms have emerged as a major battlefront for deepfake-fueled misinformation. Cybercriminals often use deepfakes to create fake celebrity endorsements for fraudulent products or sometimes promote political ideologies (Maras and Alexandrou, 2019).

One of the major examples involved deepfake videos of Elon Musk manipulated to endorse cryptocurrency scams. Such videos circulated on different platforms, including Twitter, YouTube, and TikTok, and fooled many users into participating in and investing in these scams (Floridi, 2020). Likewise, Tom Cruise made headlines in 2021 with his viral deepfake on TikTok, demonstrating AI's power to misdirect audiences in the right way (Suwajanakorn et al. 2017).

The advancing technology behind deepfakes has increased difficulty in separating the real from the fake. Tech platforms have rolled out AI-driven detection systems such as DFDC (Deepfake Detection Challenge) classifiers, but the constant refinements take the battle to the realm of the impossible (Dolhansky et al., 2020).

4.2 Corporate Espionage

4.2.1 Deepfake Phishing Attacks on Executives

Deepfake technology's most alarming application in corporate environments is CEO voice fraud, generating voice synthesis imitated by cybercriminals impersonating an executive. This method, which is audio deepfake phishing, literally leads to huge financial losses.

Noteworthy is the event in 2019 when fraudsters impersonated the CEO's voice of a UK energy firm using an AI-generated deepfake. They then directed one of their employees to transfer €220,000 to a fake account (Mirsky & Lee, 2021). The employee, believing in the power of the superior, complied and later discovered the scam.

Such types of deepfake phishing attacks thrive with increased dependency on voice communication in distance work scenarios, where old verification techniques have gone obsolete. Companies have now resorted to voice authentication systems and multi-factor verification protocols, a counterstrategy against such threats (Korshunov & Marcel, 2018). Table 4. Shows the comparison.

Table 4. Comparison of traditional and deepfake phishing attacks

Phishing Type	Attack Method	Difficulty of Detection	Mitigation Strategies
Email Phishing	Spoofed emails requesting credentials	Medium	Spam filters, training
Traditional Vishing	Phone based social engineering	High	Caller ID verification
Deepfake Vishing	Artificially generated voice mimicking executives	Very High	Voice biometrics, multi-factor authentication

4.3 National Security Breaches

4.3.1 Military Impersonation and Fake Crisis Scenarios

Deepfake technology has been used to create false crisis scenarios as well as disinformation in the context of national security. The potential of deepfake videos to be used for military deception, psychological operations, and for diplomatic conflicts is of concern to governments and intelligence services (Helmus et al., 2020).

One such incident was recorded in the year 2020 when a Ukrainian government official was impersonated on a deepfake video imparting a false statement with regards to military movements. The truth about the original video was revealed very soon, but this just spread like wildfire across Telegram, Twitter, and YouTube, showing how the technology could be weaponized in geopolitical conflicts (Schick, Fan & Schütze, 2021).

Military analysts mentioned that relevant issues would pertain to war-related deepfakes used to manipulate evidence, e.g., for fabricated war crimes or altered battlefield communications. In light of these threats, defense agencies are investing in AI-driven detection frameworks along with blockchain-based systems for content verification to stop the spread of deepfake disinformation (Gupta et al., 2021).

Figure 4. shows Deepfake Impact on National Security illustrates the major areas wherein deepfake technologies have found application regarding military deception, misinformation campaigns, and cyber warfare.

Figure 4. Deepfake impact on national security

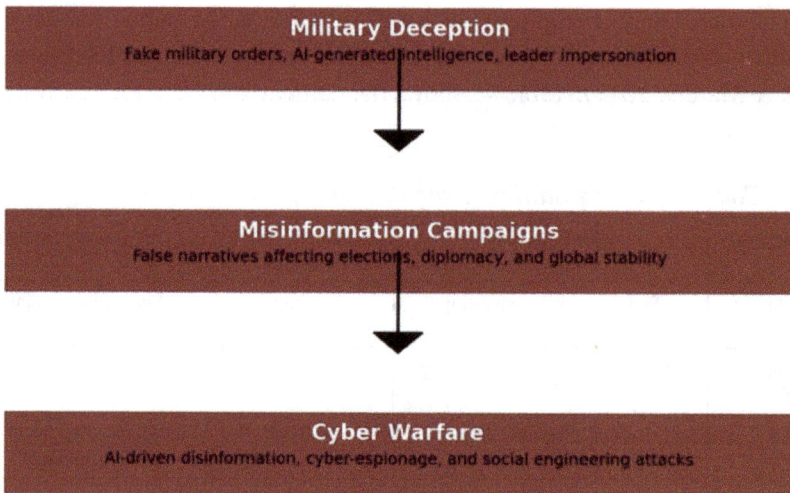

5. CHALLENGES IN CURRENT APPROACHES

5.1 Technical Limitations

A major hindrance to dealing with deepfake threats is the increasingly fast evolution of AI-generated engines which quickly develop newer versions most current detection ones cannot detect. Current modern techniques for deepfake video generation include Generative Adversarial Networks (GAN) and Transformers, which are increasingly sophisticated techniques and produce fake content which then becomes more difficult to separate from real media (Tolosana et al., 2020). The earlier detection models relied on artifact-based forensics, such as inconsistent facial expressions, shadows, and unnatural lighting, while modern deepfakes rely on new inclusion of adversarial training making them very resilient to detection even in popular literature (Rossler et al., 2019).

Deepfake detection algorithms are confronted with huge computational costs. Most of the high-accuracy models require extremely high-processing power to analyze massive datasets since they are deep neural network architectures. Thus, it becomes a challenge in real-time detection on social media platforms and live broadcasts (Chai et al., 2021).

Another hit is that there are a lot of false positives and false negatives associated with deepfake detection. Some legitimate videos could be classified as deepfakes, thus harming reputation and sources of information conflict (Mirsky & Lee, 2021). On the flip side, high-level deepfakes might evade detection altogether, thus allowing adversaries to mold public opinion and manipulate key decision-making processes. Table 5. Show the comparison.

Table 5. Comparison of deepfake detection techniques and their limitations detection approach strengths weaknesses computational cost

Detection Approach	Advantages	Disadvantages	Computational Cost
CNN-Based Forensics	Pixel-level artifacts are detectable	Training can undermine detection methods	High
Optical Flow Analysis	Contradiction in motion is detected	The method does not work with pristine deep-fake videos	Medium
Deep Learning Classifiers	Learning to represent complex features	Needs large training datasets	Very high
Blockchain Authentication	Ensures integrity of content	In the real world it has seen very little adoption	Low

5.2 Ethical and Legal Gaps

While the growing threat of deepfakes has caught the attention of the media and policy makers, the lack of any global regulation or legal standardization on their misuse is alarming. Countries around the globe have taken different approaches to tackle crimes related to deepfake: content moderation policies developed in the United States, and criminalization defined in legislation in Asia, Europe, and elsewhere

(Westerlund, 2019). However, many legal frameworks remain quite fragmented and reactive since they cannot keep pace with the fast-moving evolution of synthetic media technology.

For example, under the European Union's Digital Services Act, there are provisions specific to the detection of AI-generated content, but the real challenge lies in its implementation through a consistent provision for such detection across borders. A similar case is with the Deepfake Report Act of 2019 in the United States, mandating that federal agencies study the implications of deepfakes, but there remains a vacuum for other more comprehensive legislative frameworks (Chesney & Citron, 2021).

Deepfakes compromise privacy; this is another issue that surfaces imminently whenever one raises the issue of deepfake detection. Most detection systems rely on facial recognition databases and biometric analysis, leading to the ethical dilemmas of surveillance overreach and data misuse (Whittaker et al., 2020). For instance, the Clearview AI facial recognition software has been quite contentious: its system engaged in scraping images off social media without user consent, posing a security-versus-right-to-privacy dilemma (Vincent, 2020).

5.3 Societal Vulnerabilities

One of the major hurdles in fighting against the deepfake threats is the lack of public awareness which may cause atrocities. A lot of people cannot tell the difference between real and fake, thus falling prey to psychological manipulations and misinformation campaigns (Vaccari & Chadwick, 2020). Research states that even when exposed to a warning that says, "it might be AI-generated," people still tend to trust that which appears convincing to the eye (Pennycook & Rand, 2019).

Deepfakes pose big threats even to social trust and related processes of democracy. The independent creation of fictional testimonies, political speeches, and crisis events drains trust in digital information; consequently, the more people polarize and fight misinformation with conflict (Helmus et al., 2020). An illuminating example is "liar's dividend," where public figures dismiss real evidence as deepfake, diminishing accountability (Chesney & Citron, 2021).

Media literacy campaigns, fact-checking initiatives, and other efforts designed to lessen such vulnerabilities have yet emerged. However, they are not too much in operation yet today because of other causes that include biases about algorithms against content being moderated and generally low uptake by the larger public (Hancock & Bailenson, 2021). Table 6. Shows the percentage comparison.

Table 6. Popular public perception towards deepfakes and associated misinformation dangers

Survey Response	Percentage (%)
Believe they can detect deepfakes	42%
Have unknowingly shared deepfake content	28%
Trust information on social media	54%
Support government regulation of deepfakes	67%

6. THE FUTURE DEVELOPMENTS IN CYBERSECURITY IMPROVEMENT

6.1 High-tech Innovations

Innovations in deepfake technology are moving a fast pace than frontline applications and develop in detecting modern deepfake techniques, such as adaptive AI models that perform dynamic effectiveness improvements in their detection. One such benefit is federation learning, which advances the collaborative capability to develop AI models by way of raw data-sharing, thus keeping the identification capacity privacy-enabling (McMahan et al., 2017). Expanded use of federated learning in incorporating distributed data sources reduces bias in respective deepfake detection and improves detection across different content platforms (Hard et al., 2019).

Another emerging area is in the explainable AI (XAI), allowing more transparency in deepfake detection with interpretable ways of how such decisions get made. Unlike traditional black-box AI models which are difficult to decipher for security analysts, XAI will let them understand how and why a detection algorithm classifies content as synthetic (Gunning & Aha, 2019). It will also avail itself to enforcement by giving regulatory authorities the access they require to make evidence-based AI decisions.

Cross-modal detecting methods, which attempt to multi-aspect analyze audio, video, and metadata for joint viewing, are expected to significantly increase deep fake identification efficiency. Recent advancements have demonstrated that the merging of facial expression inconsistencies, anomalies in voiceprints, and metadata of context improves the strength of detection models (Agarwal et al., 2020). Cybersecurity systems are strengthened in their relia-bility against false positives and negatives through the input of multiple modalities.

The multimodal deepfake detection framework illustrated in Figure 6. indicates how different factors contribute to the detection of the deepfake: image analysis, voice analysis, and metadata analysis.

Figure 6. Multimodal deepfake detection framework

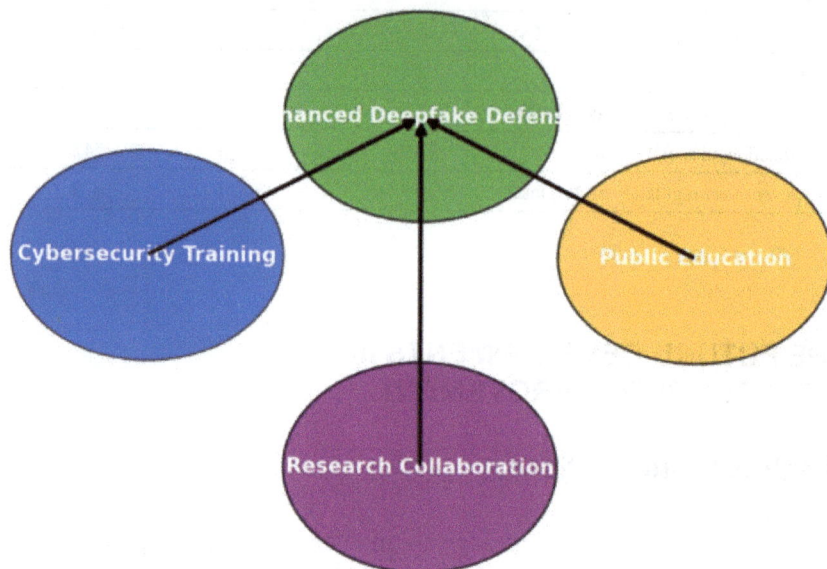

6.2 Policy Design and Collaboration

The rapid proliferation of deepfake threats accentuates the need for some form of international regulative sanctioning, capable of binding its signatories to a uniform standard of political accountability. At the moment, such international regulations are in discord among countries and regions regarding enforcement and much less about accountability for deepfake threats (Chesney & Citron, 2021). Developing sensible governance policies for AI on deepfakes under the auspices of the UN, European Commission, and U.S. Federal Trade Commission would provide some meaningful legal structures that could enable nation-states to address deepfake threats properly (Westerlund, 2019).

Public-private partnerships provide the impetus for several advances in cybersecurity. Technology companies working with academics and government programs led to initiatives, such as the Facebook Deepfake Detection Challenge (DFDC) and the Google FaceForensics++ dataset, aimed at improving detection schemes by large-scale sharing of online data (Rossler et al., 2019). Multiplying such partnerships could propel the efforts to counter deepfake-driven cyber threats even faster.

It is also important to have ethical guidelines for AI development and deployment to ensure that the technologies to fight deepfakes will not infringe on privacy rights. Detection systems using biometrics can be said to infringe on the rights of individuals, posing real threats of mass surveillance and abuses at the hands of authoritarian regimes (Whittaker et al., 2020). An ethical framework that sets out clear guidelines on how to balance security need with personal rights will give life to such propositions. Table 7. shows regulations summary.

Table 7. Comparative overview of global deepfake regulations

Region	Legislation/Policy	Focus Area	Implementation Status
EU	Digital Services Act (DSA)	AI content moderation	Enforced (2024)
US	Deepfake Report Act (2019)	AI-generated misinformation	Limited enforcement
China	Online Audio-Visual Information Regulation	Deepfake disclosure requirement	Enforced (2023)
UK	Online Safety Bill	Social media deepfake detection	Pending approval

6.3 Capacity Building

Deepfake menace has warranted training for the cybersecurity workforce and public education campaigns on the new digital threat. Organizations should throw deepfake detection modules into their cybersecurity training programs which teach professionals how to identify and mitigate threats (Mirsky & Lee, 2021). Those programs deal with emerging AI-driven attack vectors, forensic detection techniques, and legal implications associated with synthetic media.

Public awareness raises awareness of false deepfake content, thus making it less likely to lead to material being misrepresented. Media literacy campaigns have emphasized teaching users to critically assess content online, such as those authored by fact-checking companies like Snopes and PolitiFact (Pennycook & Rand, 2019). Governments and tech companies should invest in interactive tools and awareness workshops to enhance public resilience against deepfake-mediated deception.

Further, there could be joint research between universities and cybersecurity firms, to speed up advances in countermeasures against deepfakes. It involves open-access research initiatives, creating pathways for stakeholders to develop collectively better methodologies of detection and enhanced security frameworks digitally (Hancock & Bailenson, 2021).

7. CONCLUSION

7.1 Urgency in Countering Deepfake Threat

Deepfake technology is evolving rather fast and provides one huge cybersecurity challenge that can be addressed only through urgent and collaborative responses. Advanced generative models like GANs and other transformer-based architectures that facilitate fast generation of hyper-realistic synthetic media are increasingly becoming accessible. While such innovations might be explored for legitimate and creative purposes, countermeasures must immediately be instated against their misuse in heinous cyber activities including cyberattacks, misinformation campaigns, and fraud (Chesney & Citron, 2021). These kinds of deepfakes are able to manipulate public discourse, financial markets, and even geopolitical stability, which highlights the dire need of strong detection, mitigation, and regulatory frameworks (Westerlund, 2019).

7.2 Synthesis of Key Findings

The study established that deepfake detection and countermeasures remain a complex and evolving warfare. Comparing detection mechanisms shows that while forensic tools and AI-based classifiers have achieved a promising level of accuracy, the adversarial deepfake techniques seem to be on top of the game in that regard (Agarwal et al., 2020). Such a study on the real-life deepfake instances appears from election interference to corporate fraud elucidating how far-reaching are the implications given by synthetic media threats. Furthering the divide, policy loopholes and the ethical discourse in AI governance complicate counter-deepfake efforts, making coordinated legislative action and standardized ethical guidelines imperative on a global scale (Whittaker et al., 2020).

A multimodal approach that synergizes analysis of image, voice, and metadata as potential combination candidates is thought to hold significant promise and avert adversarial deepfakes with enhanced resilience (Rossler et al., 2019). However, the cost computation of these models and the possibility of adversarial attacks make it an ongoing problem. The quest for a scalable, real-time detection solution remains crucial for cybersecurity practitioners, social media platforms, and government institutions (Mirsky & Lee, 2021).

7.3 Call to Action for Multidisciplinary Collaboration

An efficient response to threats posed by deepfakes needs a multidisciplinary consortium involving technology, policy, law enforcement, media literacy, and

236

education in cybersecurity. Governments must create a regulatory framework to counter the malicious use of synthetic media while aiming at this technology with accountability and traceability (Westerlund, 2019). Social media platforms and AI companies should monitor and remove fake deepfake content through real-time detection algorithms and watermarking techniques (Gunning & Aha, 2019).

Further, public-private partnerships could entail sharing insights on generating open-source deepfake detection models, as apparent in Facebook's Deepfake Detection Challenge (DFDC) and Google's Deepfake Dataset (Rossler et al., 2019). Universities should teach AI ethics and media literacy so people may learn skills that enable them to detect and assess deepfake content critically (Pennycook & Rand, 2019).

7.4 Vision for a Secure Digital Ecosystem

The future sustenance of cybersecurity resilience against deepfakes depends on accelerating technological innovation, cooperation worldwide, and continued public education. Much promise is offered by emerging advances in explainable AI, federated learning, and blockchain-based authentication, toward improving the detection and attribution of deepfakes (McMahan et al., 2017). Through collaborative research, ethical development of AI, and international alignment of policies, a safe digital ecosystem resilient to synthetic media threats shall be erected.

In as much as awareness, enhancement of AI-based defenses, and the installation of regulatory safeguards would act synergistically in mitigating the threats posed by deepfakes, it will need to be concerted. The advancement of deepfake technology would require a proactive and adaptive approach to cybersecurity ensuring the integrity of digital communications, democratic processes, and global security (Chesney & Citron, 2021).

REFERENCES

Abdullah, N. A., Hussain, F. K., & Hussain, O. K. (2021). Deepfake video detection: A systematic literature review. *IEEE Access: Practical Innovations, Open Solutions*, *9*, 140373–140391. DOI: 10.1109/ACCESS.2021.3118923

Agarwal, S., Farid, H., Gu, Y., He, M., Nagano, K., & Li, H. (2020). Protecting world leaders against deep fakes. *Proceedings of the IEEE/CVF Conference on Computer Vision and Pattern Recognition Workshops*, 38–45. DOI: 10.1109/CVPRW50498.2020.00013

Anderson, R., & Petitcolas, F. A. (2018). On the limits of steganography. *IEEE Journal on Selected Areas in Communications*, *16*(4), 474–481. DOI: 10.1109/49.668971

Aneja, D., Aneja, S., & Raman, B. (2021). Deepfake detection using convolutional neural networks. *Neural Computing & Applications*, *33*(12), 7019–7031. DOI: 10.1007/s00521-020-05531-x

Chesney, R., & Citron, D. K. (2019). Deepfakes and the new disinformation war: The coming age of post-truth geopolitics. *Foreign Affairs*, *98*(1), 147–155.

Dolhansky, B., Bitton, J., Pflaum, B., Lu, J., Howes, R., Wang, M., & Ferrer, C. C. (2020). The deepfake detection challenge dataset. *arXiv preprint arXiv:2006.07397*.

Güera, D., & Delp, E. J. (2018). Deepfake video detection using recurrent neural networks. *Proceedings of the IEEE Conference on Computer Vision and Pattern Recognition Workshops*, 39–46. DOI: 10.1109/AVSS.2018.8639163

Hsu, C. C., Chang, C. M., & Lin, H. Y. (2020). Deep learning-based forgery detection in digital videos. *Multimedia Tools and Applications*, *79*(29), 21677–21692. DOI: 10.1007/s11042-019-7318-6

Jiang, L., Li, R., Wu, W., & Kuo, C. C. J. (2020). GAN-based deepfake detection using motion magnification. *Proceedings of the AAAI Conference on Artificial Intelligence*, *34*(1), 2265–2273.

Korshunov, P., & Marcel, S. (2018). Deepfakes: A new threat to face recognition? Assessment and detection. *arXiv preprint arXiv:1812.08685*.

Li, Y., Lyu, S., & Bao, F. (2020). Exposing deepfake videos by detecting face warping artifacts. *IEEE Transactions on Information Forensics and Security*, *15*, 4263–4275. DOI: 10.1109/TIFS.2020.3019407

Matern, F., Riess, C., & Stamminger, M. (2019). Exploiting visual artifacts to expose deepfakes and face manipulations. *Proceedings of the IEEE Conference on Computer Vision and Pattern Recognition Workshops*, 1–10. DOI: 10.1109/WACVW.2019.00020

Mirsky, Y., & Lee, W. (2021). The creation and detection of deepfakes: A survey. *ACM Computing Surveys*, *54*(1), 1–41. DOI: 10.1145/3425780

Nguyen, H. H., Yamagishi, J., & Echizen, I. (2019). Capsule-forensics: Using capsule networks to detect forged images and videos. *Proceedings of the IEEE International Conference on Acoustics, Speech and Signal Processing (ICASSP)*, 2307–2311. DOI: 10.1109/ICASSP.2019.8682602

Nguyen, T., Valenzise, G., & Dufaux, F. (2021). Multimodal deepfake detection with cross-modal attention. *IEEE Transactions on Information Forensics and Security*, *16*, 3352–3367. DOI: 10.1109/TIFS.2021.3105543

Rossler, A., Cozzolino, D., Verdoliva, L., Riess, C., Thies, J., & Nießner, M. (2019). FaceForensics++: Learning to detect manipulated facial images. *Proceedings of the IEEE/CVF International Conference on Computer Vision*, 1–11. DOI: 10.1109/ICCV.2019.00009

Tolosana, R., Vera-Rodriguez, R., Fierrez, J., Morales, A., & Ortega-Garcia, J. (2020). Deepfakes and beyond: A survey of face manipulation and fake detection. *Information Fusion*, *64*, 131–148. DOI: 10.1016/j.inffus.2020.06.014

Verdoliva, L. (2020). Media forensics and deepfakes: An overview. *IEEE Journal of Selected Topics in Signal Processing*, *14*(5), 910–932. DOI: 10.1109/JSTSP.2020.3002101

Wang, X., Zhang, Y., Cao, J., & Wu, J. (2021). Adversarial training for deepfake detection: A comprehensive analysis. *IEEE Transactions on Neural Networks and Learning Systems*, *32*(10), 4723–4736. DOI: 10.1109/TNNLS.2021.3097682

Yang, X., Li, Y., Qi, H., Lyu, S., & Liu, X. (2019). Exposing GAN-synthesized faces using landmark locations. *Proceedings of the IEEE/CVF Conference on Computer Vision and Pattern Recognition Workshops*, 25–34.

Zhang, H., Yu, J., & Zhao, X. (2020). Detecting AI-generated fake videos using multimodal features. *IEEE Transactions on Multimedia*, *22*(11), 2962–2975. DOI: 10.1109/TMM.2020.2994285

Zhou, P., Han, X., Morariu, V. I., & Davis, L. S. (2019). Two-stream neural networks for tampered face detection. *Proceedings of the IEEE/CVF Conference on Computer Vision and Pattern Recognition*, 7556–7564.

Zhou, T., Lu, X., & Zhang, Y. (2021). Deepfake detection using spatiotemporal attention. *IEEE Transactions on Circuits and Systems for Video Technology, 31*(3), 919–933. DOI: 10.1109/TCSVT.2021.3054239

Zolfaghari, S., & Piramuthu, S. (2021). Blockchain-based solutions for deepfake prevention and authentication. *Journal of Cybersecurity, 7*(1), 12. DOI: 10.1093/cybsec/tyab012

Chapter 9
Deepfakes and Synthetic Media:
Challenges and Solutions in Social Engineering Attacks

Devendra Chapagain
https://orcid.org/0009-0003-6548-7112
Tribhuvan University, Nepal

Bindu Aryal
Tribhuvan University, Nepal

Bijay Bastakoti
The University of Texas at Arlington, USA

Dipendra Silwal
https://orcid.org/0009-0003-8125-4976
Oxford College of Engineering and Management, Nepal

Ayesha Arobee
https://orcid.org/0009-0003-0395-5005
Emporia State University, USA

ABSTRACT

Deepfakes and synthetic media, powered by AI technologies like Generative Adversarial Networks (GANs) and Diffusion Models, pose significant threats to digital trust and security. These tools enable the creation of highly realistic forgeries, which are increasingly exploited in social engineering attacks to spread misinformation, manipulate emotions, and impersonate trusted individuals. This chapter explores the role of deepfakes in enhancing social engineering tactics, such as phishing,

DOI: 10.4018/979-8-3373-6481-0.ch009

CEO fraud, and disinformation campaigns. It reviews current detection methods, including machine learning techniques to identify inconsistencies in synthetic media, and discusses the ethical, societal, and policy challenges posed by this emerging threat. By examining the intersection of deepfakes and social engineering, this chapter highlights the need for robust detection technologies, public awareness, and regulatory measures to address the growing risks of AI-generated content in cybersecurity.

INTRODUCTION

Overview of Deepfakes and Synthetic Media

Artificial intelligence has significantly advanced deepfakes and synthetic media, enabling the creation of highly realistic yet fabricated audio and video content. These technologies, often powered by deep learning techniques like Generative Adversarial Networks (GANs) and diffusion models, have the potential for both beneficial applications and malicious misuse. While offering creative opportunities in entertainment, education, and accessibility, synthetic media also poses a substantial threat to information integrity and societal trust. This overview explores the nature of deepfakes and synthetic media, their potential applications, the associated risks, and the ongoing efforts to mitigate their harmful impact.

Deepfakes manipulate existing images or videos to superimpose one person's likeness onto another, creating convincing forgeries of individuals saying or doing things they never did (Westerlund, 2019). Beyond facial swapping, synthetic media encompasses a broader range of manipulated or entirely computer-generated content, including AI-generated voices, manipulated images, and entirely fabricated videos (Marwick & Lewis, 2017). Easy-to-use deepfake tools have made it simpler for people to create fake content, increasing the risk of misuse.(Vaccari & Chadwick, 2020).

Synthetic media offers diverse potential applications. These applications include entertainment, such as special effects in movies and video games. They can enhance accessibility, allowing for the creation of translated content with lip-sync accuracy. They can also be used in educational settings, creating historical simulations or personalized learning experiences. However, the very features that make synthetic media powerful also create significant risks.

The primary concern surrounding deepfakes and synthetic media is their potential for malicious use in disinformation campaigns, propaganda, and fraud (Wardle & Derakhshan, 2017). Deepfake videos of public figures (e.g., politicians or community leaders) making fictitious statements can be wielded to manipulate public opinion, influence elections, or incite social conflict. By fabricating credible footage of events that never occurred, malicious actors can spread propaganda and conspiracy theories. For example, a deepfake could depict a politician appearing to confess to wrongdoing or espouse extremist views, thereby altering the political narrative. The malicious use of deepfakes can lead to the spread of false information, the manipulation of public thought, the destruction of one's reputation, and dangerous incitement of violence. The ease with which convincing forgeries can be created making it increasingly harder to differentiate between authentic and synthetic content, eroding trust in media and institutions. Furthermore, the use of synthetic media in social engineering attacks, such as CEO fraud, poses a significant threat to businesses and individuals.

AI-enabled cybercrime, exemplified by a recent deepfake audio case, has introduced a new dimension to financial fraud. According to a report by the Wall Street Journal (*The Wall Street Journal* 2024), a U.K.-based energy company fell victim to a sophisticated CEO fraud scheme, resulting in a loss of US$243,000. In this incident, cybercriminals employed AI-generated voice cloning software to impersonate the CEO of the company's Germany-based parent organization. The attackers contacted the U.K. CEO, masquerading as the parent company's executive, and directed an urgent wire transfer to a Hungary-based supplier, with assurances of reimbursement. Following the transfer, the funds were routed through multiple accounts, including one in Mexico, to obscure the transaction trail and hinder the identification of the perpetrators. This case underscores the evolving capabilities of AI in facilitating social engineering attacks and highlights the growing challenges faced by organizations in detecting and preventing such advanced fraud schemes. It also aligns with broader concerns in the cybersecurity literature regarding the misuse of deepfake technologies and the need for enhanced countermeasures to address these emerging threats (Samuel Okechukwu Omeje, 2023).

A comprehensive strategy is necessary to combat the issues raised by deepfakes and synthetic media. Technical solutions, such as deepfake detection algorithms, are being developed to identify inconsistencies in synthetic content. However, these detection methods are constantly evolving in an arms race with deepfake creation techniques. Beyond technical solutions, media literacy initiatives are crucial to educate the public about the existence and potential impact of synthetic media, empowering individuals to critically evaluate online content. Finally, policy and regulatory frameworks are needed to address the legal and ethical implications of deepfakes, including issues of consent, defamation, and the spread of misinformation (Lattanzio & Ma, 2023).

BACKGROUND AND TECHNOLOGICAL FOUNDATIONS

Evolution of Deepfake Technology

Generative AI powers deepfake by enabling creation of realistic synthetic media, such as fake images, video and audio. These deepfakes can be weaponized in social engineering attacks, where malicious actors exploit human psychology to gain trust, access sensitive information, or manipulate behavior. This convergence of generative AI, deepfakes, and social engineering poses significant risks to personal privacy, organizational security, and societal trust, highlighting the urgent need for robust detection methods and public awareness to counter these emerging threats.

This table summarizes the key findings, highlighting the prevalence, description, and examples of each category of harm caused by generative AI(Trifonova & Venkatagiri, 2024).

Table 1. Harm caused by GenAI

Harm Category	Percentage of Incidents (out of 50)	Description	Examples
Relational Harm	64%	Negatively impacts relationships through reputational damage or erosion of trust.	- Explicit deepfakes damaging reputations. - Misinformation reducing trust in information sources (e.g., AI-generated voice of Imran Khan). - AI generated non-consensual intimate images (AI-NCII) shared online.
Systematic Harm	52%	Harms systems or targets specific demographics.	- Political misinformation undermining electoral trust. - AI image generators perpetuating racial stereotypes (e.g., Meta's inability to generate multiracial images, Google Gemini producing racially diverse Nazis).
Financial Harm	36%	Involves fraud, false advertising, or lost revenue.	- AI voice scams (e.g., couple scammed by a fake voice mimicking their son). - Artists reporting lost revenue due to generative AI.

continued on following page

Table 1. Continued

Harm Category	Percentage of Incidents (out of 50)	Description	Examples
Emotional Harm	36%	Occurs in diverse contexts, often as a secondary result of other harms.	- Explicit deepfakes targeting non-public figures (e.g., teenagers generating AI-NCII of classmates). - Emotional distress linked to reputational or relational harm. - In some cases, teenagers have used AI tools to bully classmates by generating inappropriate images, leading to emotional and mental health consequences.
Physical Harm	0%	This remains a theoretical category with no confirmed cases at the time of the study.	-No instance recorded While Trifonova & Venkatagiri (2024) did not record instances of this in their sample, one can imagine scenarios such as deepfakes provoking violence (e.g., a fake video of a community leader inciting riots could lead to real-world violence), or false emergency messages leading to physical dangers.

The origins of deepfake technology can be traced back to a long history of manipulating visual media. Early methods, such as airbrushing in photography and basic montage techniques in film, were some of the first steps in altering how we perceive reality. In late 2017, a machine learning algorithm was developed that enabled the swapping of faces, particularly those of public figures (Tolosana et al., 2020). This innovation is widely regarded as the earliest concept of what we now know as deepfake technology. As technology advanced, the rise of computer graphics in the late 20th century took these possibilities even further, enabling the creation of entirely synthetic images through digital tools. These developments set the stage for the sophisticated deepfake technology we see today.

Early Computer Graphics: The genesis of computer graphics in the mid-20th century provided the initial tools for creating and manipulating digital images. While primitive by today's standards, early CGI demonstrated the potential for synthetic visuals(Sutherland, 1964).

Image and Video Editing Software: The advent of user-friendly image and video editing software, such as Photoshop, democratized the ability to manipulate digital media. While initially used primarily for artistic expression, these tools also facilitated more deceptive alterations.

Face Replacement Techniques: Early attempts at face replacement and video manipulation were complex, time-consuming processes often confined to specialized film and television production.

Key Breakthroughs in AI and Machine Learning

The recent surge in deepfake capabilities is directly attributable to advancements in AI and machine learning, particularly in deep learning and generative models.

Deep Learning: The evolution of highly sophisticated deep learning models has been made possible by the accessibility of vast datasets and increased computational resources. Deep learning itself is a subdiscipline of machine learning that uses multi-layered artificial neural networks to uncover intricate patterns in data (LeCun et al., 2015).

Generative Adversarial Networks (GANs): Introduced by Goodfellow (Goodfellow et al., 2020), GANs have revolutionized synthetic media creation. Comprising a generator and a discriminator network engaged in adversarial training, GANs have become a cornerstone of deepfake generation. GANs are widely utilized for generating images, transferring styles, and enhancing data. They also have applications in healthcare (e.g., medical imaging), entertainment (e.g., deepfakes), and art (e.g., creating novel designs). Their ability to generate high-quality, realistic data makes them a powerful tool across various industries.

Autoencoders: Autoencoders, neural networks designed for data compression and reconstruction, facilitate learning compressed representations of visual elements, enabling manipulation and combination for deepfake creation (Hinton & Salakhutdinov, 2006). In the context of deepfakes, autoencoders are particularly useful for learning compressed representations of faces and other visual elements (Fernando et al., 2025). This allows for efficient manipulation and recombination of these elements to create synthetic media. For example, an autoencoder can be trained to learn the essential features of a person's face, such as its shape, texture, and expression (Solomon et al., 2023). These features can then be swapped with the features of another person's face to create a deepfake.

Diffusion Models: Emerging as a powerful alternative to GANs, diffusion models have gained prominence for generating high-quality synthetic media. They operate by progressively adding noise to an image and training a network to reverse this process, effectively learning image generation from noise (Ho et al., 2020). Diffusion models are particularly relevant to deepfakes because of their ability to generate highly realistic images and videos (Bhattacharyya et al., 2024). This makes them a powerful tool for creating convincing synthetic media. Their ability to generate subtle details and complex textures makes them very effective at creating convincing facial manipulations. As the technology continues to develop, diffusion models are likely to play an increasingly significant role in the creation of deepfakes.

Advanced Speech Synthesis and Voice Cloning: Beyond visual content, the evolution of text-to-speech (TTS) and voice cloning models has been critical for audio deepfakes. AI models such as Google's WaveNet and Tacotron series, and more recent transformer-based TTS systems, can generate human-like speech from text, capturing the prosody and accent of a target speaker when trained on samples of that person's voice. By analyzing a person's vocal patterns, these models enable highly realistic voice replication – an attacker can produce an audio clip of someone speaking any scripted lines, in a voice that listeners might believe is authentic. The improvement in voice quality and the reduction of data needed for cloning (recent models can clone voices with just seconds of audio sample) have made voice phishing using AI a tangible threat.

The Convergence and Recent Advances

The rapid advancement of deepfake technology is a direct result of the confluence of sophisticated AI/ML techniques, the availability of extensive datasets, and increased computational power. Recent research has prioritized enhancing both the realism and controllability of deepfakes, with a particular focus on identity preservation, expression cloning, and seamless visual integration. Specifically, ongoing development aims to refine the rendering of facial details, lighting, and motion to achieve greater authenticity. Moreover, efforts are dedicated to enabling precise manipulation of facial features, expressions, and actions, thereby increasing the level of control over generated content (Daniel, 2022). Parallel to these advancements in visual deepfakes, significant progress has been made in the generation of realistic synthetic speech, which introduces new concerns regarding audio-based manipulation.

How AI Has Enhanced Deepfake Realism

One of the reasons deepfakes have become such a potent tool for adversaries is the dramatic increase in their realism and believability, driven by the AI advances described above. Today's AI models can generate synthetic faces with photorealistic detail, clone voices with the correct accent and intonation, and even synthesize realistic body movements. Several key improvements in AI have directly enhanced deepfake realism:

Higher-fidelity Generators: Improvements in GAN training techniques (such as newer loss functions, regularization methods, and the introduction of models like StyleGAN) have yielded generators that produce faces with fewer obvious artifacts. Modern GAN-generated faces have correct lighting, sharp edges (e.g., around eyes and teeth), and consistent detailing (like hair texture and skin pores) that earlier attempts lacked. This reduction in tell-tale glitches makes detection much harder.

Better Identity Preservation: Early face-swap deepfakes sometimes produced a blended look that failed to perfectly capture the target's identity or had warped facial proportions. Newer deepfake algorithms incorporate identity loss functions and multi-angle training data to ensure the generated face looks exactly like the target person from all angles. They can preserve unique facial quirks and expressions of the target, improving the illusion that it's really them in the video.

Lip-sync and Speech Alignment: AI systems now excel at matching synthesized speech to mouth movements in video. By using techniques like audio-driven facial reenactment, a deepfake video can have the target's lips and facial muscles move convincingly in sync with any dubbed speech. This creates fake videos where the person appears to be speaking naturally, significantly boosting credibility. For instance, one can take an audio clip of an impersonated voice and generate a video of the target saying those exact words with matching lip motions.

Emotion and Tone Reproduction: Beyond just the content of speech, deepfakes now capture the emotional tone and body language. If the goal is to create a fake video of someone giving an angry speech, the AI can adjust the facial expressions (furrowed brows, lip movements) and even gestures to reflect anger. This is achieved by training models on not just neutral faces, but a range of emotional states, or by using motion transfer techniques where an actor's performance is mapped onto the target's face and body.

Multimodal Integration: Cutting-edge projects integrate multiple modalities – video, audio, and sometimes text – to improve consistency. By jointly modeling how a person looks when they speak certain words (audio-visual correlation), deepfake systems reduce mismatches that could give away fakery. Some deepfakes are now so coherent that even subtle features like eye blinking patterns and breathing motions (which early deepfakes often overlooked) are properly rendered.

SOCIAL ENGINEERING

Social engineering is a psychological manipulation that uses human behavior and the vulnerabilities within it to achieve access to sensitive information or execute unauthorized activities. In contrast to traditional hacking, which exploits the weaknesses in technology, social engineering takes advantage of trust, emotions, and cognitive biases in humans to succeed. (Mitnick & Simon, 2003). This form of attack is often more effective than technical breaches because people are inherently more susceptible to deception than well-secured systems (Hadnagy, 2018).

Social engineering takes several forms like phishing, pretexting, baiting, and impersonation. Most attackers go through a very convincing process to let the victim give away sensitive information they hold, thus making the security breach look like a legit interaction. (Jagatic et al., 2007). In recent years, advancements in artificial intelligence (AI) and machine learning have further enhanced these tactics, with deepfake technology emerging as one of the most dangerous tools for cyber deception.

Evolution of Social Engineering

Pre-Digital Era: Social engineering has existed for centuries, with early examples found in deception-based fraud schemes. One of the most famous historical cases is that of Frank Abagnale Jr., a con artist who forged checks and assumed false identities to manipulate banks and airlines in the 1960s (Abagnale & Redding, 2000). Traditional social engineering tactics involved impersonating authority figures, exploiting trust, and fabricating emergencies to manipulate victims.

Rise of Telecommunications: The introduction of the telephone gave rise to new forms of social engineering. Attackers used vishing (voice phishing) to impersonate trusted individuals and manipulate victims over the phone. Scams such as the "grandparent scam", in which fraudsters pretend to be distressed relatives, became common during this period (Ch, 2014).

Internet & Email: The enhancement of the internet and e-mail communication has upped the number of phishing attacks. It is an attack that uses a fake organization to dupe users into giving sensitive information. In the past, phishing emails used to impersonate banks, government agencies, or tech support services, while telling users to enter their credentials on a false website (Jagatic et al., 2007). As social media gained popularity, attackers began harvesting personal data from public profiles to create more convincing scams (Mitnick & Simon, 2003).

AI-Driven Social Engineering: Modern cybercriminals have adopted artificial intelligence (AI) and automation to enhance their deception tactics. Spear-phishing campaigns use AI to craft personalized messages, while chatbots engage in real-time conversations to manipulate victims into revealing sensitive data. AI-powered scams have made social engineering more scalable and difficult to detect (Zuboff, 2023).

The Social Engineering Process

Social engineering attacks exploit human psychology to manipulate individuals into revealing confidential information or compromising security. These attacks typically progress through several key stages, which have been well-described by Hadnagy (2010).

Figure 1. The four major social engineering attacks sequence

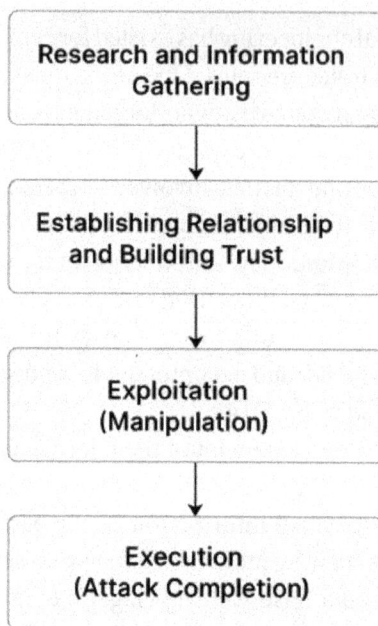

```
┌─────────────────────────────┐
│  Research and Information   │
│         Gathering           │
└─────────────────────────────┘
              │
              ▼
┌─────────────────────────────┐
│  Establishing Relationship  │
│      and Building Trust     │
└─────────────────────────────┘
              │
              ▼
┌─────────────────────────────┐
│       Exploitation          │
│       (Manipulation)        │
└─────────────────────────────┘
              │
              ▼
┌─────────────────────────────┐
│        Execution            │
│    (Attack Completion)      │
└─────────────────────────────┘
```

Research and Information Gathering:

Attackers first collect sufficient information that they can use against the target. The process begins by gathering personal and professional details of the person, organizational details, and sometimes even vulnerability points, through social networking profiles, public records, and company websites. The idea behind all this is to have deep information so that an attack strategy, well-crafted and personalized, can be worked out properly.

Establishing Relationship and Building Trust:

With the acquired information, attackers proceed to build rapport with the target by impersonating trusted individuals or authoritative figures. They create convincing narratives or scenarios (pretexting) to lower the target's defenses and increase the likelihood of compliance.

Exploitation (Manipulation):

Once trust is established, the attacker manipulates the victim into divulging sensitive information or performing actions that facilitate unauthorized access. This could involve persuading the target to share passwords, click on malicious links, or grant access to restricted areas, leveraging the trust and authority perceived by the victim.

Execution (Attack Completion):

In the final stage, the attacker utilizes the acquired information or access to achieve their objective, such as data theft, financial fraud, or further infiltration into an organization's systems. The execution phase capitalizes on the groundwork laid in the previous stages, culminating in the realization of the attacker's goals

HOW DEEPFAKES ENHANCE THE EFFECTIVENESS OF SOCIAL ENGINEERING

The human element remains the most vulnerable link in the cybersecurity chain, as social engineering tactics exploit psychological vulnerabilities to extract confidential information. This manipulation of human behavior often proves more effective than purely technical breaches, resulting in a higher success rate for social engineering attacks compared to those targeting system vulnerabilities (Bhusal, 2021).

Deepfakes take deception to a new level by making social engineering attacks incredibly realistic. For example, imagine getting a video call from your boss asking you to transfer funds urgently. The voice and face look and sound exactly like them, making it hard to tell it's fake. As note, deepfakes can mimic people we trust—like CEOs, coworkers, or even family-making us more likely to act without questioning.

It gets even more concerning. Deepfakes can create emotional situations that exploit our instincts. For instance, a deepfake video might show a friend in distress, urgently asking for help. The emotional impact can override our logical thinking, pushing us to act impulsively (Jagatic et al., 2007).

We also tend to trust what we see and hear, especially if it aligns with what we already believe. Even if we have doubts, a convincing deepfake can easily dismiss them. Attackers can also use personal details from social media to make these scams feel even more real(Mitnick & Simon, 2003).

The danger goes further. Deepfakes can be used for long-term manipulation, slowly influencing our opinions or beliefs. They can even create fake "evidence" to support scams, making them powerful tools for blackmail or compulsion (Samuel Okechukwu Omeje, 2023). In short, deepfakes blur the line between reality and fiction, making it extremely hard to tell what's real. This makes social engineering attacks much more effective—and dangerous.

CASE STUDIES OF DEEPFAKE-BASED SOCIAL ENGINEERING ATTACKS

Publicly documented cases of deepfake-based social engineering attacks—especially those causing major financial losses or clear harm—are still relatively rare.

This scarcity is likely due to several reasons: the technology is still new, it's often hard to prove an attack used deepfakes, and organizations may avoid reporting such incidents to protect their reputation. Many cases are probably handled privately or through law enforcement, so they don't make headlines. But the absence of public reports does not necessarily imply the absence of incidents. Experts warn that these attacks are on the rise (Marwick & Lewis, 2017). What we do see are smaller-scale examples, like disinformation campaigns or proof-of-concept demonstrations, which show just how dangerous deepfakes could become in larger, more targeted attacks.

While concrete, widely publicized cases of deepfake-driven social engineering attacks resulting in significant, quantifiable losses are still somewhat limited (likely due to factors like underreporting and difficulty in attribution), research and emerging trends paint a concerning picture. The intersection of deepfakes and social engineering is being actively studied, and while full-blown, large-scale attacks might not be dominating headlines yet, the building blocks and potential for such attacks are becoming increasingly clear ("Deepfakes: The latest weapon in the cyber security arms race," 2024).

A deepfake video could be used to establish a false identity or create a believable backstory (pretexting), making it easier for an attacker to gain the trust of their target (*The Impact of Deepfake Fraud: Risks, Solutions, and Global Trends*, 2024). Or, a deepfake could be used to create a seemingly irresistible offer or opportunity (baiting), luring the target into a trap. These combined tactics, leveraging the power of deepfakes, can be incredibly effective. As Vaccari and Chadwick (2020) discuss, the combination of deepfakes with existing disinformation and manipulation tactics represents a significant challenge for individuals and society.

Despite the limited number of widely publicized large-scale attacks, significant financial losses attributed to deepfakes have been reported. In March 2023, a UK energy firm reported a loss of €220,000 (approximately US$240,000) due to a deepfake voice cloning attack (Breacher.ai, 2024). The perpetrators used AI voice synthesis technology to precisely mimic the CEO's voice, including speech patterns and accent nuances, to call a senior financial manager and request an urgent transfer to a supposed supplier. The convincing nature of the voice clone, combined with the apparent urgency, bypassed standard verification procedures, highlighting the particular vulnerabilities posed by audio deepfakes in business environments where voice communication carries inherent authority.

More recently, in January 2024, a finance worker at a multinational company in Hong Kong was deceived into transferring HK$200 million (approximately US$25.6 million) to fraudsters (Heather Chen, 2024). The attackers used deepfake technology to impersonate the company's chief financial officer during a video conference call, which was part of a series of fraudulent communications. The finance employee was convinced they were participating in a confidential transaction, demonstrating how deepfakes exploit established trust in executive communications and organizational hierarchies. The sophisticated attack combined technological deception with social engineering tactics that preyed on corporate protocols and employee psychology.

Beyond direct financial losses, deepfakes have already made a noticeable impact in areas like disinformation and manipulation. While not always a direct social engineering attack aimed at stealing money or information, deepfakes are increasingly used to create fake videos of politicians or public figures. These videos spread false narratives, damage reputations, and influence public opinion (Wardle & Derakhshan, 2017). For example, during political campaigns, manipulated videos have been used to discredit opponents or sway voters. Even though these videos are often debunked quickly, they can spread rapidly on social media, causing significant short-term damage. These examples highlight how deepfakes can manipulate human perception and behavior—a core element of social engineering.

Another growing concern is the use of deepfakes in personalized attacks. While large-scale breaches aren't widely reported yet, experts predict that deepfakes are being used in targeted phishing campaigns and other forms of personalized social engineering. For instance, a deepfake audio clip of a trusted colleague could trick an employee into sharing sensitive information. Similarly, a deepfake video impersonating a client or business partner could deceive someone into revealing confidential data. These targeted attacks are harder to detect and trace, making them a serious threat. With advancements in deepfake technology, the frequency and complexity of such attacks are expected to rise.

One area of active research focuses on the psychological impact of deepfakes and how they can manipulate trust and decision-making (Reardon, 2024). A study by (Westerlund, 2019) explored how deepfakes can erode trust in established institutions and create an environment ripe for manipulation. This erosion of trust, coupled with the convincing nature of deepfakes, makes individuals more susceptible to social engineering tactics (*The Psychology of Deepfakes in Social Engineering*, 2025). The research suggests that even if individuals are aware of the existence of deepfakes, the realistic presentation can still influence their perceptions and judgments, making them more vulnerable to manipulation. This is a crucial element of how deepfakes enhance social engineering: they exploit our reliance on visual and auditory cues, even when we know those cues might be deceptive.

Another relevant area involves the use of deepfakes in spear-phishing attacks. From 2012 to 2022, spear-phishing attacks surged in frequency and sophistication, becoming a dominant cyber threat. Key incidents include the 2012 Shamoon attack on Saudi Aramco, the 2014 Sony Pictures hack, the 2016 DNC breach, and the 2017 Yahoo and Equifax breaches. By 2020, 88% of global organizations faced spear-phishing attempts, with high-profile attacks like the Twitter hack and SolarWinds breach. In 2021, spear phishing made up 65% of all phishing attacks, targeting systems like Microsoft Exchange and Colonial Pipeline (Birthriya et al., 2025).

It's important to recognize that the threat landscape is constantly evolving. While large-scale, widely reported deepfake social engineering attacks may not be commonplace today, the research and emerging trends clearly indicate a growing risk. The potential for deepfakes to enhance existing social engineering techniques and create new avenues for manipulation is undeniable. This necessitates ongoing research, development of detection technologies, and increased public awareness to mitigate the risks associated with this powerful technology.

THE INTERSECTION OF DEEPFAKES AND SOCIAL ENGINEERING ATTACKS

Deepfake-driven social engineering doesn't only work by tricking our eyes and ears; it also exploits deep-seated cognitive biases and psychological tendencies that govern human trust and decision-making (Hancock & Bailenson, 2021).Understanding these human factors is crucial to grasp why deepfakes can be so effective:

Trust Bias in Visual/Audio Information: Humans are naturally inclined to trust what they perceive through sight and sound. We evolved to use facial recognition and voice tone as key indicators of someone's identity and intent. This "seeing is believing" heuristic means that if we see a person we know saying something on video, we generally accept it as truth. Deepfakes prey on this bias by providing artificial visual or auditory stimuli that appear authentic, thereby instantly lowering our skepticism. People instinctively let their guard down when confronted with a familiar face or voice (especially of an authority figure or loved one), which makes deepfake-based requests or claims very persuasive. In essence, deepfakes hijack the brain's normal trust calibration, which was not designed to account for the existence of perfectly mimicked humans by a machine.

Confirmation Bias: People tend to be more trusting of information that already fits what they believe or hope is true, making them less likely to question it. (Eynern, 2024). Deepfakes can be crafted to feed into what a target is inclined to think. For example, in a politically charged environment, a person who already distrusts a politician might readily accept a deepfake video of that politician making a scandalous comment as genuine, because it confirms their suspicions. Similarly, an employee who expects a certain type of directive from their boss is less likely to question a deepfake delivering that directive. Attackers can utilize this bias by tailoring deepfakes to narratives the target audience is subject to accept. This exacerbates the spread of disinformation: once a deepfake "fits" someone's worldview, they may even help propagate it without verifying it.

Cognitive Overload and Distraction: Deepfake technology's realism overwhelms critical thinking, making people more vulnerable to social engineering attacks. High-fidelity deepfakes demand significant cognitive processing, causing cognitive overload – where the brain prioritizes absorbing the message over questioning its authenticity. Attackers amplify this by creating urgent, emotionally charged scenarios, such as emergency directives or distressed pleas, which flood victims with stress and impair their ability to detect subtle inconsistencies like lip-sync errors or unnatural intonations. This overload discourages precautionary actions, such as verifying requests through alternative channels, as victims feel compelled to act immediately. Modern multitasking and information anxiety exacerbate this vulnerability (Kirsh, 2000). Constant information demands reduce focus, making individuals prone to hasty decisions and oversight of red flags. Combined with emotional manipulation, cognitive overload creates a perfect storm for attackers to exploit.

Authority and Authenticity Cues: Social engineers have long exploited perceived authority – for instance, pretending to be a CEO, police officer, or IT administrator – because people tend to obey authority figures. Deepfakes bolster this tactic by adding convincing authenticity cues to the impersonation. The uniform of an authority (face, voice, demeanor) is digitally cloned, not just claimed. Research in psychology (as Reality Defender's report in 2025 highlights) notes how people are conditioned to comply with requests from those they recognize as authority or familiar (Cialdini's principles of influence include authority and liking). A deepfake of a known superior combine both: an authority figure whom the victim also personally knows and likes. This can be more compelling than a stranger's voice asserting authority.

Fear and Urgency: Many social engineering attacks rely on creating a sense of urgency or fear to push people into quick action (e.g., "act now or something bad happens"). Deepfakes make the fear and urgency more tangible. Seeing a "family member" in danger on video or hearing terror in their voice is far more visceral than reading a text. Fear appeals delivered through deepfakes can short-circuit rational thought almost instantly. This is especially powerful in scams like fake kidnappings or bogus emergency directives. The victim's physiological stress response (fight-or-flight) is triggered by the realistic stimuli, reducing their ability to think logically – exactly what the attacker wants.

Erosion of Baseline Trust (Societal Impact): On a broader scale, even people who are not directly targeted by a deepfake attack may experience a psychological toll. As deepfakes become more common knowledge, the average person may start feeling unsure about the veracity of information in general. This can lead to anxiety, cynicism, or apathy – responses that can be damaging to society's information integrity. For example, constant exposure to the idea that "anything could be fake" might make people disengage from news or distrust important warnings, a sort of fatigue or learned helplessness in discerning In the context of social engineering, this widespread distrust can either help (people become more cautious) or hinder (people stop believing even legitimate communications, which can be dangerous in crises). It's a double-edged effect but certainly a significant psychological ripple effect of deepfakes.

Social engineering attacks rely on psychological manipulation to trick individuals into divulging sensitive information or performing actions that compromise security. Deepfakes amplify these attacks by adding a layer of realism and credibility, making them even more effective. Here's how you can connect the two:

DEEPFAKES AS A TOOL FOR SOCIAL ENGINEERING

While traditional social engineering relies on psychological manipulation through text, voice, and limited visual cues, deepfakes elevate these tactics to an unprecedented level of realism and believability. By creating convincing synthetic media that impersonates trusted individuals or fabricates compelling scenarios, deepfakes significantly amplify the effectiveness and potential harm of social engineering attacks.

Deepfake technology enhances traditional social engineering techniques by making attacks more sophisticated and harder to detect. AI-generated forgeries can convincingly mimic the appearance or voice of trusted figures, thereby increasing the likelihood of successful social engineering attacks. This technological advancement has transformed conventional phishing attempts into highly personalized and credible deceptions.

The specific ways deepfakes are being and can be weaponized in various social engineering contexts are.

- **Impersonation**: Deepfakes can be used to impersonate trusted individuals (e.g., CEOs, government officials, or family members) in phishing or vishing (voice phishing) attacks. For example, a deepfake audio or video call could convince an employee to transfer funds or share confidential information.
- **Credibility Enhancement**: Deepfakes make social engineering attacks more believable. For instance, a fake video of a CEO announcing a policy change could trick employees into complying with malicious requests.
- **Emotional Manipulation**: Deepfakes can exploit emotions like fear, urgency, or trust to manipulate victims. For example, a deepfake video of a family member in distress could be used to extort money.

APPLICATIONS OF DEEPFAKES IN SOCIAL ENGINEERING

Deepfakes, synthetic media creations using sophisticated artificial intelligence, present a double-edged sword. While offering potential benefits in fields like entertainment and accessibility, they also pose a significant threat to information integrity and societal trust. One of the particularly concerning area is the application of deepfakes in social engineering. SE relies on exploiting human psychology. Deepfakes significantly amplify the effectiveness of these manipulative tactics by adding a layer of unprecedented realism and believability (*Deepfakes: The New Threat to Cybersecurity*). This section explores deepfakes in social engineering attacks, showcasing their diverse applications. From enhanced impersonation to evidence fabrication and automation, deepfakes transform deception and manipulation.

Business Email Compromise (BEC): Deepfake technology enables the creation of convincing audio and video impersonations of executives, which can be exploited to authorize fraudulent transactions. Recent incidents, such as those involving a multinational company in Hong Kong and a UK energy firm, demonstrate how effectively deepfake audio and video can mimic high-ranking officials. During video conferences or phone calls, attackers utilizing these forgeries can instruct subordinates to execute fraudulent actions, including the transfer of funds or the disclosure of confidential information.

Political Manipulation: Deepfake videos could spread misinformation to influence public opinion or destabilize organizations. In 2023, deepfake videos of several European politicians making controversial statements circulated on social media platforms prior to elections, potentially influencing voter opinions and creating political instability (European Union Agency for Cybersecurity).

Enhanced Impersonation: Deepfakes can create highly realistic impersonations of trusted figures, such as CEOs, colleagues, clients, or even family members. This allows attackers to craft believable scenarios and requests, significantly increasing the likelihood of victims complying. Imagine a deepfake audio call from a "CEO" urgently requesting a wire transfer, or a deepfake video of a "colleague" asking for login credentials. The perceived authority and familiarity make these manipulations far more potent.

Fabricated Evidence and Narratives: Deepfakes can be used to create fabricated "evidence" to support a social engineering narrative. For example, a deepfake video could be used to falsely implicate someone in wrongdoing, making them vulnerable to blackmail or coercion. Similarly, deepfakes can be used to create entirely fabricated scenarios, such as a deepfake video of a "witness" confirming a false narrative. This "evidence" can be used to manipulate individuals into taking specific actions.

Personalized Attacks: Deepfakes can be tailored to specific individuals, incorporating personal details gleaned from social media or other sources. This level of personalization makes the attack feel more genuine and less generic, increasing its effectiveness. For example, a deepfake video could be crafted to appeal to a specific individual's interests or vulnerabilities, making them more susceptible to manipulation. Multiple celebrities have had their likenesses used in deepfake videos endorsing fraudulent investment schemes, resulting in financial losses for consumers who trusted the apparent endorsements (Federal Bureau of Investigation, 2024).In 2023, deepfake videos of several European politicians making controversial statements circulated on social media platforms prior to elections, potentially influencing voter opinions and creating political instability (European Union Agency for Cybersecurity).

Emotional Manipulation: Deepfakes can be used to create emotionally charged scenarios designed to bypass critical thinking and induce impulsive reactions. For example, a deepfake video of a "loved one" in distress could be used to manipulate someone into revealing sensitive information or transferring money. The emotional appeal can override rational judgment, making the target more vulnerable. Deepfake videos or images could be used to create fake personas in online dating scams.

Long-Term Manipulation and Influence: Deepfakes can subtly influence opinions and beliefs over time. By gradually introducing fabricated content, attackers can manipulate a target's perception of reality, making them more vulnerable to future social engineering attempts. This can involve everything from subtly shifting political opinions to influencing purchasing decisions.

Automated Social Engineering: As deepfake technology becomes more sophisticated, it could be combined with AI-powered chatbots and other automation tools to create highly scalable social engineering attacks (Shu et al., 2017). Imagine a system that automatically generates personalized deepfake messages and distributes them to thousands of potential victims. This could significantly amplify the reach and impact of social engineering campaigns.

Circumventing Multi-Factor Authentication: While multi-factor authentication (MFA) adds an extra layer of security, deepfakes can potentially be used to circumvent even this protection. For example, a deepfake voice recording could be used to bypass voice-based authentication systems. This highlights the need for more robust authentication methods that are resistant to deepfake manipulation.

Disinformation Campaigns: Deepfakes are increasingly central to large-scale disinformation campaigns. The creation of convincingly fabricated videos featuring public figures, celebrities, and politicians, often through techniques like LinkedIn profile manipulation and voice cloning, enables the manipulation of public opinion and the sowing of discord (Helmus, 2022). This practice fosters an environment of distrust, rendering individuals more susceptible to various forms of manipulation, including social engineering.

Visual Communication Power: Research indicates that visual communication, such as videos, has a stronger persuasive power compared to text (Vaccari & Chadwick, 2020). This is particularly relevant in political communication, where "image bites" can shape voter opinions more effectively than traditional "sound bites". The ability of deepfakes to manipulate visual content makes them a potent tool for deception.

DETECTION METHODS FOR DEEPFAKE-BASED SOCIAL ENGINEERING

Deepfakes pose a substantial threat to cybersecurity and erode trust in digital media. Effectively combating deepfake-based social engineering requires robust detection mechanisms. This section explores a variety of such methods, combining technical approaches with human-centric strategies focused on behavioral analysis and awareness.

Artifact-Based Detection:

These methods capitalize on subtle inconsistencies often introduced during deepfake generation. Deepfakes, despite their realism, frequently leave behind telltale signs, such as unnatural blinking patterns, inconsistencies in facial features (e.g., blurring around the hairline or mouth), or artifacts detectable in the frequency domain. Machine learning and computer vision algorithms are employed to detect these artifacts, but the evolving nature of deepfake technology necessitates continuous refinement and adaptation of these algorithms.

Behavioral Biometrics:

This approach analyzes behavioral patterns, like micro-expressions, lip movements, and head gestures, which are often difficult for deepfakes to perfectly replicate. Xie et al. (2022) illustrated the Facial Action Coding System (FACS), introduced by Ekman and Friesen is the most widely used method for analyzing facial expressions.

Contextual Analysis:

Contextual analysis examines the surrounding information and context of the media for inconsistencies. Verifying the source, cross-referencing information, and analyzing metadata can reveal discrepancies indicative of manipulation. For example, a deepfake video claiming to show a newsworthy event might be contradicted by other news sources or lack supporting evidence. This method relies on access to reliable information and the ability to effectively synthesize it. Platforms like Twitter's Community Notes program have demonstrated that crowdsourced fact-checking can reduce the spread of misleading content by up to 50% (Renault et al., 2024), highlighting the importance of collaborative efforts in addressing this issue.

Hybrid Approaches:

Hybrid deepfake detection methods combine different techniques such as artifact-based detection, behavioral biometric, and contextual analysis to improve identification. Hybrids offer an integration of diverse kinds of detection strategies against the number of false positives and negatives, hence making detection more robust. For example, integration of facial feature analysis and audio-visual cues improves the system's capability to identify deepfakes.

Human Awareness and Media Literacy:

Human awareness and media literacy are critical components of deepfake detection. Educating individuals about deepfakes and their potential impact is essential. Promoting critical thinking and skepticism towards online content empowers individuals to identify suspicious cues. This includes training individuals to look for common deepfake artifacts, to be wary of emotionally charged content, and to verify information from multiple sources.

Adversarial Attacks and Defense:

The deepfake detection field is engaged in a continuous arms race. Researchers develop adversarial attacks to probe the vulnerabilities of detection algorithms, leading to improvements in resilience against increasingly sophisticated deepfakes (Goodfellow et al., 2020). This ongoing cycle of attack and defense drives progress in both deepfake generation and detection.

Source Camera Attribution:

This technique tries to identify the camera that was used to create a particular video. This can be helpful in identifying deepfakes, as the deepfake may not have the same camera characteristics as the original video.

Combining Audio-Visual Cues:

Combining audio and visual cues is a crucial area of research in deepfake detection. By leveraging the synergy between these modalities, detection systems can become more accurate and robust, making it harder for deepfakes to evade detection. The importance of combining audio and visual cues for deepfake detection. Behavioral analysis, specifically related to lip synchronization and facial expressions during speech, plays a crucial role in this multimodal approach. Models like SyncNet are effective at detecting lip-sync errors, which are common in deepfake videos (Chung & Zisserman, 2017). However, advances in voice cloning technologies make audio cues less reliable, highlighting the importance of integrating both audio and visual analysis for more accurate detection.

Physiological Cues:

Hui in his paper (Guo, 2022) emphasizes the use of physiological cues, specifically focusing on the consistency of pupil shapes. GAN-generated faces often exhibit irregular pupil shapes due to the lack of physiological constraints in the models used to create them. This inconsistency can be a reliable indicator for identifying fake faces.

Blockchain and Provenance Tracking:

By recording metadata and content fingerprints on a decentralized ledger, blockchain offers immutability and transparency, enabling effective tracking of media origins and subsequent alterations. This approach ensures that any tampering with digital content becomes detectable through inconsistencies in the provenance record (Neisse et al., 2017).

Projects such as Project Origin and the Content Authenticity Initiative (CAI) have implemented frameworks that embed cryptographic signatures and content credentials at the point of media creation. These metadata can be verified downstream to detect manipulation and ensure the integrity of digital assets (Islam et al., 2024). Such systems are particularly valuable in contexts like journalism, legal evidence, and electoral communication, where establishing trust in digital content is critical.

Additionally, recent research has proposed smart contract-enabled deepfake detection networks, which automate the validation process and reduce reliance on centralized authorities (Hasan & Salah, 2019). These decentralized mechanisms help combat the dissemination of manipulated media by providing transparent, tamper-proof audit trails for verification.

MITIGATION STRATEGIES

There is no single solution will completely eliminate the threat of deepfakes. Mitigating the threat of deepfakes requires a multi-faceted approach, combining technological advancements, educational initiatives, policy considerations and ethical safeguards. Here are some possible mitigation strategies with supporting in-text citations:

Technical Solutions:

Deepfake Detection Technologies: Continued research and development of robust deepfake detection algorithms are crucial. These technologies should focus on identifying artifacts, inconsistencies, and behavioral anomalies in synthetic media. This includes exploring AI-powered detection methods that can keep pace with evolving deepfake generation techniques.

Blockchain and Digital Watermarking: Implementing blockchain-based systems for media provenance can help track the origin and modifications of digital content, making it easier to verify authenticity. Digital watermarking can also be used to embed verifiable information within media files. Heidari et al. (2024) proposed a framework aimed at improving fake video detection by leveraging blockchain technology to identify deepfakes in both images and videos. They also conducted a comparative analysis with other existing methods.

Media Authentication Platforms: Developing platforms that allow users to easily verify the authenticity of online content enabling people to critically evaluate the content they see and hear.

Robust Authentication Methods: Strengthening authentication methods, including multi-factor authentication and biometric verification, can make it more difficult for deepfakes to be used to impersonate individuals. Exploring methods resistant to voice and facial mimicry is crucial.

Educational and Awareness Initiatives:

Media Literacy Programs: Integrating media literacy into education and workforce training can help individuals critically evaluate what they see and hear. People should learn to "trust but verify" digital media, especially when it prompts high-stakes actions or strong emotional responses. Training modules or workshops can show examples of deepfakes and how they can be identified (for instance, looking for unnatural eye movement, odd transitions, or asking oneself if the scenario makes logical sense). By seeing how easily a face or voice can be faked, individuals may become more cautious about unverified communications. Organizations are beginning to include deepfake awareness in their cybersecurity awareness programs, alongside phishing awareness. For example, employees might be taught to verify any financial transaction requests through a secondary channel, even if they come via an apparent voice note from the CEO.

Simulated Deepfake Drills: Just as companies run phishing simulations to test and teach employees (sending fake phishing emails to see if users click), a forward-thinking idea is to run deepfake simulation drills. An organization could simulate a deepfake attack in a controlled manner – e.g., send a fake voicemail from a "manager" asking for a password – and then debrief staff on how to handle such a situation. While logistically more challenging, it could drive the lesson home and make employees more vigilant.

Training for Professionals: Specialized training programs are essential for cybersecurity professionals, journalists, and individuals handling sensitive information to effectively address the threats posed by deepfakes. These programs should focus on deepfake detection techniques and prevention strategies. Regular training sessions can enhance employee awareness of deepfakes, equipping them with the knowledge to identify potentially manipulated content, which is critical for early detection and proactive prevention (Kapoor & Rahman, 2024). Training curricula should incorporate practical case studies and establish clear verification protocols for communications originating from leadership.

Public Awareness Campaigns: On the societal level, governments and non-profits can run campaigns to inform the public about deepfakes. Public service announcements, documentaries, or social media campaigns that highlight the existence of deepfakes and showcase notable instances can inoculate the public to some degree. When people know this technology exists, they may be more likely to question sensational media. For example, ahead of major elections, warnings that adversaries might release fake videos of candidates could prepare voters to be skeptical of any last-minute "scandal video" that hasn't been verified by trusted news outlets. Several countries have issued such warnings and even social media companies often remind users that "manipulated media" circulates online (Cybersecurity agencies like Singapore's MAS (2024) have released advisories on generative AI risks, urging caution).

Policy and Legal Frameworks:

Regulation of Deepfake Creation: A comprehensive strategy to address deepfakes requires a balanced approach, integrating technological safeguards with policy and educational interventions (Leibowicz, 2025). Furthermore, public trust in the efficacy and integrity of governance solutions is essential. This necessitates careful consideration of regulatory frameworks, particularly regarding the creation and distribution of malicious deepfakes, while simultaneously safeguarding freedom of expression.

Legislation against Deepfake-Facilitated Crimes: Laws should be enacted to address the use of deepfakes in criminal activities, such as fraud, defamation, grooming, stalking, and harassment. Experts agree that existing surface web crimes will likely migrate and become more complex in these immersive digital spaces (Stavola & Choi, 2023). The lack of current legal frameworks for the metaverse necessitates an urgent call for policymakers and stakeholders to develop and implement legislation and preventative measures before these crimes become widespread and entrenched. The experts emphasize the vulnerability of younger users and the need for proactive, systematic approaches to detection and sanctioning of such harmful behavior in the metaverse.

International Cooperation: Given the global nature of online disinformation and manipulation, international cooperation is essential to develop effective strategies for combating deepfakes.

Industry Collaboration:

Social Media Platform Responsibility: Social media platforms should take greater responsibility for identifying and flagging potentially manipulated content, including deepfakes. This includes investing in detection technologies and implementing clear policies for handling deepfake content (Bradshaw & Howard, 2018).

Collaboration between Technology Companies and Researchers: Closer collaboration between technology companies and academic researchers is essential to accelerate the development of deepfake detection and prevention technologies.

Monitoring and Intelligence: Staying informed about the latest deepfake incidents and tools can help an organization anticipate what might hit them. There are services that monitor the dark web for chatter about targeting a certain company or searches for employee data that could precede an attack. If a company knows, for example, that their executives' public speeches are being downloaded (possibly to train a voice model), they could raise an alert. Also, keeping an ear to employee reports – if someone receives a strange call that felt "off," even if nothing bad happened, investigating it could uncover an attempted deepfake scam in the reconnaissance stage.

Ethical Considerations:

Responsible AI Development: Promoting the responsible development and use of AI technologies, including those used to create and detect deepfakes, is crucial. This includes considering the ethical implications of these technologies and developing guidelines for their use.

Human-Centric Strategies:

Critical Thinking Skills: Encouraging the development of critical thinking skills in individuals can help them to better evaluate online information and resist manipulation.

Trust but Verify: Promoting a "trust but verify" mindset can help individuals to be more cautious about the information they consume online and to seek out reliable sources of verification (Wardle & Derakhshan, 2017).

THE FUTURE LANDSCAPE

The evolution of deepfake technology continues to advance rapidly, with future research focusing on creating more robust and efficient generation methods, enhancing the quality and resolution of deepfakes, and addressing the ethical and societal implications of this powerful tool. As the technology progresses, it presents a dual-edged sword, offering transformative opportunities across various fields while also posing significant challenges. Balancing innovation with responsible use will be crucial to harnessing its potential for positive impact while mitigating risks.

On one hand, deepfake technology could revolutionize fields such as criminal investigations by enabling the strategic deployment of synthetic media for data collection, provided ethical considerations are addressed (Al-Mulla, 2022). It also holds promise in governance, where its misuse could ironically lead to improved authentication mechanisms and stronger security protocols (*Cyber Risks Associated with Generative Artificial Intelligence* 2024). Additionally, deepfakes could play a vital role in assisting individuals with disabilities, such as helping visually impaired individuals navigate their surroundings through real-time image recognition and audio feedback systems (Cecílio et al., 2015).

In healthcare, deepfakes could enhance disease diagnosis and streamline the management of patient medical records (Chen et al., 2021). Educational institutions could also benefit, with medical students practicing on simulated patients and commerce students replicating high-stakes transactions in a risk-free environment . Furthermore, deepfake technology could strengthen copyright protection through advanced techniques like hashing and digital watermarking (Zhao et al., 2023).

However, the potential for misuse remains a critical concern. On a more positive note, the technology could break language barriers by enabling real-time multilingual announcements and eliminating the need for subtitles in movies (Chen et al., 2021). While deepfake and synthetic media hold immense potential to innovate various sectors, their ethical and malicious applications must be carefully managed to ensure they serve as tools for progress rather than harm. Balancing innovation with regulation will be key to shaping a future where deepfake technology benefits society as a whole.

AI-Synthesized Documents and Legal/Financial Records

Although deepfake is concerned mostly with visuals and audio, it could also generate fake documents like legal contracts, invoices, transcripts, bank statements or identification papers (*Synthetic Document Generation for NLP and Document AI* 2024). An AI could be trained on templates of official documents (say, passports, bank statements, or corporate letterheads. For instance, a social engineer attempting a corporate data breach might present a fake court order or attorney letter (generated by AI in the right format and language) via email to pressure an employee into releasing data. Or criminals could use AI to produce fraudulent tax filings, insurance claims, or other paperwork to cause financial harm. Financial institutions that rely on scanned documents could be at risk if they cannot detect AI-forged PDFs or images that look authentic. In short, any process that trusts documents or text without robust verification could be attacked with AI-generated forgeries. This extends the deepfake problem beyond human sensory deception into procedural deception – fooling bureaucratic or organizational protocols through fake documentation.

Looking ahead, one of the most concerning prospects is **self-propagating, AI-driven disinformation**. We touched on personalized propaganda; expanding that concept, future malicious AI agents could run largely autonomously, continuously generating and disseminating false content across platforms without direct human guidance. These could be multifaceted campaigns where an AI agent creates a network of fake personas (complete with deepfake profile photos and backgrounds), posts coordinated content daily (news articles, videos, memes, forum posts), and even engages in debates with real users or other bots to sway opinion. Because the AI can learn from the responses, it might iteratively improve its persuasiveness, finding the most effective lies to achieve its goals.

Such an AI could potentially simulate an entire grassroots movement online – producing leaders (via deepfake videos), followers (via social bots), and propaganda – all fictitious yet interacting with real people and each other as if a real social movement exists. This goes beyond one-off social engineering and into society-wide manipulation. It's an extrapolation of current trends like troll farms and botnets, supercharged by AI's ability to adapt and scale. The challenge with an autonomous campaign is that it might be difficult to shut down; even if some accounts or content are flagged, the AI can create new ones or shift strategy faster than defenders can respond. This cat-and-mouse dynamic is already seen in spam bots; with smarter AI, it could be like fighting a hydra – cut off one head and two new ones (new lies, new fake personas) appear.

As digital and virtual environments (often dubbed the "metaverse") become more prevalent for work and social interaction, deepfakes might find new vectors there. In virtual worlds, users are represented by avatars, which could be customized to look like anyone or anything. It's conceivable that people could deploy unauthorized avatar skins of real individuals (a kind of deepfake in VR) to impersonate them in virtual meetings or communities. If business meetings move to VR spaces, verifying identity becomes even harder if the avatar visuals and voice are deepfaked.

Furthermore, generative AI might enable dynamic environment manipulation. For example, in a virtual storefront, an AI could show different fake product images or reviews to different viewers to influence their buying (an evolution of personalized scam). Or in a virtual political rally, a deepfake of a notable figure could appear and endorse a cause, misleading attendees. While these scenarios are speculative, they underscore that as technology domains evolve, the core issue – verifying what is real vs AI-generated – will remain, just in new forms.

Another future trend is the commodification of deepfake capabilities. We may see the rise of Deepfake-as-a-Service (DFaaS) platforms on the dark web, where anyone with ill intent but limited technical skill can simply pay for a customized deepfake creation. Already, some open websites allow users to create novelty deepfakes (e.g., face swap yourself into a movie scene). In the underground market, this could take the form of a service where an attacker uploads target footage/audio and gets back a polished deepfake tailored for whatever scam they plan. If such services become widespread, the volume of deepfake attacks could surge, as the barrier to entry shifts from technical expertise to just a small fee. This democratization of deception technology means even minor criminals or individuals with personal vendettas could access highly sophisticated fake media, not just well-funded groups.

On the flip side, improvements in detection and authentication technology (discussed next) might curb some of these threats. For each emerging threat, researchers are actively working on countermeasures. Nonetheless, it is clear that the threat landscape is constantly evolving. What seems like science fiction today (like real-time holographic deepfakes or fully autonomous fake news ecosystems) could become a pressing security issue in a few years given the rapid pace of AI innovation. Hence, continuous vigilance and adaptation are required from defenders.

CONCLUSION

Deepfakes exploit human trust mechanisms and cognitive biases to an alarming degree. They illustrate that cybersecurity is not just a technical challenge but a human psychology challenge. The psychological impact amplifies the technical threat: even a perfectly crafted deepfake requires the human target to fall for it, and understanding these biases helps explain why they often do. Addressing deepfake threats will thus require not only better detection tools but also training and awareness to bolster the human defenses against being psychologically manipulated.

Understanding the historical development and the technological drivers behind deepfakes is essential for developing effective strategies to mitigate their potential misuse and harness their beneficial applications. It also underscores the importance of taking proactive steps to protect against deepfake-based social engineering. Organizations should educate employees about the risks of deepfakes and strengthen their security measures. At the same time, developing better deepfake detection tools and promoting media literacy are essential to combat the spread of misinformation and manipulation enabled by this technology.

These findings highlight the transformative potential of collaboration between human intelligence and AI. However, it is equally important to learn how to leverage the power of AI while safeguarding against its potential abuses.

In conclusion, deepfakes and synthetic media represent a double-edged sword. While offering potential benefits, they also pose significant risks to information integrity and societal trust. Mitigating these risks requires a combined effort involving technical advancements, public awareness, and appropriate policy interventions. Only through such a comprehensive approach can we hope to harness the potential of synthetic media while minimizing its harmful impact.

REFERENCES

Abagnale, F. W., & Redding, S. (2000). *Catch me if you can: The true story of a real fake*. Crown.

Al-Mulla, M. S. (2022). Deepfakes: Criminalization And Legalization Analytical Descriptive Study. *Webology, 19*(2).

Bhattacharyya, C., Wang, H., Zhang, F., Kim, S., & Zhu, X. (2024). Diffusion deepfake. *arXiv preprint arXiv:2404.01579*.

Bhusal, C. S. (2021). Systematic review on social engineering: Hacking by manipulating humans. *Journal of Information Security, 12*(1), 104–114. DOI: 10.4236/jis.2021.121005

Birthriya, S. K., Ahlawat, P., & Jain, A. K. (2025). Detection and Prevention of Spear Phishing Attacks: A Comprehensive Survey. *Computers & Security, 104317*, 104317. 10.1016/j.cose.2025.104317. DOI: 10.1016/j.cose.2025.104317

Bradshaw, S., & Howard, P. N. (2018). Challenging truth and trust: A global inventory of organized social media manipulation. *The computational propaganda project, 1*, 1-26.

Breacher.ai. (2024). *Deepfake Attacks Examples*. https://breacher.ai/deepfake/deepfake-attack-examples/

Cecílio, J., Duarte, K., & Furtado, P. (2015). BlindeDroid: An information tracking system for real-time guiding of blind people. *Procedia Computer Science, 52*, 113–120. DOI: 10.1016/j.procs.2015.05.039

Ch, H. (2014). *Social Engineering: The Science of Human Hacking*. Wiley.

Chen, R. J., Lu, M. Y., Chen, T. Y., Williamson, D. F., & Mahmood, F. (2021). Synthetic data in machine learning for medicine and healthcare. *Nature Biomedical Engineering, 5*(6), 493–497. 10.1038/s41551-021-00751-8. DOI: 10.1038/s41551-021-00751-8 PMID: 34131324

Chung, J. S., & Zisserman, A. (2017). Out of Time: Automated Lip Sync in the Wild. In C.-S. Chen, J. Lu, & K.-K. Ma, *Computer Vision – ACCV 2016 Workshops* Cham.

Cyber Risks Associated with Generative Artificial Intelligence (2024). https://www.mas.gov.sg/-/media/mas-media-library/regulation/circulars/trpd/cyber-risks-associated-with-generative-artificial-intelligence.pdf

Daniel, J. F. (2022). First order motion model for image animation and deep fake detection: Using deep learning. 2022 International Conference on Computer Communication and Informatics (ICCCI), *Deepfakes for good? How synthetic media is transforming business*. (2023). https://techinformed.com/deepfakes-for-good-how-synthetic-media-is-transforming-business/

Deepfakes: The latest weapon in the cyber security arms race. (2024). https://www.beazley.com/en-US/news-and-events/deepfakes-the-latest-weapon-in-the-cyber-security-arms-race/

Deepfakes: The New Threat to Cybersecurity. Retrieved March 1, 2025 from https://www.blackberry.com/us/en/solutions/endpoint-security/ransomware-protection/deepfakes

Eynern, C. (2024). *Olaf Scholz Deepfake: How a Deepfake impacts Public Trust* University of Twente]. https://purl.utwente.nl/essays/101675

Fernando, T., Priyasad, D., Sridharan, S., Ross, A., & Fookes, C. (2025). Face Deepfakes-A Comprehensive Review. *arXiv preprint arXiv:2502.09812*.

Goodfellow, I., Pouget-Abadie, J., Mirza, M., Xu, B., Warde-Farley, D., Ozair, S., Courville, A., & Bengio, Y. (2020). Generative adversarial networks. *Communications of the ACM, 63*(11), 139–144. DOI: 10.1145/3422622

Guo, H. (2022). Exposing GAN-generated faces using deep neural network. https://scholarsarchive.library.albany.edu/legacy-etd/2917

Hadnagy, C. (2010). *Social engineering: The art of human hacking*. John Wiley & Sons.

Hancock, J. T., & Bailenson, J. N. (2021). The social impact of deepfakes. In (Vol. 24, pp. 149-152): Mary Ann Liebert, Inc., publishers 140 Huguenot Street, 3rd Floor New. DOI: 10.1089/cyber.2021.29208.jth

Hasan, H. R., & Salah, K. (2019). Combating deepfake videos using blockchain and smart contracts. *IEEE Access : Practical Innovations, Open Solutions, 7*, 41596–41606. DOI: 10.1109/ACCESS.2019.2905689

Heather Chen, K. M. (2024). *Deepfake CFO scam hits Hong Kong*. https://edition.cnn.com/2024/02/04/asia/deepfake-cfo-scam-hong-kong-intl-hnk/index.html

Heidari, A., Navimipour, N. J., Dag, H., Talebi, S., & Unal, M. (2024). A novel blockchain-based deepfake detection method using federated and deep learning models. *Cognitive Computation, 16*(3), 1073–1091. DOI: 10.1007/s12559-024-10255-7

Helmus, T. C. (2022). Artificial intelligence, deepfakes, and disinformation. *Rand Corporation*, 1-24.

Hinton, G. E., & Salakhutdinov, R. R. (2006). Reducing the dimensionality of data with neural networks. *science, 313*(5786), 504-507.

Ho, J., Jain, A., & Abbeel, P. (2020). Denoising diffusion probabilistic models. *Advances in Neural Information Processing Systems, 33*, 6840–6851.

Islam, M. B. E., Haseeb, M., Batool, H., Ahtasham, N., & Muhammad, Z. (2024). AI threats to politics, elections, and democracy: A blockchain-based deepfake authenticity verification framework. *Blockchains, 2*(4), 458–481. DOI: 10.3390/blockchains2040020

Jagatic, T. N., Johnson, N. A., Jakobsson, M., & Menczer, F. (2007). Social phishing. *Communications of the ACM, 50*(10), 94–100. DOI: 10.1145/1290958.1290968

Kapoor, J., & Rahman, N. A. A. (2024). Organizational Security Improvement in Preventing Deepfake Ransomware. In *Digital Innovation Adoption: Architectural Recommendations and Security Solutions* (pp. 58-78). Bentham Science Publishers. DOI: 10.2174/9789815079661124010009

Kirsh, D. (2000). A few thoughts on cognitive overload. *Intellectica, 30*(1), 19–51. DOI: 10.3406/intel.2000.1592

Lattanzio, G., & Ma, Y. (2023). Cybersecurity risk and corporate innovation. *Journal of Corporate Finance, 82*, 102445. DOI: 10.1016/j.jcorpfin.2023.102445

LeCun, Y., Bengio, Y., & Hinton, G. (2015). Deep learning. *nature, 521*(7553), 436-444. https://www.nature.com/articles/nature14539

Leibowicz, C. R. (2025). Regulating Reality: Exploring Synthetic Media Through Multistakeholder AI Governance. *arXiv preprint arXiv:2502.04526*.

Marwick, A., & Lewis, R. (2017). Media manipulation and disinformation online. *New York. Data & Society Research Institute, 359*, 1146–1151.

Mitnick, K. D., & Simon, W. L. (2003). *The art of deception: Controlling the human element of security*. John Wiley & Sons.

Neisse, R., Steri, G., & Nai-Fovino, I. (2017). A blockchain-based approach for data accountability and provenance tracking. Proceedings of the 12th international conference on availability, reliability and security, *The Psychology of Deepfakes in Social Engineering*. (2025). Reality Defender. https://www.realitydefender.com/blog/the-psychology-of-deepfakes-in-social-engineering

Reardon, S. (2024). *How Deepfakes Are Impacting Public Trust in Media*. Pindrop. https://www.pindrop.com/article/deepfakes-impacting-trust-media/

Renault, T., Amariles, D. R., & Troussel, A. (2024). Collaboratively adding context to social media posts reduces the sharing of false news. *arXiv preprint arXiv:2404.02803*.

Samuel Okechukwu Omeje, B. O. Mary Onyedikachi Chukwuka. (2023). Artificial Intelligence on Social Media: Use, Misuse, And Impacts. In *Emergence of Social Media: Shaping the Digital Discourse of the Next Generation* (pp. 38-46). Routledge.

Shu, K., Sliva, A., Wang, S., Tang, J., & Liu, H. (2017). Fake news detection on social media: A data mining perspective. *SIGKDD Explorations*, *19*(1), 22–36. DOI: 10.1145/3137597.3137600

Solomon, E., Woubie, A., & Emiru, E. S. (2023). Autoencoder based face verification system. *arXiv preprint arXiv:2312.14301*.

Stavola, J., & Choi, K.-S. (2023). Victimization by deepfake in the metaverse: Building a practical management framework. *International Journal of Cybersecurity Intelligence & Cybercrime*, *6*(2), 2. DOI: 10.52306/2578-3289.1171

Sutherland, I. E. (1964). Sketch pad a man-machine graphical communication system. Proceedings of the SHARE design automation workshop, *Synthetic Document Generation for NLP and Document AI*. (2024). Medium. Retrieved 3/21/2025 from https://medium.com/@tagx20/synthetic-document-generation-for-nlp-and-document-ai-9b04bb5008db

The Impact of Deepfake Fraud: Risks, Solutions, and Global Trends. (2024). Regula. https://regulaforensics.com/blog/impact-of-deepfakes-on-idv-regula-survey/#:~:text=Criminals%20can%20now%20easily%20create,on%20a%20screen%20during%20verification

The Wall Street Journal (2024). https://www.wsj.com/search?query=CEO%20fraud

Tolosana, R., Vera-Rodriguez, R., Fierrez, J., Morales, A., & Ortega-Garcia, J. (2020). Deepfakes and beyond: A survey of face manipulation and fake detection. *Information Fusion*, *64*, 131–148. DOI: 10.1016/j.inffus.2020.06.014

Trifonova, P., & Venkatagiri, S. (2024). Misinformation, Fraud, and Stereotyping: Towards a Typology of Harm Caused by Deepfakes. Companion Publication of the 2024 Conference on Computer-Supported Cooperative Work and Social Computing.

Wardle, C., & Derakhshan, H. (2017). *Information disorder: Toward an interdisciplinary framework for research and policymaking* (Vol. 27). Council of Europe Strasbourg.

Westerlund, M. (2019). The emergence of deepfake technology: A review. *Technology Innovation Management Review*, *9*(11), 39–52. http://doi.org/10.22215/timreview/1282. DOI: 10.22215/timreview/1282

Xie, H.-X., Lo, L., Shuai, H.-H., & Cheng, W.-H. (2022). An overview of facial micro-expression analysis: Data, methodology and challenge. *IEEE Transactions on Affective Computing*, *14*(3), 1857–1875. DOI: 10.1109/TAFFC.2022.3143100

Zhao, Y., Liu, B., Ding, M., Liu, B., Zhu, T., & Yu, X. (2023). Proactive deepfake defence via identity watermarking. Proceedings of the IEEE/CVF winter conference on applications of computer vision, Zuboff, S. (2023). The age of surveillance capitalism. In *Social theory re-wired* (pp. 203-213). Routledge. DOI: 10.1109/WACV56688.2023.00458

KEY TERMS AND DEFINITIONS

Behavioral Biometrics: Unique physical or behavioral traits (e.g., voice patterns, typing rhythm) used to authenticate identity or detect anomalies in synthetic media.

Cognitive Overload: A state where excessive information or stress impairs critical thinking, making individuals more susceptible to manipulation (e.g., by urgent or emotional deepfake content).

Deepfake: Synthetic media created using AI to manipulate or generate realistic images, audio, or video, often to impersonate individuals or fabricate events.

Deepfake-as-a-Service (DFaaS): Dark web platforms offering customizable deepfake creation tools for malicious actors, lowering the technical barrier to misuse.

Disinformation Campaigns: Coordinated efforts to spread false or misleading information, often amplified by deepfakes, to influence public opinion or destabilize trust.

Media Literacy: The ability to critically evaluate digital content, recognize manipulation techniques (e.g., deepfakes), and verify sources before sharing or acting on information.

Multimodal Detection: Combining analysis of multiple data types (e.g., audio + video) to identify inconsistencies in deepfakes, such as mismatched lip-syncing or unnatural gestures.

Social Engineering: Psychological manipulation tactics used to deceive individuals into divulging sensitive information or performing actions that compromise security.

Synthetic Media: Any digital content (e.g., images, videos, audio) generated or altered using AI, including deepfakes, AI-generated text, or computer-simulated voices.

Chapter 10
Deepfakes Unleashed:
Exploring the Role of Blockchain in Managing AI–Generated Content

M. Sridevi
Rajalakshmi Engineering College, India

P. Madhavasarma
iD https://orcid.org/0000-0003-0485-8111
SASTRA University, India

Jayaprakash J. Stanly
Mahendra Institute of Technology, India

Kumar M. Santhosh
iD https://orcid.org/0009-0009-6623-0558
Nandha Engineering College, India

ABSTRACT

Deepfakes, which are driven by generative AI, have revolutionized synthetic media, presenting both exciting opportunities and formidable obstacles. Deepfakes may be utilized for immersive experiences and imaginative storytelling, but they also present risks including false information, identity theft, and a decline in public confidence. The crucial role that blockchain technology plays in controlling AI-generated material and reducing the dangers of deepfakes is examined in this study. Digital media authenticity and provenance may be effectively verified thanks to blockchain's decentralized, unchangeable ledger. Blockchain and generative AI may be used to provide a strong foundation for content authentication, manipulation detection, and media production and distribution responsibility.

DOI: 10.4018/979-8-3373-6481-0.ch010

INTRODUCTION

Digital content generation, modification, and distribution have been completely transformed by the quick developments in deep learning and artificial intelligence (AI). Using generative adversarial networks (GANs) and other deep learning models, deepfake technology is one of the most revolutionary yet contentious advancements in this field. It produces incredibly lifelike synthetic media, such as images, videos, and audio, that are frequently indistinguishable from authentic recordings. Originally seen as a breakthrough in AI-driven content creation, deepfakes have turned into a double-edged sword that presents significant ethical, legal, and societal problems in addition to new opportunities in the creative, digital storytelling, and customized media sectors. The ease with which modified media may be produced has increased worries about political deceit, identity theft, disinformation, and the decline in confidence in digital material. It is becoming more and more difficult to distinguish between real and artificially created material as deepfake technology advances, which increases the need for strong systems to confirm authenticity and stop harmful use cases. By offering decentralized, unchangeable, and transparent ways to confirm the authenticity and provenance of AI-generated content, blockchain technology shows promise in this area. In order to demonstrate how the confluence of deepfake technology, generative AI, and blockchain-based verification frameworks may guarantee media integrity, improve accountability, and promote an ethical digital environment, this chapter examines the complex relationships between these three technologies.

The fundamental component of deepfake technology is sophisticated machine learning models, which produce artificial media with a previously unheard-of degree of realism. Iteratively improving the quality of generated outputs, these models, especially GANs (Generative Adversarial Networks), work by competing two neural networks, the discriminator and the generator. Although this technology has made major strides in the fields of virtual reality (VR), augmented reality (AR), filmmaking, gaming, and automated dubbing, its rapid development and accessibility have also made it easier for malicious activities like political disinformation campaigns, cyber fraud, revenge pornography, and the spread of fake news. The spread of this kind of material has highlighted the shortcomings of conventional verification methods, making a decentralized, impenetrable system for content authentication necessary. Here, blockchain technology is essential for documenting the provenance, ownership, and alteration history of digital assets, giving AI-generated content a layer of trust. By capturing transactions in an unchangeable and verifiable way, blockchain technology—basically a distributed and decentralized ledger system—ensures security and transparency. Blockchain functions on a trustless network, which means that no one organization has authority over data verification and authentication, in contrast to centralized content verification techniques. Blockchain is a great option for timestamping content production, certifying AI-generated media, and confirming media authenticity in a decentralized setting because of its feature. To ensure that any later changes are readily identified, one of the main ways to use blockchain in deepfake detection is to insert the cryptographic hashes of the original media files into a blockchain network. By preventing the transmission of false information, this unchangeable record not only safeguards digital rights and ownership but also aids in differentiating between authentic and modified content. Blockchain-based media verification platforms and a number of new decentralized apps (DApps) are already investigating this strategy, employing smart contracts to automate authenticity checks and stop unwanted changes. Blockchain technology with AI-generated content may be used in a variety of sectors, such as social media, cybersecurity, entertainment, and news media. By ensuring that news agencies' media material is unaltered, blockchain-based verification frameworks can lower the possibility of false news spreading in the journalism industry. Filmmakers and other content providers may safeguard their intellectual property and stop illegal deepfake manipulations in the entertainment sector by using blockchain-powered digital watermarks.

Blockchain-based verification layers may be included into social media platforms to validate user-generated content and stop the spread of dangerous deepfake films that might instigate violence or destroy people's reputations. Furthermore, forensic investigators and law enforcement organizations may use blockchain technology to record forensic evidence in a tamper-proof ledger, guaranteeing that crimes involving deepfakes can be successfully tracked down and punished. A crucial element in the fight against deepfakes is the implementation of moral standards, legal regulations, and content control techniques. Blockchain offers a technological framework for authenticity verification, but legal frameworks are just as important for regulating the moral use of material produced by AI. Globally, governments and regulatory agencies are starting to understand the ramifications of deepfake technology and are attempting to create regulations that would make the use of malevolent deepfakes illegal while maintaining innovative and legal uses. By linking verified digital signatures to media material, blockchain-based decentralized identity management systems (DID) can aid in content creator authentication and guarantee that altered or artificial intelligence (AI)-generated media can be appropriately identified and classified. Furthermore, blockchain networks may be combined with AI-powered deepfake detection algorithms to automatically identify synthetic media and warn questionable material before it reaches large audiences. The combination of blockchain technology and AI-generated content verification is not without its difficulties, despite its potential.

Since storing massive amounts of audiovisual material on blockchain can be computationally costly and inefficient, one of the main issues is the scalability of blockchain networks. The real media files are kept in decentralized storage systems (like IPFS or Arweave), while only cryptographic hashes and metadata are saved on the blockchain. This is being addressed by hybrid solutions that combine off-chain storage and on-chain verification. The creation of standardized protocols for digital content verification is necessary to address the issue of interoperability across various blockchain networks and AI platforms. Furthermore, since storing private or sensitive deepfake detection data on an immutable ledger poses issues with data ownership and consent, privacy problems must be addressed.

In order to mitigate deepfakes using blockchain technology, politicians, media specialists, cryptographers, and AI researchers must work together across academic boundaries. Differential privacy (DP) and federated learning (FL) in AI models may assist improve generative AI's security and privacy without sacrificing speed, according to emerging trends. Furthermore, research is being done on zero-knowledge proofs (ZKPs) as a way to confirm the legitimacy of information without disclosing private details. Proof-of-Stake (PoS) and Proof-of-Authority (PoA) are two consensus techniques that, as blockchain technology advances, can aid in the development of more scalable and energy-efficient blockchain solutions for digital media verification.

STATE OF ART MODELS

Fan Yang et al (2024) says that the hazards of false information endangering market integrity are among the issues raised by the growing amount of AI-generated content (AIGC) on digital platforms. It highlights that in order to encourage responsible AI usage, experts, regulators, and AI developers must work together and implement efficient regulatory measures, such as systems for identifying errors and guaranteeing adherence to rules. In order to improve the security of AIGC, the paper suggests a blockchain-based regulatory framework that incorporates data encryption, access control, safe identity verification for content owners, and an effective caching mechanism for AIGC information. Additionally, it presents a customized data supervision system designed to preserve data security, secure the identities of content authors, and guarantee efficient monitoring in the AIGC environment.

Islam et al (2024) studies addresses the increasing risks that artificial intelligence (AI) technologies pose to the integrity of international elections, emphasizing how AI can affect political processes by producing deepfakes that can sway voter perceptions and weaken opposition parties, generative AI for disseminating misleading information, and biased language models. The authors suggest a Blockchain-based Deepfake Authenticity Verification Framework (B-DAVF) to resolve these issues by identifying and authenticating deepfake content instantly. They also suggest extensive countermeasures like improved laws, technological advancements, and public awareness campaigns.

Jordan et al (2024) suggests using blockchain technology as a safety measure to deal with issues including generative AI toxicity, biases, hallucinations, misaligned interests, AI as a black box, and abuse. It highlights how the creation and application of AI can be made more transparent, verifiable, and decentralized through the convergence of blockchain and AI, which will increase the dependability and accountability of AI for businesses and encourage responsible and transparent AI use.

Liu et al (2024) addresses issues with service latency, security, and reliability by presenting a blockchain-powered architecture for controlling the lifespan of AIGC products in edge networks. It implements an incentive mechanism for safe ownership swaps among anonymous users and suggests a protocol called Proof-of-AIGC to safeguard ownership and copyright.

The system also has a multi-weight subjective logic-based reputation mechanism to assist AIGC producers in locating reliable edge service providers. The study suggests possible avenues for further research in this field and provides numerical findings demonstrating the efficacy of the suggested methodology.

Adru et al (2024) discusses an innovative platform that utilizes artificial intelligence and blockchain technology to empower content creators by enabling them to share and monetize their work through Non-Fungible Tokens (NFTs). It highlights the challenges and opportunities faced by content creators in the digital era and how this platform can address these issues. Key features of the platform include text-to-image generation for creative inspiration, a recommendation engine for content discovery, and a collaborative chat room that facilitates direct interaction between creators and their audiences, aiming to enhance the overall content creation ecosystem.

UNDERSTANDING DEEPFAKE TECHNOLOGY

In the area of generative models, where neural networks are taught to create hyper-realistic audiovisual material, deepfake technology is a major advancement in artificial intelligence (AI). Deepfakes produce believable-looking photos, movies, and sounds by utilizing deep learning algorithms, especially Generative Adversarial Networks (GANs). Combining the words "deep learning" with "fake," the phrase "deepfake" emphasizes the technology's fundamental idea of employing AI to create realistic-looking but misleading media. Originally created for AI and computer vision research, deepfake technology has now spread to a number of industries, including politics, digital marketing, education, entertainment, and cybersecurity. Deepfake creation relies heavily on a kind of neural networks called GANs, which function as a two-network system consisting of a discriminator and a generator.

Samples of synthetic media are produced by the generator, and their authenticity is assessed by the discriminator, which separates authentic from fake material. Over several cycles, the generator becomes more adept at creating material that is so lifelike that the discriminator is unable to distinguish between false and genuine. The creation of extremely complex deepfake models that can imitate human voices, facial emotions, and body language with previously unheard-of precision has been made possible by this adversarial learning process. Other designs, such as Diffusion Models and Variational Autoencoders (VAEs), improve on GANs by improving the produced content's texture quality, motion consistency, and contextual awareness. Deepfake technology has led to substantial breakthroughs in the methods for creating synthetic media that improve accessibility, realism, and efficiency. One of the most popular techniques is face-swapping, which involves replacing a subject's face in a video with that of another person while preserving realistic facial emotions and gestures. This is usually accomplished by using deep learning models that have been trained on big collections of videos and pictures of people. This enables the AI to map important face traits and create smooth transitions. Voice synthesis and cloning is another well-liked deepfake approach in which artificial intelligence (AI) models simulate human speech by analyzing a speaker's tone, pitch, and speech patterns.

Voice cloning is made possible by AI-powered text-to-speech (TTS) models, including Microsoft's VALL-E and OpenAI's WaveNet, which need little input data to produce speech that sounds almost exactly like the original speaker. Another approach is lip-syncing deepfakes, where AI alters a video's lip movements to match a completely other audio track, giving the impression that the person is uttering things they have never really said. Because it enables more precise lip synchronization in translated content, this has been frequently employed in media localization and dubbing. AI can now also change a person's body gestures and motions in films thanks to the development of full-body deepfake generation, which has uses in gaming, augmented reality, and virtual reality.

AI-driven deepfake technology has advanced beyond simple face-swapping to create completely new images, animated sequences, and photorealistic videos from textual descriptions thanks to the development of text-to-image and text-to-video generation models like DALL-E, Stable Diffusion, and RunwayML's Gen-2. While these advances are transforming artistic expression and content production, they also raise ethical questions about identity fraud, disinformation, and digital trust.

Applications of deepfake technology have been identified in a variety of sectors, with both favorable and contentious results. Film studios may now de-age performers, bring back historical characters, or substitute stunt doubles in films and television shows thanks to deepfakes, which are changing visual effects (VFX) in the entertainment sector. In popular movies, AI-powered face reanimation has been used to change actors' performances without needing to reshoot. Deepfake technology is being utilized in virtual reality and gaming to produce individualized in-game characters, incredibly lifelike avatars, and immersive narrative experiences that allow players to engage with artificial intelligence (AI)-generated virtual people. Digital marketing and advertising have also adopted deepfake-driven AI for customized brand endorsements, in which deepfake-powered virtual influencers present viewers with dynamic and interactive material.

Brands also use artificial intelligence (AI)-generated voices and synthetic avatars for automated customer support, which improves engagement by using lifelike digital assistants. Artificial intelligence (AI)-powered tutors, historical reenactments, and interactive learning environments with multilingual virtual lecturers are all made possible by deepfakes in the education and training industry. But among the most revolutionary uses is in therapy and healthcare, where AI-created digital people help patients with speech impairments by creating customized voice synthesis solutions, help with mental health support, and mimic medical procedures for training.

Deepfake technology has advantages, but there are also serious hazards, especially with regard to cybersecurity and disinformation. The public's faith and the integrity of the media are seriously threatened by malicious actors who have used deepfake methods to promote political propaganda, fake news, and social engineering campaigns. Deepfake-produced films of political figures making false claims have swayed public opinion and elections, underscoring the pressing need for strong blockchain-based authentication systems and AI-driven detection tools. Deepfake technology is used by cybercriminals to alter biometric authentication systems in the context of fraud and identity theft, granting them unlawful access to bank accounts and sensitive data. Cybercriminals are using AI-generated speech deepfakes to pose as CEOs in fraudulent schemes, including CEO fraud and business email compromise (BEC) frauds, which has led to an increase in corporate security concerns. Global regulatory organizations are investigating ways to create frameworks for digital content verification and use watermarking systems to differentiate between actual and artificial intelligence-generated material, while the ethical and legal ramifications of deepfake technology remain a topic of discussion.

The necessity for proactive solutions, ethical concerns, and legal frameworks to prevent possible risks and embrace the creative potential of deepfake technology is highlighted by its fast progress. Blockchain technology, which uses digital ledgers and cryptographic verification to provide unchangeable evidence of content validity, is being investigated more and more as a decentralized way to combat deepfake manipulation. When paired with blockchain-based content provenance tracking, AI-driven deepfake detection algorithms can be extremely helpful in guaranteeing accountability and transparency in digital media. In order to establish a safe, moral, and reliable digital environment where AI-generated content can be used sensibly without jeopardizing societal security and trust, researchers, legislators, tech companies, and digital media platforms must work together as deepfake technology develops.

CHALLENGES POSED BY DEEPFAKE TECHNOLOGY

Although deepfake technology has brought about revolutionary improvements in AI and media production, it has also brought about a number of problems that jeopardize public confidence and digital security. The growing complexity of AI-generated material prompts worries about false information, invasions of privacy, moral and legal quandaries, and the decline of online trust. Widespread social, political, and economic upheavals might result from the abuse of deepfakes as they get more realistic and available. The capacity to create incredibly lifelike movies, pictures, and audio recordings allows bad actors to trick viewers, sway public opinion, and carry out cybercrimes with previously unheard-of speed. Traditional approaches to digital forensics and content authentication are being challenged by the combined effects of artificial intelligence (AI), deep learning, and generative adversarial networks (GANs), which have made it harder to discern between legitimate and fake information. Because deepfake technology is developing so quickly, stakeholders from a variety of industries, including governments, media outlets, and tech companies, must address these issues through technological advancements, legislative actions, and public awareness campaigns to guarantee the moral and responsible use of content produced by artificial intelligence. One of the most pressing challenges posed by deepfake technology is its role in spreading misinformation and disinformation. The ability to generate convincing yet entirely fabricated content has serious implications for digital media, as fake videos, manipulated images, and synthetic audio recordings can be weaponized to influence public discourse, destabilize governments, and incite social unrest. Political deepfakes have already been used to fabricate speeches, alter historical narratives, and create misleading news stories that manipulate voter behavior. The rapid dissemination of deepfake-generated misinformation through social media platforms amplifies the risk of mass deception, as algorithms prioritize engagement over accuracy, allowing misleading content to reach millions of users within minutes. Journalism and fact-checking groups have additional difficulties as a result of deepfake technology, since they need to create sophisticated instruments to identify and refute AI-generated falsehoods. The sheer amount of deepfake content is too great for traditional fact-checking procedures to handle, thus blockchain-based verification systems and AI-driven forensic techniques must be integrated to validate digital media. Audiences now find it more difficult to distinguish between real and manipulated information, and the emergence of synthetic media has further blurred the boundaries between fact and fiction, eroding confidence in news sources. Democratic institutions are under risk from this decline in media trust as deepfake-generated false material may be used to defame public figures, create scandals, and skew public opinion on important social issues.

In the corporate and financial sectors, where bogus movies and artificial voice recordings may affect stock prices, slander companies, and carry out massive financial schemes, the effects of deepfake-driven disinformation go beyond politics and media. AI-generated speech deepfakes are used in business email compromise (BEC) scams and deepfake phishing attempts to pose as executives and approve fraudulent transactions in corporate settings. Organizations targeted by deepfake fraud schemes have suffered multi-million dollar losses as a result of cybercriminals' successful use of AI-generated voice clones to trick employees. Deepfake-driven misinformation may potentially affect financial markets, since AI-produced films can be used to manipulate investor mood, invent CEO remarks, and cause stock market swings.

Because AI-generated material may be used to create sexual or libelous information without authorization, alter biometric identification systems, and impersonate people, deepfake technology poses serious risks to individual privacy. The capacity to create lifelike voice and face clones presents significant concerns for identity theft, as cybercriminals may use deepfake technology to circumvent security measures, obtain unauthorized access to private accounts, and commit fraud. Deepfake assaults are increasingly targeting biometric authentication systems, such voice verification and face recognition, because AI-generated copies may accurately imitate a person's biometric traits. Financial institutions, governmental organizations, and internet platforms that depend on biometric authentication for safe access control are alarmed by this, underscoring the pressing need for multi-factor authentication and AI-driven fraud detection systems to protect user identities.

A serious privacy infringement that mostly affects public figures, celebrities, and private persons is the abuse of deepfake technology to produce sexual and non-consensual content. Commonly known as "deepfake pornography," AI-generated pornographic deepfakes have been used as a weapon to take advantage of victims, resulting in harm to their reputations, emotional suffering, and legal issues. Because deepfake films may spread quickly across several internet channels, victims of deepfake harassment frequently find it difficult to delete AI-generated sexual content from digital platforms, rendering content removal attempts futile. Legal and legislative debates over digital consent, privacy rights, and the control of AI-generated pornographic material have been triggered by the spread of deepfake pornography.

Recognizing the serious harm that non-consensual deepfake pornography does to victims and the larger digital ecosystem, lawmakers in a number of nations are contemplating passing legislation to make its production and dissemination illegal.

Beyond worries about personal privacy, deepfake technology has sparked concerns in cybersecurity, as AI-generated impersonations might jeopardize business espionage, diplomatic relations, and national security. Cyberattacks targeting government leaders, military personnel, and intelligence agencies have employed deepfake-driven identity fraud, underscoring the necessity of sophisticated AI-driven detection frameworks to recognize and counteract synthetic media threats. The cybersecurity community must create proactive defensive mechanisms, such as blockchain-based identity verification, AI-powered fraud detection, and digital watermarking technologies, to differentiate genuine information from artificial intelligence-generated forgeries as deepfake capabilities continue to advance. Since current laws are unable to adequately handle the complexity of synthetic media, the emergence of deepfake technology has spurred much discussion on the moral and legal ramifications of AI-generated material. Concerns over responsibility, digital rights, and freedom of speech in the AI era are raised by the absence of established legislative frameworks for deepfake detection, content authenticity, and liability. Determining the legal limits of deepfake content presents difficulties for governments and legal organizations, especially when it comes to issues involving defamation, invasions of privacy, and disinformation operations. Different jurisdictions have different laws governing deepfake technology; some have strong laws prohibiting the production and dissemination of deepfakes, while others rely on industry-wide voluntary guidelines and moral AI standards. Another area of legal dispute is intellectual property (IP) rights, as AI-generated content makes it harder to distinguish between machine-generated art and human ingenuity. Because deepfake-driven content production may be created without direct human interaction, it presents concerns around copyright ownership, credit, and fair use. Legislators and legal professionals are investigating frameworks for AI-generated intellectual property, such as ways to assign authorship rights to AI models, provide digital provenance monitoring, and ensure openness in the attribution of AI-generated output. Deepfake technology's ethical ramifications also include the possibility of algorithmic bias, manipulation, and social effect; hence, addressing ethical AI governance, digital media responsibility, and responsible innovation in AI and blockchain convergence calls for a multidisciplinary approach.

The ubiquitous availability of AI-generated media undermines faith in the validity of digital material, making deepfake technology a serious threat to public trust and digital credibility. In the digital era, viewers find it difficult to discern between reality and deceit due to the capacity to make realistic-looking but fake movies, pictures, and audio recordings. This decline in trust impacts a number of industries, such as social media, journalism, and law enforcement, as disinformation and artificial media manipulation erode democratic institutions and public debate. Deepfake technology's long-term effects on digital trust necessitate all-encompassing solutions, such as blockchain-based content authentication, AI-powered deepfake detection, and public awareness campaigns to inform consumers of the dangers of AI-generated material.

To rebuild confidence in digital material, media enterprises, tech firms, and legislators must work together to create open AI ethics, digital verification systems, and accountability procedures. Digital watermarking, cryptographic authentication systems, and AI-driven forensic tools can all improve the integrity of digital media by enabling viewers to confirm the veracity of information before taking it at face value. Researchers, regulatory agencies, and industry stakeholders must work together to combat disinformation, safeguard privacy, support ethical AI norms, and strengthen digital credibility as deepfake technology develops. The ethical and responsible use of deepfake technology is essential to the future of AI-generated media. Innovation and responsibility must be balanced to build a digital environment that promotes security, transparency, and trust.

BLOCKCHAIN AS A SOLUTION FOR DEEPFAKE DETECTION AND MANAGEMENT

Robust systems to recognize and regulate AI-generated material have become critical as deepfake technology continues to advance, bringing both innovation and disruption to digital media. Concerns regarding disinformation, identity theft, privacy invasion, and the decline in public confidence in digital material have been sparked by the appearance of hyper-realistic deepfakes. The fast improvements in generative adversarial networks (GANs) are making it harder for traditional detection approaches, such as AI-driven forensic tools, to distinguish between real and fake material. In this regard, blockchain technology offers a viable way to improve the accountability, traceability, and validity of digital material. Utilizing the core ideas of immutability, decentralization, and cryptographic security, blockchain may be a dependable foundation for content authentication and deepfake detection. A transparent and impenetrable system that reduces the dangers of deepfake technology may be established by combining blockchain-based digital identity verification, cryptographic watermarking, and decentralized media storage. The potential of blockchain as a deepfake detection and management tool is examined in this chapter, with particular attention paid to its fundamental ideas, safeguards for openness and confidence, function in digital identity verification, and decentralized authentication systems for AI-generated material.

Blockchain technology is a distributed ledger that securely, decentralized, and irreversibly records transactions. Blockchain works via a peer-to-peer (P2P) network, where data is stored across numerous nodes, negating the need for centralized control that characterizes traditional databases. The blockchain records every transaction or data input in a "block," which is then connected to earlier blocks chronologically to create an ongoing, safe "chain" of records. Due to its decentralized structure, which requires network-wide consent to change any record, blockchain is impervious to data manipulation. Additionally, digital signatures and cryptographic hashing protect the integrity and validity of data that is stored by thwarting unwanted changes. The consensus mechanism of blockchain is one of its distinguishing characteristics; it guarantees that every transaction is validated prior to being included into the ledger. Different ways to preserving network security and stopping fraudulent activity are offered by different consensus algorithms, including Proof of Work (PoW), Proof of Stake (PoS), and Delegated Proof of Stake (DPoS). In the context of deepfake detection, metadata, digital fingerprints, and provenance information of media files may be stored using blockchain's immutability and consensus-driven verification, which facilitates authenticity verification. Blockchain smart contracts, which are self-executing agreements stored inside the blockchain, may also be used to automate content verification procedures, guaranteeing that only validated and authenticated media assets are shared on digital platforms.

Loss of confidence in digital material is one of the main problems caused by deepfake technology. People, organizations, and governments are finding it more and more difficult to tell the difference between authentic and altered media due to the capacity to create incredibly lifelike but entirely fake movies, photos, and audio recordings. This has resulted in a crisis of confidence in law enforcement, entertainment, journalism, and social media, where it is simple to spread misleading narratives in an effort to mislead audiences and sway public opinion. Blockchain provides a workable answer to this issue by using decentralized verification techniques to guarantee transparency and trust.

Through the use of blockchain technology into digital media authentication processes, content producers and distributors may register media files on an impenetrable ledger, guaranteeing that every piece of material has a history that can be verified. By recording media files with cryptographic proofs, blockchain-based timestamping enables the tracking of the creation date, location, and creator of a piece of information. This method greatly lowers the possibility of disinformation caused by deepfakes since blockchain allows consumers to track the source of digital content and confirm its legitimacy before taking it at face value. Furthermore, the openness of blockchain guarantees that an open and verifiable system for content authentication is available to all stakeholders, including consumers, regulatory bodies, journalists, and content providers. By distributing verification duties throughout a decentralized network, blockchain prevents any one institution from controlling the legitimacy of material, in contrast to centralized verification systems that establish faith in a single authority. By guaranteeing that no person or group may sway the verification process to suit their own objectives, this decentralized method increases confidence.

AI-generated voice clones and face swaps may be used to impersonate people, get around authentication systems, and conduct fraud, which has led to new challenges to digital identity security from deepfake technology. The rising susceptibility of conventional identity verification techniques, such passwords, biometric authentication, and two-factor authentication, to deepfake assaults calls for a more safe and impenetrable solution. Blockchain-based digital identity verification, which offers a decentralized and cryptographically secure framework for identity identification, presents a possible strategy to reduce these dangers. People may build digital identities that are self-governing and preserved on a safe, unchangeable ledger using blockchain technology. In contrast to centralized identity management solutions that depend on outside parties, blockchain-based identity verification gives individuals complete control over their personal data, lowering the possibility of identity theft and data breaches. A cryptographic key is associated with each identity recorded on the blockchain, guaranteeing that only the legitimate owner may view and alter their identity information. In order to tackle deepfake-related fraud, this decentralized identity system is especially helpful since it offers a trustworthy way to confirm people's legitimacy in online interactions. Blockchain-based digital IDs may be utilized for social media verification and internet security to validate user-generated material and stop the spread of false information produced by artificial intelligence. Blockchain technology guarantees accountability and transparency in content creation by establishing a chain of trust between digital material and verified identities. To lessen the possibility of misinformation fueled by deepfakes, social media companies and news outlets should use blockchain-based identity verification systems to verify the origins of photos, videos, and audio recordings. Additionally, deepfake assaults may be used to carry out fraudulent operations and impersonate people, which has important ramifications for legal and financial transactions including blockchain-based identity verification. Blockchain-powered smart contracts may be configured to confirm digital identities prior to transaction execution, guaranteeing that only verified users have access to private financial services. This method reduces the dangers of AI-generated identity fraud while enhancing security and confidence in digital transactions. Conventional approaches to content authentication are failing to identify AI-generated forgeries as deepfake technology develops. Blockchain-based decentralized authentication provides a scalable and reliable way to instantly confirm the legitimacy of AI-generated material. Blockchain technology may be integrated with digital signatures, cryptographic watermarking, and AI-driven forensic analysis to create a complete framework for content authentication and deepfake detection. Adding media file cryptographic hashes to the blockchain at the time of creation is one method of decentralized authentication. To make sure that any later changes or edits can be identified, every media file is given a distinct digital fingerprint that is stored on the blockchain ledger.

A user can check the legitimacy of a questionable piece of media by comparing its digital fingerprint with the blockchain's original record. In order to stop deep-fake false information from spreading, any inconsistencies in the material might be reported as perhaps altered. Automating content verification procedures with blockchain-based smart contracts is another decentralized authentication technique. Media files' information, timestamps, and digital signatures may be cross-referenced with validated blockchain records to enable smart contracts to verify their legitimacy. While requiring less human involvement, this automated method improves deepfake detection's effectiveness and precision. Decentralized content verification networks with blockchain technology, including those based on Ethereum and Hyperledger, offer scalable ways to identify deepfake material on many platforms. These networks use the combined processing capacity of dispersed nodes to authenticate material and conduct deepfake analysis in real time. Blockchain makes that deepfake detection is not dominated by one organization by dividing up verification duties across a decentralized ecosystem, which lowers the possibility of bias, censorship, and manipulation.

REAL-WORLD IMPLEMENTATIONS AND USE CASES

Artificial intelligence (AI) and blockchain integration has started to change the digital media market by providing strong solutions for content security, media authentication, and deepfake identification. Numerous practical applications have shown how effective these technologies can be in thwarting false information, safeguarding intellectual property, and promoting confidence in digital media. Blockchain-based media authentication systems are becoming a vital line of defense against deepfakes because they offer unchangeable records of the source of material, confirm its legitimacy, and make it possible to monitor digital assets transparently. By storing information, timestamps, and cryptographic hashes of digital material using decentralized ledger technology, these systems make it almost hard to change or edit media files covertly. These solutions make use of blockchain's tamper-proof structure to guarantee that digital material is unchangeable and verifiable at every stage of its existence. In order to curb the dissemination of false information and fake news, a number of businesses and organizations have implemented blockchain-based authentication frameworks that allow media outlets, journalists, and content producers to attest to the validity of their work. Businesses like Truepic and Project Origin have used blockchain technology to protect visual material, guaranteeing that photos and movies don't change from where they were taken. In a similar vein, Adobe is spearheading the Content Authenticity Initiative (CAI), which is collaborating with prominent media organizations to develop blockchain-supported methods for tracking the origin of digital media assets. This will ensure accountability and transparency in the production and dissemination of content. Along with authentication, deepfake detection driven by AI and integrated with blockchain is becoming more popular as a useful technique for detecting and lessening the effects of synthetic media. Machine learning models enable deepfake detection techniques, which examine audio and visual patterns to distinguish between authentic and altered information. Even then, adversarial assaults, biases in datasets, and changing deepfake creation methods pose problems for standalone AI-based detection systems. By establishing a decentralized and verifiable record of discovered deepfakes, blockchain integration improves existing detection frameworks and stops fraudsters from evading detection systems or falsifying evidence. In order to boost efforts to prevent disinformation and digital fraud, forensic professionals and policymakers may obtain an unchangeable record of modified material by putting the results of deepfake research on a blockchain. Deepware Scanner and Sensity AI, two decentralized AI-powered verification networks, are using blockchain technology to record deepfake analysis. This ensures that any manipulations found are clearly documented and unchangeable. Because fewer false positives or intentional suppression of acceptable content are likely to occur, this method increases confidence in AI-driven content management. Blockchain and artificial intelligence are being used more quickly in the journalism, entertainment, and social media sectors as businesses want to preserve consumer confidence and preserve digital integrity. Major media companies are using blockchain-based verification tools in the news industry to fight false information and boost trustworthiness. Blockchain-backed metadata stamping, for instance, has been tested by Reuters and The New York Times to confirm the legitimacy of news photos and videos. By preventing the dissemination of falsified news, these initiatives assist media companies in protecting journalistic integrity. Film studios and content producers are using blockchain technology in the entertainment sector to monitor content distribution, protect digital rights management, and fight piracy. Automated royalty distribution made possible by blockchain-based smart contracts guarantees that authors and artists are fairly compensated for their labor while avoiding illegal copying of digital goods. Blockchain technology is used by platforms such as Audius and Myco to facilitate decentralized content sharing and offer clear income arrangements to artists and video producers.

In order to address the rising worries of disinformation and the spread of deepfakes, social media platforms—which are frequently at the forefront of content dissemination—are also looking at blockchain solutions. Blockchain-based verification techniques are being investigated by companies such as Twitter and Meta (previously Facebook) to validate user-generated content and stop the spread of misleading information. Blockchain-driven content authentication is being pioneered by decentralized social networks like Minds and Steemit, which enable users to confirm the authenticity of media and posts published on their networks. Furthermore, reputation systems powered by blockchain technology are being created to identify and penalize disseminators of false information while rewarding reliable content producers. These deployments point to a change toward a digital media ecosystem that is more responsible and transparent and places a higher value on reliability and authenticity. The broad use of blockchain and AI-powered media authentication solutions is nonetheless fraught with difficulties, notwithstanding the advancements. Concerns like scalability, interoperability, and regulatory approval are crucial issues that need to be resolved to guarantee these technologies' efficacy. Researchers and business executives must work together to improve detection techniques, boost blockchain performance, and create standardized standards for media verification as deepfake tactics continue to advance. Future developments in federated learning, zero-knowledge proofs, and decentralized AI models may improve the security and dependability of deepfake detection systems based on blockchain technology.

CONCLUSION

The generative AI-driven rapid development of deepfake technology has drastically changed the digital media ecosystem, posing both ground-breaking new possibilities and formidable obstacles. The public's confidence, identity security, and information integrity are seriously threatened by the potential exploitation of deepfakes, even as they allow for imaginative storytelling and immersive experiences. This study emphasizes how crucial blockchain technology is to reducing these risks since it offers a decentralized, unchangeable structure for content verification and authentication. The transparency, security, and traceability of blockchain technology may be used to efficiently monitor AI-generated media, guaranteeing ethical licensing, responsible content production, and safe media dissemination. Blockchain and generative AI together present a viable way to protect digital identities, identify deepfake manipulation, and build confidence in synthetic media. Multidisciplinary cooperation and more study into blockchain-based authentication methods will be crucial in resolving the security and ethical issues related to deepfakes as technology develops. Blockchain and AI working together can lead to a more open and reliable digital media ecosystem in the future by striking a balance between innovation and responsible governance.

REFERENCES

Adru, S. L., Johnson, S., & Hemalatha, M. (2023). AI and Blockchain Based Platform for Empowering Content Creators: Enabling NFT – Driven Content Sharing, Inspiration Generation, and Collaborative Interaction. 666–673. .DOI: 10.1109/ICOSEC58147.2023.10276305

Brewer, J., Patel, D., Kim, D., & Murray, A. (2024). Navigating the challenges of generative technologies: Proposing the integration of artificial intelligence and blockchain. *Business Horizons*, *67*(5), 525–535. Advance online publication. DOI: 10.1016/j.bushor.2024.04.011

Islam, M., Haseeb, M., Batool, H., Ahtasham, N., & Muhammad, Z. (2024). AI Threats to Politics, Elections, and Democracy: A Blockchain-Based Deepfake Authenticity Verification Framework. *Blockchains*, *2*(4), 458–481. DOI: 10.3390/blockchains2040020

Liu, Y., Du, H., Niyato, D., Kang, J., Xiong, Z., Miao, C., Shen, X. S., & Jamalipour, A. (2023). Blockchain-Empowered Lifecycle Management for AI-Generated Content (AIGC) Products in Edge Networks. arXiv.Org, abs/2303.02836. /arXiv.2303.02836. DOI: 10.48550

Yang, F., Abedin, M. Z., Qiao, Y., & Ye, L. (2024). Towards Trustworthy Governance of AI-Generated Content (AIGC): A Blockchain-Driven Regulatory Framework for Secure Digital Ecosystems. *IEEE Transactions on Engineering Management*, *71*, 1–18. DOI: 10.1109/TEM.2024.3472292

Chapter 11
Secure and Intelligent Computation Offloading Between Edge and Cloud Servers Using Generative AI and Blockchain

C. P. Shabariram

https://orcid.org/0000-0001-6136-9862

PSG Institute of Technology and Applied Research, India

N. Shanthi

Kongu Engineering College, India

P. Ponnuswamy Priya

https://orcid.org/0000-0003-1511-9226

Vellore Institute of Technology, India

ABSTRACT

Due to the increased demand of intelligent edge applications, efficient computational offloading schemes and secure communication between edge and cloud server has become essential. This chapter presents an intelligent framework that integrates Blockchain technology and Generative AI to achieve intelligent computation offloading in an edge computing. The framework includes generative models to encode the sensitive data and blockchain based smart contract infrastructure. To ensure confidentiality, the generative adversarial network is used to encode the data into images or audio files. The smart contract is applied to log task metadata and verify the data integrity. The immutable execution logs are ensured by blockchain based

DOI: 10.4018/979-8-3373-6481-0.ch011

infrastructure. The framework allows seamless computational offloading between edge and cloud server with end-to-end security. The experimental results depict the system overhead with respect to interception, latency and tampering. The fusion of AI-driven data masking provides a secure and intelligent computation offloading mechanism in the decentralized manner.

1. INTRODUCTION

With the recent development in edge computing devices and Industrial Internet of Things, the need for secure, energy efficient computation offloading has significantly increased. The traditional edge computing architecture reduces the usage on resource-constrained edge devices by offloading the computational tasks to the cloud environment. However, the computational offloading process introduces the challenges in terms of data security, integrity and trust in execution and transmission between the devices.

The impact of Generative Artificial Intelligence (Gen AI) gives the solutions for secure transmission and the data representation. The Generative Adversarial Network (GAN) is used to encode the sensitive data similar to traditional steganography techniques. The model enhances the confidentiality aspects and minimizes the risk of interception in data transmission. The diffusion model is also used to achieve data encoding on sensitive data in data transmission.

In the decentralized computing environment, trust and integrity plays a major role. Blockchain technology is considered as a powerful tool to achieve transparency, trust and integrity in decentralized systems. The application of distributed ledgers and smart contracts, the blockchain can log and verify the computational offloading process. Blockchain transaction covers the data encoding in edge devices to the result validation at the cloud server. The proposed framework integrates Gen AI for data encoding and Blockchain for secure, trustworthy and verifiable transmission of data.

2. RELATED WORK

The computation offloading strategies to address the limitations of edge devices were explored (Dong et al., 2024). Mobile edge computing focuses on transmission time, data insecurity and energy consumption. Task offloading is a key technology in Mobile edge computing. The offloading decision is based on minimal computational delay and energy consumption. The methodologies range from partial task offloading to dynamic offloading based on network conditions.

An energy efficient offloading based on reinforcement learning and deep learning was achieved. Energy consumption and task completion are considered as key parameters. To achieve Quality of service, data characteristics such as latency, energy and reliability are analyzed. The system focuses on the Industrial Internet of Things and its development. Edge computing is utilized to optimize task management (Chouikhi et al., 2024). However, the approach considers a secure communication channel used between the edge and cloud server. During the transmission, data integrity and confidentiality are neglected

The traditional steganography techniques use media signals to encode the sensitive data (AlSabhany et al., 2020). The media signals cover audio and image-based methods. These data masking techniques lack adaptability and resilience against the Gen AI based detection systems. Moreover, the traditional systems fail to scale with dynamic offloading in edge and cloud ecosystems. The system focuses on perceptual transparency, hiding capacity and Robustness. The balance challenge is considered as a major concern in the steganography techniques.

In recent years, Generative adversarial networks (Goodfellow et al., 2020) and variational autoencoders are used for data masking in steganography-based applications. The deep steganography embeds the sensitive data in AI-generated image and audio files (Magdy et al., 2025). The AI-generated media files are used instead of normal media files. The high level of adaptability is achieved by deep learning-based technique. The generative models can learn to bypass steganalysis. The deep learning aggregation (DLA34) is used to detect multiple objects in a video frame. In the final stage, data embedded into objects using Discrete Wavelet Transform (DWT) and Singular Value Decomposition (SVD). The average Peak Signal-to-Noise Ratio (PSNR) is 73.57.

The security, computational delay and energy efficiency are the major factors in the Internet of Things enabled systems (Nguyen et al., 2024). The edge and blockchain are integrated to provide a better system. The environmental security parameters such as access control, integrity, confidentiality, availability are considered. The blockchain is used in Mobile edge computing systems and enhances the security parameters. The blockchain system prevents unauthorized access during the computation offloading process. The effectiveness of blockchain based methods are compared with various parameter settings.

The generic architecture for edge-blockchain integrated environments is provided in the edge-based applications (Xue et al., 2023). The resource constraints are enhanced by computation, memory and security. The application specific paradigms are involved in resource management. The existing solutions are evaluated in the generalized architecture. The research explores the primary concerns in the integration and insights into data masking and offloading.

The current generation of Gen AI depends on the cloud computing environment and requires high performance computing. The edge computing environment is needed for handling high latency specific Gen AI services. The edge and cloud integration have proven low latency and give appropriate computational resources. The lifecycle of Gen AI services is implemented in the collaborative infrastructure. The various design patterns in the integrated environment are considered. (Wang et al., 2023).

The 5G communication enables the application of cloud and edge computing on a large scale. In the case of cloud servers, centralized systems suffer from a single point of failure and biased actions. The decentralized system with application of block chain allows anti-tampering and transparency. The key metrics specific to centralized and decentralized systems are considered as environmental factors (Baranwal et al., 2023). The results are compared with respect to cloud systems, distributed edge systems and hybrid systems. The blockchain based resource management is achieved using consensus mechanisms. The integration of blockchain and AI ensures enhanced cyber security, trustworthiness and security concerns.

The digital twin technology is used to provide intelligent offloading decisions. The edge computing paradigm addresses the key challenges such as delay, availability and bandwidth. The real-time systems are represented in the form of virtual instances in digital twins (Tran-Dang & Kim, 2025). The optimal resource allocation gives the guaranteed decision making at the edge nodes. The system compared with the fundamental edge computing environment. The results indicate the inclusion of digital twins significantly improves resource management. Digital twins are used to improve resource allocation, decision making and situational awareness.

The edge computing and IoT based edge detection integrates blockchain to achieve trusted data transmission and computation verification. The reliable task offloading framework allows a balanced workflow in the Internet of Medical Things. Task offloading process enhanced by Software Defined Network and Blockchain technology. The smart contract ensures the guaranteed security in the system (Li et al., 2024). To enable the trust between edge device and edge server, trust-based caching system was adapted. The blockchain is used to secure the caching process (Bounaira et al., 2024). The bidirectional trust established by the management system. Deep learning techniques are used to perform decision making in the offloading process. The system achieves better performance in terms of data integrity and security in edge caching.

EtherEdge and BlockEdge are used to achieve trust in the distributed edge-cloud ecosystems. The Peer-to-Peer transactions are enabled by blockchain adoption in the middleware (Nawaz et al., 2020).

Edge based Blockchain of Things provides interaction between the nodes and external entities. The system excluded the usage of intermediaries in the environment. The immutable characteristics, decentralized factors and smart contracts are considered in the peer transactions. The system gives significant results with respect to computational resource utilization.

The integration of Blockchain and Gen AI is an emerging research area. The collaboration between these technologies is examined (Kshetri, 2025). Data security and integrity are considered as key factors in the adoption of blockchain. On the other hand, The development in AI-driven technologies (Martín et al., 2023) focuses on decentralized development and safe learning. The blockchain technology is used to secure AI-generated media files. However, the application of these integration in the context of computational offloading remains unexplored

3. SYSTEM IMPLEMENTATION

An intelligent computation offloading is designed to offload computational tasks from edge devices to cloud servers. Secure communication ensured by the integration of Gen AI and Blockchain. The data encoding achieved using Gen AI. The immutable task verification and traceability achieved by blockchain technology. The system is composed of four layers that includes edge layer, generative encoding layer, blockchain integration layer, cloud layer. Figure 1 shows the layer architecture of the proposed framework.

Figure 1. Layered architecture

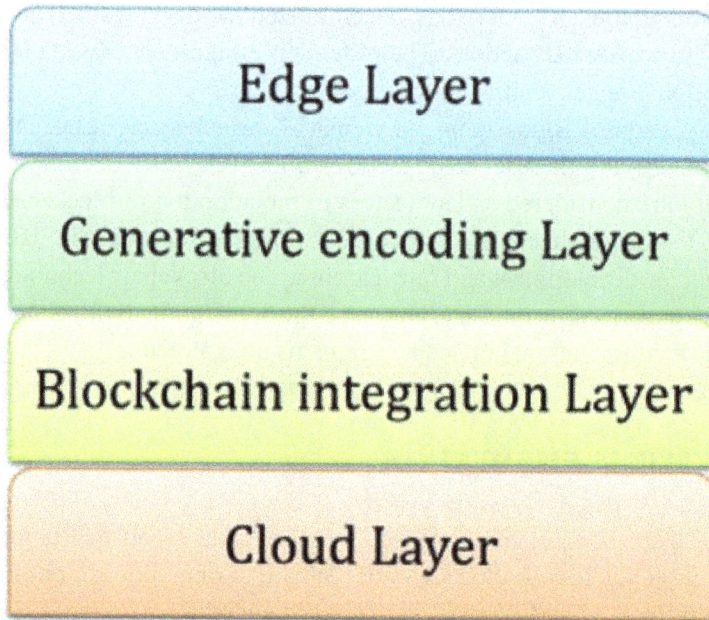

The edge layer consists of edge devices which are responsible for task computation, data generation and initiate computation offloading. The basic operations are performed due to its resource limitations. Input image capturing, data preprocessing, encoding and decoding, blockchain registration are implemented as basic operations. The generative encoding layer conceals the data during the transmission using Generative Adversarial Network. The model embeds the information in the media files. StyleGAN2 is used for image-based encoding and WaveGAN is used for audio-based data encoding. The sensitive data is encoded as a latent variable in a trained model. The model synthesizes an image and audio file. The encoded media is transferred over the communication channel.

Algorithm: Secure and Intelligent computation offloading using Gen AI and Blockchain

Input: Sensitive Data from Edge Device (D), Trained Generative Model (G), Blockchain Smart Contract (SC), Cloud Server (CS)

Output: Offloaded task result (R)

Step 1: Data preprocessing at Edge level

Generate the task data (D) in Edge device and Normalize the task data (D')

Extract metadata such as time stamp, task id, priority and edge device id

Step 2: Secure data encoding using Generative AI

Train the model using Generative Adversarial Network

Encode D into Media file (M) using StyleGAN2 or WaveGAN

Step 3: Blockchain logging and verification

Generate hash value H(M) using SHA-256 and Sign with edge device private key

Submit a transaction to Smart Contract (SC) on Blockchain

Wait for confirmation and transaction id (TX_ID)

Step 4: Offloading to Cloud Server

Transmit M to cloud server (CS) with TX_ID and Verify TX_ID

Retrieves H(M) from blockchain and Compute H'(M), Compare with H(M).

Step 5: Computation at Cloud Server

Decode the media file D" =G'(M) and Perform computation R using D"

Sign and submit result hash H(R) back to blockchain

Step 6: Result retrieval at Edge level

Edge device listens for result event on block chain

Retrieve H(R) and download R, Validate hash and signature

Present R to user or trigger next task

In the computation offloading life cycle, blockchain integration layer ensures transparency, trust and privacy. Ganache is used as a private Ethereum blockchain. Solidity is used for defining smart contracts. Secure Hash Algorithm (SHA-256) is included for hashing the sensitive data. The hash value and metadata are stored on a blockchain. The blockchain metadata consists of timestamp, edge device id and task id.

Figure 2. Technological stack

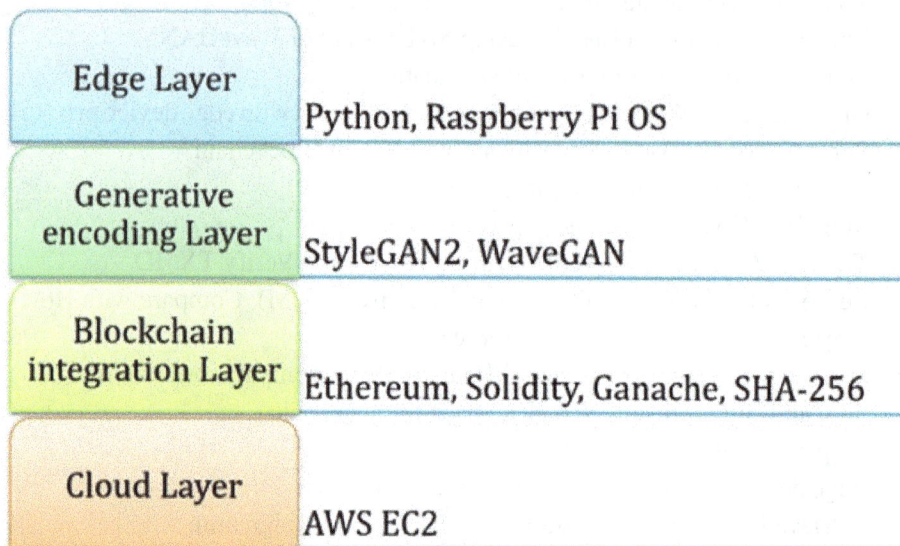

Edge Layer	Python, Raspberry Pi OS
Generative encoding Layer	StyleGAN2, WaveGAN
Blockchain integration Layer	Ethereum, Solidity, Ganache, SHA-256
Cloud Layer	AWS EC2

The smart contracts are providing the validation of the tasks and results are verifiable. Metadata is added to the on-chain after the task is offloaded. The topmost layer receives the encoded media. The generative model is used for decoding the sensitive data and processing the computational tasks. Figure 2 depicts the technologies used in the various layers. The communication between edge device and cloud server is achieved using secure HyperText Transfer Protocol and RESTful services. The mutual authentication is performed using public and private key infrastructure.

The task data includes image classification, file processing, sensor data analysis and audio transcoding. Generative AI based encoding on media files focuses on confidentiality. The usage of SHA-256 ensures integrity and authenticity. The blockchain logs and smart contracts maintain trust and traceability. An immutable blockchain transaction enables the tampering-proof logs in the edge and cloud integrated ecosystem. Based on the application, the Graphical Processing Unit is used for training and encoding. The accuracy of the decoding depends on the trained model. The consensus mechanism in blockchain technology introduces negligible latency compared to the computational latency. The comparison over the baseline offloading scheme given in table 1.

Table 1. Traditional offloading vs intelligent computation offloading

Feature	Traditional Offloading	Intelligent Computation Offloading
Data Confidentiality	Moderate	High
Integrity Assurance	Low	High
Tamper Detection	Manual	Automated via Blockchain
Flexibility	Low	High

4. RESULT ANALYSIS

To evaluate the effectiveness of the proposed framework, a simulation was conducted. The simulation environment includes an edge device, a cloud server and a
private Ethereum to enable the blockchain. The pretrained StyleGAN2 was used for
generative data encoding. The SHA-256 was implemented for hashing. The performance of the framework was evaluated based on Encoding Time (ET), Blockchain
Latency (BL), Transmission Delay (TD), Computation Time (CT), End-to-End Delay
(E2E) and Security Success Rate (SSR). The existing system was simulated using
Advanced Encryption Standard and HyperText Transfer Protocol based computation
offloading. The simulation configuration setting listed in Table 2.

Table 2. Simulation parameter setting

Parameter	Value
Batch Size	32
Network Bandwidth	10 Mbps uplink, 50 Mbps downlink
Learning Rate	0.001
Data Size per Task	5–20 MB
Average Block Generation Time	15 seconds
Optimizer	Adam
Encoding Format	WAV, 16-bit mono
Training Epochs	10

Figure 3. Evaluation metrics vs task types

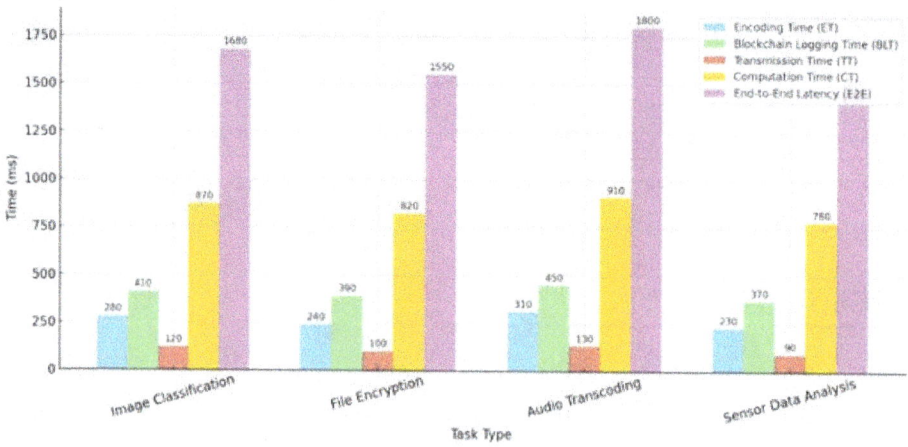

Figure 3 indicates the encoding time ranges from 230 ms to 310 ms across four different task types. The complexity of generative encoding for audio formats gives the highest encoding time. The sensor data analysis gives minimal blockchain logging time as 370 ms. The blockchain metadata increases the blockchain logging time. The proposed system gives minimal transmission time compared to all other evaluation metrics. Computation time ranges from 780 ms to 910 ms. The audio transcoding and image classification tasks take higher computation time and reflect the usage of cloud servers. Despite the added security and encoding steps, the E2E latency remains within acceptable limits for most edge applications. The graph signifies computation and blockchain logging time introduce latency in the proposed system. Audio transcoding tasks take higher overhead due to the complexity.

Figure 4. Generative model accuracy and loss

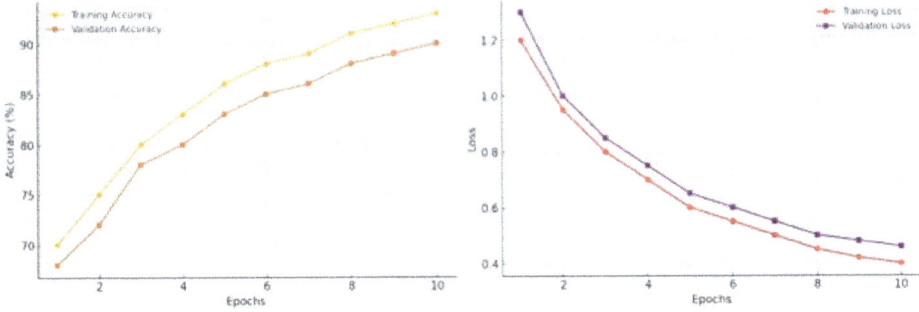

The consistent improvement of accuracy and good convergence of the generative model are represented in Figure 4. The training accuracy of the generative model improves from 70% to 93%. The validation accuracy ranges from 68% to 90%. The minimal overfitting ensured by the gap exists in the training and validation accuracy. The accuracy range indicates the model is learning effectively and generalizing to new data. In the convergence, training loss reduces from 1.2 to 0.4 and validation loss optimized to 0.46. The decline in training and validation loss indicates the model is optimizing the error.

Figure 5. Proposed framework vs existing methods

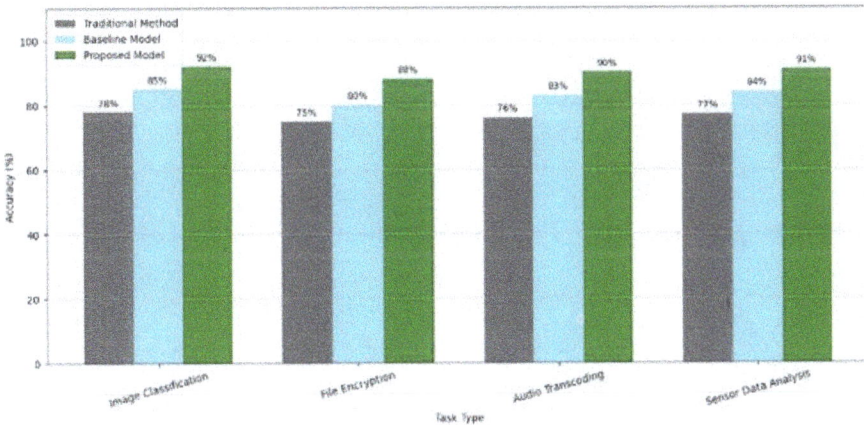

The performance accuracy with respect to four different task types given in Figure 5. The cloud based computation and generative model enables the proposed system to 92% in image classification and 91% in sensor data analysis. The proposed framework gives better results compared to traditional and baseline systems. The improvements indicated the effectiveness of data encoding using Gen AI and secure offloading using Blockchain. The performance gain represents the strength of the proposed system in terms of security, trust and accuracy.

5. CONCLUSION

In this study, a novel intelligent offloading framework is proposed using generative adversarial network and blockchain technology. The system ensures secure and intelligent computation offloading between edge and cloud server. The approach used a generative model to encode the sensitive data which significantly improves the confidentiality during the data transmission. An immutable logs and smart contracts in blockchain achieves data integrity and authenticity in the edge network. The framework was implemented using Gen AI and private blockchain networks. The system demonstrates the effective protection against the interception and tampering. The performance analysis indicates the practicality and robustness of the framework in an edge-cloud environment. The fusion of Gen AI and blockchain gives a new dimension in secure offloading. In the future, lightweight generative models for edge devices and cross-chain interoperability are considered in heterogeneous environments.

REFERENCES

AlSabhany, A. A., Ali, A. H., Ridzuan, F., Azni, A. H., & Mokhtar, M. R. (2020). Digital audio steganography: Systematic review, classification, and analysis of the current state of the art. *Computer Science Review*, *38*(100316), 100316. DOI: 10.1016/j.cosrev.2020.100316

Baranwal, G., Kumar, D., & Vidyarthi, D. P. (2023). Blockchain based resource allocation in cloud and distributed edge computing: A survey. *Computer Communications*, *209*, 469–498. DOI: 10.1016/j.comcom.2023.07.023

Bounaira, S., Alioua, A., & Souici, I. (2024). Blockchain-enabled trust management for secure content caching in mobile edge computing using deep reinforcement learning. *Internet of Things : Engineering Cyber Physical Human Systems*, *25*(101081), 101081. DOI: 10.1016/j.iot.2024.101081

Chouikhi, S., Esseghir, M., & Merghem-Boulahia, L. (2024). Energy-efficient computation offloading based on multi-agent deep reinforcement learning for industrial internet of things systems. *IEEE Internet of Things Journal*, *11*(7), 1–1. DOI: 10.1109/JIOT.2023.3333044

Dong, S., Tang, J., Abbas, K., Hou, R., Kamruzzaman, J., Rutkowski, L., & Buyya, R. (2024). Task offloading strategies for mobile edge computing: A survey. *Computer Networks*, *254*(110791), 110791. DOI: 10.1016/j.comnet.2024.110791

Goodfellow, I., Pouget-Abadie, J., Mirza, M., Xu, B., Warde-Farley, D., Ozair, S., Courville, A., & Bengio, Y. (2020). Generative adversarial networks. *Communications of the ACM*, *63*(11), 139–144. DOI: 10.1145/3422622

Kshetri, N. (2025). Building trust in AI: How blockchain enhances data integrity, security, and privacy. *Computer*, *58*(2), 63–70. DOI: 10.1109/MC.2024.3505012

Li, J., Zhu, M., Liu, J., Liu, W., Huang, B., & Liu, R. (2024). Blockchain-based reliable task offloading framework for edge-cloud cooperative workflows in IoMT. *Information Sciences*, *668*(120530), 120530. DOI: 10.1016/j.ins.2024.120530

Magdy, S., Youssef, S., Fathalla, K. M., & ElShehaby, S. (2025). DeepSteg: Integerating new paradigms of cascaded deep video steganography for securing digital data. *Alexandria Engineering Journal*, *116*, 483–501. DOI: 10.1016/j.aej.2024.12.034

Martín, A., Hernández, A., Alazab, M., Jung, J., & Camacho, D. (2023). Evolving Generative Adversarial Networks to improve image steganography. *Expert Systems with Applications*, *222*(119841), 119841. DOI: 10.1016/j.eswa.2023.119841

Nawaz, A., Peña Queralta, J., Guan, J., Awais, M., Gia, T. N., Bashir, A. K., Kan, H., & Westerlund, T. (2020). Edge computing to secure IoT data ownership and trade with the ethereum blockchain. *Sensors (Basel)*, *20*(14), 3965. DOI: 10.3390/s20143965 PMID: 32708807

Nguyen, T., Nguyen, H., & Nguyen Gia, T. (2024). Exploring the integration of edge computing and blockchain IoT: Principles, architectures, security, and applications. *Journal of Network and Computer Applications*, *226*(103884), 103884. DOI: 10.1016/j.jnca.2024.103884

Tran-Dang, H., & Kim, D.-S. (2025). Digital Twin-empowered intelligent computation offloading for edge computing in the era of 5G and beyond: A state-of-the-art survey. *ICT Express*, *11*(1), 167–180. DOI: 10.1016/j.icte.2025.01.002

Wang, Y.-C., Xue, J., Wei, C., & Kuo, C.-C. J. (2023). An overview on generative AI at scale with edge–cloud computing. *IEEE Open Journal of the Communications Society*, *4*, 2952–2971. DOI: 10.1109/OJCOMS.2023.3320646

Xue, H., Chen, D., Zhang, N., Dai, H.-N., & Yu, K. (2023). Integration of blockchain and edge computing in the internet of things: A survey. *Future Generation Computer Systems*, *144*, 307–326. DOI: 10.1016/j.future.2022.10.029

Chapter 12
Mint, Tokenize, Authenticate:
An NFT Perspective

Trisha Nirav Rami

https://orcid.org/0009-0004-7773-5993

Unitedworld Institute of Technology, India

ABSTRACT

This chapter delves into the transformative power of Non-Fungible Tokens (NFTs) as foundational components of the Web3 ecosystem. It examines the way tokenization is disrupting the digital asset ownership vector to bring decentralized exchange of assets and the redesign of industries like creative arts, real estate to finance. The chapter provides the whole picture of technical, legal and operational frameworks using which the NFT adoption takes place through a deep dive into token standards, smart contract architecture, decentralized storage, and cross chain interoperability. It also examines how security and authentication protocols, security mechanisms, and maintenance practices of decentralized systems work together to make sure of trust, provenance and usability in decentralized environments. Furthermore, the chapter investigates the integration of NFTs with metaverse platforms, the emergence of advanced token protocols, and the broader implications for identity, governance, and digital economies.

DOI: 10.4018/979-8-3373-6481-0.ch012

1. INTRODUCTION

1.1. The Evolution of Digital Assets: From Concept to Reality

The concept of ownership has changed much these days in the digital age. Wealth (owning) in the earlier centuries was a physical thing. Due to technological improvements, we are witnessing the birth of digital assets that redefined value and exchange. In the broadest sense, digital assets can function as a medium of exchange, or of payment, as a record of rights, whether ownership or usage of underlying assets or future economic value, or as providing access to other services. Financial instruments can be digital assets and it depends on the nature of the asset and applicable regulatory determination (J.P. Morgan, 2024).

During the 1900s, plenty of digital assets began forming on the internet and on computers. In his 1982 dissertation, David Chaum, an expert in cryptography, wrote about a protocol that is similar to blockchain (Freeman Law, 2022). In 1998, Nick Szabo developed "bit gold," a kind of digital currency based on decentralized decentralization that operated in a way that did not involve centralization of control, as the name suggests. It incorporated security through cryptographic techniques and used a proof of work (CFTE, 2023).

The first decentralized cryptocurrency, Bitcoin, officially introduced blockchain technology in the year of its release, 2009. This development proved the existence of digital value apart from money, and that it could be used to record transactions (TechTarget, 2023). Besides cryptocurrencies, blockchain's possible applications grew to a number of areas including supply chains, digital identities, and others because of its tamper-resistant and decentralised nature (Library of Congress, 2020).

1.2. Blockchain Infrastructure: The Backbone of the Digital Economy

NFTs are one of the biggest of the milestones in the development of digital assets. NFTs differ from cryptocurrencies, in that they are unique, and digital assets on the blockchain that give proof of ownership or proof of authenticity of a particular good, either virtual or real (World Economic Forum, 2023). Blockchain technology made the emergence of the digital asset markets. Digital asset markets are achieved using cryptocurrency and decentralized technology of the Internet era. While blockchain makes the stock transfer and securities offering with all attributes of the physical transfer of stock, blockchain stock transfer is completely virtual and digital (Kaal, 2020).

The first one is blockchain infrastructure that is used to create, deploy, and manage your decentralized applications and what are known as digital assets (Androulaki et al., 2018). It consists of interconnected nodes validating and recording transaction, consensus mechanism ensuring network agreement and smart contracts that automate certain or predefined actions (Farooq et al., 2024). This architecture is very secure, transparent and immutable, making it mandatory for such Applications like Non-fungible Tokens (NFTs). NFT can be minted, tokenized, and authenticated using blockchain infrastructure (Solouki & Bamakan, 2023), so that it is verifiable who owns it and that there exists only one (original) instance of it.

2. A COMPREHENSIVE REVIEW

2.1. Contemporary NFT Ecosystem and Technological Framework

Blockchain technology, digital ownership and creator's economy make up the contemporary NFT ecosystem. An NFT (Non Fungible Token) is a unique digital asset, digitally recorded on a blockchain, most common being Ethereum, that certifies a person owns or created a particular item (Wang et al., 2021). Unlike cryptocurrencies, use cases for NFTs include art, music, virtual real estate, and in-game or gaming assets: In all these use cases they are very distinct, indivisible things, and if notably physically distinct are fungible within their own set.

NFTs are based on technological standards such as ERC-721 and ERC-1155 which specify the rules of token creation, storing metadata and possession transferability. Without any intermediaries, they are the contracts of decentralized and transparent ownership (Ethereum Foundation, n.d.a). Much like how platforms like OpenSea, Rarible and Foundation allow people around the world to mint, showcase and trade NFTs, creators also gained access to ease of use while doing the same.

These days interoperability and metadata permanence are critical aspects in eco-system. Most NFTs store their metadata in an off chain off chain (IPFS or Arweave) to save gas and keep the data live. Layer 2 solutions and other alternative blockchains (e.g. Polygon, Solana and Flow) are proliferating as the facilitating network for NFT creation which is more environmentally and economically feasible.

2.2. Innovation Trajectories and Implementation Challenges

Innovation in utility, interoperability and industry integration among the other things is driving the NFT space in a rapid way. NFTs started out as a play on digital art and digital collectibles and of course, it has expanded to other domains like gaming, virtual real estate, IP rights, event ticketing, academic certification and so forth. On the emerging trends for NFTs, dynamic NFTs (dNFT), which are NFTs that are dynamic according to real world inputs, as well as soulbound tokens (SBT) which are supposed to represent non transferable credentials and affiliations that expand the use of NFTs on identity and reputation systems (Buterin, 2022).

However, NFTs are still on the move despite this momentum, and they have a lot of challenges to be implemented in the real world. H. It is still a concern of scalability on networks such as Ethereum, that have high gas fees that can make the creator and user inaccessible. Layer 2 solutions and other blockchains are somewhat an improvement, but standardization and interoperability between chains are still growing. Finally, as the ecosystem faces more risks of phishing, counterfeit NFT's, and rug pulls, security and fraud prevention are also key. In addition, issues related to intellectual property rights, royalties, as well as jurisdiction specific regulations contribute to the friction in adoption, in particular in institutional contexts (Nadini et al., 2021).

The maturation of supporting infrastructure and legal frameworks has a big influence on the development of NFT innovation as much as technological break-throughs. Now that NFTs have started their hype cycle, it will be up to ecosystem players to tackle these fundamental challenges together and transparently, if NFTs are to build into the long tail beyond hype.

3. MINTING: THE GENESIS OF DIGITAL ASSETS

3.1. Foundational Architecture of NFT Creation

Minting means transforming digital files into cryptographically verifiable assets on a blockchain. The start of this NFT creation process involves defining the metadata, which are usually terms such as the title, description, creator information, as well as a reference to the artwork contained in it, usually formatted as JSON. The asset has this metadata stored either on chain or off chain using decentralized storage setups e.g IPFS (InterPlanetary File System) to continue making the asset accessible and available for future (IPFS Documentation, n.d.).

When it comes to minting, smart contracts are deployed at the core and usually are using Ethereum's ERC-721 or ERC-1155 standards. ERC-721 works for the creation of individually unique tokens while ERC-1155 is used for semi fungible tokens such that they allow for more efficient minting and batch transfers. In the case when a user mints an NFT, the smart contract picks an ID unique to that NFT and relates to the received metadata, put to the blockchain ledger. This makes the NFT's origin, ownership, authenticity, and timeliness publicly verifiable (Ethereum Foundation, n.d.a).

It can be decentralized where the creators communicate with smart contracts directly (via Remix, custom dApps or Web3 interfaces) or centralized (through Rarible or OpenSea platforms) and progresses through the minting phase alike. Minting costs and speed can be impaired by gas fees and network congestion, so many creators of DeFi projects will search for faster and cheaper alternatives, which means layer 2 or alternative chain.

3.2. Smart Contract Protocols and Implementation Framework

NFTs obtain the operational backbone from the smart contracts that are governing the mint, transfer and interactions of tokens on the blockchain. Speakers write these self-executing contracts in Ethereum smart contracts supported languages those being Solidity and are deployed mostly on Ethereum and other alternative chains like Solana and Tezos have their own contract languages with their own standards. ERC-721 standard supports unique NFTs while ERC-1155 allows minting NFTs in batch with Hybrid fungibility. The purpose is these protocols define the functions need to work—such as ownerOf, transferFrom and tokenURI that always work same way in marketplaces (Ethereum Foundation, n.d.b).

An NFT smart contract's implementation includes the contract structure, handling token metadata, and ownership and royalty logic. Some recent innovation includes customizable royalty splits, whitelist on chain for the exclusive drops, and event emissions support live tracking. OpenZeppelin provides pre-audited contract templates which are very useful to improve security and reduce the time of deployment. These contracts can be interfaced with via Web3 libraries (eg: Ethers.js or Web3.js) to enable secure and trusted interface between block chain logic and frontends (OpenZeppelin, n.d.).

This remains critical as smart contract implementation is still vulnerable to vulnerabilities that can end in irreversible loss of asset. Then there are those who try to cope with the adaptability by applying the patterns of auditing and upgradable contracts through proxy patterns to remain decentralize.

3.3. Economic Dynamics and Platform Optimization

Scarcity, creator royalties, market demand, these things define the NFT economy, as well as all the platform driven incentives. The scarcity determined through perceived uniqueness of items and their utility impacts the primary sales and secondary market performance. OpenSea and Blur make use of various fee structures, curation strategies, and visibility algorithm which impact top performer discoverability and creator profitability. That once considered a key value proponent for artists: royalties, have become the subject of a debate, as platforms are offering optional or zero royalty models to gain high frequency traders (OpenSea, n.d.).

Platform optimization is achieved through improving user experience whilst keeping the process of decentralization on the move. Other techniques like lazy minting (minting upon purchase) and batch listing combined with gas efficient chains such as Polygon or Arbitrum reduce entry barriers. In addition, platforms are inevitably token gated for access, are rewarding loyalty through rewards, and are liquidity mining in order to stimulate community engagement and sustained economic activity. NFT fractionalization is also finding appeal as a way to increase liquidity while expanding participation (Nadini et al., 2021).

It is upholding the economy of NFTs to be transparent, fair revenue sharing and technical reliability. Platforms that are maturing will need to understand and align creator interests with from user incentives in order to be a long term viable.

4. TOKENIZATION: DIGITAL ASSET TRANSFORMATION

Tokenization is transforming how people own and interact with the term 'ownership' in the era of the digital. We unlock new possibilities to transparency, liquidity and access by turning the real world assets such as property, stocks, or intellectual property into digital tokens for specific blockchain. changing this streamlines the exchanging of resources by isolating them into digital programmable, checkable, and moveable units. And the great part is that these tokens can be fractionalized, shareable, and exchangeable globally, overcoming geographical, intermediary hurdles, and manual paperwork typically (Chainlink, n.d.).

In this chapter, we give an example of how tokenization works through the three main concepts that make tokenization work: the asset digitization protocols, the cross chain interoperability protocols, and the decentralized storage protocols to make sure that there is secure and easy access without applying the centralized decentralized application.

4.1. Asset Digitization and Representation Protocols

The essence of tokenization lies in asset digitization — the process of digitizing the tangible or intangible assets with the help of digital tokens living in a blockchain. These tokens aren't digital files, they are real value represented with code that implements all the rules, ownership and transfer rights.

Figure 1. Tokenization workflow architecture

Tokenization Workflow Architecture

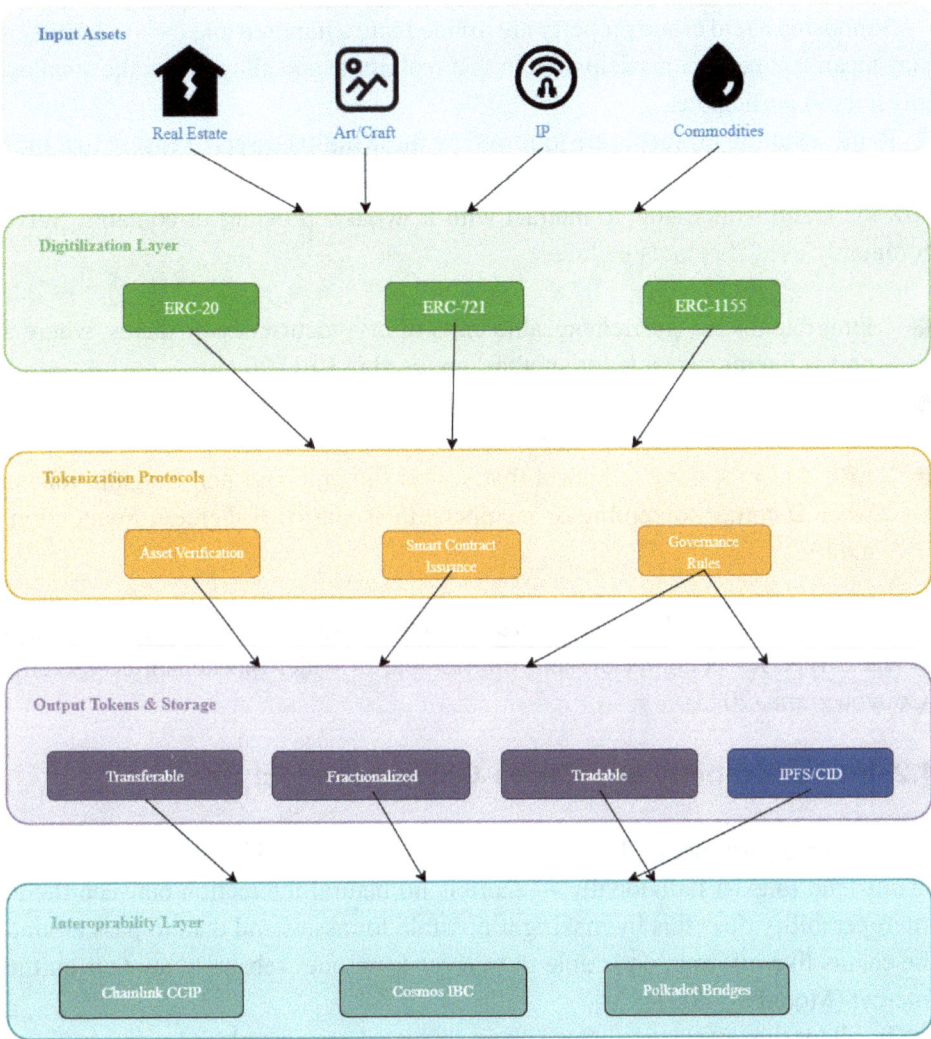

Figure 1 is a diagram of the Tokenization Workflow shows the entire process from assets in the real world to digital tokens. Physical and Ip Assets, for example, real estate, artwork, IP, are considered for digitization it starts at the Input Assets layer. These assets are represented on chain by the token standards like ERC20 (fungible) ERC721 (non fungible), ERC1155 (semi fungible) in the Digitization Layer. Ensuring asset verification, the Tokenization Protocols layer assures a brand new way of issuing token through smart contracts, and enforce governance rules. Thirdly, the Output Tokens & Storage layer makes these tokens transferable, fractionalized,

tradable, and stored using decentralized solutions like IPFS/CID. Furthermore, it employs Chainlink CCIP, Cosmos IBC and Polkadot Bridges to enable token bridging across various blockchain platforms for simple token travelling and communication.

Supposing a real estate property are divided into a hundred tokens — each token may mean one percent participation in that real estate and allows even the smallest investors to participate.

Representation protocols are followed by these digital assets to ensure that they will work well in different platforms. They are predefined sets of rules which define how the token works, how to interact with it, what it provides or contains. Some commonly used standards include:

- Fungible tokens (interchangeable units of cryptocurrency or shares, where a unit is interchangeable for another) are used in ERC-20.
- ERCs 721: Used for non fungible tokens (unique assets like he digital art, or certificates, etc.) (Ethereum Foundation, n.d.a)
- ERC-1155: A flexible hybrid that serves fungible and non fungible tokens when it comes to gaming or membership scenarios (Ethereum Foundation, n.d.b).

These protocols make that tokenized assets are suitable for wallets, exchanges and dApps for being usable and transferable in wider blockchain ecosystems (Cointelegraph, 2023).

4.2. Interoperability and Cross-Chain Architecture

Another big stumbling block in the blockchain world is that different blockchains tend to exist individually — there is no natural interaction between them. Interoperability does this by making it possible for assets and data to pass around the chains like information is able to transfer from one website to another on the internet (MoonPay, 2023).

To allow this interaction, cross chain architecture is employed using bridges, wrapped tokens, or interoperability protocols specifically for this purpose. For instance:

- Wrapped version of the token issued on Ethereum can be used on Binance Smart Chain.
- To this end, current projects building out ecosystems where different blockchains can communicate with one another, sharing data and tokens quickly are building upon the ideas of Polkadot, and later on, more likely Cosmos.

- Chainlink CCIP (Cross Chain Interoperability Protocol) is creating a standardized method of instructing and moving value securely from one blockchain to another (Chainlink, n.d.).

For tokenized asset to achieve its true potential, interoperability is important. That is because it provides for the global liquidity, meaning that users can easily buy, sell, or trade their assets from multiple blockchains and ecosystems while not being tied down to just one (Cambridge University Press, 2021).

4.3. Decentralized Storage Solutions and IPFS Integration

The blockchain stores data about the tokens such as ownership, transfer history, but it's not good at storing something big such as image, certificate, or a legal document. If you need to store decentralized, it becomes an issue of decentralized storage solutions like IPFS (InterPlanetary File System) (IPFS Docs, n.d.).

Instead of forcing files to reside in centralized servers, IPFS is a peer to peer file storage system which disperses files across the network. When we upload a file to IPFS, it will have a permanent content hash (CID) that locates this exact version of the file, as opposed to a URL. In doing so, data is immutable, when a file is added it can't be changed without changing the CID.

If IPFS is tied to tokenization, it makes it a secure way for large or sensitive data such as digital certificates, land registry documents or artwork files to connect to tokens. For example, any digital certificate of authenticity can point to its blockchain based tokenized version that represents the attended university degree on IPFS (IPFS Docs, n.d.).

This concept is built on other platforms like Filecoin or Arweave, which give users incentives to host data and hence maintain durability and accessibility over long periods of time. These solutions maintain the decindical form of Web3 where even the supporting data behind Token cannot be lost, tampered with and censored (Filecoin, n.d.).

5. AUTHENTICATION: SECURING DIGITAL PROVENANCE

In the digital age, you need to be sure of authenticity above all. In instances where assets, identities, interactions, etc. are becoming more and more automated to blockchain based systems we can guarantee secure and reliable provenance by a fundamental basis of trust. There's no shortage of 'authenticate' related to logging in, but in this context it's more about cryptography to prove that an asset is genuine, ownership is provable and fraudulent activities are precluded systemically. Without the proper authentication procedure, tokenization and digital asset management would be exposed as especially insecure and without credibility. The first part to this section covers the core building blocks of securing digital provenance through blockchain.

Figure 2 is a diagram explaining the lifecycle of an NFT in a royalty enabled smart contract. Specifically, it defines the core interactions: minting the NFT, creating and defining the metadata associated with it, and establishing the royalty terms by embedding in smart contract logic. The original creator automatically earns a percentage of the NFT whenever it is sold or transferred. Not only does this mechanism secure creator's compensation on secondary sales, but also it safeguards the trust and inventory of the decentralized ecosystem. This flow of how NFTs become programmable assets with smart contracts turned into revenue generating instruments.

Figure 2. Secure NFT authentication stack

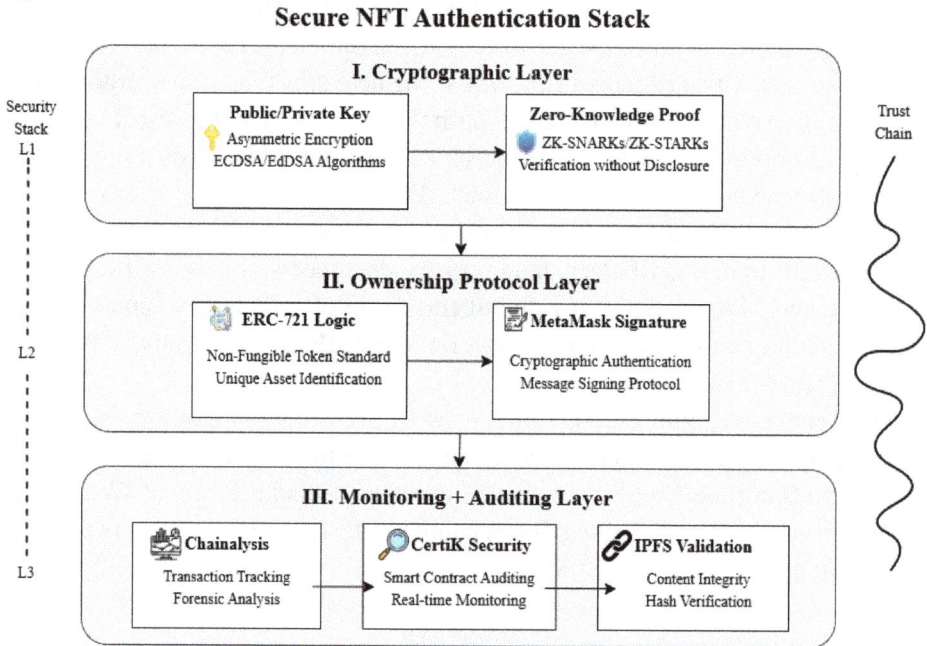

Secure NFT Authentication Stack

5.1. Cryptographic Validation Mechanisms

Public-key cryptography is basically at the heart of digital provenance security (Boneh & Shoup, 2020). Private key is used to sign every transaction on a blockchain and the public key validates it (Nakamoto, 2008). This means that only the rightful owner of a digital asset can start transferring the asset or updating its metadata. The best part about this system in its current form is that there does not need to be a third party involved to validate an action.

In addition, hashing functions ensure the content (i.e. metadata or linked files) hasn't been tampered. Take for example a certificate or artwork that would be sent as a token, its cryptographic hash works like a e digital fingerprint in which any change would instantly change the hash and wreck the trust chain.

They are also being used in addition to privacy and security through Zero Knowledge Proofs (ZKPs) (Zyskind et al., 2015). In particular, these mechanisms enable one party to prove possession of some data, without itself revealing the data at all — a powerful way of verifying identity and performing transactions in a distributed environment.

These two mechanisms combined constitute a tamper evident system that enables authentication of not only who did what, but also that the said asset or information was not manipulated or was verifiable.

5.2. Ownership Verification and Transfer Protocols

Supposing you're betting crypto Palace, ownership on the blockchain is binary and absolute, you have the token or you don't. With this level of clearness, also backed up by cryptographic signatures it is very simple to verify asset ownership (Wood, 2014; Boneh & Shoup, 2020). While these come very close in name for interfacing with the host protocol and setting up configurable state, ERC standards (for example ERC721 for NFTs, ERC20 for fungible tokens) are not limited to token creation, but are protocols which determine how ownership is recorded, transferred and queried (Buterin, 2015).

The blockchain is updated every time a token is transferred immutably and publicly. The provenance is easily auditable because this provides a traceable history of ownership. In addition, each smart contract adds this custom logic to ownership, giving you the ability to grant time-based access, royalties on resale, or access control among other things, which are critical for digital collectibles, licenses, and credentials.

This means that the interacting wallets have to be authenticated; which is often done by requesting signature for transfer via platforms like MetaMask (Nadini et al., 2021), making sure that only the owner who owns it can give consent for a transfer, in case the owner loses his ownership, all the money can be stolen. In this self sovereign model, we do not rely on centralized authorities, and do belong to peer to peer movement of assets with provable integrity.

However, blockchain inherently secure, but mining real world threats like phishing, wallet robbery, and the smart contracts you expose to the same. As a result, a complete security framework should be wider than just on-chain validation.

5.3. Security Framework and Fraud Prevention Systems

Fraud prevention is an island made up of multiple layers. Instead, multi-signature wallets, or multisig as it's known colloquially, safeguard the majority of wallets by requiring many participants before access can be granted (CertiK, n.d.). Security firms where they undergo contract audits, guard smart contracts against exploits and bugs (Parity Technologies, n.d.). Finally, reputation based systems also are formed, and addresses with verified behaviors or badges are more reputable.

By integrating identity checks (single KYC or verifiable credentials) into NFT marketplaces or digital identity platforms, this prevents the illegal content–either forged content or without authorisation–from being sold. Also, on chain analytics tools such as Chainalysis or CertiK may indicate weird behavior or stay tracks of the stolen assets in real time (CertiK, n.d.; Chainalysis, n.d.).

All together, a grandma's mentality about security secures provenance from origin to transaction and long beyond.

6. TECHNICAL IMPLEMENTATION ARCHITECTURE

In any blockchain based system, this technical implementation architecture lays the foundation of the system and therefore is the determinant of how robust, scalable and secure the solution will be. Each technical choice in turn affects the system's success not only in terms of writing the actual code that defines asset ownership and interaction, but in terms of integrating and 24/7 operability with decentralized tools. This section gets into what a smart contract is developed, deployed and how Web3 tools power the interaction in a decentralized way, and how the monitoring and maintenance protocols can remain sustainable in the long term.

6.1. Smart Contract Development and Deployment

The Decentralized application consists of smart contracts. These self-executing programs encode the logic behind token transfers, governance rules, access permissions, and economic models. Smart contracts, which are lines of code written most often in Solidity (for Ethereum based ecosystems), are deployed into a blockchain fighting to not be able to be altered once done (Buterin, 2015).

The logic of any specific asset and interactions of users with it, determines the beginning of development. For instance, a token contract (ERC 20, ERC 721) of supply, rules of transfer and triggers of events. Generally, the developers use frameworks like Hardhat, Truffle, or Foundry to build, test and simulate how a contract will behave on local or test network before deploying (Truffle Suite, 2023; Antonopoulos & Wood, 2018).

It deploys on a chosen blockchain network, for example on Ethereum Mainnet or any-other testnet. In this case, Remix IDE or Ethers.js/Web3.js scripts push the contract live interacting with those wallets through tools like MetaMask (ConsenSys, 2023). Once deployed smart contracts are immutable, as it is, the critical thing to note is to make sure to test them into inedibility (rigorously) and to make use of third party audits, tools like Slither or MythX, so there are no vulnerabilities (Ethereum Foundation, n.d.a. n.d.b; OpenZeppelin, n.d.).

Figure 3 depicts a smart contract designed using Solidity and OpenZeppelin library was developed to exercise its practical deployment of tokenization and decentralized ownership. It shows a contract creating ERC721 compliant NFTs with royalty logic ambient inside by using ERC2981 standard. Royalties ensure that creators get secondary market sale benefits because there is demand for them, which is extremely good for creative and entertainment industries. The owner has a contract for the NFTs to mint, metadata assignment through a base URI and default royalty to the percentage of token. This is a real world, technically functional example of tokenization being the means for providing economic incentives, traceability and creative control to the asset originator within blockchain ecosystems.

Figure 3. Royalty-Enabled NFT smart contract for transparent ownership and revenue sharing

```
// SPDX-License-Identifier: MIT
pragma solidity ^0.8.26;

import "@openzeppelin/contracts/token/ERC721/extensions/ERC721Enumerable.sol";
import "@openzeppelin/contracts/access/Ownable.sol";

contract RoyaltyNFT is ERC721Enumerable, Ownable {
    uint256 public nextTokenId;
    uint256 public royaltyFee;
    address public royaltyRecipient;

    constructor(string memory name, string memory symbol, uint256 _royaltyFee, address _royaltyRecipient)    // infinite gas 2063800 gas
        ERC721(name, symbol)
        Ownable(msg.sender)
    {
        royaltyFee = _royaltyFee;
        royaltyRecipient = _royaltyRecipient;
    }

    function mint() external {    // infinite gas
        uint256 tokenId = nextTokenId;
        _safeMint(msg.sender, tokenId);
        nextTokenId++;
    }

    function getRoyaltyInfo(uint256 /* tokenId */, uint256 salePrice) external view returns (address, uint256) {    // infinite gas
        uint256 royaltyAmount = (salePrice * royaltyFee) / 100;
        return (royaltyRecipient, royaltyAmount);
    }
}
```

6.2. Web3 Infrastructure Integration

After coming live with the smart contract, users have to be able to interact with it. Web3 infrastructure picks up on that: Web3 is the distributed internet that stacks the front end with a backend on top of the blockchain.

In order to create a smooth and secure user experience, dApps have libraries, like Web3.js, Ethers.js or frameworks like RainbowKit and wagmi to connect wallets (ConsenSys, 2023). They allow the users to either sign in with Metamask, asking to send them transactions, to get token data from blockchain. If large files (e.g. certificates or documents) need to be stored off-chain, then integration with IPFS or Filecoin may also be made use of (IPFS Documentation, n.d.).

React.js is one of the popular libraries taken along with Tailwind CSS to develop the UI as responsive, visually appealing interface. At the same time, APIs and event listeners monitor changes in the smart contract state as it occurs in real time. Furthermore, The Graph can provide benefits in form of indexing and querying blockchain data so that Dapps can be more responsive and usable (The Graph, 2022).

A strong Web3 integration makes it easy for the user to transition from decentralized backend to work seamlessly in their natural behavior of interaction, with secure and trustless operations.

6.3. System Monitoring and Maintenance Protocols

While smart contracts are immutable and decentralized, the surrounding eco-system just like any other ecosystem, remains new and requires clear maintenance and health checks. Since the dApp is used by many, system monitoring is done to make sure that the dApp is running smoothly, errors are caught in time, and users trust can be maintained.

Tenderly, Alchemy, or Infura etc have deep analytics + gas usage patterns and real time transaction tracking (Alchemy, 2023; Tenderly, 2023). In addition, they allow to simulate a way contract will behave before transaction comes to an end. Notifications are frequently added from both devs and a web tools in order to alert you when key metrics exceed thresholds (such as failed transactions, high gas used, or a contract error).

Secondly, smart contracts also interact with oracles, bridges and third party APIs, all of which need uptime tracking. frontend or backend make their way into the git repository and are logged either by logs or version control systems (GitHub, GitLab).

Maintenance also deals with ensuring user experience, for example if the wallet works, if the documentation stays on the page, and if errors are not thrown from supporting infrastructure. Together, the combination of live analytics, security pro-tocols and pre-emptive updates of the operational backbone acts as the operational backbone making the whole ecosystem sheer trustworthy.

7. NFT APPLICATIONS ACROSS INDUSTRIES

Non Fungible Tokens (NFTs) have gone way past digital collectibles and profile pictures. As they have provided their core function of verifiable ownership of unique digital or physical assets on a blockchain, they can be applied to a wide range of real world industries. NFTs were quietly starting to shape the new wave of decentralized economies that have secured ownership in the arts, that have broken down barriers in finance and that even have the potential to revolutionize property rights in the real world. In this section, we don't only look to where NFTs are being used but how they are eliminating some of the oldest problems by using blockchain logic and smart contracts (Regner et al., 2019).

7.1. Creative Industries: Art, Music, and Entertainment

For the creative sector, NFTs serve as digital certificate of originality and own-ership (andноï biological ownership) that solves the century old challenge of trusted provenance (and royalties), free from piracy (Dowling, 2022). The traditional system for digital artists and musicians is predicated upon a service economy, where interme-diaries (galleries, labels and the like) of whose scale cuts are gargantuan, yet provide next to no transparency or returns (Dowling, 2022). NFTs flip this power dynamic.

The issue stems from the fact that minting an artwork or a song as an NFT means the ownership, who created the artist, and the sale history are all recorded immutably on the blockchain (Regner et al., 2019). This results in artists being able to avoid the third parties that normally serve as intermediaries between collectors and artists. What makes programmable royalties the real game changer? Well, these are smart contracts in which artists get to be paid a percentage whenever their NFT is resold in the secondary market (Kugler, 2021).

Musicians, for instance, he made available on platforms such as Sound.xyz or Audius, released tracks as NFTs that give fans ownership access to the tracks, behind the scenes content, or even governance of future albums. Rather in entertainment, film studios and indie creators are using NFTs to finance productions through NFT backed memberships, early access pass, and scene level ownership (Dickson, 2021).

7.2. Financial Services: DeFi Integration and Asset Fractionalization

NFTs, in fact, are becoming used as pivotal instruments in the interface of decentralized finance (DeFi), where they are not replacing fungible tokens but are tokenizing unique positions, contracts and assets with unique identities. For example, the liquidity position in the protocol like Uniswap V3, is represented as an NFT because each user has a different price range and token pair (Adams et al., 2021).

A strong use case for this is asset collateralization. Taking advantage of such platforms as NFTfi or Arcade, NFT holders can borrow providing their tokens as collateral. These are systems that use floor price, rarity or historic trading volume to value NFT but apply repayment conditions if so and all this automatically enforced with smart contracts. On the other hand, if the loan defaults, the NFT is liquidated (Schär, 2021).

Finally, NFTs are foundational to fractional ownership over properties that are too costly (physically or financially) or illiquid. NFTs can be divided using protocols like Fractional.art or Tessera into ERC-20 tokens representing fractional shares of high value assets and thus small investors can own and trade fractions of already expensive assets. This makes liquidity, accessible democratization and market driven pricing possible to such previously scarce markets (Kugler, 2021).

The fact that NFTs are not confined to static assets that can be static and present variables which are retained so it not necessarily static over time, these third parties are evolved, financial, instruments which can be integrated, insured, and monetized within wider DeFi ecosystems (Schär, 2021).

7.3. Real-World Asset Tokenization: Real Estate and Physical Assets

The most promising — and probably the most complex – application of NFTs are on tokenizing the physical world, and a large part of it is real estate. The property transaction is traditionally slow, heavily intermediated and bureaucratically inefficient. Converting legal rights, and other documentation of property ownership to programmable digital record can be simply represented as NFTs and thus can be transferred, leased, or sold with fewer intermediaries compared to property ownership today (Zambrano et al., 2021).

Let's take for example a real estate company which will tokenize the property deed to be NFT with legal metadata, geographical coordinates, and ownership rights in the smart contract. These tokens could be bought by the verified KYC/AML compliant platforms and even the fractional NFTs could enable investors purchase parts of commercial property that would democratize real estate investment (Zambrano et al., 2021).

Propy and RealT among startups are experimenting with these models already, providing the fully tokenized real estate sales with blockchain verified records. Properties can range from what's beyond just property, including luxury watches, vintage cars, or even commodities, and in these cases, an NFT is a token used to convey digital representation of goods, which is connected to attestation or storage services (Propy, 2023; RealT, 2022).

Nevertheless, clarification is needed in regard to regulatory recognition, enforcement by law, and custody. However, the trajectory is clear: NFTs provide for transparent, programmable, and liquid approach to treating access to physical assets as a dynamic, tradeable, digital interaction (Schär, 2021).

8. CHALLENGES AND TECHNICAL LIMITATIONS

Though so efficient, their legal challenges, environmental issues, and technical obstacles make blockchain based systems and NFTs potentially wonderful, but in fact they continue to be highly problematic. Ultimately these are not just limitations, they are what makes the technology fast, dispensable, and, yes, sustainable. It's important for people looking to develop real world blockchain apps from the ground up that have confidence and integrity in their app for them to understand these friction points from scalability issues to environmental concerns and to legal gray zones. We then dive in this section to go beyond problems identification to the trade offs, actual problems and how they can be solved.

8.1. Scalability and Performance Optimization

That security and trustlessness enables decentralization is a paradox, as decentralization is essential in order to achieve them, but it significantly impacts performance. Ethereum is one of the most popular smart contract platforms in its base layer; for example, it processes only around 15–30 transactions per second (TPS). For example, compare this approach of handling 24,000 TPS with traditional such as Visa. While the throughput bottleneck may seems as if it's just about throughput, gas fees, transaction delays, and to some degree, user adoption (Ethereum Foundation, n.d.a, n.d.b; Buterin, 2015) are also affected.

To tackle this, Layer 2 solutions such as Optimistic Rollups and ZK Rollup consolidate (bundle) multiple off chain transactions onto on chain second layer, as a way of estimating their hash. The basic methods leave you with security whilst reducing congestion dramatically. On the same hand, sharded, multichain architectures such as platforms which are based on Polkadot and Substrate, optimize their scalability across verticals (Farooq et al., 2024; Parity Technologies, n.d.).

Generally speaking, scalability is inherently lacking when the technical debt in this problem is attracted by the weighted average standardized discount rate. On the other hand, developers must profile and gas optimize code using tools such as Slither, Hardhat or Tenderly. Also, off chain indexing and querying solutions like The Graph lighten the performance loads on the chain. On the other hand considering this landscape, performance tuning becomes a system level responsibility that involves selection of a consensus algorithm, ensuring that the frontend dApp behavior is performant.

8.2. Environmental Impact and Sustainability Measures

One of the things blockchain is most criticized for is energy consumption. Problems arise from mass adoption of mass data science operations on legacy proof-of-work (PoW), where bitcoin keeps using Disc the same amount electricity as small nations (Library of Congress, 2020; Nakamoto, 2008). Despite the reduction of Ethereum's energy usage through its shift from Proof of Work (PoW) to Proof of Stake (PoS via "The Merge) by 99.95%, many chains and mining based platforms that continue to operate under an energy heavy model (Buterin, 2022).

Currently, the focus is on green blockchain infrastructure. For example, networks such as Tezos, Algorand, and Chia, as well as Filecoin make active attempts to juggle low carbon footprint decentralized data hosting with incentive schemes (Filecoin invests a lot into this, and IPFS Docs do as well amongst other things). Adding sustainability into token economics (Chainlink, n.d.) means that developers and DAOs are introducing carbon offset tracking mechanisms directly into smart contracts for the purposes of driving carbon footprint reduction efforts.

The aim of sustainability in blockchain goes beyond consensus and includes reducing blockchain bloat. It is discouraged to store large metadata or asset files on the blockchain. Different from IPFS and Arweave, IPFS and Arweave provide off-chain file solutions with tamper resistant content addressing thereby reducing redundant node replication and ecological efficiency (Chainlink, n.d.; IPFS Docs, n.d.).

In this way, sustainability in the Web3 is not only about energy but rather is about how data moves, settles, and retains accessibility over time.

8.3. Regulatory Compliance and Legal Frameworks

Blockchain brings a new model of decentralization, however it presents as a new critical bottleneck: the legal ambiguity. The regulatory bodies across the world are still adapting to what constitutes a digital asset or a security or an unregulated instrument (J.P. Morgan, 2024; Kaal, 2020). International operations are risky without unified standards and benign NFT is a term used so loosely without good reason that they can unintentionally violate securities laws or intellectual property rights.

Due to the pseudonymous nature of wallets, AML (Anti Money Laundering) and KYC (Know Your Customer) protocols are made very difficult to enforce due to the compliance nature of it. Countries such as the U.S., EU, Singapore etc are building roof friendly frameworks of smart contracts that merge verifiable credentials and decentralized identifiers (DIDs), as well as zero knowledge proofs (Zyskind et al., 2015) to protect privacy and legality at the same time.

Further, data protection regulations like GDPR conflict with blockchain's immutability. If a user has a "right to be forgotten" what allows one to parcel that with an immutable on chain record? Off-chain storage with on-chain reference emerged as a solution which can record revocation without blockchain tampering (Solouki & Bamakan, 2023; Wang et al., 2021).

Legal clarity is not a burden in back office—it is the base of mass trust. As projects continue to embark on their journey forward, they need to design smart contract and dApp projects to instantiate legal audit trails that are embedded, permissioned by role, and have the necessary KYC workflows defined based on region.

9. FUTURE TRAJECTORIES: NFTs IN Web3

NFTs became building blocks of the Web3 experience as we continue further into the decentralized internet. As advancements in token standards come, as token standards have been integrated into immersive virtual environments, and as token standards converge with other frontier technologies like AI and AR, this is thus how their evolution is shaped. PTC, which stands for programmable truth, fits nicely into the current trend of changing the foundation of the Web to define a new sort of web connection – programmatic personality and dynamic, composable assets are going to expand the eliminate of digital possession on top of reworking the essence of web communication. This section looks beyond theory and on to the real builders steering in that direction now.

9.1. Advanced Token Standards and Protocols

Having established the way to tokenize an NFT via traditional token standards such as ERC-721 and ERC-1155, their drawbacks are now more and more obvious as use cases are maturing. Generally they operate on static metadata and rigid ownership. The new generation of NFTs requires higher flexibility, composability and programmability.

Token Bound Accounts (ERC-6551) idea is to convert NFTs into smart wallets. This gives NFTs the opportunity to own other NFTs, tokens or even interact with protocols, making it an agent, where an NFT is not just a passive asset, rather an agent in the Web3 ecosystem, more specifically in the Ethereum Foundation (Ethereum Foundation, n.d.a., n.d.b). Such a thing is monumentous for gaming, identity, and composable art.

Projects like Soulbound Tokens (SBTs) created by Vitalik Buterin combine the benefits of NFTs as non-transferable and linked to a person's identity that also comprise credentials, affiliations or achievements as a digital resume of membership and governance rights (Buterin, 2022).

In addition, the design of modular token is evolving to standards which allow in real time metadata updates and dynamic royalties and cross chain compatibility (e.g. CIP-68 on Cardano). These changes are being driven by developers, but also by user need for NFTs that can have multiple use cases within metaverses, DeFi and DAOs (OpenSea, n.d.; Chainlink, n.d.).

9.2. Metaverse Integration and Digital Identity

NFTs as a digital identity has become part of the fabric of the emerging metaverse platforms. Since everything lives in the virtual world, ownership, presence and interaction needs to be verifiable, and where NFTs act as the enablers of that framework.

For example, imagine logging into one of those lucrative metaverse worlds with your NFT wallet that does more than just hold art, passing skin avatars, cheap keys to private lounges or virtual land deeds, you might even have credentials into

DAOs you're part of. Decentraland, The Sandbox, and Spatial already have NFTs as identity primitives being integrated as a part of platforms, enabling the users to bring personalized assets into shared environments (World Economic Forum, 2023; Propy, 2023).

Digital identity goes beyond avatars. With verifiable credentials as NFTs, users can have their diplomas, certifications, social rep etc. in their pockets. We are abandoning the logins of usernames and wallets…and you will have a persistent, portable, and privacy oriented identity that revolves around NFTs, you own, who you are, and what access you have a right to.

Except that the friction is interoperability. For instance, the activities of Lens Protocol, Ceramic Network, and other teams are building decentralized identity graphs for connecting ownership of NFTs, reputation and activities across a variety of dApps and chains as in Chainlink (IPFS Documentation, n.d.; Chainlink, n.d.; IPFS Docs, n.d.). Now that we get to NFTs, that become dynamic and bound to real-time identity layers, social, financial and digital presence will completely blur.

9.3. Emerging Technologies and Innovation Pathways

While, a new wave of technologies increasingly interconnect with NFTs, their boundaries are about to be pushed to unchartable spaces. For the above layers to continue to make progress, AI, AR/VR, IoT, and quantum computing, NFTs are more likely to absorb these layers which are becoming more and more autonomous, intelligent, and real time aware.

A near real case would be that of the AI generated NFT's such as Altered State Machine, the platform ties the neural network where NFTs feed the intelligent characters that are trained and learn. This will enable 'living NFTs' whose behavior changes over time and offer access to intelligent companions, AI based DAO agents, or changing digital artworks (Nadini et al., 2021).

Another new trend within the world of NFTs is Augmented Reality NFTs. NFTs are about to become tangible and even have their very own applications built with Apple's Vision Pro and other spatial computing devices, making tangible distinct from digital.

However, such integration with the real world could enable updating NFT states based on real-world sensors — an actual NFT for a plant, for instance, whose health's state is reflected by moisture sensors in the real word. In parallel, in supply chain tracking, real world events can trigger smart contract updates, and hence make NFTs verifiable proof of origin and authenticity (Solouki & Bamakan, 2023).

In the next run, the innovation path will be towards NFT based governance, AI integrated DAOs, and fully on chain built on any composable economy. The maturity of these technologies together will help NFTs mature from tokens-> infrastructure-> the atomic unit of Web3 life.

10. CONCLUSION

As this is our last section, we consolidate our insights into how NFTs shape the future of digital ownership, and how we should perceive the technical footprint of NFTs, and forecast the next steps for research and development of NFTs. NFTs from collectibles to the foundational components of the Web3 infrastructure is the reason why NFT's impact, and particularly influence is continuing to grow across the industries, technology ecosystems, and regulatory landscapes. This part, looking past, with clarity, relevance, and a forward-looking mindset, suggests where we are, where we've been technically, and where we're going.

10.1. Impact Assessment and Technical Implications

NFTs are both disruptive and constructive to the technical impact of NFTs in digital ecosystems. First of all, NFTs have opened up the verifiable digital ownership, fractionalized asset representation and creator-led economy. On one, they have disrupted what is to follow by insisting for blockchain native design pattern which put decentralisation, user control and transparency first.

From a development point, NFTs have standardized smart contract protocols such as ERC-721 and ERC-1155 which help in the cross application compatibility and opening up for the composable dApps. On the front end Web3 tooling (for example Ethers.js, wagmi, RainbowKit), they've also asked for change because these forced developers to build interfaces that are secure but yet intuitive to the end user without having familiarity with wallets or private keys.

From a deeper implication, NFTs need to be stored on IPFS, Arweave; indexing protocols (The Graph) to query blockchain state; relies multi chain bridges to deal with operating on multiple networks. This bumps up the technical stack of Web3 a couple levels, making NFTs endpoints and conduits in a distributed digital architecture.

In fact, NFT based ecosystems have also provided imitations in 'real time' metadata updates, gas optimization and ownership (and ownership change) authentication with using zero knowledge proofs and wallet signatures. In this way, the NFT movement is not merely about introducing a new class of the digital assets but also changing the entire stage of the life cycle development of the decentralized applications.

10.2. Future Research Directions and Development Roadmap

It is in this maturing of the landscape that we are beginning to see, which will define the next decade of NFTs emerging, several key research and development pathways. Key among these is the need of sustainability in scaling factors like rollups layer 2 (Optimism, zkSync) and new consensus models that lower the energy costs and fees in such a way that mass NFT adoption does not compromise the ideals of the decentral.

The other promising avenue is on semantic metadata and on chain AI interaction. Take a world where NFTs aren't just storing data but to do the opposite, to interpret, to learn, and interact using intelligent agents. To this, the combination of decentralized identity (DID), soulbound tokens (SBTs), and AI protocol that can ask context questions in a privacy and sovereignty respect is required.

In fact, there is an increasing evolution of regulatory aware NFT frameworks. To support global regulators, and keep up with the race, research must also focus on how NFT's can include KYC, AML and legal metadata in a decentralized compliant way, especially for financial and real estate use cases. RealT and Propy are already projects that are offering blueprints for such compliant tokenization models.

But finally, as the development will lead towards standardization for composability, NFTs will flow freely across dApps, metaverses, and DeFi layers. The luckiest ones are likely to think about open NFT operating systems with their smart contract templates that are modular, royalties that are DAO governed, and logic baked right into their core.

For all intents and purposes, the future of NFTs is to go beyond use cases, they're going to make them more useful and insert them into the digital economy as programmable, interoperable, and intelligent assets.

REFERENCES

Adams, H., Zinsmeister, N., Salem, M., Keefer, D., & Robinson, D. (2021). Uniswap v3 Core. Uniswap. https://uniswap.org/whitepaper-v3.pdf

Alchemy. (2023). Web3 developer tools and APIs. Retrieved from https://www.alchemy.com/

Androulaki, E., Barger, A., Bortnikov, V., Cachin, C., & Christidis, K. (2018). Hyperledger Fabric: A Distributed Operating System for Permissioned Blockchains. *Proceedings of the Thirteenth EuroSys Conference*, 1–15. DOI: 10.1145/3190508.3190538

Antonopoulos, A. M., & Wood, G. (2018). *Mastering Ethereum: Building smart contracts and DApps*. O'Reilly Media.

Boneh, D., & Shoup, V. (2020). A graduate course in applied cryptography. Version 0.5. Stanford University. https://toc.cryptobook.us/

Buterin, V. (2015). A next-generation smart contract and decentralized application platform. Ethereum Whitepaper. https://ethereum.org/en/whitepaper/

Buterin, V. (2022). Soulbound. Ethereum Blog. https://ethereum.org/en/community/blog/

Cambridge University Press. (2021). Cross-chain interoperability among blockchain-based systems using transactions. *The Knowledge Engineering Review*, *36*, e22. DOI: 10.1017/S0269888921000016

Certi, K. (n.d.). Blockchain Security and Smart Contract Audits. https://www.certik.com/

CFTE. (May 15,2023). The history of digital assets. https://blog.cfte.education/the-history-of-digital-assets

Chainalysis. (n.d.). Blockchain Data Platform. https://www.chainalysis.com/

Chainlink. (n.d.). Asset Tokenization Explained. Chainlink. Retrieved April 10, 2025, from https://chain.link/education/asset-tokenization

Cointelegraph. (2023). Asset tokenization: What it is and how it works. Cointelegraph. Retrieved April 10, 2025, from https://cointelegraph.com/learn/articles/asset-tokenization

ConsenSys. (2023). A guide to Web3.js and Ethers.js: Connecting to Ethereum networks. Retrieved from https://consensys.net/h/

Dickson, B. (2021). How NFTs are impacting the music and movie industries. TechTalks. https://bdtechtalks.com/2021/03/29/nfts-music-movie-industry/

Docs, I. P. F. S. (n.d.). How IPFS works. InterPlanetary File System Documentation. Retrieved April 10, 2025, from https://docs.ipfs.tech/concepts/how-ipfs-works/

Documentation, I. P. F. S. (n.d.). https://docs.ipfs.io/

Dowling, M. (2022). Fertile LAND: Pricing non-fungible tokens. *Finance Research Letters*, *44*, 102096. DOI: 10.1016/j.frl.2021.102096

Ethereum Foundation. (n.d.a). ERC-721 Non-Fungible Token Standard. https://ethereum.org/en/developers/docs/standards/tokens/erc-721/

Ethereum Foundation. (n.d.b). ERC-1155 Multi Token Standard. https://ethereum.org/en/developers/docs/standards/tokens/erc-1155/

Farooq, M. S., Jamil, H., & Riaz, H. S. (2024). A Multichain Based Marketplace Architecture. arXiv preprint arXiv:2402.06636. https://arxiv.org/abs/2402.06636

Filecoin. (n.d.). Store and retrieve data with decentralized storage. Filecoin. Retrieved April 10, 2025, from https://filecoin.io/

Kaal, W. A. (2020). Digital asset market evolution. *The Journal of Corporation Law*, *46*, 909.

Kugler, L. (2021). Non-fungible tokens and the future of art. *Communications of the ACM*, *64*(9), 19–20. DOI: 10.1145/3474355

Law, F. (2022). The history of the blockchain and Bitcoin. https://freemanlaw.com/the-history-of-the-blockchain-and-bitcoin/

Library of Congress. (May, 2020). Cryptocurrency & blockchain technology. https://guides.loc.gov/fintech/21st-century/cryptocurrency-blockchain

MoonPay. (2023). Blockchain interoperability: How do blockchains communicate? MoonPay. Retrieved April 10, 2025, from https://www.moonpay.com/learn/blockchain/blockchain-interoperability

Morgan, J. P. (Oct, 2024). Evolution of digital assets. J.P. Morgan. https://www.jpmorgan.com/content/dam/jpm/cib/complex/content/securities-services/regulatory-solutions/evolution-of-digital-assets.pdf

Nadini, M., Alessandretti, L., Di Giacinto, F., Martino, M., Aiello, L. M., & Baronchelli, A. (2021). Mapping the NFT revolution: Market trends, trade networks, and visual features. *Scientific Reports*, *11*(1), 20902. DOI: 10.1038/s41598-021-00053-8 PMID: 34686678

Nakamoto, S. (2008). Bitcoin: A peer-to-peer electronic cash system. https://bitcoin.org/bitcoin.pdf

Nakamoto, S. Bitcoin: A Peer-to-Peer Electronic Cash System, BITCOIN.ORG (May 24, 2009), https://bitcoin.org/bitcoin.pdf (PDF).

OpenSea Developer Docs. https://docs.opensea.io/

OpenZeppelin Contracts Documentation. https://docs.openzeppelin.com/contracts/

Propy. (2023). NFT Real Estate Transactions. https://propy.com/browse/

Real, T. (2022). Real Estate on the Blockchain. https://realt.co/

Regner, F., Urbach, N., & Schweizer, A. (2019). NFTs in practice – Applications and implications of non-fungible tokens for artists, investors, and marketplaces. *Business & Information Systems Engineering, 61*(6), 546–550.

Schär, F. (2021). Decentralized finance: On blockchain- and smart contract-based financial markets. *Review - Federal Reserve Bank of St. Louis, 103*(2), 153–174. DOI: 10.20955/r.103.153-74

Solouki, M., & Bamakan, S. M. H. (2023). A Review of the Key Challenges of Non-Fungible Tokens. *Technological Forecasting and Social Change, 187*, 122297. DOI: 10.1016/j.techfore.2022.122297

Suite, T. (2023). Smart contract development tools. Retrieved from https://trufflesuite.com/

Technologies, P. (n.d.). Substrate: Blockchain Framework. https://substrate.io/

TechTarget. (2023). A timeline and history of blockchain technology. https://www.techtarget.com/whatis/feature/A-timeline-and-history-of-blockchain-technology

Tenderly. (2023). Real-time monitoring and debugging for smart contracts. Retrieved from https://tenderly.co/

The Graph. (2022). Decentralized querying protocol for blockchains. Retrieved from https://thegraph.com/

Wang, Q., Li, R., Wang, Q., & Chen, S. (2021). Non-Fungible Token (NFT): Overview, Evaluation, Opportunities and Challenges. arXiv preprint arXiv:2105.07447.

Wood, G. (2014). Ethereum: A secure decentralised generalised transaction ledger. https://ethereum.github.io/yellowpaper/paper.pdf

World Economic Forum. (2023). What are non-fungible tokens (NFTs) and are they useful? https://www.weforum.org/stories/2023/10/nfts-non-fungible-tokens-blockchain/

Zambrano, R., Jani, A., & Lakhanpal, S. (2021). Blockchain in land administration: A review of potential and challenges. *Land Use Policy*, *100*, 104893. DOI: 10.1016/j.landusepol.2020.104893

Zyskind, G., Nathan, O., & Pentland, A. (2015). Decentralizing privacy: Using blockchain to protect personal data. 2015 IEEE Security and Privacy Workshops (SPW), 180–184. DOI: 10.1109/SPW.2015.27

Compilation of References

Abagnale, F. W., & Redding, S. (2000). *Catch me if you can: The true story of a real fake*. Crown.

Abdullah, N. A., Hussain, F. K., & Hussain, O. K. (2021). Deepfake video detection: A systematic literature review. *IEEE Access: Practical Innovations, Open Solutions*, 9, 140373–140391. DOI: 10.1109/ACCESS.2021.3118923

Adams, H., Zinsmeister, N., Salem, M., Keefer, D., & Robinson, D. (2021). Uniswap v3 Core. Uniswap. https://uniswap.org/whitepaper-v3.pdf

Adru, S. L., Johnson, S., & Hemalatha, M. (2023). AI and Blockchain Based Platform for Empowering Content Creators: Enabling NFT – Driven Content Sharing, Inspiration Generation, and Collaborative Interaction. 666–673. .DOI: 10.1109/ICOSEC58147.2023.10276305

Agarwal, S., Farid, H., Gu, Y., He, M., Nagano, K., & Li, H. (2020). Protecting world leaders against deep fakes. *Proceedings of the IEEE/CVF Conference on Computer Vision and Pattern Recognition Workshops*, 38–45. DOI: 10.1109/CVPRW50498.2020.00013

Aichroth, P., Cuccovillo, L., & Gerhardt, M. (2021). Audio Forensics and provenance analysis: Technologies for media verification and asset management. *Journal of Digital Media Management*, 9(4), 348. DOI: 10.69554/CEXG6223

AJUZIEOGU, U. C. Towards Hallucination-Resilient AI: Navigating Challenges, Ethical Dilemmas, and Mitigation Strategies.

Alchemy. (2023). Web3 developer tools and APIs. Retrieved from https://www.alchemy.com/

Ali Linkon, A., Shaima, M., & Uddin Sarker, M. S. (2024). Advancements and applications of generative artificial intelligence and large language models on Business Management: A comprehensive review. *Journal of Computer Science and Technology Studies, 6*(1), 225–232. DOI: 10.32996/jcsts.2024.6.1.26

Alisha, S. K., & Krishna, B. V. (2024). FAKE NEWS, DISINFORMATION, AND DEEP FAKES LEVERAGING DISTRIBUTED LEDGER TECHNOLOGIES. *International Journal of Management Research and Business Strategy, 14*(2), 275–288.

Alkhard, A. (2024). Leveraging Digital Asset Management and meta-data integration for enhanced asset management. *Construction Economics and Building, 24*(3). DOI: 10.5130/AJCEB.v24i3.8741

Al-Mulla, M. S. (2022). Deepfakes: Criminalization And Legalization Analytical Descriptive Study. *Webology, 19*(2).

Alrubei, S. M., Ball, E. A., Rigelsford, J. M., & Willis, C. A. (2020). Latency and performance analyses of real-world wireless IoT-blockchain application. *IEEE Sensors Journal, 20*(13), 7372–7383. DOI: 10.1109/JSEN.2020.2979031

AlSabhany, A. A., Ali, A. H., Ridzuan, F., Azni, A. H., & Mokhtar, M. R. (2020). Digital audio steganography: Systematic review, classification, and analysis of the current state of the art. *Computer Science Review, 38*(100316), 100316. DOI: 10.1016/j.cosrev.2020.100316

Alzoubi, M. M. (2024). Investigating the synergy of blockchain and AI: Enhancing security, efficiency, and transparency. *Journal of Cyber Security Technology,* 1–29. DOI: 10.1080/23742917.2024.2374594

Amazeen, M. A. (2015). Revisiting the epistemology of fact-checking. *Critical Review, 27*(1), 1–22. DOI: 10.1080/08913811.2014.993890

Anderson, R., & Petitcolas, F. A. (2018). On the limits of steganography. *IEEE Journal on Selected Areas in Communications, 16*(4), 474–481. DOI: 10.1109/49.668971

Androulaki, E., Barger, A., Bortnikov, V., Cachin, C., & Christidis, K. (2018). Hyperledger Fabric: A Distributed Operating System for Permissioned Blockchains. *Proceedings of the Thirteenth EuroSys Conference,* 1–15. DOI: 10.1145/3190508.3190538

Aneja, D., Aneja, S., & Raman, B. (2021). Deepfake detection using convolutional neural networks. *Neural Computing & Applications, 33*(12), 7019–7031. DOI: 10.1007/s00521-020-05531-x

Angelova, M. (2019). Application of blockchain technology in the cultural and Creative Industries. *2019 II International Conference on High Technology for Sustainable Development (HiTech)*, 1–4. DOI: 10.1109/HiTech48507.2019.9128267

An, K., Lu, Z. M., Sun, X. C., & Wang, Z. H. (2024a). Multipurpose video watermarking algorithm for copyright protection and tamper detection. *Multimedia Tools and Applications*, *83*(17), 51647–51668. DOI: 10.1007/s11042-023-17558-1

Antonopoulos, A. M., & Wood, G. (2018). *Mastering Ethereum: Building smart contracts and DApps*. O'Reilly Media.

Authors Guild v. Google, Inc., 804 F.3d 202 | Casetext Search + Citator. (n.d.). Retrieved January 31, 2025, from https://casetext.com/case/guild-v-google-inc-1

Banerjee, P., Govindarajan, C., Jayachandran, P., & Ruj, S. (2020). Reliable, fair and decentralized marketplace for content sharing using blockchain. *2020 IEEE International Conference on Blockchain (Blockchain)*, 365–370. DOI: 10.1109/ Blockchain50366.2020.00053

Baranwal, G., Kumar, D., & Vidyarthi, D. P. (2023). Blockchain based resource allocation in cloud and distributed edge computing: A survey. *Computer Communications*, *209*, 469–498. DOI: 10.1016/j.comcom.2023.07.023

Bayer, J. (2024). Legal implications of using generative AI in the media. *Information & Communications Technology Law*, *33*(3), 310–329. DOI: 10.1080/13600834.2024.2352694

Benaich, I., & Hogarth, N. (2023). *State of AI Report 2023*. Air Street Capital. Retrieved from https://www.stateof.ai

Bengesi, S., El-Sayed, H., Sarker, M. K., Houkpati, Y., Irungu, J., & Oladunni, T. (2024). Advancements in generative AI: A comprehensive review of gans, GPT, autoencoders, diffusion model, and Transformers. *IEEE Access : Practical Innovations, Open Solutions*, *12*, 69812–69837. DOI: 10.1109/ACCESS.2024.3397775

Benhamou, M. (2023). The Security Threat of "Polisario". *Horizons: Journal of International Relations and Sustainable Development*, (23), 122–135.

Bertie County Center. (2025). Digital literacy for the age of deepfakes: Recognizing misinformation in AI-generated media. North Carolina State University. https://bertie.ces.ncsu.edu/2025/03/digital-literacy-for-the-age-of-deepfakes-recognizing-misinformation-in-ai-generated-media/

Bhardwaj, A., Sharma, K., & Mehta, R. (2023). Integrating blockchain with generative AI for ethical media governance. *Journal of Digital Ethics and Technology*, *11*(1), 55–70. DOI: 10.1080/25741292.2023.1142785

Bhattacharyya, C., Wang, H., Zhang, F., Kim, S., & Zhu, X. (2024). Diffusion deepfake. *arXiv preprint arXiv:2404.01579*.

Bhumichai, D., Smiliotopoulos, C., Benton, R., Kambourakis, G., & Damopoulos, D. (2024). The convergence of artificial intelligence and blockchain: The state of play and the road ahead. *Information (Basel)*, *15*(5), 268. DOI: 10.3390/info15050268

Bhusal, C. S. (2021). Systematic review on social engineering: Hacking by manipulating humans. *Journal of Information Security*, *12*(1), 104–114. DOI: 10.4236/jis.2021.121005

Binns, R. (2018). Fairness in machine learning: Lessons from political philosophy. *Proceedings of the 2018 Conference on Fairness, Accountability and Transparency (FAT)**, 149–159. DOI: 10.1145/3287560.3287598

Birthriya, S. K., Ahlawat, P., & Jain, A. K. (2025). Detection and Prevention of Spear Phishing Attacks: A Comprehensive Survey. *Computers & Security, 104317*, 104317. 10.1016/j.cose.2025.104317. DOI: 10.1016/j.cose.2025.104317

Bitcoin: A peer-to-peer electronic cash system. (n.d.). https://bitcoin.org/bitcoin.pdf

Blockchain and smart contracts in supply chain management: A game theoretic model—ScienceDirect. (n.d.). Retrieved February 1, 2025, from https://www.sciencedirect.com/science/article/abs/pii/S0925527320302188?via%3Dihub

Boneh, D., & Shoup, V. (2020). A graduate course in applied cryptography. Version 0.5. Stanford University. https://toc.cryptobook.us/

Bounaira, S., Alioua, A., & Souici, I. (2024). Blockchain-enabled trust management for secure content caching in mobile edge computing using deep reinforcement learning. *Internet of Things : Engineering Cyber Physical Human Systems*, *25*(101081), 101081. DOI: 10.1016/j.iot.2024.101081

Bradshaw, S., & Howard, P. N. (2018). Challenging truth and trust: A global inventory of organized social media manipulation. *The computational propaganda project, 1*, 1-26.

Bragazzi, N. L., & Garbarino, S. (2024). Understanding and Combating Misinformation: An Evolutionary Perspective. *JMIR Infodemiology*, *4*(1), e65521. DOI: 10.2196/65521 PMID: 39466077

Breacher.ai. (2024). *Deepfake Attacks Examples*. https://breacher.ai/deepfake/deepfake-attack-examples/

Brewer, J., Patel, D., Kim, D., & Murray, A. (2024). Navigating the challenges of generative technologies: Proposing the integration of artificial intelligence and blockchain. *Business Horizons*, *67*(5), 525–535. Advance online publication. DOI: 10.1016/j.bushor.2024.04.011

Brown, I., & Marsden, C. T. (2023). *Regulating Code: Good Governance and Better Regulation in the Information Age* (2nd ed.). MIT Press., DOI: 10.7551/mitpress/13764.001.0001

Brown, T., Mann, B., Ryder, N., Subbiah, M., Kaplan, J. D., Dhariwal, P., & Amodei, D. (2020). Language models are few-shot learners. *Advances in Neural Information Processing Systems*, *33*, 1877–1901.

Buccafusco, C. (2016). A Theory of Copyright Authorship. *Virginia Law Review*, *102*, 1229.

Butcher, J., & Beridze, I. (2022). Policy, legal and regulatory implications of AI: Understanding the challenges. *AI and Ethics*, *2*(3), 531–545. DOI: 10.1007/s43681-021-00082-2

Buterin, V. (2014). A next-generation smart contract and decentralized application platform. *Ethereum White Paper*.

Buterin, V. (2015). A next-generation smart contract and decentralized application platform. Ethereum Whitepaper. https://ethereum.org/en/whitepaper/

Buterin, V. (2022). Soulbound. Ethereum Blog. https://ethereum.org/en/community/blog/

Bu incu, C. N., & Alexandrescu, A. (2023). Blockchain-based platform to fight disinformation using crowd wisdom and artificial intelligence. *Applied Sciences (Basel, Switzerland)*, *13*(10), 6088. DOI: 10.3390/app13106088

Cambridge University Press. (2021). Cross-chain interoperability among blockchain-based systems using transactions. *The Knowledge Engineering Review*, *36*, e22. DOI: 10.1017/S0269888921000016

Carlini, N., Tramer, F., Wallace, E., Jagielski, M., Herbert-Voss, A., Lee, K., & Song, D. (2021). Extracting training data from large language models. *Proceedings of the 30th USENIX Security Symposium*, 2633–2650. DOI: 10.48550/arXiv.2012.07805

Catalini, C., & Gans, J. (2016). *Some Simple Economics of the Blockchain*. DOI: 10.3386/w22952

Catalini, C., & Gans, J. S. (2018). *Initial coin offerings and the value of crypto tokens* (No. w24418). National Bureau of Economic Research.

Cecílio, J., Duarte, K., & Furtado, P. (2015). BlindeDroid: An information tracking system for real-time guiding of blind people. *Procedia Computer Science*, *52*, 113–120. DOI: 10.1016/j.procs.2015.05.039

Certi, K. (n.d.). Blockchain Security and Smart Contract Audits. https://www.certik .com/

CFTE. (May 15,2023). The history of digital assets. https://blog.cfte.education/the -history-of-digital-assets

Chainalysis. (n.d.). Blockchain Data Platform. https://www.chainalysis.com/

Chainlink. (n.d.). Asset Tokenization Explained. Chainlink. Retrieved April 10, 2025, from https://chain.link/education/asset-tokenization

Chakraborty, D. (2023). *Copyright Challenges in the Digital Age: Balancing Intellectual Property Rights and Data Privacy in India's Online Ecosystem* (SSRN Scholarly Paper No. 4647960). Social Science Research Network. DOI: 10.2139/ ssrn.4647960

Chakraborty, S., & Gupta, R. (2022). Blockchain for responsible AI: A framework for transparent and traceable content creation. *Journal of Ethics and Information Technology*, *24*(3), 389–405. DOI: 10.1007/s10676-022-09634-w

Chander, A., & Parmar, M. (2022). Digital sovereignty and AI regulation in India: A comparative study. *Indian Journal of Law and Technology*, *18*(2), 127–149. DOI: 10.2139/ssrn.4094321

Chatterjee, R., & Singh, M. (2023). Generative AI in Indian media: Opportunities and ethical considerations. *Journal of Emerging Media Technologies*, *12*(2), 155–169. DOI: 10.1016/j.jemt.2023.06.009

Chen, H., Wang, X., Zhou, Y., Huang, B., Zhang, Y., Feng, W., Zhu, W. (2024). Multi-modal generative ai: Multi-modal llm, diffusion and beyond. arXiv preprint arXiv:2409.14993.

Chen, R. J., Lu, M. Y., Chen, T. Y., Williamson, D. F., & Mahmood, F. (2021). Synthetic data in machine learning for medicine and healthcare. *Nature Biomedical Engineering*, *5*(6), 493–497. 10.1038/s41551-021-00751-8. DOI: 10.1038/s41551-021-00751-8 PMID: 34131324

Chesney, R., & Citron, D. (2019). Deep Fakes: A Looming Challenge for Privacy, Democracy, and National Security. *California Law Review*, *107*(6), 1753–1820. DOI: 10.15779/Z38RV0D15J

Chesney, R., & Citron, D. K. (2019). Deepfakes and the new disinformation war: The coming age of post-truth geopolitics. *Foreign Affairs*, *98*(1), 147–155.

Chevalier, M. (2021). From smart contract litigation to Blockchain Arbitration, a new decentralized approach leading towards the blockchain arbitral order. *Journal of International Dispute Settlement*, *12*(4), 558–584. DOI: 10.1093/jnlids/idab025

Ch, H. (2014). *Social Engineering: The Science of Human Hacking*. Wiley.

Chopra, R., & Singh, V. (2023). Blockchain-powered NFTs and the Indian creative economy: Opportunities and regulatory challenges. *Journal of Digital Law and Policy*, *4*(1), 34–48. DOI: 10.2139/ssrn.4348712

Chouikhi, S., Esseghir, M., & Merghem-Boulahia, L. (2024). Energy-efficient computation offloading based on multi-agent deep reinforcement learning for industrial internet of things systems. *IEEE Internet of Things Journal*, *11*(7), 1–1. DOI: 10.1109/JIOT.2023.3333044

Christidis, K., & Devetsikiotis, M. (2016). Blockchains and smart contracts for the internet of things. *IEEE Access : Practical Innovations, Open Solutions*, *4*, 2292–2303. DOI: 10.1109/ACCESS.2016.2566339

Chugh, R., & Srivastava, M. (2022). Blockchain in Creative Industries: Protecting Intellectual Property in the Age of AI. *Journal of Intellectual Property and Technology Law*, *17*(2), 95–110. DOI: 10.2139/ssrn.4078143

Chung, J. S., & Zisserman, A. (2017). Out of Time: Automated Lip Sync in the Wild. In C.-S. Chen, J. Lu, & K.-K. Ma, *Computer Vision – ACCV 2016 Workshops* Cham.

Ciriello, R. F., Torbensen, A. C. G., Hansen, M. R. P., & Müller-Bloch, C. (2023). Blockchain-based digital rights management systems: Design principles for the music industry. *Electronic Markets*, *33*(5), 5. DOI: 10.1007/s12525-023-00628-5

Citron, D. K., & Pasquale, F. (2014). The scored society: Due process for automated predictions. *Washington Law Review (Seattle, Wash.)*, *89*, 1.

Cointelegraph. (2023). Asset tokenization: What it is and how it works. Cointelegraph. Retrieved April 10, 2025, from https://cointelegraph.com/learn/articles/asset-tokenization

Columbia Data Science Institute. (2023). AI art is here to stay: How blockchain can help creators gain control over their work. Columbia University. https://datascience.columbia.edu/news/2023/ai-art-is-here-to-stay-how-blockchain-can-help-creators-gain-control-over-their-work/

ConsenSys. (2023). A guide to Web3.js and Ethers.js: Connecting to Ethereum networks. Retrieved from https://consensys.net/h/

Crawford, K. (2021). *Atlas of AI: Power, Politics, and the Planetary Costs of Artificial Intelligence*. Yale University Press.

Croman, K., Decker, C., Eyal, I., Gencer, A. E., Juels, A., Kosba, A., Wattenhofer, R. (2016, February). On Scaling Decentralized Blockchains: (A Position Paper). In *International conference on financial cryptography and data security* (pp. 106-125). Berlin, Heidelberg: Springer Berlin Heidelberg. DOI: 10.1007/978-3-662-53357-4_8

Cvetkovski, T. (2013). Copyright developments in popular media: Doctrinal and statutory challenges. Copyright and Popular Media, 121–142. DOI: 10.1057/9781137024602_4

Cyber Risks Associated with Generative Artificial Intelligence (2024). https://www.mas.gov.sg/-/media/mas-media-library/regulation/circulars/trpd/cyber-risks-associated-with-generative-artificial-intelligence.pdf

Daniel, J. F. (2022). First order motion model for image animation and deep fake detection: Using deep learning. 2022 International Conference on Computer Communication and Informatics (ICCCI), *Deepfakes for good? How synthetic media is transforming business*. (2023). https://techinformed.com/deepfakes-for-good-how-synthetic-media-is-transforming-business/

Darwish, S. M., Abu-Deif, M. M., & Elkaffas, S. M. (2024). Blockchain for video watermarking: An enhanced copyright protection approach for video forensics based on perceptual hash function. *PLoS One*, *19*(10), e0308451. DOI: 10.1371/journal.pone.0308451 PMID: 39436935

Das, P. (2023). Digital provenance and blockchain: Protecting originality in AI-generated media. *Indian Journal of Law and Technology*, *19*(1), 33–51. DOI: 10.2139/ssrn.4532107

Datta, P., Whitmore, M., & Nwankpa, J. K. (2021). A Perfect Storm: Social Media News, Psychological Biases, and AI. *Digital Threats, 2*(2), 15:1-15:21. DOI: 10.1145/3428157

De Filippi, P., & Wright, A. (2018). *Blockchain and the law: The rule of code*. Harvard University Press.

Deepfakes: The latest weapon in the cyber security arms race. (2024). https://www
.beazley.com/en-US/news-and-events/deepfakes-the-latest-weapon-in-the-cyber
-security-arms-race/

Deepfakes: The New Threat to Cybersecurity. Retrieved March 1, 2025 from https://
www.blackberry.com/us/en/solutions/endpoint-security/ransomware-protection/
deepfakes

Diakopoulos, N., & Johnson, S. (2022). Credibility and blockchain: The use of
immutable records in news verification. *Digital Journalism (Abingdon, England)*,
10(2), 233–251. DOI: 10.1080/21670811.2021.1925429

Dickson, B. (2021). How NFTs are impacting the music and movie industries.
TechTalks. https://bdtechtalks.com/2021/03/29/nfts-music-movie-industry/

DIRECTIVE (EU) 2019/790 OF THE EUROPEAN PARLIAMENT AND OF THE
COUNCIL - of 17 April 2019—On copyright and related rights in the Digital Single
Market and amending Directives 96/9/EC and 2001/29/EC. (n.d.).

Docs, I. P. F. S. (n.d.). How IPFS works. InterPlanetary File System Documentation.
Retrieved April 10, 2025, from https://docs.ipfs.tech/concepts/how-ipfs-works/

Documentation, I. P. F. S. (n.d.). https://docs.ipfs.io/

Dolhansky, B., Bitton, J., Pflaum, B., Lu, J., Howes, R., Wang, M., & Ferrer, C. C.
(2020). The deepfake detection challenge dataset. *arXiv preprint arXiv:2006.07397*.

Dong, S., Tang, J., Abbas, K., Hou, R., Kamruzzaman, J., Rutkowski, L., & Buyya,
R. (2024). Task offloading strategies for mobile edge computing: A survey. *Computer
Networks*, *254*(110791), 110791. DOI: 10.1016/j.comnet.2024.110791

Doshi-Velez, F., & Kim, B. (2017). Towards a rigorous science of interpretable
machine learning. *arXiv preprint arXiv:1702.08608*.

Dowling, M. (2022). Fertile LAND: Pricing non-fungible tokens. *Finance Research
Letters*, *44*, 102096. DOI: 10.1016/j.frl.2021.102096

Eastern Book Company & Ors vs D.B. Modak & Anr on 12 December, 2007. (2007).

Ec, L. (n.d.). IN THE HIGH COURT OF JUSTICE BUSINESS AND PROPERTY
COURTS OF ENGLAND AND WALES INTELLECTUAL PROPERTY LIST.

Elgammal, A., Liu, B., Elhoseiny, M., & Mazzone, M. (2017). *CAN: Creative Adversarial Networks, Generating "Art" by Learning About Styles and Deviating from Style Norms.* In *Proceedings of the Eighth International Conference on Computational Creativity* (pp. 96–103). Association for Computational Creativity. DOI: 10.48550/arXiv.1706.07068

Empowering the Commons. Blockchain for IP Protection in Generative AI by Gabriela Fuentes, Assel Omarova: SSRN. (n.d.). Retrieved February 1, 2025, from https://papers.ssrn.com/sol3/papers.cfm?abstract_id=4803536

Ernst, E., Merola, R., & Samaan, D. (2019). Economics of Artificial Intelligence: Implications for the Future of Work. *IZA Journal of Labor Policy*, *9*(1), 20190004. DOI: 10.2478/izajolp-2019-0004

Ethereum Foundation. (n.d.a). ERC-721 Non-Fungible Token Standard. https://ethereum.org/en/developers/docs/standards/tokens/erc-721/

Ethereum Foundation. (n.d.b). ERC-1155 Multi Token Standard. https://ethereum.org/en/developers/docs/standards/tokens/erc-1155/

European Broadcasting Union. (2023). Navigating the digital frontier: The impact of AI on media literacy. https://www.ebu.ch/news/2023/10/navigating-the-digital-frontier--the-impact-of-ai-on-media-literacy

European Commission. (2021). Proposal for a Regulation of the European Parliament and of the Council Laying Down Harmonised Rules on Artificial Intelligence (Artificial Intelligence Act) and Amending Certain Union Legislative Acts. COM/2021/206 final. https://eur-lex.europa.eu/legal-content/EN/TXT/?uri=CELEX%3A52021PC0206

Eynern, C. (2024). *Olaf Scholz Deepfake: How a Deepfake impacts Public Trust* University of Twente]. https://purl.utwente.nl/essays/101675

Fan, M.-Q., & Wang, H.-X. (2007). A novel multipurpose watermarking scheme for copyright protection and content authentication. *Second Workshop on Digital Media and Its Application in Museum & Heritage (DMAMH 2007)*. DOI: 10.1109/DMAMH.2007.34

Farooq, M. S., Jamil, H., & Riaz, H. S. (2024). A Multichain Based Marketplace Architecture. arXiv preprint arXiv:2402.06636. https://arxiv.org/abs/2402.06636

Felzmann, H., Villaronga, E. F., Lutz, C., & Tamò-Larrieux, A. (2019). Transparency you can trust: Transparency requirements for artificial intelligence between legal norms and contextual concerns. *Big Data & Society*, *6*(1), 2053951719860542. DOI: 10.1177/2053951719860542

Fernando, T., Priyasad, D., Sridharan, S., Ross, A., & Fookes, C. (2025). Face Deepfakes-A Comprehensive Review. *arXiv preprint arXiv:2502.09812.*

Ferro, E., Saltarella, M., Rotondi, D., Giovanelli, M., Corrias, G., Moncada, R., Cavallaro, A., & Favenza, A. (2023). Digital Assets Rights Management through smart legal contracts and smart contracts. *Blockchain: Research and Applications*, *4*(3), 100142. DOI: 10.1016/j.bcra.2023.100142

Fetzer, J. H. (2002). Peirce and the philosophy of AI. *Digital Encyclopedia of Charles S. Peirce. URL:* http://www. digitalpeirce. fee. unicamp. br/ai_fetzer. htm

Fichtner, J. (2016). The anatomy of the Cayman Islands offshore financial center: Anglo-America, Japan, and the role of hedge funds. *Review of International Political Economy*, *23*(6), 1034–1063. DOI: 10.1080/09692290.2016.1243143

Filecoin. (n.d.). Store and retrieve data with decentralized storage. Filecoin. Retrieved April 10, 2025, from https://filecoin.io/

Floridi, L., Cowls, J., Beltrametti, M., Chatila, R., Chazerand, P., Dignum, V., Luetge, C., Madelin, R., Pagallo, U., Rossi, F., Schafer, B., Valcke, P., & Vayena, E. (2018). AI4People—an ethical framework for a good AI society: Opportunities, risks, principles, and recommendations. *Minds and Machines*, *28*(4), 689–707. DOI: 10.1007/s11023-018-9482-5 PMID: 30930541

Floridi, L., Cowls, J., Beltrametti, M., Chatila, R., Chazerand, P., Dignum, V., & Vayena, E. (2018). An Ethical Framework for a Good AI Society: Opportunities, Risks, Principles, and Recommendations. DOI: 10.31235/osf.io/2hfsc

Frattolillo, F. (2024). Blockchain and smart contracts for digital copyright protection. *Future Internet*, *16*(5), 169. DOI: 10.3390/fi16050169

Fredenslund, M. (2013, May 17). *Denmark: Infopaq-case finally decided after eight years.* Kluwer Copyright Blog. https://copyrightblog.kluweriplaw.com/2013/05/17/denmark-infopaq-case-finally-decided-after-eight-years/

Frontiers | Investigating generative AI models and detection techniques: Impacts of tokenization and dataset size on identification of AI-generated text. (n.d.). Retrieved February 1, 2025, from https://www.frontiersin.org/journals/artificial-intelligence/articles/10.3389/frai.2024.1469197/full

Fuentes, G., & Omarova, A. (2024). Empowering the commons: Blockchain for IP protection in generative AI. *SSRN.* https://ssrn.com/abstract=4803536 DOI: 10.2139/ssrn.4803536

G, A. K., A, H., & Sasikala, M. D. (2018). Avoiding data piracy in artworks using blockchain. International Journal of Trend in Scientific Research and Development, Volume-2(Issue-3), 1005–1012. DOI: 10.31142/ijtsrd11244

Gervais, D. (2020). AI and Copyright: Assessing the Challenge of Human-Machine Creativity. *Houston Law Review*, *57*(3), 803–843. DOI: 10.2139/ssrn.3359524

Ginsburg, J. C. (2018). People Not Machines: Authorship and What It Means in the Berne Convention. *IIC - International Review of Intellectual Property and Competition Law, 49*(2), 131–135. DOI: 10.1007/s40319-018-0670-x

Goodfellow, I., Bengio, Y., & Courville, A. (2022). *Deep learning* (Vol. 1). MIT Press., DOI: 10.7551/mitpress/12094.001.0001

Goodfellow, I., Pouget-Abadie, J., Mirza, M., Xu, B., Warde-Farley, D., Ozair, S., & Bengio, Y. (2014). Generative adversarial nets. *Advances in Neural Information Processing Systems*, 27.

Goodfellow, I., Pouget-Abadie, J., Mirza, M., Xu, B., Warde-Farley, D., Ozair, S., Courville, A., & Bengio, Y. (2020). Generative adversarial networks. *Communications of the ACM*, *63*(11), 139–144. DOI: 10.1145/3422622

Graves, L. (2016). *Deciding what's true: The rise of political fact-checking in American journalism*. Columbia University Press. DOI: 10.7312/grav17506

Güera, D., & Delp, E. J. (2018). Deepfake video detection using recurrent neural networks. *Proceedings of the IEEE Conference on Computer Vision and Pattern Recognition Workshops*, 39–46. DOI: 10.1109/AVSS.2018.8639163

Guo, H. (2022). Exposing GAN-generated faces using deep neural network. https://scholarsarchive.library.albany.edu/legacy-etd/2917

Gupta, N., & George, A. (2024). Digital Personal Data Protection Act, 2023: Charting the Future of India's Data Regulation. In *Data Governance and the Digital Economy in Asia*. Routledge. DOI: 10.4324/9781003505723-3

Gupta, R., Sharma, A., & Das, P. (2023). Blockchain and AI in media verification: An integrated framework. *Journal of Information Security Research*, *11*(2), 78–91. DOI: 10.1016/j.jisr.2023.04.005

Gupta, R., & Srivastava, M. (2023). Generative AI and multimodal content: Emerging trends in media communication. *Journal of Media Innovation*, *14*(2), 120–137. DOI: 10.1016/j.jmi.2023.03.005

Gurumurthy, A., & Bharthur, D. (2022). Platform governance and digital rights: Regulating the online public sphere in India. *International Journal of Communication, 16*, 1506–1525. https://ijoc.org/index.php/ijoc/article/view/18630

Hadnagy, C. (2010). *Social engineering: The art of human hacking.* John Wiley & Sons.

Hancock, J. T., & Bailenson, J. N. (2021). The social impact of deepfakes. In (Vol. 24, pp. 149-152): Mary Ann Liebert, Inc., publishers 140 Huguenot Street, 3rd Floor New. DOI: 10.1089/cyber.2021.29208.jth

Haq, S. A., & Yunanto, Y. (2024, May). Yunanto2, Syaif Al Haq1. "Legal Implications of Using Artificial Intelligence (AI) Technology in Electronic Transactions.". *International Journal of Social Science and Human Research, 07*(05), 2024. DOI: 10.47191/ijsshr/v7-i05-108

Hasan, H. R., & Salah, K. (2018). Proof of delivery of digital assets using blockchain and smart contracts. *IEEE Access : Practical Innovations, Open Solutions, 6*, 65439–65448. DOI: 10.1109/ACCESS.2018.2876971

Hasan, H. R., & Salah, K. (2019). Combating deepfake videos using blockchain and smart contracts. *IEEE Access : Practical Innovations, Open Solutions, 7*, 41596–41606. DOI: 10.1109/ACCESS.2019.2905689

Heather Chen, K. M. (2024). *Deepfake CFO scam hits Hong Kong.* https://edition.cnn.com/2024/02/04/asia/deepfake-cfo-scam-hong-kong-intl-hnk/index.html

Hegnauer, T. (2019). Design and development of a blockchain interoperability api. Zürich, Switzerland, February.

Heidari, A., Navimipour, N. J., Dag, H., Talebi, S., & Unal, M. (2024). A novel blockchain-based deepfake detection method using federated and deep learning models. *Cognitive Computation, 16*(3), 1073–1091. DOI: 10.1007/s12559-024-10255-7

Helmus, T. C. (2022). Artificial intelligence, deepfakes, and disinformation. *Rand Corporation*, 1-24.

Heymann, L. A. (2012). *Everything Is Transformative: Fair Use and Reader Response* (SSRN Scholarly Paper No. 1148379). Social Science Research Network. https://papers.ssrn.com/abstract=1148379

Hinton, G. E., & Salakhutdinov, R. R. (2006). Reducing the dimensionality of data with neural networks. *science, 313*(5786), 504-507.

Hodge, V., & Austin, J. (2004). A survey of outlier detection methodologies. *Artificial Intelligence Review, 22*(2), 85–126. DOI: 10.1023/B:AIRE.0000045502.10941.a9

Hofmann, J., & Kamps, J. (2021). Smart copyrights: Blockchain technology and copyright management. *Journal of Intellectual Property Law & Practice, 16*(6), 561–569. DOI: 10.1093/jiplp/jpab055

Ho, J., Jain, A., & Abbeel, P. (2020). Denoising diffusion probabilistic models. *Advances in Neural Information Processing Systems, 33*, 6840–6851.

Hooda, A., Hooda, A., & Yadav, D. (2024). *Integrating Blockchain with Big Data for Secure Data Sharing: A Comprehensive Methodology.* DOI: 10.21203/rs.3.rs-5005857/v1

Hsu, C. C., Chang, C. M., & Lin, H. Y. (2020). Deep learning-based forgery detection in digital videos. *Multimedia Tools and Applications, 79*(29), 21677–21692. DOI: 10.1007/s11042-019-7318-6

Hu, J., Jia, Y., & Qi, Y. Using Blockchain and Digital Watermarking to Enhance Open-Source Code Copyright Confirmation and Traceability. *Available at SSRN* 4936584. DOI: 10.2139/ssrn.4936584

Hussain, A. A., & Al-Turjman, F. (2021). Artificial intelligence and blockchain: A review. *Transactions on Emerging Telecommunications Technologies, 32*(9), e4268. DOI: 10.1002/ett.4268

Hussain, S., Luo, J., & Kim, S. (2023). Decentralized provenance tracking for AI-generated content using blockchain and smart contracts. *Journal of Digital Ethics and Technology, 6*(1), 33–47. DOI: 10.1016/j.jdet.2023.01.004

Islam, M. B. E., Haseeb, M., Batool, H., Ahtasham, N., & Muhammad, Z. (2024). AI threats to politics, elections, and democracy: A blockchain-based deepfake authenticity verification framework. *Blockchains, 2*(4), 458–481. DOI: 10.3390/blockchains2040020

Jagatic, T. N., Johnson, N. A., Jakobsson, M., & Menczer, F. (2007). Social phishing. *Communications of the ACM, 50*(10), 94–100. DOI: 10.1145/1290958.1290968

Jain, A., Bhattacharya, R., & Menon, S. (2023). AI for inclusive education: Opportunities and challenges of multimodal generative systems. *International Journal of Educational Technology in Higher Education, 20*(1), 18–32. DOI: 10.1186/s41239-023-00412-z

Jiang, L., Li, R., Wu, W., & Kuo, C. C. J. (2020). GAN-based deepfake detection using motion magnification. *Proceedings of the AAAI Conference on Artificial Intelligence, 34*(1), 2265–2273.

Jing, N., Liu, Q., & Sugumaran, V. (2021). A blockchain-based code copyright management system. *Information Processing & Management*, *58*(3), 102518. DOI: 10.1016/j.ipm.2021.102518

Jobin, A., Ienca, M., & Vayena, E. (2019). The global landscape of AI ethics guidelines. *Nature Machine Intelligence*, *1*(9), 389–399. DOI: 10.1038/s42256-019-0088-2

Joshi, V., & Arora, P. (2023). Bias and fairness in Indian language NLP: Challenges and future directions. *Journal of South Asian Digital Humanities*, *5*(1), 88–105. DOI: 10.33675/dhsa.005.03

Kaal, W. A. (2020). Digital asset market evolution. *The Journal of Corporation Law*, *46*, 909.

Kaminski, M. E. (2019). The right to explanation, explained. *Berkeley Technology Law Journal*, *34*(1), 189–218. DOI: 10.15779/Z38F47HV20

Kapoor, J., & Rahman, N. A. A. (2024). Organizational Security Improvement in Preventing Deepfake Ransomware. In *Digital Innovation Adoption: Architectural Recommendations and Security Solutions* (pp. 58-78). Bentham Science Publishers. DOI: 10.2174/9789815079661124010009

Kaur, N., & Kshetri, N. Blockchain Technology: Aiding Transformation in the Healthcare and Medical Industry. In *Blockchain Technology for Cyber Defense, Cybersecurity, and Countermeasures* (pp. 34-54). CRC Press.

Kaur, A., Noori Hoshyar, A., Saikrishna, V., Firmin, S., & Xia, F. (2024). Deepfake video detection: Challenges and opportunities. *Artificial Intelligence Review*, *57*(6), 159. DOI: 10.1007/s10462-024-10810-6

Kearns, L., Alam, A., & Allison, J. (2023). Synthetic Media Authentication Threats: Detection Using a Combination of Neural Network and Blockchain Technology. DOI: 10.2139/ssrn.4658121

Kesan, J. P., & Hayes, C. (2022). Cross-border legal challenges in AI and blockchain regulation. *Journal of International and Comparative Law*, *9*(1), 54–78. DOI: 10.2139/ssrn.3918755

Khan, M. H. (2023). *The Impact of AI on the Media Industry.* https://urn.kb.se/resolve?urn=urn:nbn:se:uu:diva-516624

Khan, A. A., Laghari, A. A., Li, P., Dootio, M. A., & Karim, S. (2023). The collaborative role of blockchain, artificial intelligence, and industrial internet of things in digitalization of small and medium-size enterprises. *Scientific Reports*, *13*(1), 1656. DOI: 10.1038/s41598-023-28707-9 PMID: 36717702

Khare, A., Singh, U. K., Kathuria, S., Akram, S. V., Gupta, M., & Rathor, N. (2023). Artificial intelligence and blockchain for copyright infringement detection. In *2023 International Conference on Edge Computing and Applications (ICECAA)* (pp. 1–6). IEEE. DOI: 10.1109/ICECAA58104.2023.10212277

Khurana, D., Koli, A., Khatter, K., & Singh, S. (2023). Natural language processing: State of the art, current trends and challenges. *Multimedia Tools and Applications*, *82*(3), 3713–3744. DOI: 10.1007/s11042-022-13428-4 PMID: 35855771

Kim, S., Chen, J., Cheng, T., Gindulyte, A., He, J., He, S., Li, Q., Shoemaker, B. A., Thiessen, P. A., Yu, B., Zaslavsky, L., Zhang, J., & Bolton, E. E. (2023). PubChem 2023 update. *Nucleic Acids Research*, *51*(D1), D1373–D1380. DOI: 10.1093/nar/gkac956 PMID: 36305812

Kim, S., Deka, G. C., & Zhang, P. (2019). *Role of blockchain technology in IOT Applications*. Academic Press.

Kirsh, D. (2000). A few thoughts on cognitive overload. *Intellectica*, *30*(1), 19–51. DOI: 10.3406/intel.2000.1592

Korshunov, P., & Marcel, S. (2018). Deepfakes: A new threat to face recognition? Assessment and detection. *arXiv preprint arXiv:1812.08685*.

Kosba, A., Miller, A., Shi, E., Wen, Z., & Papamanthou, C. (2016, May). Hawk: The blockchain model of cryptography and privacy-preserving smart contracts. In *2016 IEEE symposium on security and privacy (SP)* (pp. 839-858). IEEE.

Kouhizadeh, M., Saberi, S., & Sarkis, J. (2021). Blockchain technology and the sustainable supply chain: Theoretically exploring adoption barriers. *International Journal of Production Economics*, *231*, 107831. DOI: 10.1016/j.ijpe.2020.107831

Koutroumpis, P., Leiponen, A., & Thomas, L. D. (2020). Markets for data. *Industrial and Corporate Change*, *29*(3), 645–660. DOI: 10.1093/icc/dtaa002

Krafft, P. M., Osoba, O. A., & Richards, A. (2023). Authentication at scale: Blockchain-based verification for synthetic media. *AI & Society*, *38*(1), 145–161. DOI: 10.1007/s00146-022-01423-6

Krishnamurthy, A., & Ghosh, S. (2023). Synthetic news and cultural narratives: A study on AI in Indian regional media. *Journal of Media Ethics and Society*, *15*(2), 66–81. DOI: 10.1080/2470912X.2023.1950491

Kritikos, M. (2022). Artificial Intelligence and Dispute Resolution: The Role of Blockchain in Ensuring Accountability. *European Journal of Law and Technology*, *13*(1), 1–18. DOI: 10.2139/ssrn.4207161

Kshetri, N., Bhusal, C. S., Kumar, D., & Chapagain, D. (2023). SugarChain: Blockchain technology meets Agriculture—The case study and analysis of Indian sugarcane farming. *arXiv preprint arXiv:2301.08405*.

Kshetri, N., Hutson, J., & Revathy, G. (2023, December). healthAIChain: Improving security and safety using Blockchain Technology applications in AI-based health-care systems. In *2023 3rd International Conference on Innovative Mechanisms for Industry Applications (ICIMIA)* (pp. 159-164). IEEE.

Kshetri, N. (2025). Building trust in AI: How blockchain enhances data integrity, security, and privacy. *Computer, 58*(2), 63–70. DOI: 10.1109/MC.2024.3505012

Kugler, L. (2021). Non-fungible tokens and the future of art. *Communications of the ACM, 64*(9), 19–20. DOI: 10.1145/3474355

Kumar, A., & Arora, R. (2021). Blockchain-based digital forensics in India: Legal and technological perspectives. *Indian Journal of Law and Technology, 17*(2), 102–120. DOI: 10.2139/ssrn.3869122

Kumar, A., & Ramesh, V. (2023). Regulating AI and data privacy in India: An analysis of the Digital Personal Data Protection Act, 2023. *Indian Journal of Law and Technology, 19*(1), 45–61. DOI: 10.2139/ssrn.4569987

Kumar, A., & Rana, S. (2023). GANs and creativity: Reframing content generation in digital storytelling. *AI & Society, 38*(1), 91–105. DOI: 10.1007/s00146-022-01472-4

Kumar, A., & Tripathi, R. (2023). Artificial intelligence and legal accountability in India: Policy lag or regulatory void? *Journal of Law and Emerging Technologies, 5*(1), 45–61. DOI: 10.2139/ssrn.4359893

Kumar, D., & Suthar, N. (2024). Assessing the prospects and constraints of blockchain technology for Intellectual Property Management. *The Journal of World Intellectual Property*. DOI: 10.1111/jwip.12324

Kumar, S., & Deshmukh, R. (2024). The Digital Personal Data Protection Act 2023: Implications for AI governance in India. *Indian Journal of Law and Technology, 20*(1), 44–59. DOI: 10.1007/s12553-024-00119-8

Kumar, S., Musharaf, D., Musharaf, S., & Sagar, A. K. (2023). A comprehensive review of the latest advancements in large generative AI models. *Communications in Computer and Information Science, 1920*, 90–103. DOI: 10.1007/978-3-031-45121-8_9

Kuye, A. (2023). Blockchain ecosystem governance frameworks: Unlocking the value of blockchain ecosystems. SSRN Electronic Journal. DOI: 10.2139/ssrn.4590414

Kuznetsov, O., Sernani, P., Romeo, L., Frontoni, E., & Mancini, A. (2024). On the integration of artificial intelligence and blockchain technology: A perspective about security. *IEEE Access: Practical Innovations, Open Solutions, 12*, 3881–3897. DOI: 10.1109/ACCESS.2023.3349019

Lattanzio, G., & Ma, Y. (2023). Cybersecurity risk and corporate innovation. *Journal of Corporate Finance, 82*, 102445. DOI: 10.1016/j.jcorpfin.2023.102445

Law, F. (2022). The history of the blockchain and Bitcoin. https://freemanlaw.com/the-history-of-the-blockchain-and-bitcoin/

LeCun, Y., Bengio, Y., & Hinton, G. (2015). Deep learning. *nature, 521*(7553), 436-444. https://www.nature.com/articles/nature14539

Lee, J., & Choi, H. (2023). Smart contracts and AI content governance: A hybrid legal-technical approach. *Computer Law & Security Review, 49*, 105772. DOI: 10.1016/j.clsr.2023.105772

Leekha, S. (2018). Book review: Don Tapscott and Alex Tapscott, blockchain revolution: How the technology behind Bitcoin is changing money, business, and the world. *FIIB Business Review, 7*(4), 275–276. DOI: 10.1177/2319714518814603

Leibowicz, C. R. (2025). Regulating Reality: Exploring Synthetic Media Through Multistakeholder AI Governance. *arXiv preprint arXiv:2502.04526.*

Leung, T., & Narayanan, P. (2023). Consent and identity in AI-generated content: A blockchain-based framework. *Journal of Technology Law & Policy, 26*(3), 145–163. DOI: 10.2139/ssrn.4573264

Levendowski, A. (2023). AI authorship and the copyright conundrum. *Journal of Intellectual Property Law & Practice, 18*(5), 325–336. DOI: 10.1093/jiplp/jpad033

Liang, X., Shetty, S., Tosh, D., Kamhoua, C., Kwiat, K., & Njilla, L. (2017, May). Provchain: A blockchain-based data provenance architecture in cloud environment with enhanced privacy and availability. In *2017 17th IEEE/ACM International Symposium on Cluster, Cloud and Grid Computing (CCGRID)* (pp. 468-477). IEEE. DOI: 10.1109/CCGRID.2017.8

Library of Congress. (May,2020). Cryptocurrency & blockchain technology. https://guides.loc.gov/fintech/21st-century/cryptocurrency-blockchain

Li, J., & Wang, Y. (2023). Regulating deep synthesis technologies in China: Governance mechanisms and challenges. *Journal of Cyber Policy, 8*(1), 59–78. DOI: 10.1080/23738871.2023.2172763

Li, J., Zhu, M., Liu, J., Liu, W., Huang, B., & Liu, R. (2024). Blockchain-based reliable task offloading framework for edge-cloud cooperative workflows in IoMT. *Information Sciences, 668*(120530), 120530. DOI: 10.1016/j.ins.2024.120530

Lilova, S. (2021). *Copyright or Copyleft for AI-Generated Works: Private Ordering Solutions for the Benefit of Content Creators* (SSRN Scholarly Paper No. 4271966). Social Science Research Network. DOI: 10.2139/ssrn.4271966

Linoy, S., Stakhanova, N., & Matyukhina, A. (2019). Exploring Ethereum's Blockchain Anonymity Using Smart Contract Code Attribution. *2019 15th International Conference on Network and Service Management (CNSM)*, 1–9. DOI: 10.23919/CNSM46954.2019.9012681

Liu, T., Lai, S. N., Yuan, X., Liu, Y., & Lam, C. T. (2024b). A novel blockchain-watermarking mechanism utilizing interplanetary file system and fast walsh hadamard transform. *iScience, 27*(9), 110821. DOI: 10.1016/j.isci.2024.110821 PMID: 39314242

Liu, X., Xu, R., & Chen, Y. (2024). A Decentralized Digital Watermarking Framework for Secure and Auditable Video Data in Smart Vehicular Networks. *Future Internet, 16*(11), 390. DOI: 10.3390/fi16110390

Liu, Y., Huang, J., Li, Y., Wang, D., & Xiao, B. (2024). Generative AI model privacy: A survey. *Artificial Intelligence Review, 58*(1), 33. DOI: 10.1007/s10462-024-11024-6

Li, Y., Lyu, S., & Bao, F. (2020). Exposing deepfake videos by detecting face warping artifacts. *IEEE Transactions on Information Forensics and Security, 15*, 4263–4275. DOI: 10.1109/TIFS.2020.3019407

Luo, H., Luo, J., & Vasilakos, A. V. (2023). Bc4llm: Trusted artificial intelligence when blockchain meets large language models. arXiv preprint arXiv:2310.06278.

Lustig, C. (2019). Intersecting Imaginaries: Visions of Decentralized Autonomous Systems. *Proc. ACM Hum.-Comput. Interact., 3*(CSCW), 210:1-210:27. DOI: 10.1145/3359312

Madushanka, T., Kumara, D. S., & Rathnaweera, A. A. (2024). SecureRights: A Blockchain-Powered Trusted DRM Framework for Robust Protection and Asserting Digital Rights. *arXiv preprint arXiv:2403.06094.*

Magdy, S., Youssef, S., Fathalla, K. M., & ElShehaby, S. (2025). DeepSteg: Integerating new paradigms of cascaded deep video steganography for securing digital data. *Alexandria Engineering Journal, 116*, 483–501. DOI: 10.1016/j.aej.2024.12.034

Malik, A., & Joshi, P. (2021). Legal challenges of blockchain-based smart contracts in India. *International Journal of Law and Management Studies*, *3*(2), 45–54. DOI: 10.2139/ssrn.3791645

Malik, N., Wei, Y., Appel, G., & Luo, L. (2023). Blockchain technology for Creative Industries: Current State and Research Opportunities. *International Journal of Research in Marketing*, *40*(1), 38–48. DOI: 10.1016/j.ijresmar.2022.07.004

Martín, A., Hernández, A., Alazab, M., Jung, J., & Camacho, D. (2023). Evolving Generative Adversarial Networks to improve image steganography. *Expert Systems with Applications*, *222*(119841), 119841. DOI: 10.1016/j.eswa.2023.119841

Marwick, A., & Lewis, R. (2017). Media manipulation and disinformation online. *New York. Data & Society Research Institute*, *359*, 1146–1151.

Matern, F., Riess, C., & Stamminger, M. (2019). Exploiting visual artifacts to expose deepfakes and face manipulations. *Proceedings of the IEEE Conference on Computer Vision and Pattern Recognition Workshops*, 1–10. DOI: 10.1109/WACVW.2019.00020

McCutcheon, J. (2022). Authors and AI: Challenges to copyright law in the digital era. *The Modern Law Review*, *85*(3), 612–640. DOI: 10.1111/1468-2230.12712

McGregor, L., Murray, D., & Ng, V. (2022). Deepfakes and the content authenticity initiative: A technological and ethical analysis. *Journal of Media Ethics*, *37*(2), 95–110. DOI: 10.1080/23736992.2022.2049375

Mehrabi, N., Morstatter, F., Saxena, N., Lerman, K., & Galstyan, A. (2021). A survey on bias and fairness in machine learning. *ACM Computing Surveys*, *54*(6), 1–35. DOI: 10.1145/3457607

Mehta, A., & Singh, R. (2022). Regulatory challenges of AI in India: A policy review of NITI Aayog's approach. *Indian Journal of Law and Technology*, *18*(1), 1–27. DOI: 10.5555/ijlt.18.1.1

Menon, R., & Suresh, A. (2023). Smart contracts for academic publishing: Securing AI-generated educational resources with NFTs. *Indian Journal of Educational Technology*, *17*(2), 78–92. DOI: 10.5958/2230-7135.2023.00008.9

Mirsky, Y., & Lee, W. (2021). The creation and detection of deepfakes: A survey. *ACM Computing Surveys*, *54*(1), 1–41. DOI: 10.1145/3425780

Mitnick, K. D., & Simon, W. L. (2003). *The art of deception: Controlling the human element of security*. John Wiley & Sons.

Mittal, M., Rahman, K. F., Jha, C. K., Bali, V., & Khanna, T. (2024). Bridging policy and practice: A systematic review of blockchain adoption for copyright protection. In 2024 International Conference on Communication, Computing and Energy Efficient Technologies (I3CEET) (pp. 1–6). IEEE. DOI: 10.1109/I3CEET61722.2024.10993987

Mohan, K., & Shetty, P. (2022). Cultural ethics and bias in generative AI systems in Indian media. *Asian Journal of Ethics and Technology*, 9(1), 45–62. DOI: 10.23856/ajet.2022.90105

MoonPay. (2023). Blockchain interoperability: How do blockchains communicate? MoonPay. Retrieved April 10, 2025, from https://www.moonpay.com/learn/blockchain/blockchain-interoperability

Morgan, J. P. (Oct,2024). Evolution of digital assets. J.P. Morgan. https://www.jpmorgan.com/content/dam/jpm/cib/complex/content/securities-services/regulatory-solutions/evolution-of-digital-assets.pdf

Muhammad, I. (2023). COMMUNAL INTELLECTUAL PROPERTY IN THE DIGITAL AGE: EXPLORING THE RELEVANCE, REGULATION, AND IMPACT OF CREATIVE COMMONS LICENSES. *Indonesian Law Journal*, 16(1), 1. DOI: 10.33331/ilj.v16i1.127

Mukherjee, A., & Sanyal, S. (2023). Blockchain for ethical verification in AI-generated media: A regulatory perspective. *AI and Ethics*, 4(3), 243–258. DOI: 10.1007/s43681-023-00262-6

Mukherjee, S., & Ghosh, T. (2022). Trusting local journalism: The case for blockchain watermarking in Indian media. *Asian Journal of Communication and Technology*, 4(3), 55–66. DOI: 10.1080/15504435.2022.1876335

Murray, J. (2022). Smart contracts and NFTs: Copyright enforcement in the age of AI and blockchain. *Journal of Intellectual Property Law & Practice*, 17(4), 273–281. DOI: 10.1093/jiplp/jpac020

Muthukumar, R., & Reddy, V. (2022). Algorithmic bias in multimodal AI: An Indian perspective on data justice. *AI & Society*, 37(4), 1221–1236. DOI: 10.1007/s00146-021-01247-5

Nadini, M., Alessandretti, L., Di Giacinto, F., Martino, M., Aiello, L. M., & Baronchelli, A. (2021). Mapping the NFT revolution: Market trends, trade networks, and visual features. *Scientific Reports*, 11(1), 20902. DOI: 10.1038/s41598-021-00053-8 PMID: 34686678

Nakamoto, S. (2008). Bitcoin: A peer-to-peer electronic cash system.

Nakamoto, S. (2008). Bitcoin: A peer-to-peer electronic cash system. https://bitcoin .org/bitcoin.pdf

Nakamoto, S. (2008). Bitcoin: A peer-to-peer electronic cash system. SSRN *Electronic Journal*. DOI: 10.2139/ssrn.3977007

Nakamoto, S. Bitcoin: A Peer-to-Peer Electronic Cash System, BITCOIN.ORG (May 24, 2009), https://bitcoin.org/bitcoin.pdf (PDF).

Nakamoto, S. (2008). *Bitcoin: A peer-to-peer electronic cash system*. Satoshi Nakamoto.

Narayanan, A., Bonneau, J., Felten, E., Miller, A., Goldfeder, S., & Clark, J. (2016). *Bitcoin and cryptocurrency technologies*. Princeton University Pres.

Narayanan, P., & Gupta, A. (2023). The ethics of synthetic media in the era of AI: Policy challenges in India. *Indian Journal of Law and Technology*, *19*(1), 27–45. DOI: 10.5281/zenodo.8101456

Nassar, A., & Kamal, M. (2021). Ethical Dilemmas in AI-Powered Decision-Making: A Deep Dive into Big Data-Driven Ethical Considerations. *International Journal of Responsible Artificial Intelligence*, *11*(8), 8.

Nawaz, A., Peña Queralta, J., Guan, J., Awais, M., Gia, T. N., Bashir, A. K., Kan, H., & Westerlund, T. (2020). Edge computing to secure IoT data ownership and trade with the ethereum blockchain. *Sensors (Basel)*, *20*(14), 3965. DOI: 10.3390/ s20143965 PMID: 32708807

Nazer, L. H., Zatarah, R., Waldrip, S., Ke, J. X. C., Moukheiber, M., Khanna, A. K., Hicklen, R. S., Moukheiber, L., Moukheiber, D., Ma, H., & Mathur, P. (2023a). Bias in artificial intelligence algorithms and recommendations for mitigation. *PLOS Digital Health*, *2*(6), e0000278. DOI: 10.1371/journal.pdig.0000278 PMID: 37347721

Neisse, R., Steri, G., & Nai-Fovino, I. (2017). A blockchain-based approach for data accountability and provenance tracking. Proceedings of the 12th international conference on availability, reliability and security, *The Psychology of Deepfakes in Social Engineering*. (2025). Reality Defender. https://www.realitydefender.com/ blog/the-psychology-of-deepfakes-in-social-engineering

Nguyen, A. T., Kharosekar, A., Krishnan, S., Krishnan, S., Tate, E., Wallace, B. C., & Lease, M. (2018). Believe it or not. *Proceedings of the 31st Annual ACM Symposium on User Interface Software and Technology*. DOI: 10.1145/3242587.3242666

Nguyen, H. H., Yamagishi, J., & Echizen, I. (2019). Capsule-forensics: Using capsule networks to detect forged images and videos. *Proceedings of the IEEE International Conference on Acoustics, Speech and Signal Processing (ICASSP)*, 2307–2311. DOI: 10.1109/ICASSP.2019.8682602

Nguyen, T., Lee, Y., & Kim, J. (2022). Blockchain as a trust protocol in media authentication: A review of opportunities and challenges. *ACM Transactions on Multimedia Computing Communications and Applications*, *18*(2), 1–19. DOI: 10.1145/3429457

Nguyen, T., Nguyen, H., & Nguyen Gia, T. (2024). Exploring the integration of edge computing and blockchain IoT: Principles, architectures, security, and applications. *Journal of Network and Computer Applications*, *226*(103884), 103884. DOI: 10.1016/j.jnca.2024.103884

Nguyen, T., Valenzise, G., & Dufaux, F. (2021). Multimodal deepfake detection with cross-modal attention. *IEEE Transactions on Information Forensics and Security*, *16*, 3352–3367. DOI: 10.1109/TIFS.2021.3105543

Nyhan, B., & Reifler, J. (2015). Displacing misinformation about events: An experimental test of causal corrections. *Journal of Experimental Political Science*, *2*(1), 81–93. DOI: 10.1017/XPS.2014.22

Oakley, K. (2006). Include Us Out—Economic Development and Social Policy in the Creative Industries. *Cultural Trends*, *15*(4), 255–273. DOI: 10.1080/09548960600922335

OECD. (2019). OECD Principles on Artificial Intelligence. OECD Legal Instruments. https://legalinstruments.oecd.org/en/instruments/OECD-LEGAL-0449

OpenSea Developer Docs. https://docs.opensea.io/

OpenZeppelin Contracts Documentation. https://docs.openzeppelin.com/contracts/

Pal, A.Ashutosh Pal Singh. (2024). Safeguarding authenticity in the Digital Realm: A holistic approach integrating content provenance, secure watermarking, and transparent labeling to combat deepfakes. *International Journal For Multidisciplinary Research*, *6*(3), 21580. DOI: 10.36948/ijfmr.2024.v06i03.21580

Panda, L., Jena, S. K., Rath, S. S., & Misra, P. K. (2020). Heavy metal removal from water by adsorption using a low-cost geopolymer. *Environmental Science and Pollution Research International*, *27*(19), 24284–24298. DOI: 10.1007/s11356-020-08482-0 PMID: 32306254

Pareek, S., van Berkel, N., Velloso, E., & Goncalves, J. (2024). Effect of explanation conceptualisations on trust in AI-Assisted Credibility Assessment. *Proceedings of the ACM on Human-Computer Interaction, 8*(CSCW2), 1–31. DOI: 10.1145/3686922

Pasquale, F. (2015). *The Black Box Society: The Secret Algorithms That Control Money and Information*. Harvard University Press. DOI: 10.4159/harvard.9780674736061

Patel, O. (2019). Blockchain - integrated AI for Decentralized Autonomous Organizations (daos). [IJSR]. *International Journal of Science and Research (Raipur, India), 8*(4), 2010–2019. DOI: 10.21275/SR24806045716

Pathak, A., & Sundararajan, M. (2023). Blockchain for Media Integrity: Indian Context and Applications. *Indian Journal of Law and Technology, 19*(1), 77–94. DOI: 10.2139/ssrn.4462219

Picha Edwardsson, M., & Al-Saqaf, W. (2022). Drivers and barriers for using blockchain technology to create a global fact-checking database. *Online Journal of Communication and Media Technologies, 12*(4), e202228. DOI: 10.30935/ojcmt/12381

Pillai, S., & Thomas, J. (2022). Algorithmic fairness and ethical AI in India: The role of blockchain for traceable accountability. *Indian Journal of AI Ethics and Law, 4*(2), 88–103. DOI: 10.1007/s12553-022-00510-7

Portillo, N. (2024a). Bitcoin: A Peer-to-Peer Electronic Cash System. DOI: 10.2139/ssrn.4993270

Portmann, E. (2018). Rezension „Blockchain: Blueprint for a new economy". *HMD Praxis der Wirtschaftsinformatik, 55*(6), 1362–1364. DOI: 10.1365/s40702-018-00468-4

Potluri, J., Gummadi, H., Alladi, K., & Ramesh, G. (2023). Securing intellectual property in the digital age through blockchain innovation. In *2023 Global Conference on Information Technologies and Communications (GCITC)* (pp. 1–6). IEEE. DOI: 10.1109/GCITC60406.2023.10426242

Propy. (2023). NFT Real Estate Transactions. https://propy.com/browse/

Qureshi, A., & Megias, D. (2020). Blockchain-based multimedia content protection: Review and open challenges. *Applied Sciences (Basel, Switzerland), 11*(1), 1. DOI: 10.3390/app11010001

Radhakrishnan, R., & Shilpa, P. (2022). Blockchain and smart contracts in Indian media and entertainment: Opportunities and regulatory concerns. *Journal of Medical Law and Ethics, 10*(1), 33–49. DOI: 10.5281/zenodo.7529478

Radziwill, N. (2018). Blockchain Revolution: How the technology behind Bitcoin is changing money, business, and the world. *The Quality Management Journal*, *25*(1), 64–65. DOI: 10.1080/10686967.2018.1404373

Rahwan, I., Cebrian, M., Obradovich, N., Bongard, J., Bonnefon, J. F., Breazeal, C., & Lazer, D. (2019). Machine behaviour. *Nature*, *568*(7753), 477–486. DOI: 10.1038/s41586-019-1138-y PMID: 31019318

Rajagopal, R., & Mishra, V. (2022). Smart contracts and digital rights management in India's media sector. *Journal of Media Innovation and Law*, *5*(1), 31–47. DOI: 10.2139/ssrn.4452112

Rajput, A., & Agrawal, A. (2024). Blockchain for privacy-preserving data distribution in healthcare. *Proceedings of the 10th International Conference on Information Systems Security and Privacy*, 621–631. DOI: 10.5220/0012470500003648

Raman, A., & Dubey, A. (2022). Legal enforceability of blockchain evidence in Indian courts: Challenges and prospects. *Indian Bar Review*, *49*(2), 203–220. DOI: 10.2139/ssrn.4341216

Ramesh, A., Pavlov, M., Goh, G., Gray, S., & Agarwal, S. (2022). Hierarchical text-conditional image generation with CLIP Latents. NeurIPS Proceedings, 35, 31315–31327. /arXiv.2204.06125DOI: 10.48550

Ramesh, S., & Iyer, V. (2023). Policy and regulation for AI-generated multimedia content in India. *Indian Journal of Law and Technology*, *19*(1), 67–84. DOI: 10.52370/ijlt.v19i1.2023.004

Rana, M. S., Nobi, M. N., Murali, B., & Sung, A. H. (2022). Deepfake detection: A systematic literature review. *IEEE Access : Practical Innovations, Open Solutions*, *10*, 25494–25513. DOI: 10.1109/ACCESS.2022.3154404

Ravichandar, A., & Narayan, A. (2022). Artificial Intelligence and Intellectual Property in India: Regulatory Dilemmas and Future Directions. *NUJS Law Review*, *15*(2), 202–223. DOI: 10.2139/ssrn.4145722

Real, T. (2022). Real Estate on the Blockchain. https://realt.co/

Reardon, S. (2024). *How Deepfakes Are Impacting Public Trust in Media*. Pindrop. https://www.pindrop.com/article/deepfakes-impacting-trust-media/

Regner, F., Urbach, N., & Schweizer, A. (2019). NFTs and the future of digital content licensing. *Business & Information Systems Engineering*, *61*(6), 553–558. DOI: 10.1007/s12599-019-00600-9

Regner, F., Urbach, N., & Schweizer, A. (2019). NFTs in practice – Applications and implications of non-fungible tokens for artists, investors, and marketplaces. *Business & Information Systems Engineering, 61*(6), 546–550.

Renault, T., Amariles, D. R., & Troussel, A. (2024). Collaboratively adding context to social media posts reduces the sharing of false news. *arXiv preprint arXiv:2404.02803.*

Roehrs, A., Da Costa, C. A., da Rosa Righi, R., & De Oliveira, K. S. F. (2017). Personal health records: A systematic literature review. *Journal of Medical Internet Research, 19*(1), e5876. DOI: 10.2196/jmir.5876 PMID: 28062391

Rosenblatt, B. (2022). Blockchain and copyright: Protecting AI-generated works in the digital domain. *Journal of Intellectual Property Law & Practice, 17*(5), 377–388. DOI: 10.1093/jiplp/jpac019

Rossler, A., Cozzolino, D., Verdoliva, L., Riess, C., Thies, J., & Nießner, M. (2019). FaceForensics++: Learning to detect manipulated facial images. *Proceedings of the IEEE/CVF International Conference on Computer Vision*, 1–11. DOI: 10.1109/ICCV.2019.00009

Ryan, M. D., Macrossan, P., Wright, S., & Adams, M. (2021). Blockchain and publishing: Towards a publisher-centred distributed ledger for the Book Publishing Industry. *Creative Industries Journal, 16*(1), 2–21. DOI: 10.1080/17510694.2021.1939541

Saad, M., Ahmad, A., & Mohaisen, A. (2019, June). Fighting fake news propagation with blockchains. In *2019 IEEE Conference on Communications and Network Security (CNS)* (pp. 1-4). IEEE.

Samuel Okechukwu Omeje, B. O. Mary Onyedikachi Chukwuka. (2023). Artificial Intelligence on Social Media: Use, Misuse, And Impacts. In *Emergence of Social Media: Shaping the Digital Discourse of the Next Generation* (pp. 38-46). Routledge.

Samuelson, P. (2022). Allocating ownership rights in AI-generated works. *Berkeley Technology Law Journal, 37*(2), 455–498. DOI: 10.2139/ssrn.3924653

Sarkar, S., & Menon, R. (2023). Legal Challenges of AI-Generated Content in India: Ownership and Accountability. *Indian Journal of Law and Technology, 19*(1), 47–67. DOI: 10.2139/ssrn.4389214

Saxena, N. (2023). Harmonizing data protection frameworks for AI-driven media platforms: A comparative study of GDPR and Indian data laws. *Journal of Cyber Policy and Governance, 8*(2), 115–133. DOI: 10.1080/23738871.2023.2234020

Schär, F. (2021). Decentralized finance: On blockchain- and smart contract-based financial markets. *Review - Federal Reserve Bank of St. Louis*, *103*(2), 153–174. DOI: 10.20955/r.103.153-74

Schoren, M., Ghose, A., & Xu, S. (2023). Blockchain and AI: Complementary Technologies for Ethical Governance in Digital Content Creation. *AI & Society*, *38*(1), 99–115. DOI: 10.1007/s00146-022-01376-0

Shae, Z., & Tsai, J. (2019, July). AI blockchain platform for trusting news. In *2019 IEEE 39th International Conference on Distributed Computing Systems (ICDCS)* (pp. 1610-1619). IEEE. DOI: 10.1109/ICDCS.2019.00160

Shang, W., Li, H., Ni, X., Chen, T., & Liu, T. (2025). BlockGuard: Advancing digital copyright integrity with blockchain technique. *Computers & Electrical Engineering*, *122*, 109897. DOI: 10.1016/j.compeleceng.2024.109897

Sharma, S. R., & Kshetri, N. (2025). BCT4C4: Blockchain Technology for Cyber-security, Cyber Data, and Cyber Communication in Today's Cyber World. Chapter 6, In book *Blockchain Technology for Cyber Defense, Cybersecurity, and Counter-measures: Techniques, Solutions, and Applications*, 94, CRC Press.

Sharma, S. R., & Kshetri, N. (2025). BCT4C4: Blockchain Technology for Cy-bersecurity, Cyber Data, and Cyber Communication in Today's Cyber World. In *Blockchain Technology for Cyber Defense, Cybersecurity, and Countermeasures* (pp. 94-105). CRC Press.

Sharma, S. R., Kshetri, N., & Poudel, S. R. (2025). SHSBchain: Blockchain Technology Solutions for Smart Homes and Smart Business. Chapter 13, In book *Blockchain Technology for Cyber Defense, Cybersecurity, and Countermeasures: Techniques, Solutions, and Applications* (pp. 211-221), CRC Press.

Sharma, S. R., Kshetri, N., & Poudel, S. R. (2025). SHSBchain: Blockchain Tech-nology Solutions for Smart Homes and Smart Business. In *Blockchain Technology for Cyber Defense, Cybersecurity, and Countermeasures* (pp. 211-221). CRC Press.

Sharma, N., & Dey, A. (2023). Rethinking authorship in the age of generative AI: A comparative legal analysis. *The Journal of Law and Technology*, *8*(1), 23–38. DOI: 10.5958/2349-4829.2023.00003.0

Sharma, R., & Dey, N. (2022). Ethical considerations in Indian AI systems: A focus on caste and regional representation. *Indian Journal of Ethics in Technology*, *3*(2), 55–72. DOI: 10.25027/IJET.2022.032.05

Sharma, R., & Iyer, V. (2023). Ethical AI frameworks in multimedia production: A comparative policy study. *Media Culture & Society*, *45*(6), 1021–1038. DOI: 10.1177/01634437231123109

Shekhar, A., Prabhat, P., Yandrapalli, V., Umar, S., Abdul, F., & Wakjira, W. D. (2023). Generative AI in Supply Chain Management.

Shokri, R., Stronati, M., Song, C., & Shmatikov, V. (2017). Membership inference attacks against Machine Learning Models. *2017 IEEE Symposium on Security and Privacy (SP)*, 3–18. DOI: 10.1109/SP.2017.41

Shu, K., Sliva, A., Wang, S., Tang, J., & Liu, H. (2017). Fake news detection on social media: A data mining perspective. *SIGKDD Explorations*, *19*(1), 22–36. DOI: 10.1145/3137597.3137600

Siddiqui, F., & Chang, H. (2023). NFTs and the redefinition of digital media ownership. *International Journal of Digital Art & Blockchain*, *2*(1), 12–27. DOI: 10.1080/27663312.2023.1965031

Singh, A., Kumar, A., & Touthang, J. (2022, November). Detection of Tampering in Multimedia Using Blockchain Technology. In *Advances in Manufacturing Technology and Management: Proceedings of 6th International Conference on Advanced Production and Industrial Engineering (ICAPIE)—2021* (pp. 492-500). Singapore: Springer Nature Singapore.

Singh, N., Pandey, R., & Krishnan, M. (2022). Algorithmic bias in generative AI: An Indian perspective. *Journal of Digital Ethics and Society*, *7*(2), 110–125. DOI: 10.26529/jdes.2022.11072

Singh, O. P., Singh, K. N., Singh, A. K., & Agrawal, A. K. (2024). Watermarking with blockchain: A survey. In *Digital Image Security* (pp. 200–224). CRC Press. DOI: 10.1201/9781003468974-10

Sinha, R. (2023). Artificial intelligence and copyright law in India: Navigating uncharted waters. *NUJS Law Review*, *16*(1), 78–94. DOI: 10.2139/ssrn.4567892

Sinnappan, S., & Zutshi, A. (2022). The role of metadata and blockchain in digital content authentication. *Journal of Emerging Technologies in Media*, *5*(2), 88–104. DOI: 10.1016/j.jetm.2022.05.002

Smith, T. (2023). State-level regulatory responses to synthetic media in the United States. *Yale Journal of Law & Technology*, *25*(2), 135–162. DOI: 10.2139/ssrn.4321210

Solomon, E., Woubie, A., & Emiru, E. S. (2023). Autoencoder based face verification system. *arXiv preprint arXiv:2312.14301*.

Solouki, M., & Bamakan, S. M. (2022). An in-depth insight at digital ownership through dynamic nfts. *Procedia Computer Science*, *214*, 875–882. DOI: 10.1016/j.procs.2022.11.254

Solouki, M., & Bamakan, S. M. H. (2023). A Review of the Key Challenges of Non-Fungible Tokens. *Technological Forecasting and Social Change*, *187*, 122297. DOI: 10.1016/j.techfore.2022.122297

Stavola, J., & Choi, K.-S. (2023). Victimization by deepfake in the metaverse: Building a practical management framework. *International Journal of Cybersecurity Intelligence & Cybercrime*, *6*(2), 2. DOI: 10.52306/2578-3289.1171

Stix, C. (2021). A survey of the European Union's Artificial Intelligence Act: Risk-based regulation in practice. *Nature Machine Intelligence*, *3*(12), 1032–1034. DOI: 10.1038/s42256-021-00425-3

Suite, T. (2023). Smart contract development tools. Retrieved from https://trufflesuite.com/

Sundaram, A., & Rao, T. (2023). Localizing generative AI: A case for Indic language models. *International Journal of AI and Society*, *12*(3), 201–216. DOI: 10.1007/s13178-023-00678-w

Sundararajan, K., & Ramesh, M. (2021). Blockchain applications in Indian governance and creative sectors: Potential and policy perspectives. *Journal of South Asian Policy Studies*, *6*(2), 112–128. DOI: 10.1007/s13531-021-00129-w

Suthar, S., & Pindoriya, N. M. (2020). Blockchain and smart contract based Decentralized Energy Trading Platform. *2020 21st National Power Systems Conference (NPSC)*. DOI: 10.1109/NPSC49263.2020.9331883

Sutherland, I. E. (1964). Sketch pad a man-machine graphical communication system. Proceedings of the SHARE design automation workshop, *Synthetic Document Generation for NLP and Document AI*. (2024). Medium. Retrieved 3/21/2025 from https://medium.com/@tagx20/synthetic-document-generation-for-nlp-and-document-ai-9b04bb5008db

Taddeo, M., & Floridi, L. (2020). The ethics of digital well-being: A thematic review. *Science and Engineering Ethics*, *26*(4), 2313–2343. DOI: 10.1007/s11948-020-00175-8 PMID: 31933119

Tapscott, D., & Tapscott, A. (2016). *Blockchain revolution: how the technology behind bitcoin is changing money, business, and the world.* Penguin.

Tapscott, D., & Tapscott, A. (2019). *Blockchain.* Rewolucja, Wydawnictwo PWN.

Technologies, P. (n.d.). Substrate: Blockchain Framework. https://substrate.io/

TechTarget. (2023). A timeline and history of blockchain technology. https://www.techtarget.com/whatis/feature/A-timeline-and-history-of-blockchain-technology

Tenderly. (2023). Real-time monitoring and debugging for smart contracts. Retrieved from https://tenderly.co/

The Graph. (2022). Decentralized querying protocol for blockchains. Retrieved from https://thegraph.com/

The Impact of Deepfake Fraud: Risks, Solutions, and Global Trends. (2024). Regula. https://regulaforensics.com/blog/impact-of-deepfakes-on-idv-regula-survey/#:~:text=Criminals%20can%20now%20easily%20create,on%20a%20screen%20during%20verification

The Wall Street Journal (2024). https://www.wsj.com/search?query=CEO%20fraud

Thorne, J., Vlachos, A., Christodoulopoulos, C., & Mittal, A. (2018). FEVER: a large-scale dataset for fact extraction and VERification. *arXiv preprint arXiv:1803.05355.* DOI: 10.18653/v1/N18-1074

Tian, F. (2017, June). A supply chain traceability system for food safety based on HACCP, blockchain & Internet of things. In *2017 International conference on service systems and service management* (pp. 1-6). IEEE.

Tolosana, R., Vera-Rodriguez, R., Fierrez, J., Morales, A., & Ortega-Garcia, J. (2020). Deepfakes and beyond: A survey of face manipulation and fake detection. *Information Fusion, 64,* 131–148. DOI: 10.1016/j.inffus.2020.06.014

Tran-Dang, H., & Kim, D.-S. (2025). Digital Twin-empowered intelligent computation offloading for edge computing in the era of 5G and beyond: A state-of-the-art survey. *ICT Express, 11*(1), 167–180. DOI: 10.1016/j.icte.2025.01.002

Trifonova, P., & Venkatagiri, S. (2024). Misinformation, Fraud, and Stereotyping: Towards a Typology of Harm Caused by Deepfakes. Companion Publication of the 2024 Conference on Computer-Supported Cooperative Work and Social Computing.

Tripathi, A., & Joshi, D. (2023). Challenges in regulating generative AI in digital media: A legal outlook. *South Asian Journal of Law and Policy, 12*(1), 25–39. DOI: 10.2139/ssrn.4388291

Tripathi, K., & Bansal, M. (2023). Blockchain as an Intellectual Property Management Tool in India's Creative Sector. *Journal of Intellectual Property Rights*, 28(4), 167–175. DOI: 10.56042/jipr.v28i4.125273

Truong, V. T., Le, H. D., & Le, L. B. (2024). Trust-free blockchain framework for AI-generated content trading and management in metaverse. *IEEE Access: Practical Innovations, Open Solutions*, 12, 41815–41828. DOI: 10.1109/ACCESS.2024.3376509

Tyagi, A. K., Kukreja, S., Richa, , & Sivakumar, P. (2024). Role of blockchain technology in smart era: A review on possible smart applications. *Journal of Information & Knowledge Management*, 23(03), 2450032. DOI: 10.1142/S0219649224500321

Varadarajan, M. N., & Seeni, S. K. (2024). Innovative Digital ownership and collectibles via proof of stake (POS) and non-fungible tokens (NFTS). *INTERNATIONAL JOURNAL OF ADVANCES IN SIGNAL AND IMAGE SCIENCES*, 10(1), 22–34. DOI: 10.29284/IJASIS.10.1.2024.22-34

Vaswani, A. (2017). Attention is all you need. *Advances in Neural Information Processing Systems*.

Veale, M., & Borgesius, F. Z. (2021). Demystifying the draft EU Artificial Intelligence Act. *Computer Law Review International*, 22(4), 97–112. DOI: 10.9785/cri-2021-220402

Verdoliva, L. (2020). Media forensics and deepfakes: An overview. *IEEE Journal of Selected Topics in Signal Processing*, 14(5), 910–932. DOI: 10.1109/JSTSP.2020.3002101

Verma, N., & Iyer, S. (2023). Adoption of AI-generated content tools in Indian digital media. *South Asian Journal of Media Studies*, 8(3), 201–217. DOI: 10.1177/09763500231123865

Voigt, P., & von dem Bussche, A. (2017). *The EU General Data Protection Regulation*. GDPR., DOI: 10.1007/978-3-319-57959-7

Wang, Q., Li, R., Wang, Q., & Chen, S. (2021). Non-Fungible Token (NFT): Overview, Evaluation, Opportunities and Challenges. arXiv preprint arXiv:2105.07447.

Wang, H., Zheng, Z., Xie, S., Dai, H. N., & Chen, X. (2018). Blockchain challenges and opportunities: A survey. *International Journal of Web and Grid Services*, 14(4), 352–375. DOI: 10.1504/IJWGS.2018.095647

Wang, L., & Chen, Y. (2023). Blockchain-enabled provenance tracking for AI-generated multimedia. *Multimedia Systems*, 29(3), 467–482. DOI: 10.1007/s00530-022-00983-9

Wang, X., Ban, T., Chen, L., Usman, M., Guan, Y., Lyu, D., Cheng, J., Chen, H., Leung, C., & Miao, C. (2024). Decentralised knowledge graph evolution via blockchain. *IEEE Transactions on Services Computing*, *17*(1), 169–182. DOI: 10.1109/TSC.2023.3337873

Wang, X., Zhang, Y., Cao, J., & Wu, J. (2021). Adversarial training for deepfake detection: A comprehensive analysis. *IEEE Transactions on Neural Networks and Learning Systems*, *32*(10), 4723–4736. DOI: 10.1109/TNNLS.2021.3097682

Wang, Y.-C., Xue, J., Wei, C., & Kuo, C.-C. J. (2023). An overview on generative AI at scale with edge–cloud computing. *IEEE Open Journal of the Communications Society*, *4*, 2952–2971. DOI: 10.1109/OJCOMS.2023.3320646

Wardle, C., & Derakhshan, H. (2017). *Information disorder: Toward an interdisciplinary framework for research and policymaking* (Vol. 27). Council of Europe Strasbourg.

Westerlund, M. (2019). The emergence of deepfake technology: A review. *Technology Innovation Management Review*, *9*(11), 39–52. http://doi.org/10.22215/timreview/1282. DOI: 10.22215/timreview/1282

Whittlestone, J., Nyrup, R., Alexandrova, A., & Cave, S. (2019). The role and limits of principles in AI ethics: Towards a focus on tensions. Proceedings of the 2019 AAAI/ACM Conference on AI, Ethics, and Society, 195–200. DOI: 10.1145/3306618.3314289

Wischmeyer, T., & Rademacher, T. (2020). Regulating artificial intelligence in the European Union. *Common Market Law Review*, *57*(5), 1149–1180. DOI: 10.54648/COLA2020061

Wood, G. (2014). Ethereum: A secure decentralised generalised transaction ledger. https://ethereum.github.io/yellowpaper/paper.pdf

World Economic Forum. (2023). What are non-fungible tokens (NFTs) and are they useful? https://www.weforum.org/stories/2023/10/nfts-non-fungible-tokens-blockchain/

Wright, C. S. (2008). Bitcoin: A peer-to-peer electronic cash system. SSRN Electronic Journal, 3440802, 10-2139.

Wu, L., Zhang, M., & Zhou, T. (2023). From uni-modal to multi-modal: Evolution of large language models for digital content generation. *ACM Transactions on Multimedia Computing Communications and Applications*, *19*(3), 1–19. DOI: 10.1145/3589387

Wu, X., Ma, P., Jin, Z., Wu, Y., Han, W., & Ou, W. (2022). A novel zero-watermarking scheme based on NSCT-SVD and blockchain for video copyright. *EURASIP Journal on Wireless Communications and Networking*, *2022*(1), 20. DOI: 10.1186/s13638-022-02090-x

Xiao, L., Huang, W., Xie, Y., Xiao, W., & Li, K.-C. (2020). A blockchain-based traceable IP copyright protection algorithm. *IEEE Access: Practical Innovations, Open Solutions*, *8*, 49532–49542. DOI: 10.1109/ACCESS.2020.2969990

Xiao, X., He, X., Zhang, Y., Dong, X., Yang, L. X., & Xiang, Y. (2023). Blockchain-based reliable image copyright protection. *IET Blockchain*, *3*(4), 222–237. DOI: 10.1049/blc2.12027

Xie, H.-X., Lo, L., Shuai, H.-H., & Cheng, W.-H. (2022). An overview of facial micro-expression analysis: Data, methodology and challenge. *IEEE Transactions on Affective Computing*, *14*(3), 1857–1875. DOI: 10.1109/TAFFC.2022.3143100

Xie, R., & Tang, M. (2024). A digital resource copyright protection scheme based on blockchain cross-chain technology. *Heliyon*, *10*(17), e36830. DOI: 10.1016/j.heliyon.2024.e36830 PMID: 39281489

Xu, X., Weber, I., & Staples, M. (2019). Architecture for Blockchain Applications. DOI: 10.1007/978-3-030-03035-3

Xue, H., Chen, D., Zhang, N., Dai, H.-N., & Yu, K. (2023). Integration of blockchain and edge computing in the internet of things: A survey. *Future Generation Computer Systems*, *144*, 307–326. DOI: 10.1016/j.future.2022.10.029

Xue, X., Shang, G., Ma, Z., Xu, M., Guo, H., Li, K., & Cheng, X. (2024, November). DataSafe: Copyright Protection with PUF Watermarking and Blockchain Tracing. In *Blockchain and Web3 Technology Innovation and Application Exchange Conference* (pp. 256–268). Springer Nature Singapore.

Xu, R., Nikouei, S. Y., Nagothu, D., Fitwi, A., & Chen, Y. (2020). BlendSPS: A blockchain-enabled Decentralized Smart Public Safety System. *Smart Cities*, *3*(3), 928–951. DOI: 10.3390/smartcities3030047

Yadav, K. K. (2023). Unmasking The Lies: How Information Technology is Fighting Fake News and Viral Deception. *Journal of Data Acquisition and Processing*, *38*(2), 3183. DOI: 10.5281/zenodo.777149

Yang, F., Abedin, M. Z., Qiao, Y., & Ye, L. (2024). Towards Trustworthy Governance of AI-Generated Content (AIGC): A Blockchain-Driven Regulatory Framework for Secure Digital Ecosystems. *IEEE Transactions on Engineering Management*, *71*, 14945–14962. DOI: 10.1109/TEM.2024.3472292

Yang, F., Shi, Y., Wu, Q., Li, F., Zhou, W., & Hu, Z. (2019). The survey on intellectual property based on blockchain technology. In *2019 IEEE International Conference on Industrial Cyber Physical Systems (ICPS)* (pp. 1–6). IEEE. DOI: 10.1109/ICPHYS.2019.8780125

Yang, X., Li, Y., Qi, H., Lyu, S., & Liu, X. (2019). Exposing GAN-synthesized faces using landmark locations. *Proceedings of the IEEE/CVF Conference on Computer Vision and Pattern Recognition Workshops*, 25–34.

Yazdinejad, A., Parizi, R. M., Srivastava, G., & Dehghantanha, A. (2020). Making sense of blockchain for AI deepfakes technology. 2020 IEEE Globecom Workshops (GC Wkshps, 1–6. DOI: 10.1109/GCWkshps50303.2020.9367545

Yli-Huumo, J., Ko, D., Choi, S., Park, S., & Smolander, K. (2016). Where is current research on blockchain technology?—A systematic review. *PLoS One*, *11*(10), e0163477. DOI: 10.1371/journal.pone.0163477 PMID: 27695049

Yuan, S., Yang, W., Tian, X., & Tang, W. (2024). A Blockchain-Based Privacy Preserving Intellectual Property Authentication Method. *Symmetry*, *16*(5), 622. DOI: 10.3390/sym16050622

Zambrano, R., Jani, A., & Lakhanpal, S. (2021). Blockchain in land administration: A review of potential and challenges. *Land Use Policy*, *100*, 104893. DOI: 10.1016/j.landusepol.2020.104893

Zen, Y. (2021). Type 2 autoimmune pancreatitis: Consensus and controversies. *Gut and Liver*, *16*(3), 357–365. DOI: 10.5009/gnl210241 PMID: 34670874

Zhang, X., Tang, Z., Xu, Z., Li, R., Xu, Y., Chen, B., . . . Zhang, J. (2024). OmniGuard: Hybrid Manipulation Localization via Augmented Versatile Deep Image Watermarking. *arXiv preprint arXiv:2412.01615*.

Zhang, H., Yu, J., & Zhao, X. (2020). Detecting AI-generated fake videos using multimodal features. *IEEE Transactions on Multimedia*, *22*(11), 2962–2975. DOI: 10.1109/TMM.2020.2994285

Zhang, P., White, J., Schmidt, D. C., Lenz, G., & Rosenbloom, S. T. (2018). FHIR CHAIN: Applying blockchain to securely and scalably share clinical data. *Computational and Structural Biotechnology Journal*, *16*, 267–278. DOI: 10.1016/j.csbj.2018.07.004 PMID: 30108685

Zhao, Y., Liu, B., Ding, M., Liu, B., Zhu, T., & Yu, X. (2023). Proactive deepfake defence via identity watermarking. Proceedings of the IEEE/CVF winter conference on applications of computer vision, Zuboff, S. (2023). The age of surveillance capitalism. In *Social theory re-wired* (pp. 203-213). Routledge. DOI: 10.1109/ WACV56688.2023.00458

Zheng, Z., Xie, S., Dai, H., Chen, X., & Wang, H. (2017, June). *An overview of blockchain technology: Architecture, consensus, and future trends. In 2017 IEEE international congress on big data (BigData congress).* Ieee.

Zhou, P., Han, X., Morariu, V. I., & Davis, L. S. (2019). Two-stream neural networks for tampered face detection. *Proceedings of the IEEE/CVF Conference on Computer Vision and Pattern Recognition*, 7556–7564.

Zhou, T., Lu, X., & Zhang, Y. (2021). Deepfake detection using spatiotemporal attention. *IEEE Transactions on Circuits and Systems for Video Technology*, *31*(3), 919–933. DOI: 10.1109/TCSVT.2021.3054239

Zhou, X., Li, T., & Zhang, Y. (2022). Multimodal transformers in generative AI: Frameworks and applications. *AI Review Quarterly*, *45*(4), 345–369. DOI: 10.1007/ s10462-022-10102-7

Zolfaghari, S., & Piramuthu, S. (2021). Blockchain-based solutions for deepfake prevention and authentication. *Journal of Cybersecurity*, *7*(1), 12. DOI: 10.1093/ cybsec/tyab012

Zubiaga, A., Aker, A., Bontcheva, K., Liakata, M., & Procter, R. (2018). Detection and resolution of rumors in social media: A survey. *ACM Computing Surveys*, *51*(2), 1–36. DOI: 10.1145/3161603

Zyskind, G., Nathan, O., & Pentland, A. (2015). Decentralizing privacy: Using blockchain to protect personal data. 2015 IEEE Security and Privacy Workshops, 180–184. DOI: 10.1109/SPW.2015.27

Zyskind, G., Nathan, O., & Pentland, A. (2015). Decentralizing Privacy: Using Blockchain to Protect Personal Data. In *2015 IEEE Security and Privacy Workshops* (pp. 180-184).

Zyskind, G., & Nathan, O. (2015, May). *Decentralizing privacy: Using blockchain to protect personal data. In 2015 IEEE security and privacy workshops.* IEEE.

About the Contributors

G Revathy has been working as a academic professional for past 15 years. She has numerous publications in the field of Artificial intelligence and wireless mesh networks. She has also been an editor for the book "Advanced Applications of Osmotic Computing" by IGI Publishers.

Arul Kumar Natarajan currently serves as an Assistant Professor in the Department of Computer Science at the Samarkand International University of Technology in Uzbekistan. He earned his Doctor of Philosophy degree in Computer Science from Bharathidasan University, India, in 2017. Concurrently, he is engaged in postdoctoral research in Generative AI for Cybersecurity at the Singapore Institute of Technology, Singapore. Throughout his 14-year teaching career, Dr. Arul has held esteemed positions at various institutions, including Christ University, Bishop Heber College in India, and Debre Berhan University in Ethiopia. Dr. Arul has made significant contributions to academia, specializing in cybersecurity and artificial intelligence, as evidenced by his portfolio of scholarly works. He has authored 52 peer-reviewed and internationally indexed publications and delivered 35 conference presentations. Additionally, he has edited and published 04 books with IGI Global, USA, which are indexed in Scopus and focus on Artificial Intelligence and Cybersecurity. He also has 04 more books in the processing stage with IGI Global, Wiley, and Springer. In addition to his academic pursuits, Dr. Arul is a prolific innovator. He has 17 patents granted in India and 1 granted in the United Kingdom, spanning diverse fields such as communication and computer science. His latest work involves 1 copyrighted research (Govt. of India) in Artificial Intelligence and Machine Learning, specifically focused on segmenting, classifying, and tracking issue nuclei in images. Dr. Arul also exhibits notable proficiency in networking and cybersecurity, having completed the CCNA Routing and Switching Exam from CISCO and the Networking Fundamentals exam from Microsoft. He continues to demonstrate a strong interest in Generative AI for Cybersecurity.

***

Ayesha Arobee is a dual master's student in Business Administration and Information Technology at Emporia State University. Originally from Bangladesh, she is passionate about tech innovation, strategic leadership, and sustainable development.

Bindu Aryal is a dedicated educator and IT professional, currently serving as a full-time faculty member at Birendra Multiple Campus, Tribhuvan University, Nepal. With a strong academic background, she holds a Master of Computer Applications (MCA) from IGNOU and a Bachelor of Computer Applications (BCA) from Pokhara University. Recognized for her academic contributions, she has received awards such as the Best Result Award and a Certificate of Appreciation for excellence in bachelor-level programs. Beyond teaching, Bindu has actively contributed to IT research, demonstrating her commitment to advancing knowledge in computer science. Known for her leadership, problem-solving skills, and ability to manage multiple responsibilities, she continues to inspire students and peers in Nepal's academic and technical community.

C.P. Shabariram is pursuing his PhD at Anna University. He is an Assistant Professor at PSG Institute of Technology and Applied Research, Coimbatore, Tamil Nadu, India. His research interests include cloud computing, edge computing and deep learning.

Devendra Chapagain is an accomplished academic and researcher with a strong foundation in computer science. He boasts a distinguished educational background, having earned his Master of Computer Applications (MCA) from Lovely Professional University (LPU) in Punjab, India, in 2014, and his Bachelor of Computer Applications (BCA) from Pokhara University (PU) in Pokhara, Nepal, in 2010. Currently, Mr. Chapagain serves as an Associate Lecturer at Birendra Multiple Campus (BMC), Bharatpur, Chitwan, Nepal. This accredited college is affiliated with Tribhuwan University, Nepal's largest university. At BMC, he inspires the next generation of computer scientists by sharing his extensive knowledge and expertise. Prior to his current role, Mr. Chapagain held the position of DHOD at Oxford College of Engineering and Management (OCEM) in Gaindakot, Nepal. He also served as a lecturer at Lord Buddha Education Foundation (LBEF) in Maitidevi, Kathmandu. Mr. Chapagain's research interests lie in the critical fields of cybersecurity, blockchain technology, and information security. He has actively contributed to these areas by publishing several academic papers and presenting his research findings at national and international conferences. His work is respected within the academic community and demonstrably advances the field of computer science. In addition to his academic work, Devendra is also involved in various community activities and initiatives that promote the use of technology for the betterment of society. He is a respected member of the academic community and a valuable contributor to the field of Computer Science.

Naresh Kshetri (BCA '10, MCA '14, MS '17, PhD '22) is currently a full time faculty at Department of Cybersecurity, Rochester Institute of Technology (RIT), Rochester, New York, USA. With more than ten years of experience and interests in Cybersecurity, AI Security, Blockchain technology, he has published in various journals, conferences, & book chapters. Dr. Kshetri has taught various CS & CSEC courses at both the undergraduate and graduate levels. Dr. Kshetri is the Senior Member of IEEE (M '19, SM '25) and Professional Member of ACM (M '25).

Kunal Lanjewar is a distributed systems engineer with a background in planetary scale infrastructure and online multiplayer games. He has contributed to various NASA projects involving geospatial visualization and machine learning, and currently leads platform-scale backend architecture at Riot Games, where he builds resilient systems supporting millions of concurrent players.

P. Madhavasarma is a faculty at the Department of Electronics & Instrumentaion Engineering, SASTRA Deemed University, Thanjavur. Prior to joining the institute, he was with Saraswathy College of Engineering &Technology, Tindivanam. His research interests span the fields of model prediction and fracture healing analysis, process modeling and simulation, control relevant process identification, biomedical engineering and soft computing techniques. His main focus is to impart value based quality education in the field of engineering and do research which is useful to the society. His current research interst in the field of interdicilpinary work along with medical practitioners for fracture healing analysis using soft computing and image processing based 3D pinting for scaffold for fracture treatment. He has worked with electrical related companies as a consultant to improve their product quality. He has been reviewer for the international journals such as 1)Transaction of the Institute of Measurement and Control 2) Instrumentation science and technology 3) Computer Methods in Biomechanics and Biomedical Engineering 4) Ain Shams Engineering Journal-Elsevier 5) Brazilian Journal of

N. Shanthi is a Professor of Computer Science and Engineering at Kongu Engineering College, Tamil Nadu, India. She received her B.E. and M.E. degrees from Bharathiar University and her Ph.D. from Periyar University. She has published over 90 journal papers, authored two books, and guided 13 Ph.D. scholars. Her research interests include Image Processing, Optical Character Recognition, data mining, edge computing and machine learning. She is a Life Member of ISTE and a Fellow of IEI.

P. Nagaraj is currently serving as an Associate Professor in the Department of Computer Science and Engineering at SRM Institute of Science and Technology, Tiruchirappalli. He holds a Ph.D. in Computer Science and Engineering and has over 16 years of rich teaching and research experience. His research interests span across Data Science and Analytics, Computational Intelligence, and Recommendation Systems. Dr. Nagaraj has published more than 200 research articles in reputed international journals and conferences, including International Journal of Imaging Systems and Technology (IMA), Diabetes, Metabolic Syndrome and Obesity: Targets and Therapy, and International Journal of Healthcare Information Systems and Informatics (IJHISI). He has also contributed to several book chapters published in renowned Springer series such as Lecture Notes on Data Engineering and Communications Technologies, Studies in Computational Intelligence, Lecture Notes in Networks and Systems, and Advances in Intelligent Systems and Computing, along with works in Elsevier books focused on healthcare data analytics. He serves as a Guest Editor for Frontiers in Artificial Intelligence and actively reviews for high-impact journals such as IEEE Access and Applied Soft Computing. His work primarily focuses on applications of data analytics in healthcare, diabetes management, optimization techniques, and intelligent systems for engineering applications. In his academic career, Dr. Nagaraj has guided over 30 UG projects, 5 PG projects, and is currently supervising 8 Ph.D. scholars in the domain of Data Science and Analytics. He has been a Resource Person for various seminars, FDPs, and workshops, and has contributed extensively to academic events across India. He previously served as the Faculty Sponsor for the KARE ACM Student Chapter (Chapter ID: 170084) and under his guidance, the chapter received the Outstanding Recruitment Program Award (2023) and Outstanding Chapter Award (2024) from ACM India. He now takes charge of the SRMIST Tiruchirappalli ACM Student Chapter and Tiruchirappalli ACM Professional Chapter . Dr. Nagaraj has been recognized among the World's Top 2% Scientists by Stanford University in both 2023 and 2024, as per Scopus-based metrics. As of now, he has 2,550 citations, an h-index of 32, and an i10-index of 60.

P. Priya Ponnuswamy received her PhD from Anna University. She is an Assistant Professor at Vellore Institute of Technology, Vellore, Tamil Nadu, India. Her research interests include edge and cloud computing.

P. VidhyaPriya is a dedicated academician with a strong foundation in both computer science and business management. She holds an MBA from Avinashilingam Deemed University, Coimbatore, and earned her Ph.D. from Bharathiar University, Coimbatore, in 2010. Before transitioning to academia, she gained valuable industry experience working with a textile firm for over three years. In 2000, she joined

Kongu Engineering College, where she has since built an illustrious career in research and teaching. With over 24 years of academic experience, Dr. VidhyaPriya's research interests lie in corporate finance, corporate governance, and behavioral finance. She has published 57 research papers in reputed national and international journals, including Scopus-indexed publications. Throughout her career, she has actively engaged with the academic community by attending numerous Faculty Development Programs (FDPs) at leading B-Schools, including IIM Bangalore, IIT Madras, Pondicherry University, and Mangalore University. Dr.VidhyaPriya has also presented papers at 30 national and international conferences and has organized multiple conferences, seminars, FDPs, workshops, and training programs. She has successfully completed two ICSSR-sponsored projects focused on start-up entrepreneurship and the Stand-Up India Scheme for entrepreneurs.

Bishwo Prakash Pokharel is a cybersecurity researcher, educator, and IT professional currently based in Toronto, Ontario, Canada. His areas of expertise include network security, cyber forensics, blockchain technology, and artificial intelligence. He is actively involved in advancing secure IT infrastructures, promoting proactive threat detection mechanisms, and addressing cybersecurity challenges in emerging domains such as smart cities and connected systems. Mr. Pokharel has contributed to several academic publications as a staff researcher and coauthor, focusing on the integration of artificial intelligence and blockchain technologies in cybersecurity frameworks. His broader research interests include smart city infrastructure security, AI-driven threat detection, IoT forensics, and data protection in distributed systems. In addition to his research contributions, Mr. Pokharel has served as a lecturer and mentor at multiple academic institutions, including Sungava College, Oxford College of Engineering and Management, Chitwan College of Technology, Presidency College of Management Sciences, and Lumbini ICT College. He has taught and supervised undergraduate and graduate students in diverse areas of information technology, with an emphasis on bridging theoretical foundations and practical applications. He is also actively engaged in mentoring international students and supporting professional development in the cybersecurity domain.

Sumit Ranjan, with over a decade of experience in technology, Sumit Ranjan has been instrumental in developing large-scale AI/ML platform products that drive efficiency and transform user experiences. He holds a Master's in Computer Science with a specialization in Machine Learning from the Georgia Institute of Technology, Atlanta, and a Bachelor's degree in Computer Science and Engineering from the National Institute of Technology, Trichy, India. Recognized for his expertise in Applied Machine Learning, Data Science, and Distributed Computing, Sumit continues to lead innovation in the AI and technology landscape.

Yazhini.S is currently pursuing her B.E CSE in V.S.B College of Engineering Technical Campus, Coimbatore. Her research area includes Machine Learning, Artificial Intelligence and Deep Learning.

S.V.Divya M.E, Ph.D., is currently working as a Professor in the Department of Computer Science & Engineering in V.S.B College of Engineering Technical Campus, Coimbatore, TamilNadu, India . She has the teaching experience of more than 16 years and had published more than 20 research papers in SCI/Scopus indexed journals, 2 Patents and 2 text books. She had published more than 15 papers in National/International Conferences.She received her B.Tech Degree in Information Technology from Jayamatha Engineering College, Aralvoimozhi and M.E Degree in Computer Science and Engineering from Mepco Schlenk Engineering College, Sivakasi in 2005 and 2007 respectively. She received her Ph.D in Computer Science and Engineering at Noorul Islam Centre for Higher Education in 2017 under the area of Cloud Computing and guiding four research scholars. Her research area includes Wireless Communications, Cloud Computing, Big Data and Cyber Security. Acted a s reviewer in many journals and IEEE conferences. She is a Life member of ISTE, The Institution of Green Engineers,IAENG.

S.Saravanaprabhu is working as an Assistant Professor in the Department of IT in Nadha College of Technology, Erode. His research interests are machine learning artificial intelligence etc.

SC Vetrivel is a faculty member in the Department of Management Studies, Kongu Engineering College (Autonomous), Perundurai, Erode Dt. Having experience in Industry 20 years and Teaching 16 years. Awarded with Doctoral Degree in Management Sciences in Anna University, Chennai. He has organized various workshops and Faculty Development Programmes. He is actively involved in research and consultancy works. He acted as a resource person to FDPs & MDPs to various industries like, SPB ltd, Tamilnadu Police, DIET, Rotary school and many. His areas of interest include Entrepreneurship, Business Law, Marketing and Case writing. Articles published more than 100 International and National Journals. Presented papers in more than 30 National and International conferences including IIM Bangalore, IIM Kozhikode, IIM Kashipur and IIM Indore. He was a Chief Co-ordinator of Entrepreneurship and Management Development Centre (EMDC) of Kongu Engineering College, he was instrumental in organizing various Awareness Camps, FDP, and TEDPs to aspiring entrepreneurs which was funded by NSTEDB – DST/GoI

Suresh Raj Sharma Address: Bihani tole 9, Bharatput Chitwan Nepal. Education Graduate: Master in Computer Application Profession: Lecturer of Tribhuvan University Currently working as lecturer of Computer Application at Birendra Multiple Campus, Bharatpur Chitwan Nepal.

Shify Antolin is currently pursuing her B.E CSE in V.S.B College of Engineering Technical Campus, Coimbatore. Her research area includes Machine Learning, Artificial Intelligence and Deep Learning.

Dipendra Silwal is an accomplished Assistant Professor at Oxford College of Engineering and Management and an experienced Software Developer with over a decade of expertise in software development and IT consulting. He possesses a strong academic and professional interest in social engineering, with a focus on cybersecurity awareness and digital risk mitigation. In addition to his teaching and development roles, he is actively engaged in conducting awareness programs, training sessions, and educational initiatives aimed at enhancing digital literacy and promoting secure online practices.

K. Muthamil Sudar is working as an Assistant Professor in the Department of Computer Science and Engineering, Mepco Schlenk Engineering College, Sivakasi, Tamil Nādu. He has 8.5 years of teaching and research experience. His research interest includes Network Security, Software Defined Networking, and Machine learning techniques

Jelin Taric.G is currently working as an Assistant Professor in the Department of CSE at Noorul Islam Centre for Higher Education Kumaracoil.. His research interests are Machine learning Artificial Intelligence etc.

V. Sabareeshwari currently serves as Assistant Professor in Department of Soil Science, Amrita School of Agricultural Sciences, Coimbatore. Having more than 5 years of research experience and more than 2 years of teaching experience. She got 7 awards in the field of agriculture. Her field of expertise are soil genesis, soil pedological studies as well as soil fertility mapping using advanced software like Arc GIS. She had published 22 research papers and more than 10 book chapters and books in high- impact reputed journals. She has actively participated and presented her papers in more than 20 conferences and seminars. She not only restrict her contribution only in the academic and research part, she had extension experience at farm level (lab to land) with varied crop research.

P. Venkadesh M.E, Ph.D., is currently working as a Professor in the Department of Artificial Intelligence & Data Science in V.S.B College of Engineering Technical Campus, Coimbatore, TamilNadu, India . He received his M.E Degree in Computer Science & Engineering from Sathyabama University, Chennai, TamilNadu, India in 2007. He completed his Ph.D at Noorul Islam Centre for Higher Education in 2017 under the area of Network Security . He is guiding five research scholars and three scholars received their Ph.D degree under his guidance. His research area includes Network Security, Image Processing, Wireless Communications and Cloud Computing. He has a teaching experience of more than 22 years and had published more than 23 research papers in SCI/Scopus indexed journals . He has published 8 Patents and two patents were granted also he has published 2 text book entitled, " Data Structures" and Problem Solving & Python Programming. He is a life member of ISTE.

V.P. Arun is a driven and accomplished professional with a diverse educational background and extensive hands-on experience across various industries. Graduating with honors, Arun earned his Master of Business Administration (M.B.A) with a specialization in Human Resources and Marketing from the renowned Sona School of Management in Salem in 2018, where he excelled academically with an impressive 8.3 Cumulative Grade Point Average (CGPA).Throughout his academic journey, Arun displayed an unwavering commitment to learning and personal growth, actively seeking opportunities to expand his knowledge and skills beyond the confines of traditional education. He sought practical experiences to complement his theoretical understanding, such as a 45-day summer internship focused on conducting a feasibility study for R-Doc Sustainability in the market. Additionally, Arun broadened his horizons through a 7-day industrial visit to Malaysia and Singapore, immersing himself in diverse cultural and professional environments. Arun's academic pursuits were further enriched by his involvement in hands-on projects, including a comprehensive study on Employee Job Satisfaction at Roots Cast Private Limited. His professional trajectory includes serving as a Growth Officer at Parle Agro Private Limited, where he played a crucial role in driving sales growth and market expansion. Arun is a dedicated professional, currently employed at JKKN Engineering College in the Management Studies Department. He holds expertise in his field and has contributed significantly to academia through the publication of two journal articles. Arun's work focuses on advancing knowledge and understanding in management studies, making valuable contributions to the academic community.

Anant Wairagade, Lead Cybersecurity Engineer, building IAM solutions for Organizational Cybersecurity with strong foundations in Enterprise Integrations and Technical Leadership. Started my career in Enterprise Middleware technology as middleware engineer, groomed by Enterprise architects early in my career helped laid strong foundation in Enterprise architecture design and patterns, early adopter of API programming built software productivity tools for companies leveraging native API methods provided by underpinning framework. Built Microservices using Spring Boot, PaaS by breaking down .NET monolithic application. Early adopter of JWT token for authentication and authorization of Microservices including interaction between UI and backend. Lead software development teams in Financial CRM, Core Banking, various Finance domains. Recent experience in Cybersecurity with focus on Identity and Access Management in Information Security.

Index

www.ingramcontent.com/pod-product-compliance
Lightning Source LLC
Chambersburg PA
CBHW080700220326
41598CB00033B/5270